Syllable inventori

Cambridge Studies in Speech Science and Communication

Patterns of sounds

In this series:

The phonetic bases of speaker recognition Francis Nolan

Patterns of sounds

Ian Maddieson
University of California at Los Angeles

With a chapter contributed by Sandra Ferrari Disner

The right of the University of Cambridge to print and sell all manner of books was granted by Henry VIII in 1534. The University has printed and published continuously since 1584.

Cambridge University Press
Cambridge
London New York New Rochelle
Melbourne Sydney

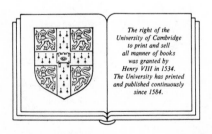

Published by the Press Syndicate of the University of Cambridge
The Pitt Building, Trumpington Street, Cambridge CB2 1RP
32 East 57th Street, New York, NY 10022, USA
P.O. Box 85, Oakleigh, Victoria 3166, Australia

First published 1984

Printed in Great Britain at the University Press, Cambridge

Library of Congress catalogue card number: 84–7753

British Library Cataloguing in Publication Data
Maddieson, Ian
Patterns of sounds. – (Cambridge studies
in speech science and communication)
1. Grammar, Comparative and general –
Phonology 2. Phonetics
I. Title II. Disner, Sandra Ferrari
414 PZ17
ISBN 0 521 26536 3

This book is dedicated to the memory of Lilian Ann Maddieson and Henry Ray Maddieson, who gave me the freedom to go my own way.

Preface

The discovery of generalizations concerning the content and structure of phonological inventories has been a significant objective of recent work in linguistics. Such generalizations have been taken into account, explicitly or implicitly, in the formulation of phonological theories, in evaluating competing historical reconstructions, in constructing models of language change and language acquisition, and they have stimulated important linguistically-oriented phonetic research. This book reports on the work done at UCLA using a computer-accessible database containing the phonological segment inventories of a representative sample of the world's languages which is designed to provide a reliable basis for such generalizations. The project has come to be referred to by the acronym UPSID - the UCLA Phonological Segment Inventory Database.

There seem to be three types of sources for observations on phonological inventories. The type with the longest tradition is an essentially impressionistic account based on a linguist's experience of a number of languages. Statements by Trubetskoy (1939), Jakobson and Halle (1956), and Ladefoged (1971) as well as incidental remarks in the papers of numerous authors are examples of this category. Although they may be based on familiarity with a very large number of languages, there is some doubt about the scope and validity of the conclusions reached, since the list of languages represented in this experience is not given and there is no quantification attached to the statements made.

The second type consists of explicit samples of languages compiled for the purpose of a single study, such as Ferguson (1963), Greenberg (1970) and Hyman (1977) on nasals, glottalic consonants and stress respectively. In these cases the quality of the sample (cf. Bell 1978) and the significance of the conclusions reached (cf. Hurford 1977) can be independently assessed by the reader.

The third kind of data source is a standardized multi-purpose survey, epitomized by the Stanford Phonology Archive (SPA), compiled at Stanford University as part of the broad Language Universals Project under the direction of J. H. Greenberg and C. A. Ferguson. A large proportion of recent work on phonological universals is either directly based on the SPA or owes an indirect debt to it. The UCLA Phonological Segment Inventory Database (UPSID) is a source of this third kind.

There are several reasons for the superiority of this third kind of data source which arise from the nature of the field of enquiry involved. The data source serves, first, to generate observations, e.g. observations concerning the frequency of segments of different types and of the phonetic attributes of segments, as well as their co-occurrence in phonological inventories, and secondly, to subject hypotheses concerning such matters as segment frequency to the test of comparison with empirical observations. The hypotheses may range from simple ones claiming that there are significant differences in the frequency of segments of different types to more elaborate ones positing contingent relationships between the occurrence of (sets of) different segments, or limitations on the distribution of phonetic attributes within inventories. The third, and perhaps most significant, purpose behind compilation of such data sources is as a stimulus to the generation of hypotheses which relate to other fields of the study of language but for which such matters as segment frequencies, inventory size, and so on, may be the point of departure. Such hypotheses can be directed at issues of production, perception, acquisition, linguistic change or language contact, but establish connections between other data and observations concerning segments and inventories.

Most of these observations and hypotheses about phonological universals necessarily concern relative rather than absolute matters. Experience has shown that few interesting things are to be said about phonological inventories that are truly universal, i.e. exceptionless. Apart from observations such as "all languages have a contrast between consonants and vowels" most of the substantive generalizations concerning segments and inventories are or can be expected to be of the form "a situation x occurs more (or less) frequently than chance leads us to predict." That is, in layman's terms, they are statistical observations. They can therefore only be meaningful if they are drawn from, or tested with respect to, a body of data appropriately designed for statistical analysis. In other words, one which is representative, extensive and uniform in analysis as far as possible. This requires establishment of a large and appropriately selected sample of languages and a standardized procedure for interpreting their phonologies. Once such a database has been established, numerous commensurate studies on the same data can be made.

This book contains nine chapters presenting analyses of aspects of the UPSID inventories. Chapter 9 is contributed by Sandra F. Disner, the rest are written by me. Each of these chapters is designed to be largely self-contained so that readers may consult a single chapter if, for example, they are interested in some particular segment type. Chapter 10 presents a relatively full account of the design of the database, including the principles governing the selection of languages, the criteria used in interpretation of the descriptive sources consulted and the set of phonetic features used to characterize segments. A full documentation of the data itself is also contained in the appendices at the end of the book, including phonemic charts of each language and full lists of the types of segments that occur. Each language is assigned an identification number which is cited whenever the language is mentioned in the text, enabling the corresponding phoneme chart to be easily found. The principles on which the identification numbers are assigned is explained in Appendix A.

Many people have assisted in making this book possible. The principal work of establishing the computer database was done by Sandra F. Disner, Vivian Flores, J. Forrest Fordyce, Jonas N. A. Nartey, Diane G. Ridley, Vincent van Heuven and myself. Help in collecting data was provided by Stephen R. Anderson, Peter Austin, Steve Franks, Bonnie Glover, Peter Ladefoged, Mona Lindau-Webb, Robert Thurman, Alan Timberlake, Anne Wingate, Andreas Wittenstein and Eric Zee. Additional assistance has come from other linguists at UCLA and elsewhere. Mel Widawsky provided valuable services in persuading the computer to accept the indigestible bulk of our input. A library of the sources from which data was drawn was compiled with assistance from Hector Javkin and Diane G. Ridley. John Crothers provided an early copy of the final report of the Stanford Phonology Archive, enabling the UCLA project to benefit from the experience accrued at Stanford. Geoffrey Lindsey and Karen Weiss did the tedious work of typing the phoneme charts and Karen Emmorey, Karen Weiss, Alice Anderton, and Kristin Precoda assisted with the preparation of the camera-ready copy of the remainder of the book. To all of these people I owe an enormous debt, which I can only pay in the coin of gratitude.

I also owe thanks to those who have shown faith in the UPSID project as it developed by making use of it, including Louis Goldstein, Pat Keating, Peter Ladefoged, Björn Lindblom and the students in Linguistics 103 at UCLA.

A considerable portion of the work reported in this book has been funded by the National Science Foundation through grants BNS 78-07680 and BNS 80-23110 (Peter Ladefoged, principal investigator). Neither the NSF nor any of the individuals named above are responsible for the errors that undoubtedly remain. If you the reader find one, please write and tell me about it.

Ian Maddieson
University of California
Los Angeles

References

Bell, A. 1978. Language samples. In J.H. Greenberg et al. (eds.) _Universals of Human Language, Vol 1, Method and Theory_. Stanford University Press, Stanford: 123-56.

Ferguson, C. A. 1963. Some assumptions about nasals. In J.H. Greenberg (ed.) _Universals of Language_. MIT Press, Cambridge: 42-7.

Greenberg, J. H. 1970. Some generalizations concerning glottalic consonants, especially implosives. _International Journal of American Linguistics_ 36: 123-45.

Hurford, J. R. 1977. The significance of linguistic generalizations. _Language_ 53: 574-620.

Hyman, L. M. 1977. On the nature of linguistic stress. In L.M. Hyman (ed.) _Studies on Stress and Accent_. (Southern California Occasional Papers in Linguistics 4) University of Southern California, Los Angeles: 37-82.

Jakobson, R. and Halle, M. 1956. Phonology and phonetics. (Part 1 of) _Fundamentals of Language_. Mouton, The Hague: 3-51.

Ladefoged, P. 1971. _Preliminaries to Linguistic Phonetics_. University of Chicago Press, Chicago.

Trubetskoy, N. 1939. _Grundzüge der Phonologie_ (Travaux du Cercle Linguistique de Prague 9). Prague.

1

The size and structure of phonological inventories

1.1 Introduction

A database designed to give more reliable and more readily available answers to questions concerning the distribution of phonological segments in the world's languages has been created as part of the research program of the UCLA Phonetics Laboratory. The database is known formally as the UCLA Phonological Segment Inventory Database, and for convenience is referred to by the acronym UPSID. UPSID has been used to investigate a number of hypothesized phonological universals and "universal tendencies". Principal among these have been certain ideas concerning the overall size and structure of the phonological inventories. The design of the database is briefly described in this chapter. A full description is given in chapter 10, and the various appendices at the end of the book report on the data contained in UPSID files. The remainder of the present chapter discusses the issues involving the overall structure and size of phonological inventories which have been examined with its use.

1.2 Design of the database

The languages included in UPSID have been chosen to approximate a properly constructed quota sample on a genetic basis of the world's extant languages. The quota rule is that only one language may be included from each small family grouping, for example, among the Germanic languages, one is included from West Germanic and one from North Germanic (East Germanic, being extinct and insufficiently documented for a reliable phonological analysis to be made, is not included). Each such small family grouping should be represented by the inclusion of one language. Availability and quality of phonological descriptions are factors in determining which language to include from within a group, but such factors as the number of speakers and the phonological peculiarity of the language are not considered. The database includes the inventories of 317 languages. In this and subsequent chapters, every language mentioned in the text is identified by a number that cross-refers to the list of these languages and the data charts at the end of the book. These numbers are assigned on the basis of the genetic affiliation of the language.

In the database each segment which is considered phonemic is represented by its most characteristic allophone, specified in terms of a set of 58 phonetic attributes. These are treated as variables which take the value 1 if the segment has the attribute and 0 if the segment lacks it. The list of attributes with the value 1 thus provides a phonetic description of the segment concerned.

For 192 of the 317 languages included, UPSID has profited from the work of the Stanford Phonology Archive (SPA). Our decisions on phonemic status and phonetic description do not always coincide with the decisions reached by the compilers of the SPA, and we have sometimes examined additional or alternative sources, but a great deal of effort was saved by the availability of this source of standardized analyses. It should be noted that UPSID, unlike the SPA, makes no attempt to include information on allophonic variation, syllable structure, or phonological rules.

In determining the segment inventories, there are two especially problematical areas. The first involves choosing between a unit or sequence interpretation of, for example, affricates, prenasalized stops, long (geminate) consonants and vowels, diphthongs, labialized consonants, etc. The available evidence which bears on the choice in each language individually has been examined but with some prejudice in favor of treating complex phonetic events as sequences (i.e. as combinations of more elementary units). The second problem area involves the choice between a segmental and a suprasegmental analysis of certain properties. Stress and tone have always been treated as suprasegmental; that is, tonal and stress contrasts do not by themselves add to the number of distinct segments in the inventory of a language, but if differences in segments are found which accompany stress or tone differences, these may be regarded as segmental contrasts if the association does not seem a particularly natural one. For example, if there is an unstressed vowel which is a little shorter or more centralized than what can be seen as its stressed counterpart, these vowels will be treated as variants of the same segment. However, larger qualitative differences between the set of stressed and unstressed vowels will lead us to enter such sets of vowels as separate segments. In all cases, sets of vowels which are divided into vowel harmony series are all entered separately; the factor which distinguishes the vowel harmony series is not extracted as a suprasegmental.

1.3 Variations in inventory size

The number of segments in a language may vary widely. The smallest inventories included in the survey have only 11 segments (Rotokas, 625; Mura, 802) and the largest has 141 (!Xũ, 918). However, it is clear that the typical size of an inventory lies between 20 and 37 segments - 70% of the languages in the survey fall within these limits. The mean number of segments per language is a little over 31; the median falls between 28 and 29. These values are very close to the number 27 ± 7 which Hockett (1955) estimated as the most likely number of segments in a language.

The variability in segment totals can be reflected in a number of statistical measures. These show that the curve formed by plotting the number of languages against the segment totals is not normally distributed. It is both positively skewed and platykurtic, that is, there is a longer tail to the distribution at the high end of the scale, and the shape of the curve is one with a low peak and heavy tails. This implies that the mean number of segments is not a good way to sum up the distribution. For this reason more attention should be paid to the range 20-37 than the mean of 31.

Whether the tendency to have from 20 to 37 segments means that this is an optimum range is an open question. It seems likely that there is an upper limit on the number of segments which can be efficiently distinguished in speech, and a lower limit set by the minimum number of segments required to build an adequate vocabulary of distinct morphemes. But these limits would appear to lie above and below the numbers 37 and 20 respectively.

Consider the following: the Khoisan language !Xũ (918) with 141 segments is related to languages which also have unusually large inventories. Comparative study of these languages (Baucom 1974; Traill 1978) indicates that large inventories have been a stable feature which has persisted for a long time in the Khoisan family. If the number of efficiently distinguished segments was substantially smaller, there would be constant pressure to reduce the number of segments. There does not seem to be any evidence of such pressure.[1]

Similarly, the facts do not seem to show that languages with small inventories (under 20 segments) suffer from problems due to lack of contrastive possibilities at the morphemic level. The symptoms of such difficulties would include unacceptably high incidence of homophony or unmanageably long morphemes. Dictionaries and vocabularies of several languages with small inventories, such as Rotokas (625, Firchow, Firchow and Akoitai 1973), Hawaiian (424, Pukui and Elbert 1965) and Asmat (601, Voorhoeve 1965: 293-361), do not provide evidence that there are symptoms of stress of these kinds in languages with small phoneme inventories. Hawaiian, for example, with 13 segments has been calculated to have an average of just 3.5 phonemes per morpheme (Pukui and Elbert 1965: xix), clearly not unacceptably long. And again, comparative evidence indicates that small inventory size may be a phenomenon which persists over time, as, for example, in the Polynesian language family, which includes Hawaiian (Grace 1959).

The restrictions on inventory size may therefore not be theoretical ones relating to message density and channel capacity in language processing. Although such considerations have been the most widely discussed, they are far from the only ones likely to influence the typical language inventory. Linguistic messages do have to be sufficiently varied to be able to deal with myriad situations and they do need to be successfully conveyed via a noisy channel, but the design of language is also subject to many pressures of a "non-functional" kind. Most languages exist in a multi-lingual social context. Limits may be placed on the size of a typical inventory through language contact, especially situations where a language is gaining speakers who are learning the language after early childhood. The mechanism may be one which approximates the following: speakers acquiring a new language make substitutions for any segment that is not matched by a closely similar segment in their own language, or is not capable of being generated by a simple process of adding familiar features (e.g. acquiring /g/ is easy if you already have /p, b, t, d / and /k/ in the first language). The resulting inventory in the acquired language contains only the segments common to both input languages, plus a few segments "generated" by the process outlined above. The smaller the inventory of the first language, the greater the probability that some segments will be generated in the fashion outlined. The greater the inventory, the smaller the probability that similar segments will coincide in the two languages and thus the greater the probability of inventory simplification.

This proposal predicts not only that upper and lower limits on inventory size will tend to be rather flexible, as is the case, but also that areal-genetic deviations from the central tendency should be expected. Thus, greater than average size inventories in Khoisan or Caucasian languages, and smaller than average in Polynesian are understandable results: local deviations are perpetuated because primary contact is with other languages tending in the same direction. This proposal also avoids a difficulty; if human processing limitations are postulated as the cause of limitations on the size of inventories, then they ought invariably to exert pressure to conform on the deviant cases. The evidence for this is lacking.

1.4 Relationship between size and structure

The data in UPSID have been used to address the question of the relationship between the size of an inventory and its membership. The total number of consonants in an inventory varies between 6 and 95 with a mean of 22.8. The total number of vowels varies between 3 and 46 with a mean of 8.7. The balance between consonants and vowels within an inventory was calculated by dividing the number of vowels by the number of consonants. The resulting ratio varies between 0.065 and 1.308 with a mean of 0.402. The median value of this vowel ratio is about 0.36; in other words, the typical language has less than half as many vowels as it has consonants. There are two important trends to observe; larger inventories tend to be more consonant-dominated, but there is also a tendency for the absolute number of vowels to be larger in the languages with larger inventories. The first is shown by the fact that the vowel ratio is inversely correlated with the number of consonants in an inventory ($r = -.40$, $p = .0001$) and the second by the fact that the total of vowels is positively correlated with the consonant total ($r = .38$, $p = .0001$). However, a large consonant inventory with a small vowel inventory is certainly possible, as, for example, in Haida (700: 46C, 3V), Jaqaru (820: 38C, 3V) or Burushaski (915: 38C, 5V). Small consonant inventories with a large number of vowels seem the least likely to occur (cf. the findings of Hockett 1955), although there is something of an areal/genetic tendency in this direction in New Guinea languages such as Pawaian (612: 10C, 12V), Daribi (616: 13C, 10V) and Fasu (617: 11C, 10V). In these cases a small number of consonants is combined with a contrast of vowel nasality. Despite some aberrant cases, however, there is a general though weak association between overall inventory size and consonant/vowel balance: larger inventories tend to have a greater proportion of consonants.

Such an association suggests that inventory size and structure may be related in other ways as well. A simple form of such a hypothesis would propose that segment inventories are structured so that the smallest inventories contain the most frequent segments, and as the size of the inventory increases, segments are added in descending order of their overall frequency of occurrence. If this were so, all segments could be arranged in a single hierarchy. Such an extreme formulation is not correct, since no single segment is found in all languages. But if we add a corollary, that larger inventories tend to exclude some of the most common segments, then there is an interesting set of predictions to investigate. We may formulate these more cautiously in the following way: a smaller inventory has a greater probability of including a given common segment than a larger one, and a larger inventory has a greater probability of including an unusual segment type than a smaller one.

The extent to which languages conform to the predictions can be tested in two straightforward ways. One is to examine inventories of some given size and see what segments they contain; the other is to examine given segment types and see how they are distributed across inventories by size. Using the second approach, the distribution of 13 of the most frequent consonants was investigated in a set of UPSID languages with relatively small inventories and in a set of languages with relatively large inventories. For the small inventory set, languages with 20-24 segments were chosen. Below 20 segments a language usually has fewer than 13 consonants, so that exclusions would occur simply because of the small numbers involved. For the large inventory set, all UPSID languages with over 40 segments were selected. These choices resulted in subsamples containing 57 and 54 languages respectively.

The set of consonants investigated and their distribution is shown in Table 1.1 below, together with three percentages. The first is the percentage of the 57 small inventory languages with the given segment, the second is the percentage of all UPSID languages which have the segment and the third is the percentage of the large inventory languages which have the segment. Note that consonants in the dental/alveolar region have not been considered here because of the frequent uncertainty as to whether they are dental or alveolar.

The consonants investigated fall into three groups. Using the overall frequency of the segment as the expected value, the first and third groups of these consonants show significant deviations ($p < .005$), while the central group shows no significant difference from the expected value (using a χ^2 test). There is a set (especially plain voiceless plosives) which are more common in the smaller inventories, for example, /p/ and /k/ occur in 90% or more of these languages but in less than 80% of the languages with larger inventories. There is also a set of these frequent consonants that are much more likely to occur in languages with larger inventories, these being notably the voiced stops /b/ and /g/ and the fricatives /f/ and /ʃ/. There is a tendency for smaller inventories to have no voicing contrast in stops and to lack fricatives apart from some kind of /s/. Note that the common nasals in the table are divided one to each group; /ŋ/ is more common in smaller inventories, /m/ is equally common in small and large, and /ɲ/ is more common in the larger inventories.

Table 1.1 Inventory size and frequency of selected segments

		"Small" percent	Total percent	"Large" percent
More likely in small inventories				
	/p/	89.5%	82.6%	77.8%
	/k/	93.0%	89.3%	79.3%
	/ŋ/	59.6%	52.7%	51.9%
Equally likely in large or small inventories				
	/m/	94.7%	94.3%	92.6%
	/w/	75.4%	75.1%	77.8%
More likely in large inventories				
	/b/	45.6%	62.8%	77.8%
	/g/	42.1%	55.2%	75.9%
	/ʔ/	33.3%	30.3%	55.6%
	/tʃ/	22.8%	44.5%	64.8%
	/f/	15.8%	42.6%	51.8%
	/ʃ/	17.5%	46.1%	70.4%
	/j/	78.9%	85.5%	94.4%
	/ɲ/	22.8%	33.8%	37.0%

From this examination, we must conclude that the relationship between the size and the content of an inventory is a matter that concerns individual types of segments, rather than being amenable to broad generalizations.

A second test of aspects of the relationship of inventory size and structure was conducted by considering what kind of consonant inventory would be formed if only the most frequent segments were included. In this case, only the number of consonants in an inventory was considered. Recall that the modal number of consonants in an inventory is 21. The most frequently occurring individual consonant segment types in the UPSID data file would form a "modal" inventory containing the 20 consonants below plus one other:

p, b	*t, *d	tʃ	k, g	ʔ
f	*s	ʃ		
m	*n	ɲ	ŋ	
w	*l, *r	j		h

A certain amount of "pooling" of similar segments is assumed to be valid for this exercise, e.g. dental or alveolar segments have been pooled, and are represented by /*t, *d, *n/ etc. The twenty-first consonant in the inventory might be one of several with rather similar frequencies, especially /z/ or /ts/ which are both about as frequent. A little less probable would be /x/, /v/ or /dʒ/ as these are a little less common. The aspirated stops /p^h/, /t^h/ and /k^h/ are about as frequent as this last group but they almost always occur as part of a series of aspirated stops and so one of them alone as the twenty-first consonant is not plausible. Because of the several possible candidates, distribution of only twenty consonants was examined.

Languages are most likely to have between 5 and 11 stops (including affricates but excluding clicks in this class for these purposes); 63% of the languages fall within the range given but the scatter is quite wide (minimum 3, maximum 36, mean 10.5). For fricatives, 1 to 4 is the most likely (58% of languages), and from 2 to 4 is most likely for nasals (91% of languages). Languages are most likely to have 2 liquids and 2 vocoid approximants (41% and 72% respectively). About 63% of the languages have the consonant /h/ which is not included in any of the categories already named.

The inventory made up from the most frequent consonant segments does conform to the predominant patterns concerning the numbers of stops, fricatives, and so on reported above. For example there are 8 (or, with /dʒ/, 9) stops, and 3 (or, with /z/, /x/ or /v/, 4) fricatives. By simply considering frequency we obtain an inventory which is typologically most plausible in its structure. This is encouraging. However, none of the 29 languages with 21 consonants contain all 20 of the segments outlined above. Bambara (105) is very close with 19 of them, having /z/ and /dʒ/ but lacking /ʔ/. Fur (203) only deviates by having /ɣ/ instead of /ʔ/ and having /dʒ/ rather than /tʃ/ and is thus also very close to the idealization generated. But at the other extreme, Wichita (755) has only 7 of the 20 segments (although two other segments are phonemically long counterparts of /s/ and /n/). Other languages with relatively few of the most common consonants include the Australian language Kariera-Ngarluma (363) with 10 and Arabana-Wanganura (366) and Mongolian (066) with 11. The majority of the languages examined have between 14 and 16 of the most frequent segments.

Leaving aside the consonants in the dental/alveolar region because of difficulties in arriving at exact counts, a calculation was done comparing the expected frequency of these consonants in any random subsample of 29 languages, and the observed frequency in the 29 languages examined. The expected frequency is simply derived from the overall frequency in the UPSID languages. For the 14 segments compared, there is only one case in which the expected and observed frequencies differ by more than 3. The difference between these frequencies is not significant (χ^2 = 1.505 for 13 d.f.). In general, the conclusion suggested is that at the modal inventory size for consonants there is no greater tendency for more frequent segments to occur than in the UPSID data file as a whole.

1.5 Phonetic salience and the structure of inventories

Although the idea of a single hierarchy cannot be sustained, there are many strong implicational hierarchies between particular types of segments (although very few are exceptionless). Some examples of these, validated by the data in UPSID and discussed in more detail in the later chapters, are given below:

(i) /k/ does not occur without /*t/. (One exception in UPSID, Hawaiian, 424.)

(ii) /p/ does not occur without /k/. (Four exceptions in UPSID, Kirghiz, 062, with /p, "t", q/, Beembe, 123, Tzeltal, 712, and Zuni, 748. These last two languages have an aspirated velar plosive /kʰ/ beside unaspirated /p/ and /t/. There are 24 languages with /k/ but no /p/; 18 of these have /b, d, g/.)

(iii) Nasal consonants do not occur unless stops (including affricates) occur at (broadly speaking) the same place of articulation. (There are 5 exceptions in UPSID. Ewe, 114, Efik, 119, and Auca, 818, have /ɲ/ but no palatal or palato-alveolar stops. Hupa, 705, has /m/ but no bilabial stops. Igbo, 116, has /m͡ŋ/ but no labial-velar stops; it does have labialized velars. There are numerous examples of languages with stops at particular places of articulation with no corresponding nasal consonant.)

(iv) Voiceless nasals and approximants do not occur unless the language has the voiced counterparts. (No exceptions in UPSID.)

(v) Mid vowels do not occur unless high and low vowels occur. (Two exceptions in UPSID; all languages have at least one high vowel but Cheremis, 051, and Tagalog, 414, are reported to lack low vowels.)

(vi) Rounded front vowels do not occur unless unrounded front vowels of the same basic height occur. (Two exceptions in UPSID, Bashkir, 063, and Khalaj, 064.)

(vii) /ø/ and /œ/ do not occur (separately or together) unless /y/ also occurs. (Hopi, 738, is a clear exception. Wolof, 107, has one front rounded vowel, /ø/, but this has allophones as high as [y]. Akan, 115, has marginal phonemes /øː/ and /œː/ but no /y/.)

Yet, as briefly illustrated in section 1.4, such observations cannot be compiled into a single composite hierarchy. At the very least, alternate choices must be built in at certain points. This is because equally valid general prohibitions on the co-occurrence of segments within an inventory can also be found. Some of these are given below:

(i) A language does not contain both (voiced) implosives and laryngealized plosives at the same place of articulation. (No counterexamples in UPSID.)

(ii) A language does not contain a voiceless lateral fricative and a voiceless lateral approximant. (No counterexamples in UPSID.)

(iii) A language does not contain both /Φ/ and /f/ or both /β/ and /v/. (2 counterexamples in UPSID, Tarascan, 747, and Ewe, 114.)

(iv) A language does not include a dental stop, fricative, nasal or lateral and an alveolar stop, fricative, nasal or lateral of the same type. (There are 22 exceptions to this observation but this number is significantly fewer than would be anticipated if the co-occurrence were unrestricted; 43 co-occurrences of /t̪/ and /t/ alone would be expected otherwise on the basis of a calculation which partitions those stops which are unspecified as being dental or alveolar into dental and alveolar plosives according to the frequency with which the plosives with known place occur.)

These statements could be subsumed under a general observation that segments do not (usually) function contrastively unless they are sufficiently phonetically distinct. The mutual exclusions cited here are all between phonetically similar segments; without defining what "phonetically similar" means with any greater precision, note that the segments referred to could be collapsed under more inclusive labels, e.g. /β/ and /v/ are both voiced labial fricatives. The distinctions between these pairs of segments verge on being noncontrastive phonetic differences of the type that have been discussed by Ladefoged (1978; 1980: 498-501).

The hypothesis referred to here is that there are measurable phonetic differences between segments which are generally similar but which occur in different languages. These differences are assumed to be found along parameters that do not serve as the basis for phonemic contrast in any language, or are of smaller magnitude than the differences which form phonemic contrasts. In this light, the difference between, say, dental and alveolar stops approaches membership in this class of distinctions which are generally unavailable for meaningful contrast in a language. (A more typical member of this class would be, say, a difference in relative timing of the release of the oral and glottal closures in the production of ejectives, cf. Lindau 1982.)

This interpretation of prohibitions on co-occurrence introduces a concept of phonetic distance or phonetic salience as an explanatory factor in the design of phonological inventories. If we can explain why certain kinds of segments never (or rarely) occur together in an inventory on the grounds that the distinctions between them are not salient enough, perhaps the favoring of certain segments can be explained on the grounds that they are the most salient, and an appropriate selection of such sounds maintains generous phonetic distance between the segments of the language involved. While such ideas have principally been discussed in relation to vowel inventories (e.g. Liljencrants and Lindblom 1972; Crothers 1978; Disner 1982), they can be extended to the whole inventory. From this perspective, implicational hierarchies can be interpreted as involving steps down in phonetic salience, with the most salient segments at the top of any hierarchical arrangement, and segments which are less distinct (distant) from each other lower down. Note that this leaves open the possibility that the mean phonetic distance between the members of an inventory is approximately constant, as an expanded inventory means the inclusion of additional members whose distance from their closest neighbor is less, even though the total phonetic space used by the language is being expanded.

It is far from a straightforward matter to determine appropriate measures of salience and phonetic distance. Nevertheless, there are probably some questions which can be answered with only an informal characterization of these notions. For example, to the question, "is maximization of distinctiveness the principle on which inventories are constructed?" the answer is obviously no. Clicks are highly salient yet few languages (about 1%) use them. Moreover, those that do, have multiple series of clicks rather than exploiting this feature to make a highly salient contrast between, say, a dental click and a velar plosive in a limited series of stops. The most frequent vowel inventory is /i, e, a, o, u/, not /i, ẽ, a̤, o̰, uˤ/ where each vowel not only differs in quality but is distinctively plain, nasalized, breathy, laryngealized and pharyngealized. Yet this second set of vowels surely provides for more salient distinctions between them and approaches maximization of contrast more than the first set whose differences are limited to only the primary dimensions conventionally recognized for vowel quality.

A more adequate theory of inventory structure must recognize that certain dimensions of contrast are preferentially used before others in ways that do not seem related to salience. For example, the world's languages only add the additional parameters of contrast to vowels if they include a fairly wide sample of simple contrasts on the primary vowel quality dimensions. In a sense, then, these additional ways of contrasting vowels are themselves involved in an implicational hierarchy whose arrangement is not predicted by a principle of selecting maximally salient contrasts.

Independent of the above discussion, it must be recognized that phonetic distance cannot explain some of the prohibitions on co-occurrence of segments. There is a class of these prohibitions that differ from those cited above in that the distinctiveness of the segments concerned is not really in doubt. An example of this is the co-occurrence restriction which applies to subinventories of laterals. A language with several lateral segments contrasts them either by manner (voiced approximant, voiceless fricative, ejective affricate, etc.) or by place (with all the laterals being voiced approximants). Only one language in UPSID (Diegueño 743) clearly violates this rule, although Irish (001) is an arguable exception too. Even two exceptions are significantly fewer than expected. Thus, while multiple-lateral subsystems almost invariably contain an apical or laminal lateral approximant, which is therefore at the top of an implicational hierarchy, at the lower end of this hierarchy there are two branches, one permitting elaboration by place and the other permitting elaboration of laterals sharing the same place of articulation by variation in the manner of production.

1.6 Compensation in inventory structure

The fact that certain types of mutual exclusions occur which do not seem to be based on principles of phonetic distance is suggestive of the position that there is a principle of "compensation" controlling the structure of inventories. Martinet (1955), for example, suggests that a historical change which simplifies an inventory in one area is counterbalanced by a compensating elaboration elsewhere. Similar ideas are discussed at length by Hagège and Haudricourt (1978).

If diachronic changes do generally follow this pattern, then the consequence should be measurable relationships between various facets of inventories which follow a pattern of negative correlation. We have already seen, though, one aspect of inventory structure in which compensation does not occur. The tendency for vowel inventories to increase in step with increases in consonant inventories (section 1.4) is the opposite of the prediction made by a compensation theory. Several other inventory sectors were investigated for general signs of the operation of a compensation process.

The stop inventories of the languages in UPSID were examined to see if there was a tendency for the elaboration of the number of place contrasts to be compensated for by reduction of the number of stop manner contrasts and vice versa. Such a compensation is suggested by the inventories of Australian languages. These typically have a rich range of places of articulation for stops (and nasals) but no contrasts of manner (such as voicing differences) within the stops (Wurm 1972; Dixon 1980). Is this a local aberration or just a particularly striking example of a basic pattern in human language? Has the atypical language Mabuiag (365) compensated for its reduction to 3 places of articulation by adding a voicing contrast, creating the stop inventory /p, "t", k; b, "d", g/?

There are a number of ways in which this comparison of places and manners could be done. In this instance, it was decided to treat doubly-articulated stops (in practice, this means labial-velars) as having a place of articulation distinct from that of either of their components, i.e. labial-velar is treated as a place of articulation. Secondary articulations on the other hand, since they are more likely to appear with a range of primary places of articulation, seem more akin to the "series-generating" nature of the differences in initiation and phonation type, and hence were treated as differences in manner (a different count is given in Chapter 2). So, of the two inventories given below, (a) is treated as having 4 places of articulation and 2 manners, whereas (b) is treated as having 3 places of articulation and 3 manners.

(a)	p	t	k	k͡p
	b	d	g	g͡b

(b)	p	t	k
	p^{w}		k^{w}
	b	d	g

The correlation was obtained between the number of places out of a list of 10 and the number of manners out of a list of 14 "series-generating" manner components for each language[2] (glottal was not included in the calculation of places because glottal stops do not (ordinarily) have contrasting manners). The numbers of languages involved are shown in Table 1.2. Those rows with very sparse representation, i.e. less than 3 and more than 5 places, or more than 4 manners, have been eliminated, removing 29 languages from the calculation. There is essentially no correlation between the numbers of places and the numbers of manners for stops, whereas the hypothesis of compensation would predict a strong negative correlation.

A similar computation was performed for fricatives relating place to manner with cases with over 5 places or over 4 manners dropped (resulting in 16 languages being excluded over and above the 21 languages which have no fricatives). The results are given in Table 1.3. The observed data are significantly different from expected ($p = .0001$), and in this case a fairly substantial positive correlation ($r = .46$) between the two variables is found. Again this is counter to the predictions of a compensation hypothesis, and more strongly so than is the case with stops.[3]

Table 1.2 Manners and places for stops

		Manners				Totals
		1	2	3	4	
Places	1	19	83	35	20	157
	2	14	28	32	21	95
	3	3	16	11	6	36
Totals		36	127	78	47	

Table 1.3 Manners and places for fricatives

		Manners			Totals
		1	2	3	
Places	1	37	8	1	46
	2	46	35	1	82
	3	21	45	8	74
	4	6	32	8	46
	5	4	22	6	32
Totals		114	142	24	

The example given by Martinet (1955) of a compensatory adjustment in segment inventories concerns elaboration of the fricative inventory by reduction of the stop inventory. Therefore a similar comparison of fricative and stop numbers was made. In this computation, languages with fewer than 5 or more than 13 stops were dropped and languages with more than 8 fricatives were dropped, resulting in 92 languages being eliminated from the total. No tabulation of these numbers is provided because the table requires an inconveniently large number of cells. Statistical tests showed a weak positive correlation between the number of fricatives and the number of stops (r = .35), but this correlation is probably not reliable as its significance level is under .05. However, the absence of an inverse correlation is still notable.

1.7 Segments and suprasegmentals

Despite the failure to find any confirmation of a compensation hypothesis in several tests involving segmental subinventories, it is possible that the compensation exists at another level. One possibility was evidently in the minds of Firchow and Firchow (1969). In their paper on Rotokas (625), which has an inventory of only 11 segments, they remark that "as the Rotokas segmental phonemes are simple, the suprasegmentals are complicated".[4] A similar view of a compensatory relationship between segmental and suprasegmental complexity seems implicit in much of the literature on the historical development of tone. For example, Hombert, Ohala and Ewan (1979) refer to "the development of contrastive tones on vowels because of the loss of a voicing distinction on obstruents". If this phenomenon is part of a pervasive relationship of compensation we would expect that, in general, languages with larger segmental inventories would tend to have more complex suprasegmental characteristics.

In order to test this prediction, the languages in UPSID which have less than 20 or more than 45 segments were examined to determine if the first group had obviously more complex patterns of stress and tone than the second. Both groups contain 28 languages. The findings on the suprasegmental properties of these languages, as far as they can be ascertained, are summarized in Table 1.4.

Table 1.4 Inventory size and suprasegmentals

	Languages with small segment inventory (< 20)	Languages with large segment inventories (> 45)
Stress		
contrastive stress	6	8
predictable stress	7	9
pitch accent (?)	2	2
no stress	5	4
inadequate data	8	5
Tone		
complex tone system	2	6
simple tone system	2	4
no tones	22	15
inadequate data	2	5

Despite some considerable uncertainty of interpretation and the incompleteness of the data, the indications are quite clear that these suprasegmental properties are not more elaborate in the languages with simpler segmental inventories. If anything, they tend to be more elaborate in the languages with larger inventories.

There are more "large" languages with contrastive stress and with complex tone systems (more than 2 tones) than "small" languages. There are more "small" languages lacking stress and tone. The overall tendency appears once again to be more that complexity of different kinds goes hand in hand, rather than for complexity of one sort to be balanced by simplicity elsewhere.

1.8 Segment inventories and syllable inventories

Another hypothesis is that the size of the segment inventory is related to the phonotactics of the language in such a way as to limit the total number of possible syllables that can be constructed from the segments and suprasegmental properties that it has. Languages might then have approximately equal numbers of syllables even though they differ substantially in the number of segments. Rough maintenance of syllable inventory size is envisaged as the function of cyclic historical processes by, for example, Matisoff (1973). He outlines an imaginary language in which, at some arbitrary starting point, "the number of possible syllables is very large since there is a rich system of syllable-initial and -final consonants". At a later stage of the language these initial and final consonantal systems are found to have simplified but "the number of vowels has increased and lexically contrastive tones have arisen" maintaining contrasting syllabic possibilities. If tone or vowel contrasts are lost, consonant clustering will increase at the syllable margins again.[5]

A brief investigation of the relationship between segmental inventory size and syllable inventory size was carried out by calculating the number of possible syllables in 9 languages. The languages are Tsou (418), Quechua (819), Thai (400), Rotokas (625), Gã (117), Hawaiian (424), Vietnamese (303), Cantonese, Higi, and Yoruba (the last three are not in UPSID but detailed data on the phonotactics are available in convenient form for these languages). The 9 languages range from those with small segment inventories (Rotokas, Hawaiian) to those with relatively large inventories (Vietnamese, Higi, Quechua) and from those with relatively simple suprasegmental properties (Tsou, Hawaiian, Quechua) to those with complex suprasegmental phenomena (Yoruba, Thai, Cantonese, Vietnamese). In calculating the number of possible syllables, general co-occurrence restrictions were taken into account, but the failure of a particular combination of elements to be attested if parallel combinations were permitted is taken only as evidence of an accidental gap, and such a combination is counted as a possible syllable. The calculations reveal very different numbers of possible syllables in these languages. The totals are given in Table 1.5.

Table 1.5 Syllable inventory size of 9 selected languages

Language	Total possible syllables
Hawaiian	162
Rotokas	350
Yoruba	582
Tsou	968
Gã	2,331
Cantonese	3,456
Quechua	4,068
Vietnamese	14,430
Thai	23,638

Even with the uncertainties involved in this kind of counting, the numbers differ markedly enough for the conclusion to be drawn that languages are not strikingly similar in terms of the size of their syllable inventories.

In following up this study, several tests were done to see which of a number of possible predictors correlated best with syllable inventory size. The predictors used were the number of segments, the number of vowels, the number of consonants, the number of permitted syllable structures (CV, CVC, CCVC, etc.), the number of suprasegmental contrasts (e.g. number of stress levels times number of tones), and a number representing a maximal count of segmental differences in which the number of vowels was multiplied by the number of suprasegmentals. Of these, the best predictor is the number of permitted syllable types ($r = .69$), an indication that the phonotactic possibilities of the language are the most important factor contributing to the number of syllables. The next best predictor is the number of suprasegmentals ($r = .59$), with the correlation with the various segmental counts all being somewhat lower. Although all the predictors tested show a positive simple correlation with the number of syllables, in a multiple regression analysis only the number of vowels contributes a worthwhile improvement to the analysis (r^2 change = .19) beyond the number of syllable types. Thus we can say that syllable inventory size does not depend heavily on segment inventory size. Nonetheless, because the predictors do have positive correlations with syllable inventory size, the picture is once again of a tendency for complexity of different types to go together.

1.9 Conclusions

Work with UPSID has confirmed that segment inventories have a well-defined central tendency as far as size is concerned. Nonetheless considerable variation in their size and structure occurs. Their structure is subject to a hierarchical organization in many particulars but cannot be substantially explained in terms of a single unified hierarchy of segment types. This is partly because segments of certain types are subject to rules of mutual exclusion. The mutual exclusions cannot all be explained as due to the avoidance of inadequate phonetic contrasts, as some involve strongly salient distinctions. A search for evidence that languages maintain a balance by compensation for complexity in one phonological respect by possessing simplicity elsewhere failed to find it in balance between classes of segments, between segments and suprasegmental contrasts, or between segments and phonotactic conditions. These investigations suggest that complexity of various kinds occurs together in languages, and that languages really do differ in their phonological complexity.

Notes

1. If languages with large phoneme inventories were approaching some kind of limit on the ability to discriminate contrasts, it would be expected that speakers of these languages would show higher error rates in tasks involving phoneme recognition than speakers of languages with small inventories. I know of no experimental data which bear on this point.
2. The manner components are: plain voiceless, plain voiced, voiceless aspirated, breathy, preaspirated, laryngealized, implosive, ejective, prenasalized, nasally-released, labialized, palatalized, velarized, pharyngealized.
3. Of course, other compensations may exist between aspects of the segmental inventories not examined here; and the failure to find evidence for gross compensatory tendencies does not affect the validity of any posited historical evolution in a particular case.
4. Rotokas is not really very complex in its suprasegmentals. It has a partially predictable stress and a contrast of vowel length that seems only partly independent of stress (Firchow, Firchow and Akoitai 1973). Long vowels are not treated as separate segments in UPSID for this language.

5. Matisoff also suggests that the morphological complexity of the language would evolve along with the phonological shifts.

References

Baucom, K.L. 1974. Proto-Central Khoisan. In E. Voeltz (ed.) Third Annual Conference on African Linguistics (Indiana University Publications, African Series, 7). Indiana University, Bloomington: 3-38.

Crothers, J. 1978. Typology and universals of vowel systems. In J.H. Greenberg et al. (eds.) Universals of Human Language, Vol. 2, Phonology. Stanford University Press, Stanford: 93-152.

Disner, S.F. 1982. Vowel Quality: the Relationship between Universal and Language-Specific Factors (UCLA Working Papers in Phonetics 58). University of California, Los Angeles.

Dixon, R.M.W. 1980. The Languages of Australia. Cambridge University Press, Cambridge.

Firchow, I. and Firchow, J. 1969. An abbreviated phoneme inventory. Anthropological Linguistics 11: 271-6.

Firchow, I., Firchow, J. and Akoitai, D. 1973. Vocabulary of Rotokas - Pidgin - English. Summer Institute of Linguistics, Papua New Guinea Branch, Ukarumpa.

Grace, G. W. 1959. The position of the Polynesian languages within the Austronesian (Malayo-Polynesian) language family (IJAL Memoir 16). Indiana University, Bloomington.

Hagège, C. and Haudricourt, A. 1978. La Phonologie Panchronique. Presses Universitaires de France, Paris.

Hockett, C.F. 1955. A Manual of Phonology (IJAL Memoir 11). Indiana University, Bloomington.

Hombert, J-M., Ohala, J.J. and Ewan, W.G. 1979. Phonetic explanations for the development of tones. Language 55: 37-58.

Ladefoged, P. 1978. Phonetic differences within and between languages. UCLA Working Papers in Phonetics 41: 32-40.

Ladefoged, P. 1980. What are linguistic sounds made of? Language 56: 485-502.

Liljencrants, J. and Lindblom, B. 1972. Numerical simulation of vowel quality contrasts: the role of perceptual contrast. Language 48: 839-62.

Lindau, M. 1982. Phonetic differences in glottalic consonants. UCLA Working Papers in Phonetics 54: 66-77.

Martinet, A. 1955. Economie des changements phonétiques (2nd ed.). Franke, Berne.

Matisoff, J.M. 1973. Tonogenesis in Southeast Asia. In L.M. Hyman (ed.) Consonant Types and Tone (Southern California Occasional Papers in Linguisticsl). University of Southern California, Los Angeles.

Pukui, M.K. and Elbert, S.H. 1965. Hawaiian - English Dictionary (3rd ed.). University of Hawaii Press, Honolulu.

Sheldon, S.N. 1974. Some morphophonemic and tone perturbation rules in Mura-Pirahã. International Journal of American Linguistics 40: 279-82.

Snyman, J.W. 1975. Zu|'hõasi Fonologie en Woordeboek. Balkema, Cape Town.

Traill, A. 1978. Research on the Non-Bantu African languages. In L.W. Lanham and K.P. Prinsloo (eds.) Language and Communication Studies in South Africa. Oxford University Press, Cape Town.

Voorhoeve, C.L. 1965. The Flamingo Bay Dialect of the Asmat Language (Verhandelingen van het Koninklijk Instituut voor Taal-, Land- en Volkenkunde 46). Nijhoff, The Hague.

Wurm, S.A. 1972. Languages of Australia and Tasmania (Janua Linguarum, Series Critica 1). Mouton, The Hague.

2

Stops and affricates

2.1 Introduction

Stops occur in the inventories of all known languages and have appropriately been regarded as the optimal consonants (e.g. by Jakobson and Halle 1956: 42). The most frequently found types of stops are plosives, that is, stops made with an egressive pulmonic airstream. Apart from differences in place of articulation, these may vary in a number of ways through variations in laryngeal settings and in the relative timing of voice onset and offset and of velic closure or opening. In addition there are stops made with glottalic and velaric airstreams, i.e. ejective stops, implosives and clicks. The principal architecture of stop systems is conveniently discussed in terms of two dimensions representing the manner series and the places of articulation that occur. In this chapter, we will therefore analyze the structure of stop systems in the languages in the UPSID database in terms of the number of series and the number of places used. We will also examine in more detail some questions concerning the frequency of stops, particularly plosives, at different places of articulation. Glottalic and laryngealized stops are discussed in more detail in a separate chapter on glottalic consonants (Chapter 7). Clicks are not the subject of any special analysis, mainly because so few of the UPSID languages contain any, and they are not included in the totals in this chapter. However, nonlateral affricates (except affricated clicks) are included in some of the analyses because of the close relationship of affricates to stops. Lateral affricates are discussed further in Chapter 5.

2.2 Stop series

A series is a set of stops (perhaps including affricates) which share in a general sense the same "manner". That is, they share the same phonation type (voiceless, voiced, breathy voiced, laryngealized), the same airstream (pulmonic, velaric, glottalic ingressive or glottalic egressive), the same relative timing of the onset of voicing (unaspirated, aspirated, pre-aspirated) and the same relative timing of velic closure (nonnasal, prenasalized, nasally-released). In this chapter, secondary articulations accompanying the production of stops, including palatalization, velarization and pharyngealization, will not be considered as creating separate series of stops. The opposite choice was made in Chapter 1 for the purposes of the computation reported in Table 1.2.

We have considered each of the "manner" differences mentioned above which occur in the stops and/or affricates of a language as establishing a series in that language. Thus, for our purposes it is not necessary for a language to show contrast between series at any given place of articulation for the series to count as distinct. For example, if a language had only two stops /k/ and /b/ it would be considered to have two series, a voiceless one and a voiced one, despite the fact that both series are defective, and voicing could be predicted from place. This decision means that the number of series contrasts is maximally represented in our counts. In some languages there may be phonological reasons to collapse certain partial series together. This has generally not been done since it is considered more important to represent the phonetic heterogeneity that exists. In general, languages with affricates have them in the same series as they have stops, or in a subset of the series in which they have stops. But a language with a series whose only representatives are affricates has been counted as adding an additional series.

All languages have at least one series of stops, but two is the most common, just over 50% having that number. Languages with more than 4 series are quite rare, and no language in our survey has more than 6 stop series (excluding clicks). The frequency with which languages with different numbers of series occur in UPSID is given in Table 2.1.

Table 2.1 Number of stop series in UPSID languages

	Number of stop series					
	1	2	3	4	5	6
No. of languages	50	162	76	25	2	2
% of languages	15.8%	51.1%	24.0%	7.9%	0.6%	0.6%

The particular types of series represented are given in Table 2.2 together with the frequency with which such series are found.

Table 2.2 Frequency of stop series

	Number of languages	Percent
Plain voiceless	291	91.8%
Plain voiced	212	66.9%
Aspirated voiceless	91	28.7%
Voiceless ejective	52	16.4%
Voiced implosive	35	11.0%
Prenasalized voiced	18	5.6%
Breathy voiced	7	2.2%
Laryngealized voiced	6	1.9%
Laryngealized voiceless	3	0.9%
Preaspirated voiceless	2	0.6%
Voiceless with breathy release	2	0.6%
Postnasalized voiced	1	0.3%
Prevoiced ejective	1	0.3%
Voiceless implosive	1	0.3%

Plain voiceless plosives series are the most frequently found, with almost 92% of languages having such a series. Keating, Linker and Huffman (1983) suggest that this type of plosive is the most widespread phonetically in languages, and argue that they are most frequent because they are the most efficient from the aerodynamic and articulatory points of view (at least in initial positions). A language with only one stop series almost invariably has plain voiceless plosives (49 out of 50) and the one exception, the Australian language Bandjalang (368), may be incorrectly reported as having voiced plosives. (Australian languages more typically have a voiceless unaspirated stop series.) In none of the languages with only one series is there an aspirated voiceless series nor do any have any glottalic or laryngealized stops. Indeed, these types of stop series do not become at all frequent until there are at least 3 series of stops. This may be seen from Table 2.3, which shows the percentage of languages with a given number of series that have a series of the particular type listed. The table only gives a partial listing of the possibilities.

Table 2.3 Frequency of stop series by number of series

	Number of series			
	1	2	3	4
Plain voiceless	98.0%	90.1%	89.5%	96.0%
Plain voiced	2.0%	81.5%	69.7%	88.0%
Aspirated voiceless	0.0%	16.0%	63.2%	52.0%
Voiceless ejective or voiceless laryngealized	0.0%	3.7%	42.1%	56.0%
Voiced implosive or voiced laryngealized	0.0%	1.2%	27.6%	48.0%

Languages with 2 stop series

A language which contrasts only 2 series of stops typically has a plain voiceless/voiced contrast. This is so for 117 of the 162 languages concerned (72.2%). A further 27 have a contrast between plosive series that differ only along what is often conceived of as a voice onset time (VOT) continuum (Lisker and Abramson 1964), that is, they have a contrast of plain voiceless and aspirated voiceless, or of plain voiced and aspirated voiceless. Altogether, then, there is a total of 88.9% of languages with 2 stop series which differentiate the series just by use of differences which have been described as voice onset time differences. The small number of remaining languages include either (i) a voiced series with a nasal onset or offset - 9 cases, of which six have plain voiceless plosives contrasting with prenasalized voiced plosives - or (ii) a series with a less usual phonation type or airstream - 9 cases of which 6 contrast plain voiceless plosives with voiceless ejectives or voiceless laryngealized plosives. There are only two languages in this group which have voiced implosives, Nyangi (207) and Maasai (204).

Languages with 3 stop series

Among the set of languages with 3 stop series, one of the series is usually a plain voiceless one (about 90% of the cases) but apart from this there is a considerable amount of variation in these languages. The single most commonly found pattern is a 3-way contrast along the VOT continuum - aspirated voiceless, plain voiceless and voiced plosives - but only 19 of the 76 languages concerned have this pattern (25.0%). The 3 next most frequent types are languages with plain voiceless and voiced plosives and an ejective series (13 languages, 17.1%), plain and aspirated voiceless plosives and an ejective series (12 languages, 15.8%), or plain voiceless and voiced plosives and a voiced implosive series (12 languages, 15.8%). However, note that all 3 of these patterns, and several others, can be summed up as consisting of two series drawn from the set of VOT contrasts plus one series with a "glottalic" element, either a glottalic airstream or laryngealization. In total, there are 50 languages which conform to this general framework, 31 of them with a voiceless glottalic series, and 19 with a voiced glottalic series. In other words, almost two thirds of the languages with 3 series of stops distinguish them in this general fashion and the "two VOT + glottalic" pattern is more common than 3 VOT contrasts. Only two of the languages with 3 series (Maidu, 708, and K'ekchi, 714) have two "glottalic" series (the decision to analyse K'ekchi as having 3 rather than 2 series of stops might be challenged, since there is no 3-way contrast at any given place of articulation; see further in Chapter 7). There are also 4 languages which have prenasalized voiced plosives plus two series contrasting along the VOT continuum.

Languages with 4 stop series

The 25 languages in the UPSID sample which have 4 series of stops are even more heterogeneous in their structure than the languages with 3 series. Four general patterns, (a)-(d) below, are about equally common:

a) plain voiceless/ plain voiced/ voiced implosive/ voiceless ejective
b) plain voiceless/ aspirated voiceless/ voiced/ voiced ejective
c) plain voiceless/ plain voiced/ prenasalized voiced/ voiced implosive or voiced laryngealized
d) plain voiceless/ aspirated voiceless/ plain voiced/ breathy voiced

There are 6 languages with the (a) pattern and 5 with each of the others. Two other languages, Zulu (126) and S. Nambiquara (816), are rather similar to the (a) group in that they have plain and aspirated voiceless plosives, ejectives and implosives. This means that the pattern of two VOT contrasts and two glottalic series is the most widespread, although it only accounts for about one third of the languages concerned. There are some strong areal patterns to recognize in these systems. All the languages with the (a) pattern and all but one with (b) are from Africa (the exception is the Austro-Asiatic language Sedang, 304). All the languages with the (c) pattern are from North America, and all the languages with the (d) pattern are from the Indian subcontinent. The (a) group includes both Nilo-Saharan and Afro-Asiatic languages from Africa, while the (b) group contains

Niger-Kordofanian (Gbeya, 129), Nilo-Saharan (Yulu, 216, Sara, 217) and Afro-Asiatic (Ngizim, 269) languages. The (d) group includes Indo-European, Dravidian and Austro-Asiatic languages. It should be noted that the (d) grouping displays the most completely filled out 4-series patterns, as in Kharia (301), with all 4 of its places of articulation filled in all 4 of its 4 series of plosives, plus a set of palato-alveolar affricates:

Kharia stop inventory:

plain voiceless plosives/affricates	p	t	tʃ	ṭ	k
aspirated voiceless plosives/affricates	pʰ	tʰ	tʃʰ	ṭʰ	kʰ
plain voiced plosives/affricates	b	d	dʒ	ḍ	g
breathy voiced plosives/affricates	b̤	d̤	d̤ʒ	ḍ̤	g̤

Compare this with the partial contrasts at each place in Hausa (266), a language from group (a) above. In Hausa there are no more than 3 series represented at any given place (velars with secondary articulations are omitted).

Hausa stop inventory:

plain voiceless plosives/affricates		t	tʃ	k
plain voiced plosives/affricates	b	d	dʒ	g
voiceless ejective stops				k'
voiced implosives	ɓ	ɗ		

In Kullo (262) the 4 series are all present only at the dental/alveolar place of articulation. At other places, one, two, or three series occur:

Kullo stop inventory:

plain voiceless plosives/affricates		"t"	"ts"	tʃ	k
plain voiced plosives/affricates	b	"d"		dʒ	g
voiceless ejective stops/affricates		"t'"	"ts'"		k'
voiced implosives		"ɗ"			

Such a system containing deficiencies at some places is quite common, particularly as the number of series increases.

Languages with 5 or 6 series

There is only a small number of languages with more than 4 series of stops. The relatively closely related languages Otomi (716) and Mazahua (717) have 5 series, contrasting 3 VOT categories and 2 glottalic series. Igbo (116) and !Xũ (918), with 6 series, add a breathy voiced series to these. Interestingly, both these last two languages have an unusual glottalic series: Igbo has voiceless implosives beside the more usual voiced ones; !Xũ has prevoiced ejectives beside the more usual voiceless ones. There are too few languages to decide if this represents a general pattern.

2.3 Summary of analysis of stop systems

In general, therefore, languages nearly always include a plain voiceless series of stops. If there is only one series it is of this kind. As the number of series expands, a contrast along the VOT dimension is added first (this is usually reported as a voiced/voiceless distinction). However a third series is more likely to be a glottalic series of one kind or another than to involve further distinctions along the VOT continuum. Systems with larger numbers of series seem about equally likely to add a second glottalic series or to add to the number of VOT contrasts.

2.4 Stop systems by place

The other main dimension along which stops vary is the place of articulation. Since affricates frequently occur at places at which there are no stops, two separate analyses of the data will be given, the first for stops alone, the second including affricates. The number of different places in which the languages in UPSID have stops of some type is summarized in Table 2.4. In this tabulation glottal stops have been omitted since this segment type differs from other stops in several ways (e.g. glottal stops cannot vary in manner). Also the one pharyngeal stop (Iraqw, 260) is omitted because of the suspicion that the same is true of pharyngeals.

Table 2.4 Frequency of sizes of stop systems by place

	Number of places for stops				
	2	3	4	5	6
No. of languages	2	171	103	35	6
Percent of sample	0.3%	53.9%	32.5%	11.0%	1.9%

The overwhelming majority of languages utilize at least 3 places of articulation for stops. The 2 languages in the survey which have stops at only 2 places are Hawaiian (424), which has no alveolar or dental stop, and Wichita (755), which has no labials. There are only 2 other languages that have no labial stop of any kind, Hupa (705) and Aleut (901). Hupa also has no velar stop, as does Kirghiz (062). All other languages have bilabial, dental or alveolar and velar stops. The number of languages in which there is one or more stop at each of the major places of articulation is given below in Table 2.5. In this tabulation, dental and alveolar places have been collapsed together, partly because they are frequently not reliably distinguished in the sources and partly because a contrast between these places is unusual. Palatal and palato-alveolar places have also been collapsed in this stop tabulation, since no language is reported with a contrast, and the choice between the two labels seems partly to result from different terminological traditions.

Table 2.5 Number of languages with stops at given places

	Bilabial	Dental or alveolar	Palatal or palato-alveolar	Retroflex	Velar	Uvular	Labial-velar
No. of languages	314	316	59	36	315	47	20
Percent	99.1%	99.7%	18.6%	11.4%	99.4%	14.8%	6.3%

Note that there are 24 languages which have stops at both dental and alveolar places, though these are not always contrastive, since the place could be redundantly predicted from a manner difference in some languages. For example Guahibo (830) is reported with aspirated dental /t̪^{h}/ but alveolar /t, d/; Sundanese (408) has /t̪/ but /d/; Yulu (216) has dental /t̪, d̪/ but its implosive and prenasalized stops are possibly produced further back and have been entered as "ɗ" and "^{n}d". It follows from the near universality of bilabial and velar places that a language with stops at only 3 places is unlikely to contrast dental and alveolar. In fact none of the languages with both dental and alveolar stops have less than 4 places and 5 or 6 is more typical (17 of 24 cases, or 70.8%). The contrast of dental and alveolar places is thus particularly associated with the use of a relatively large number of places in the stop system of the language concerned. Typically languages with stops in the palatal area or with retroflex, uvular or labial-velar stops also have 4 or more places; this is true for 58 of 59 languages in the case of palatals (98.3%), for 44 of 47 languages in the case of uvulars (93.6%), and for all the languages with retroflex or labial-velar stops (100%).

Note that the most common place system uses 3 well distinguished articulators - the lips (bilabial), the tongue tip or blade (dental or alveolar) and the tongue body (velar). An additional place is more likely to be another tongue-body articulation (either palatal or uvular) rather than another tongue tip/blade articulation (e.g. retroflex). The only other pattern that is at all common for expanding the number of places used is to combine two of the basic places through introduction of labial-velars. No other double-articulation is reported apart from a "dental-palatal" in Maung (350), which may describe an articulation with a very extensive single longitudinal contact rather than a true double articulation. Besides this marginal exception, the absence of double articulations involving the tongue tip/blade and body is understandable. These two articulators are not fully independent in the way that the lips and the tongue are, since they are both parts of the tongue. There is no similar reason for the absence of labial-alveolars (or labial-dentals), combining articulations of the lips and the tongue tip or blade. Yet they do not seem to occur; although Hoffmann (1963) has suggested that Margi (268) has labial-alveolar stops (as well as other types of labial-alveolar segments), this description is inaccurate, as these are instead sequences of labial and alveolar segments (cf. Maddieson 1983).

A more detailed analysis of the way in which place contrasts are increased shows that in a system with 4 places, a palatal (or palato-alveolar) place is a little more frequent than a uvular one (36 to 29 cases). These two tongue body places easily outrank tongue tip or blade places (retroflex 17, dental 7). Twice as many languages (60) add a place which is in front of the velar than add a post-velar place (30). Twelve languages have labial-velars. So 72 of the 103 languages with stops at 4 places (69.9%) avoid any articulation further back than velar.

A language with 5 places for stops is most likely to add one tongue blade/tip place and one tongue body place to the basic 3 (18 of the 35 languages, 51.4%). Two additional tongue body places, palatal and uvular, are next most likely (7, 20.0%) with two tip/blade articulations (dental, retroflex) or either a tip/blade or body place combined with a labial-velar place being less favored (3 or 4 cases each).

Five of the 6 languages with 6 places are uniform in the places that they use. They have bilabial, dental, alveolar, retroflex, palatal and velar stops, but not uvulars. The absence of uvulars is probably a genetic characteristic, rather than anything typical of inventories with 6 places in general. The 5 languages concerned are all Australian. The use of a larger than average number of places is a marked characteristic of this language family: 10 of the 19 Australian languages in UPSID have 5 or 6 places and an additional 6 have 4 places. Thus 84.2% of the Australian languages in UPSID have more than the usual number of places in their stop inventory. None of them is reported to have uvular stops.

2.5 Stop and affricate places

As mentioned above, languages quite frequently have affricates at places of articulation where they have no stops. If places are tabulated for stops and affricates jointly there are considerable differences from the results with stops alone. Table 2.6 gives the number and percentage of languages in UPSID with any given number of places at which stops and/or affricates occur.

Table 2.6 Number of places used for stops and affricates, by language

	Number of places for stops and/or affricates					
	2	3	4	5	6	7
No. of languages	2	62	139	87	25	2
Percent	0.6%	19.6%	43.8%	27.4%	7.9%	0.6%

When affricate places are included, a handful of languages are counted with 7 places of articulation, and the proportion of languages with 4, 5 and 6 places increases. By this count, 4 rather than 3 is the most frequent number of places to contrast (cf. Table 2.4), with the most common pattern being for palato-alveolar affricates to be added to the near-universal bilabial, dental/alveolar and velar stops. This pattern accounts for 86 languages - over a quarter of the total sample by itself.

The languages with 5 places in Table 2.6 are most likely to add palato-alveolar affricates to the 3 basic positions together with either a uvular (19 languages), palatal (12 languages) or retroflex (11 languages) stop place. Ten of this set of languages, however, have two additional places at which affricates but not stops appear. Of the 25 languages with 6 places, 17 add palato-alveolar affricates to a system with a smaller number of stop places. The languages with 6 places at which stops occur tend not to have any affricates at any place, but this too may be an Australian peculiarity rather than a general rule. Recall that these are mostly Australian languages. Note that Australian languages frequently have no fricatives as well as having no affricates (see Chapter 3).

2.6 Voicing and place of articulation for plosives

In this section, we will discuss some of the interactions of voicing and place which emerge from the examination of individual types of plosives (pulmonic egressive stops). Glottalic stops are discussed in full in

Chapter 7 and the findings there should be compared. The most common types of plosives are naturally enough the plain voiced and voiceless types at the 3 main places of articulation. Their frequencies are given in Table 2.7. Separate totals are given for dental and alveolar stops, as well as for the "unspecified dental or alveolar" category. Below, the total of these 3 categories is given. In the text, the combined category of dentals and alveolars is represented by a phonetic symbol preceded by an asterisk, i.e. *t, *d.

Table 2.7 Frequency of plain plosives by place

	Bilabial	Dental	"Dental/alveolar"	Alveolar	Velar
Plain voiceless	263	72	135	102	283
Plain voiced	199	53	77	65	175
	Plain voiceless		309		
	Plain voiced		195		

The class of segments represented by /*t/ is the most common of these, but the total of 309 /*t/'s should be "corrected" for the 19 languages that have both /t̪/ and /t/, so that only 290 languages have a /*t/ segment. Nonetheless all languages with a series of plain voiceless plosives, apart from Hawaiian, have a /*t/ segment. Note that there are about 20 more /k/'s than /p/'s. There are also about 20 fewer /g/'s than /b/'s or /*d/'s. Similar relationships between these stops can be seen not just in the raw totals, but also in the structure of the inventories of individual languages. Thus there are 24 languages that have /k/ but lack /p/. Note that these are not languages that avoid use of the bilabial place in general - most of them (18 of the 24) have a voiced series of stops including /b/. All of them include /*t/ in their inventories. On the other hand, there are only 4 languages with a /p/ but no /k/. Thus, /p/ is more likely to be "missing" than /k/ and an implicational hierarchy can be set up such that presence of /p/ implies the strong likelihood of the presence of /k/, which similarly implies presence of /*t/. With a plain voiced series, the place preferences are different. Twenty-one languages have a series of voiced stops which lacks /g/; in 6 of these /*d/ is also missing, leaving a "series" consisting of only /b/. Two languages (Gadsup, 608, and Cashinahua, 813) have a voiced series consisting of /*d/ alone. All of these languages have the velar place represented by the voiceless counterpart /k/. There are only 3 languages with /g/ but without /b/. Two of them also lack /*d/. Thus although many languages have no voiced stops, among those which do, /g/ is more likely to be "missing" than /b/ or /*d/. The implicational hierarchy for plain voiced plosives is thus: presence of /g/ implies presence of /*d/, which implies presence of /b/.

There is thus an asymmetrical distribution to be explained. One way of expressing the asymmetry is to say that the bilabial place is disfavored among voiceless plosives and the velar place is disfavored among voiced plosives. But when the ratios of voiced to voiceless plosives at the 3 places are considered, it becomes unclear if this is an appropriate way to describe the patterns. Among dental/alveolar plosives the voiced/voiceless ratio is .63; since plosives with this place are relatively common in both voiced and voiceless series, we may take this as the most typical ratio. Now, the ratio at the velar place is .62, which is quite comparable. If voicing was particularly disfavored at the velar place a lower voicing ratio would be expected. At the bilabial place the ratio is .76, substantially higher than at either the dental/alveolar or velar places. That is, there is some factor which raises the number of voiced bilabials, or some factor which lowers the number of voiceless bilabials, or, quite possibly, both. Note that velar and dental/alveolar places retain their positions relative to each other on the two hierarchies, whereas bilabial place is at the bottom of the voiceless one and at the top of the voiced one. If we assume that two processes which affect only bilabials are involved, or, alternatively, that voiceless bilabials have a tendency to turn into voiced ones, then both hierarchies can be accounted for.

There is some basis for believing that, in a language with a tendency to devoice voiced plosives, the bilabials may resist the process more than plosives at other places. This is because air can continue flowing into the oral cavity during a voiced stop for a longer time before oral air pressure equals subglottal pressure if the closure is at the lips. Hence voicing is more readily sustained in a bilabial plosive than in any other.[1] There is no particular reason for believing that this relatively greater ease in sustaining voicing during a bilabial closure should cause voiceless bilabial plosives to change to voiced ones, however. The frequency of "missing /p/" may therefore be the result of a more or less accidental convergence of several trends, perhaps including voicing but also including other processes such as sporadic shifts of /p/ to /Φ/ as in Hausa (266; Greenberg 1958; Newman 1977), etc. Stevens (cited by Ohala 1983: 195) has suggested that the relatively weaker release burst of /p/ compared to the other voiceless stops contributes to explaining its (comparative) rarity. The intra-linguistic phenomenon of a "missing" /g/ can be accounted for partly by the lesser frequency of use of the velar place in general (in comparison with dental/alveolar place), and partly by the increased number of languages with /b/, creating voiced series containing only /b/.

Although processes of the kinds referred to above may explain the patterns of occurrence, it should also be noted that there are strong associations between the occurrence of both the "gaps" where /p/ and /g/ are missing and particular areal or genetic groupings of languages. The majority of the languages with a missing /p/ are from the Afro-Asiatic and Nilo-Saharan families, which are contiguous in Africa, or from languages of New Guinea. None of the languages in UPSID from several major language families (e.g. Indo-European, Ural-Altaic, Sino-Tibetan) lacks /p/. The languages with missing /g/ are also predominantly only from certain particular areas: Austro-Asiatic and Austro-Thai languages in South East Asia and languages from the Americas account for 19 of the 21 cases. So although it is appropriate to continue the search for the reasons why gaps appear in these particular places in plosive inventories and to consider these patterns in evaluating historical reconstructions (Gamkrelidze and Ivanov 1973; Hopper 1973), the extent to which these are local aberrations should also be borne in mind. Similarities between these patterns in plosive inventories and those in glottalic stop systems will be discussed further in Chapter 7.

As for plosives in other than the major places, uvular plosives are predominantly voiceless - there are 38 languages with /q/ but only 8 with /ɢ/ for a voicing ratio of only .21. Labial-velars on the other hand have a voicing ratio of 1.05 since there is one more language with /g͡b/ than /k͡p/. Iai (422), the only non-African language with labial-velars in the database, and Temne (109) have /g͡b/ but not /k͡p/, whereas Efik (119) has /k͡p/ alone. In all other cases, /k͡p/ and /g͡b/ co-occur. The voicing ratio is .76 for palatal plosives and .82 for retroflex plosives, both of which indicate greater than usual tendency to voicing.

2.7 Secondary articulations with plosives

In the phonetic framework adopted for UPSID, appropriate segments can have secondary articulations of the following types: labialization, palatalization, velarization, pharyngealization. Of these, labialization is the most common with plosives, although it is largely confined to velars and uvulars. There are 38 languages with /kʷ/ or 13.4% of the number that have /k/. Fourteen languages have /gʷ/, which is 8.0% of the number with /g/. Nine languages have /qʷ/, which is 23.7% of the number with /q/. There are also 3 languages with /qʷʰ/ and 4 with /ɢʷ/. Only 8 of the total of 94 labialized plosives in the whole database are not velar or uvular.

Palatalization is more often found with labials (17 examples in the database) or with dental or alveolar stops (19 examples) than with velars (14 cases). Of course, historically velars in "palatalizing" contexts tend to shift their place of articulation and become palatal or palato-alveolar. Palatalization at its most frequent - with plain voiceless dental/alveolar plosives - only reaches 4.5% of the total of nonpalatalized ones. Velarized plosives are altogether rare, and pharyngealized ones are only reported in Arabic (250), Tuareg (257) and Shilha (256). Shilha has velar /kˤ/ as well as pharyngealized voiced and voiceless dental/alveolars. The other two languages have only the dentals among their pharyngealized stops.

None of the retroflex, palatal, palato-alveolar or labial-velar plosives in the UPSID languages is reported as having any secondary articulation. This may be due to the comparative rarity of plosives at these positions. Since stops with secondary articulations are less common than their simple counterparts, our survey may omit them by chance.

2.8 Affricates

The most common non-lateral and non-ejective affricates are palato-alveolar in place and sibilant in nature. The next most frequent are dental or alveolar sibilant affricates. Frequencies in the database of the major types are given in Table 2.8.

Table 2.8 Frequency of the most common affricates in UPSID

	Dental/alveolar		Palato-alveolar	
Plain voiceless	/*ts/	95	/tʃ/	141
Aspirated voiceless	/*tsʰ/	33	/tʃʰ/	42
Plain voiced	/*dz/	30	/dʒ/	80

Note that there are substantially fewer examples of the voiced dentals and alveolars /*dz/ than might be expected both on general grounds (the voicing ratio is .32) and on the basis of comparison with the palato-alveolars (where the voicing ratio is .57). However, a voicing ratio of about one third is not unusual for fricatives (see Chapter 3), and is characteristic of the pair *z/*s with which the dental/alveolar affricates obviously share acoustic and articulatory similarities. On the other hand, the voicing ratio of palato-alveolar affricates is closer to the values found for plosives. This may be related to the frequent historical descent of palato-alveolar affricates from velar or palatal stops.

Affricates at other places of articulation are relatively rare: the most common are palatal non-sibilant and retroflex sibilant voiceless affricates, but less than 10 languages have such segments. It is clear that the great majority of affricates are sibilants, and affrication rarely occurs without assibilation. Of the grand total of 522 affricate segments considered here, 485 are sibilant, that is, 92.9%.

2.9 Summary of generalizations on stops and affricates

A number of statements about the phonological patterns of stops and affricates have been made in this chapter. The most important of these are recapitulated here as summary statements, together with a fraction giving the number of cases which conform to the generalization in question over the number of relevant cases, and the percentage of conforming cases.

(i) All languages have stops. 317/317 100%.

(ii) A language is most likely to have two series of stops. 162/317 51.1%.

(iii) A language is highly likely to have a series of plain voiceless stops. 291/317 91.8%.

(iv) If a language has only one stop series, that series is plain voiceless. 49/50 98.0%.

(v) If a language has two stops series, it has a voice onset time contrast between them. 144/162 88.9%.

(vi) If a language has three stop series it is most likely to have two series with contrasting voice onset time and one "glottalic" series. 50/76 65.8%.

(vii) A language is most likely to have stops at 3 places of articulation. 171/317 53.9%.

(viii) A language most typically includes stops at bilabial, dental or alveolar, and velar places of articulation. 312/317 98.4%.

(ix) Stops at other than the 3 places mentioned in (viii) do not occur unless the language contrasts stops at 4 or more places. 206/210 98.1%.

Stops and affricates

(x) A language is most likely to have stops and/or affricates at 4 places of articulation. 139/317 43.8%.

(xi) An affricate segment is most typically a sibilant. 485/522 92.9%.

(xii) Doubly-articulated stops are labial-velar. 38/39 97.4%.

(xiii) If a language has /p/ then it has /k/, and if it has /k/ then it has /*t/ (4 counterexamples in the UPSID sample).

(xiv) If a language has /g/ then it has /*d/, and if it has /*d/ then it has /b/ (3 counterexamples in the UPSID sample).

Notes

1. This is confirmed both by direct experimentation (e.g. Ohala 1983) and by modeling the aerodynamic properties of stop production at different places (e.g Keating 1983). However, if expansion of the supraglottal cavity during the closure is as great as shown in some production data (e.g. in Westbury 1983), no differential effects of the place of articulation would be expected to occur in stops with closure durations typical of nongeminate plosives.

References

Gamkrelidze, T. and Ivanov, V. 1973. Sprachtypologie und die Rekonstruktion der gemeinindogermanischen Verschlüsse. Phonetica 27: 150-56.

Greenberg, J.H. 1958. The labial-consonants of Proto-Afro-Asiatic. Word 14: 295-302.

Hoffmann, C. 1963. A Grammar of Margi. Oxford University Press for the International African Institute, London.

Hopper, P. 1973. Glottalized and murmured occlusives in Indo-European. Glossa 7: 141-66.

Jakobson, R. and Halle, M. 1956. Fundamentals of Language. Mouton, The Hague.

Keating, P. 1983. Physiological effects on stop consonant voicing. Paper presented at 105th Meeting of the Acoustical Society of America, Cincinnati.

Keating, P., Linker, W. and Huffman, M. 1983. Patterns in allophone distribution for voiced and voiceless stops. Journal of Phonetics 11: 277-90.

Lindblom, B. 1983. Economy of speech gestures. In P.F. McNeilage (ed.), The Production of Speech. Springer, New York: 217-45.

Lisker, L. and Abramson, A. 1964. A cross-language study of voicing in initial stops: acoustical measurement. Word 20: 384-422.

Maddieson, I. 1983. The analysis of complex elements in Bura and the syllable. Studies in African Linguistics 14:285-310.

Newman, P. 1977. Chadic classification and reconstruction (Afro-Asiatic Linguistics 5.1). Undena, Malibu.

Ohala, J.J. 1983. The origin of sound patterns in vocal tract constraints. In P.F. McNeilage (ed.), The Production of Speech. Springer, New York: 189-216.

Westbury, J. 1983. Enlargement of the supraglottal cavity and its relation to stop consonant voicing. Journal of the Acoustical Society of America 73: 1322-36.

3

Fricatives

3.1 Introduction

While it is true that there are fricatives in nearly all of the world's languages, there have been relatively few studies of their precise distribution or of the patterns of occurrence which they show. Nonetheless, many linguists have expressed beliefs about universal tendencies affecting fricatives: for example, Fromkin and Rodman (1978: 331) say "If a language has fricatives (most do), it will have an /s/", and Bright (1978: 39) says:

> It is natural for a language to have at least one sibilant, namely, a voiceless alveolar [s]. Languages like Hawaiian, which lack even this single sibilant, are rare (cf. Hockett 1955: 108).

Statements such as these have been made on the basis of personal experience rather than on the kind of quantifiable research which is the only secure foundation for conclusions which depend on frequency of occurrence.

In this chapter, we will examine the fricatives in the inventories of the languages in UPSID, describe their frequency and patterns of co-occurrence, and suggest some generalizations which apply. Where possible, reasons why these generalizations hold will be suggested.

We adopt a conventional definition of fricatives, namely they are those speech sounds produced by the narrow approximation of two articulators so as to produce a turbulent airstream (Ladefoged 1971: 46). Note that this definition does not include the majority of sounds represented by the symbol /h/. Sounds transcribed with /h/ have often been labeled "glottal fricatives", but as Pike (1943) and others have pointed out, /h/ is normally a voiceless counterpart of an abutting voiced segment (most often a vowel). A brief discussion of the distribution of /h/ is given in section 3.9, but it is not included as one of the fricatives in any language in the remainder of the discussion.

Fricatives

In UPSID, fricatives are recognized as occurring at 10 places of articulation. Fricatives in the dental/alveolar region which are not described in the source as being specifically dental or alveolar are separately identified by a special variable. Fricatives also contrast in voicing and with respect to other aspects of phonation type (aspiration, breathiness, etc.). They may occur as ejectives or as laryngealized sounds, and may have a secondary articulation in addition to their primary one. A contrast is also found between central and lateral fricatives. These phonetic attributes are also features of other classes of consonants. However, one classificatory feature is restricted to fricatives and affricates. This is sibilance. Sibilance is an acoustic property, referring to a noise spectrum with comparatively strong energy at high frequencies. In many cases sibilant and nonsibilant fricatives can be produced at the same place of articulation. The articulatory difference probably involves the profile of the tongue rather than the location of the narrowest constriction. Sibilance is treated as an independent contrastive property of fricatives, and all fricative and affricate segments have been assigned a value of the variable "sibilant". Of course, the sibilant/nonsibilant distinction is only actually contrastive for segments which are articulated with the forward portion of the tongue.

3.2 The occurrence of fricatives

The great majority of the world's languages have at least one phoneme of which the representative allophone stored in UPSID is a fricative. Of the 317 languages in the sample, 296 or 93.4% have one or more fricatives. We may therefore say that it is typical of human languages that they have fricatives.

There is an important exception to this generalization. Of the 21 languages which have no fricatives, the majority are Australian. There are 19 Australian languages in UPSID and of these 15 do not have any fricatives. In a recent synthesis of work on Australian languages, Dixon (1980) shows that there is no reason to reconstruct any fricatives for Proto-Australian. Following Hale (1976), he also shows that those Australian languages with fricatives have developed them in relatively recent times from a medial laxing of stops (sometimes coupled with a loss of contrastive vowel length where length was part of the conditioning environment). It must be recognized that this family of languages is marked by an abnormal rarity of phonemic fricatives. Moreover, fricative allophones of other phonemes do not even seem to be typical.

As an aside prompted by this observation, we may note that the existence of language groups with sharply different characteristics from the rest of the world's known languages raises some doubts about the authenticity of some of the claimed universal similarities between human languages. In particular, it raises the question of to what extent "universals" are a reflection of the accidents of survival and propagation of languages, rather than of basic properties of human communication systems. A possible approach to answering this question would involve pursuing the more distant genetic relationships of the surviving languages. If all the "normal" languages turn out to be more closely related to each other than to the "deviant" languages, then apparent universals might be due to inherited similarities. As little is yet known about the remoter relationships of the recognized families of languages, this issue cannot be pursued further at this time.

3.3 Number of fricatives per language

The number of fricatives of all types found in each of the UPSID languages is summarized in Table 3.1.

Table 3.1 Number of fricatives in UPSID languages

No. of Fricatives	No. of Languages	% in Survey
0	21	6.6%
1	37	11.7%
2	62	19.6%
3	47	14.8%
4	37	11.7%
5	26	8.2%
6	28	8.8%
7	19	6.0%
8	20	6.3%
9	5	1.6%
10	4	1.3%
11	5	1.6%
12	2	0.6%
over 12	4	1.3%

The total number of fricatives in the languages surveyed ranges between 0 and 23, but the modal number is only 2, with about 20% of the languages having that number. The mean is a little over 4. Only a relative handful of languages (6.3%) have more than 8 fricatives. The structure of fricative systems with different numbers of terms will be examined in section 3.8 . However, first the overall frequency of fricatives of different types in the UPSID data file will be discussed.

The most frequent fricative type is a voiceless sibilant made with the front of the tongue. About 83% of all the languages have some kind of "s-sound". This may be dental or alveolar in its place of articulation, but for many purposes it is convenient to collapse this distinction. This decision seems justified not only because of the obvious phonetic similarity of dental and alveolar sibilants, but also because of the great rarity of contrasts between /s̪/ and /s/. There are 262 languages with an s-sound, but only 4 of these (Tzeltal 712, Karok 741, Diegueño 743, and Guarani 828) have both /s̪/ and /s/. It may also be noted that there are no languages in the survey with both /z̪/ and /z/. In the remainder of this chapter the following notation will be used: /s̪/ represents a voiceless dental sibilant fricative, /s/ represents a voiceless alveolar sibilant fricative, /"s"/ represents a sibilant with an unspecified dental or alveolar place, and /*s/ will be used to refer to all types of s-sounds together. The same conventions will be used to talk about other groups of fricatives where similar distinctions need to be made.

Apart from the 4 languages mentioned above which have both /s̪/ and /s/, 29 languages are reliably reported to have dental /s̪/ and 98 to have an alveolar /s/. However, there are 131 languages with an s-sound which is not specifically identified as dental or alveolar. In all probability, alveolar sibilants are more common than dental ones, but this cannot be definitely determined from our sample, as there are so many cases in which specific information on place of articulation is missing from our source.

We may therefore state that /*s/ is the most common fricative, with /s/ probably being the more common member of the group /*s/. The number of languages with /*s/ is 88.5% of those languages with fricatives. So Fromkin and Rodman's statement that languages with fricatives have an s-sound has relatively few exceptions. Bright's assertion that it is natural for languages to have an alveolar sibilant appears to be rather less well-founded, unless it too is construed to refer to the class /*s/ rather than strictly to the alveolar /s/.

The two next most frequent fricatives are the voiceless palato-alveolar sibilant /ʃ/ with 146 cases, and the voiceless labio-dental fricative /f/

with 135 cases. Their common occurrence is related in part to a general preference for voiceless fricatives which will be discussed further below. Next most frequent is the voiced counterpart of /*s/, namely /*z/, which is the most common voiced fricative. There are 96 languages with one or other of the members of /*z/. Next in frequency is /x/ (75 cases), followed by /v/ (67 cases) and /ʒ/ (51 cases).

There are only a little over a third as many cases of /*z/ as there are of /*s/. Such a proportion seems to be approximately the usual ratio between voiceless and voiced fricatives which are otherwise of the same type. The predominance of voiceless fricatives over voiced ones can be conveniently indicated by the ratio of voiced to voiceless, which we will call the "voicing ratio". For the total number of fricatives in the file the voicing ratio is 0.43. We may examine the separate ratios which are substantially different from this overall ratio to determine at which places voicing is more than usually favored or avoided in fricatives. The frequency of occurrence of 11 pairs of voiced and voiceless fricatives, arranged in descending order of frequency of the voiceless member of the pair, is shown in Table 3.2, together with the voicing ratio.

Table 3.2 Relative frequency of voiced and voiceless fricatives

	Voiceless				Voiced			"Voicing ratio"	
*s	/s̪/	33	266	*z	/z̪/	11	96	0.33	0.36
	/"s"/	131			/"z"/	49		0.37	
	/s/	102			/z/	36		0.35	
	/ʃ/		146		/ʒ/		51		0.34
	/f/		135		/v/		67		0.50
	/x/		75		/ɣ/		40		0.53
	/χ/		29		/ʁ/		13		0.45
	/ɸ/		21		/β/		32		1.52
*ɬ	/ɬ̪/	0	30	*ɮ	/ɮ̪/	0	7	--	0.23
	/"ɬ"/	17			/"ɮ"/	2		0.11	
	/ɬ/	13			/ɮ/	5		0.38	
	/θ/		18		/ð/		21		1.16
	/ʂ/		17		/ʐ/		3		0.17
	/ç/		16		/ǰ/		7		0.43
	/ħ/		13		/ʕ/		9		0.69

There is a high correlation between the voiceless and voiced frequencies (r^2 = .912, significant at better than .0001 level). In other words, whether a given voiced fricative is more common than another can be largely predicted from knowing which of the two voiceless counterparts is more common, and vice versa. However, certain places of articulation favor presence or absence of voicing more strongly than the general run of fricatives. Most saliently, bilabial and dental nonsibilant fricatives favor voicing, to the extent that there are more instances of /β/ than /ɸ/ and more of /ð/ than /θ/. It should also be noted that pharyngeals are more than usually likely to be voiced, and that retroflex sibilant and lateral fricatives (in the dental/alveolar area) are more than usually likely to be voiceless.

It seems to be the case that /β/ and /ð/ in many languages are of relatively recent origin and this may be related to their unexpectedly frequent occurrence. They derive historically from laxing or weakening of voiced plosives, as in Spanish (011), Atayal (407), and probably also in languages such as Kaliai (421), Gadsup (608) and Diegueño (743); and in a number of cases result from loan phonology, as in Quechua (819) and Mongolian (066). Compare Ferguson's findings in his study of the process /d/ --> /ð/. He concludes that this is "a highly context-sensitive assimilatory process which is typically part of a larger schema of spirantization (of voiced stops or all stops) which is relatively easily diffused across languages" (Ferguson 1978: 437). Since the voiceless counterparts are less common, such processes apparently either generate fewer instances of the voiceless counterparts /ɸ/ and /θ/, or once generated, these sounds are rapidly transformed into something else. It is tempting to hypothesize that /ɸ/ and /θ/ are changed into the very common voiceless fricatives /f/ and /*s/. If this hypothesis is correct, we might expect that fewer languages would have both members of the voiceless pairs /ɸ, f/ and /θ, *s/ than the voiced pairs /β, v/ and /ð, *z/. However, there are more languages with the voiceless pairs than the voiced ones. There are 13 languages with /θ, *s/ and 6 with /ð, *z/ of which 5 also have /θ, *s/. With the "labial" pairs there is also a predominance of the voiceless pair, although there are only 4 languages with both /ɸ, f/. However, there are <u>no</u> languages in UPSID with both /β, v/. The correct generalization to make in this case may therefore be from a different perspective, namely, that the absence of competing voiced fricatives may be an important factor in facilitating the adoption of /β/ (and, less clearly /ð/) into the inventory of a language. Gamkrelidze (1978) relates spirantization processes of this type to the gaps created in the stop systems, but does not discuss possible blocking of spirantization by existing fricative phonemes. Some of his observations will be discussed further in section 3.5.

3.4 Implication of voicing in fricatives

Generally, the existence of a given voiced fricative in the inventory of a language implies the presence of the voiceless counterpart in the inventory. (The converse is very far from being true, as the voicing ratios in Table 3.2 demonstrate.) This implicational relationship is subject to a fair number of exceptions.

Table 3.3 shows the number of cases which are exceptions for each voiced fricative in Table 3.2. There are altogether 78 cases out of 331 possible cases where the voiced member of a fricative pair occurs without the voiceless member, a 23.6% exception rate. In other words, for these fricatives, it is true about 76% of the time that the voiced member of the pair is accompanied by the voiceless one in the inventory. Note that this is not the number of languages involved, since a language may have more than one of the voiced fricatives being examined.

Table 3.3 Voiced fricatives without voiceless fricative

Fricative pair	Unpaired voiced fricatives/ total voiced fricatives	Exceptions as % of cases
*s, *z	0/96	0.0%
ħ, ʕ	0/9	0.0%
ʃ, ʒ	2/51	3.9%
*ɬ, *ɮ	1/8	12.5%
f, v	11/51	21.5%
ṣ, ẓ	1/3	33.3%
χ, ʁ	5/14	35.7%
x, ɣ	15/40	37.5%
θ, ð	12/21	57.1%
ç, ǰ	5/7	71.4%
ɸ, β	24/32	75.0%

As Table 3.3 indicates, there are considerable disparities between the various fricative pairs. Of the relatively large number of languages with /*z/, none lack a corresponding voiceless /*s/, and the other common voiced sibilant, /ʒ/, only occurs very rarely without /ʃ/. In addition to these sibilants, voiced dental or alveolar lateral fricatives and voiced labio-dental and pharyngeal fricatives occur only rarely or never without a voiceless counterpart. On the other hand, bilabial, dental and palatal nonsibilant fricatives are found to occur without a voiceless counterpart more often than with one. Retroflex sibilant and velar and uvular (nonsibilant) fricatives are in an intermediate group which occurs moderately often unpaired with a voiceless counterpart.

The particularly high occurrence of voiced bilabial and dental nonsibilant fricatives (in relation to the frequency of the voiceless counterparts) has been commented on above. However, the occurrence of unpaired bilabial and dental fricatives does not follow simply from the frequency. The difference between /β/ and /ɸ/ in frequency of occurrence is only 11, but there are 24 languages in which /β/ occurs unpaired with /ɸ/. Similarly, the difference in frequency of /ð/ and /θ/ is only 3 but there are 12 languages with /ð/ but without /θ/. These are significantly larger numbers than would be expected from the simple difference in frequency. This reinforces the remarks above concerning the nature of the processes which lead to the addition of /β/ and /ð/ to the inventory. Note that the strength of the implication being discussed does not necessarily relate to frequency of voicing. For pharyngeals the voicing ratio is .69 but presence of /ʕ/ always implies presence of /ħ/.

Among the group of fricatives which are intermediate in Table 3.3, voiced velar fricatives may also be derived from the same type of process as produces voiced bilabial and dental fricatives from stops. However, there are either more independent sources of the voiceless counterpart /x/ or more cases in which /x/ is developed in parallel with /ɣ/, so that a smaller percentage of exceptions to the generalization that the voiced fricative implies the presence of the voiceless counterpart is found.

The voiced uvular fricative perhaps occurs relatively frequently unpaired because of its relationship to the class of liquids. For example, /ʁ/ is the only candidate for a nonlateral "liquid" in Hebrew (253) and Sui (403), though in the latter case the historical origin seems to be from a velar stop (Li 1965).

The voiced palatal fricative /ʝ/ may derive from an approximant /j/ and seems unrelated in its occurrence to the voiceless fricative /ç/. As for the voiced labio-dental fricative /v/, this is perhaps found unpaired in some cases because it derives from the common approximant /w/ rather than from voicing of /f/.

3.5 Gamkrelidze's implicational proposals

Rather than a general implication that a voiced fricative implies the presence of the voiceless equivalent, Gamkrelidze (1978) suggests that the correct generalizations about velar and labial fricatives are opposites. He writes:

> ...the presence of the voiceless labial fricative phoneme /f/ in a system presupposes the simultaneous presence of the voiced labial fricative phoneme /w - v/... and the presence of the voiced velar fricative phoneme /ɣ/ in a system presupposes the simultaneous presence of the voiceless velar fricative /x/.

He defines /f/ to include both /ɸ/ and /f/, and its "voiced counterpart" is /w - v/ which includes /w/, /v/ and /β/. The velar fricatives are apparently conventionally defined. He claims that languages with /ɣ/ but not /x/ are "rare exceptions" (p. 30). Our finding is that over a third of the languages with /ɣ/ lack /x/. There are 75 languages in UPSID with /x/ or 23.7% of the languages. There are 40 languages with /ɣ/ or 12.6%. The percentage of languages in which these segments would co-occur if their distribution were random is thus 3% or about 10 languages, instead of the 25 languages in which they are found together. We may therefore correctly argue that presence of /ɣ/ generally implies presence of /x/, although this implication is not as strong as the implication holding between certain other voiced fricatives and their voiceless counterparts.

On the other hand, there are 139 languages or 43.8% with /f/ or /ɸ/ or both, and 288 languages with /w/ or /v/ or /β/ or a bilabial or labio-dental approximant, which Gamkrelidze would presumably also include in his /w - v/ phoneme, meaning 90.9% of the languages have a representative of his /w - v/ phoneme. Thus the percentage of languages which do not have /w - v/ is only 9.1%. Hence only 4.0% (9.1% of 43.8%) of the languages (some 12 or 13) would be expected to have his /f/ but not his /w - v/ if these phonemes were randomly distributed. There are in fact 10 languages in UPSID, about 3.2%, which have his /f/ but not his /w - v/ as construed here. Since this is close to the expected number, we must conclude that presence of /f/ does not significantly affect the occurrence of /w - v/.

3.6 Predicting frequency from intensity

It might be considered plausible that the more frequent sounds in the inventories of languages are those which have the greatest acoustic energy. These sounds would seem to be the most desirable to incorporate in a language if that language is going to have good transmission properties. As we already know, the sibilant /*s/ is the most frequent fricative, and it is the most intense. In view of this correlation it seems most appropriate to test this theory of inventory structure in relation to fricatives. Of course, what is being considered here is the intensity of the frication noise, which is greater in voiceless fricatives than in voiced ones.

There is a surprising paucity of information on relative intensity of fricatives, although some is available on the fricatives found in some individual languages. The best language-independent study remains that by Strevens (1960). Strevens examined a set of fricatives chosen "to provide a wide coverage of different places of articulation and shapes of orifice". These were [ɸ, f, θ, s, ʃ, ç, x, χ] ([h] was also included but has been discarded from consideration here). Two subjects produced a large number of tokens of each fricative at various degrees of muscular effort. Intensity readings were obtained and divided by subglottal air-pressure readings for the same tokens obtained using a nasal catheter inserted into the oesophagus. From this procedure a rank-order of intensity per unit air-pressure was obtained.

In Table 3.4 the intensity ranking of these 8 fricatives is compared with the rank-order of these fricatives by frequency in UPSID.

Table 3.4 Ranking of fricatives by intensity and frequency

	Intensity ranking	Frequency ranking
1	ç	"s"
2	ʃ	ʃ
3	x	f
4	s	x
5	χ	χ
6	f	ɸ
7	θ	θ
8	ɸ	ç

There is no significant rank-order correlation between these rankings (Spearman's rho = .1429). It does not seem that there is any strong case to be made that intensity predicts frequency. However, the tentative nature of the ranking arrived at by Strevens should be stressed. The relatively low rank for [s] and the high rank for [ç] are counter to the intuitions of most phoneticians.

3.7 Estimates of perceptual salience of fricatives

Several studies have reached conclusions concerning relative perceptual salience of fricatives of various types. Perceptual salience may involve factors other than overall intensity. It is generally measured by how successfully a segment can be identified in a listening task. These studies usually only involve comparatively limited inventories of fricatives from a single language. For example, Wang and Bilger (1973) studied responses to fricatives at the 4 places of articulation used in English. Of the 4 voiceless fricatives /f, θ, s, ʃ/, they found that /s/ was least likely to be misidentified as some other consonant. The overall ranking of the 4 is /s, ʃ, f, θ/ in terms of decreasing likelihood of being correctly identified. However, as Goldstein (1977) has pointed out, it is not easy to separate out what contribution is made by perceptual salience and what is made by response bias when the data and subjects reflect real language habits. Thus, /s/ is the most frequent of these 4 fricatives in English texts (Roberts 1965; Carterette and Jones 1974). The other 3 segments are all of relatively low frequency in English running text. In view of these facts, we may attach more importance to the fact that /ʃ/ is more reliably perceived than /f/ and that /f/ in turn is more reliably perceived than /θ/ than to the apparent salience of /s/, since this latter result may reflect listeners' expectations or some other factor related to the greater frequency of /s/ in English. Recall that /ʃ/ is a little more frequent than /f/ and both are more frequent than /θ/ in the UPSID languages.

In an experiment which involved a more varied set of consonants, including the fricatives /f, v, θ, ð, s, z, ʃ, ʒ, ʒʰ/, Singh and Black (1966) found relatively poor identification of /ð, ʒ, ʒʰ/ by all 4 groups of listeners used. Somewhat more reliably identified was the fricative /θ/, while /f, v, s, z, ʃ/ were correctly identified on the very great majority of occasions. As far as these results go, they do not contradict a hypothesis that the more common fricatives are those which are more salient, apart from the fact that /ʒ/ is considerably more common than /θ/. However, the conditions of this experiment did not provide a means of discriminating between those fricative types which are relatively frequent. Moreover, there are problems in interpreting the results of this study. The stimuli used were spoken by native speakers of English, Hindi, Japanese and Arabic. Speakers were given a short training session to enable them to approximate those sounds that were unfamiliar to them. These recordings were then played to groups of listeners who were native speakers of the same 4 languages. The listeners were given a brief training in the transcriptional conventions they were expected to use in recording their responses. Singh and Black do not report if subjects had to reach any criterion as either speakers or listeners before they were included in the study, and the design of their experiment confounds the influence of language-specific variation in the production of segments designated by the same phonetic symbol with language-dependent listener biases and with inherent salience.

As yet it seems the experimental work has not been done which can provide a sounder basis for forming a ranking of fricatives by salience. The few indications from this literature are suggestive of possible correlation of fricative salience with overall frequency in the world's languages.

3.8 The structure of systems of fricatives

Languages with one fricative

Of the 37 languages with only one fricative, 31 have some kind of /*s/ (3 /s̪/, 14 /"s"/, 14 /s/). We may therefore conclude that in languages which have one fricative, it is overwhelmingly probable that that single fricative will be a voiceless dental or alveolar sibilant. There are various ways in which a quantitative evaluation can be added to this comment: one way is to compare the ratio 31/37 to the total of /*s/'s divided by the total number of fricatives, i.e. 265/1123 (leaving aside fricatives with other than a single primary articulation and plain voiceless or voiced phonation). Of the fricatives in languages with only one fricative, the percentage of /*s/'s is 83.8%; of all the fricatives in the UPSID file the percentage of /*s/'s is 23.6%. In one sense, then, /*s/ is unusually common in these languages. However, the frequency of /*s/ in these languages is simply a function of the overall commonness of /*s/ and is not a result of any special association of /*s/ with small fricative inventories. There are 261 languages with some kind of /*s/ in their inventory, so a random selection of 37 of the 317 languages from UPSID would yield an expected number of 261/317 x 37, that is, 30.4 as the number of languages within this subsample that would have an /*s/ segment. Since 31 of the 37 one-fricative languages have an /*s/, we must conclude that /*s/ is the usual fricative in languages with only one fricative simply because /*s/ is the most common fricative.

Languages with 2 fricatives

Of the 62 languages with 2 fricatives, 56 have an /*s/ as expected. The most frequently found pair of fricatives is /*s, f/; there are 16 languages with this pairing. The percentage of these languages with this pair (25.8%) is actually less than the percentage which would be expected from consideration of the frequency of these 2 fricatives overall (35.1%). The next most frequent pair is /*s, ʃ/, found in 11 of the languages. This pair is even more infrequent (17.7%) than would be expected (37.9%). One might be tempted to argue that the pairing of these 2 voiceless sibilants is avoided in languages with a small number of fricatives, perhaps because they are phonetically similar. However, besides these 11, there are another 4 languages in this group with somewhat similar pairings of voiceless sibilants and 6 with a pair of sibilants which involve a voicing or other phonation type contrast. Altogether, then, there are 21 languages with 2 sibilants as their sole fricatives. These data provide a weak foundation for the argument that pairs of sibilants are avoided because they are too similar.

What can be said about the structure of these fricative inventories is that there is a significant tendency to prefer voiceless segments and to avoid voiced and voiceless pairs of fricatives at the same place of articulation. Only 16 of the languages contain any voiced fricatives, and only 3 contain a pair in a voicing contrast (/*s, *z/). Approximately 32% of the plain fricatives in UPSID are voiced, so a random distribution would lead us to expect about 39 or so of the total of 124 fricatives in the languages with only 2 fricatives to be voiced ones. In fact only 17 are voiced, well under half the number predicted by this calculation. As for the avoidance of voiced/voiceless pairs, a predicted number of cases can be obtained by multiplying together the separate probabilities that languages will have the voiceless and the voiced member of the pair. For the 3 most common places at which fricatives occur (dental/alveolar, labio-dental and palato-alveolar) the probabilities of the members of the fricative pair occurring together in a language are .249, .090 and .074. We may interpret these probabilities to mean that we should expect some 15 languages with the pair /*s, *z/, 5 or 6 languages with /f, v/ and 4 or 5 with /ʃ, ʒ/ from among a set of 62 languages. In the languages with 2 fricatives, there are only 3 languages with /*s, *z/ and none with either /f, v/ or /ʃ, ʒ/. It is therefore safe to say that voicing contrasts are generally avoided in fricative systems which contain only 2 fricatives.

Fricatives

Languages with 3 fricatives

In the 47 languages with 3 fricatives in UPSID the most common set is /f, *s, ʃ/, i.e. the grouping containing the 3 most common fricatives. It may be noted that there are 16 languages whose set of 3 fricatives includes the pair /f, *s/ and 22 with the pair /*s, ʃ/. These pairs are, of course, the pairs found most often in the languages with only 2 fricatives. In 29 of the 47 languages only voiceless fricatives are found: the number of voiced fricatives is less than would be expected by chance but not by such a large margin as in the 2-fricative systems. There are 8 languages in which there is a pair of fricatives contrasting in voicing (6 /*s, *z/; 1 /f, v/; 1 /ʃ, ʒ/). This is about two fifths of the expected number, compared with only about one eighth of the expected number among those languages with 2 fricatives.

Languages with 4 fricatives

When the size of a fricative inventory reaches 4 terms, there is a marked change in the extent to which voicing is used contrastively compared with smaller fricative inventories. Of the 37 languages concerned, 24 contain at least one pair of fricatives contrasting in voicing, and the most common system is one which contains 2 such pairs, that is, /f, v, *s, *z/. There are 10 languages with this inventory, plus 7 additional languages with /f, v/ and 6 with /*s, *z/. With 4 fricatives, instead of fewer voicing pairs than would be expected if fricatives occurred randomly according to their overall frequencies, there are more than expected. The expected number of languages with /*s, *z/ is only about 9, rather than the attested 16, and the expected number of languages with /f, v/ is about 3, rather than the attested 17. The probability of all 4 of these fricatives occurring together in a language is approximately .022, so only 1 language with all 4 would be expected in any random selection of 37, rather than 10.

The situation may be summed up informally as follows. There is a strong preference for voiceless fricatives in general, so languages with only a few fricatives are likely to have voiceless ones. However, if voicing is introduced into the fricative system, there is a strong likelihood that it will be extended to fricatives at more than one place of articulation. In other words, the common system /f, *s/ is converted to /f, v, *s, *z/ and the language becomes one with 4 fricatives. This may be expressed as a condition on linguistic processes in the following fashion: a process (historical or otherwise) which voices fricatives is more likely to apply to a class of fricatives than to a single fricative.

Note, however, that palato-alveolar fricatives are rarely involved in pairwise contrasts in these smaller fricative inventories. There are 2 occurrences of the pair /ʃ, ʒ/ in languages with 4 fricatives and only 1 in the languages with 3 fricatives. This is despite the fact that /ʃ/ is very common in languages with from 2 to 4 fricatives, occurring in 54 (37.0%) of the 146 languages concerned. Since the 2-fricative inventory /*s, ʃ/ is common, the 4-fricative inventory /*s, *z, ʃ, ʒ/ might also have been expected to be frequently encountered, but, as will be shown below, the pair /ʃ, ʒ/ occurs preferentially in languages with more than 4 fricatives. It is not clear why this should be so.

Languages with 5 fricatives

Of the 26 languages with 5 fricatives, 15 have a voicing contrast between one or more pairs of fricatives at the same place of articulation. Of these, 11 have /*s, *z/, 6 have /f, v/ and 3 have /ʃ, ʒ/. These are all above the number of cases expected if distribution was random (6, 2 and 2 respectively). Five languages, all from the Niger-Kordofanian family, include both pairs /*s, *z, f, v/. Nonetheless there are still 7 of these 5-fricative languages which have no voiced fricative at all.

Languages with 6 fricatives

The most common inventory for languages with 6 fricatives is one with 3 pairs of fricatives contrasting in voicing, namely /f, v, *s, *z, ʃ, ʒ/. There are only 5 languages with this inventory among the 29 concerned but they come from 3 different language families, Indo-European, Ural-Altaic and Niger-Kordofanian, so this is not just a genetically restricted phenomenon. Five languages with 6 fricatives have no voiced fricatives in their inventory, but the remaining 23 contain at least one pair contrasting in voicing. In inventories of this size, there are far more cases of /ʃ, ʒ/ than would be expected - 9 rather than the predicted 2. Other pairs of fricatives in voicing contrast are also found in greater diversity. Altogether pairs at 8 different places of articulation are found in one or more of these languages.

Languages with 7 fricatives

The typical fricative inventory with 7 terms contains 4 voiceless fricatives and 3 voiced ones which are paired with 3 of the voiceless set. Six of the 19 languages concerned contain the subset of 3 pairs /f, v, *s, *z, ʃ, ʒ/. Quileute (732) exceptionally has all of its 7 fricatives voiceless, having the set /s, ʃ, x, x^w, χ, χ^w, ɬ/. This inventory demonstrates several areal/genetic trends which are common to the languages of the Americas. These are the tendencies to have fewer voiced fricatives than other languages with fricative inventories of comparable size, to avoid labial (bilabial or labio-dental) fricatives and to have several back fricatives (velar and/or uvular).

It may be noted that voiced uvular fricatives are not found at all commonly until there are at least 7 fricatives in the inventory. Of the total of 14 voiced uvular fricatives in the UPSID languages, 3 are in languages with 7 fricatives, 6 in languages with 8 fricatives and 3 in languages with more than 8.

Languages with 8 fricatives

Twelve of the 20 languages with 8 fricatives have systems in which there are 4 voiceless and 4 voiced fricatives, although only in 4 of these is it a simple case of 4 pairs in voicing contrast. Nevertheless, in 13 of the 20, there are at least 3 pairs of fricatives at the same place of articulation with a voicing contrast. So voicing contrasts are often a major part of the content of fricative inventories of this size. However, there are 8-fricative systems which contain no voiced fricatives, for example in Iraqw (260) and Nootka (730). Yuchi (757) has 4 pairs of fricatives which are plain voiceless and ejective; there are no voiced fricatives in this language. Note that 2 of these languages are Amerindian.

Languages with 9 or more fricatives

The largest fricative inventories are fairly naturally a rather heterogeneous set, and frequently include some component such as a widely distributed secondary articulation, or a set of ejective or contrastively long fricatives. The largest system of fricatives in a language in UPSID that does not have one of these factors is Margi (268). This language has 12 fricatives composed of 6 pairs in voicing contrast, including voiced and voiceless lateral fricatives. Kabardian (911) has a total of 22 fricatives, reaching this magnitude by use of 7 places of articulation, 3 phonation types (voiceless, ejective, voiced) and 2 secondary articulations (palatalization and labialization). However, the combinatory possibilities of these various factors are very far from being exhaustively exploited. For example, as in a considerable number of other languages, labialization of fricatives in Kabardian is restricted to velars and uvulars. (Of the total number of fricatives of all types with labialization, 33 are velar or uvular in place; only 6 are reported at other places. There are also 4 cases of /hʷ/.)

3.9 The phoneme /h/

A large number of languages have a phoneme /h/. Over 63% of the languages have a segment of this type. A small number, 13, have a "voiced h". Of these, only 2 have a contrast of /h/ with /ɦ/. Clearly there is a strong tendency for /h/ and /ɦ/ not to co-occur. It should also be noted that /ɦ/ (phonetically usually a breathy voiced onset or offset to a normally voiced segment) is not limited to languages which have other breathy voiced segments (for examples, see Kashmiri, 018, Punjabi, 019, Karen, 516, Wichita, 755, Kabardian, 911). The classification of segments such as /h/ and /ɦ/ has been the subject of considerable disagreement. Although they have often been considered as members of the class of fricatives, some linguists have preferred to put them into a special class of "laryngeals" together with /ʔ/, and others have emphasized their similarity to vowels and approximants. The most extensive discussion of the issue is by Merlingen (1977) who reviews data from about 600 languages. His not very helpful conclusion is that there are several different types of /h/. This conclusion is largely based on arguments that /h/ can be associated with different kinds of consonants through examining pattern conformity and morphophonemic alternations. Although /h/ is often associated with fricatives such as /x, *s, ɬ/ by such patterns, it is also often associated with stops such as /k, p, ʔ/ as well as with nasals and other types of sounds. It remains likely that a relatively uniform phonetic characterization of /h/ is possible, but that it is best made in terms of similarities to the properties of abutting segments.

3.10 Conclusion

This chapter has presented data on the occurrence of fricatives in the languages in the UPSID sample. It has shown that patterns of frequency bear some relationship to what is known about relative intensity and salience of fricatives. It has documented more extensively some of the relationships between certain types of fricatives, such as the general tendency for voiced fricatives to occur only if the voiceless counterpart also is present. However, important limitations on this relationship apply when certain places of articulation are concerned. The structure of fricative inventories of different sizes was also examined and the connections between inventory size and types of fricatives encountered were investigated.

References

Bright, W. 1978. Sibilants and naturalness in aboriginal California. Journal of California Anthropology, Papers in Linguistics 1: 39-63.

Carterette, E.C. and Jones, M.H. 1974. Informal Speech: Alphabetic and Phonemic Texts with Statistical Analyses and Tables. University of California Press, Berkeley.

Dixon, R.M.W. 1980. The Languages of Australia. Cambridge University Press, Cambridge.

Ferguson, C.A. 1978. Phonological processes. In J.H. Greenberg et al. (eds.), Universals of Human Language, Vol. 2, Phonology. Stanford University Press, Stanford: 403-42.

Fromkin, V.A. and Rodman, R. 1978. An Introduction to Language, 2nd ed. Holt, Rinehart and Winston, New York.

Gamkrelidze, T.V. 1978. On the correlation of stops and fricatives in a phonological system. In J.H. Greenberg et al. (eds.), Universals of Human Language, Vol. 2, Phonology. Stanford University Press, Stanford: 9-46.

Goldstein, L. 1977. Three Studies in Speech Perception: Features, Relative Salience and Bias (UCLA Working Papers in Phonetics 39). University of California, Los Angeles.

Hale, K.L. 1976. Phonological developments in Northern Paman languages. In P. Sutton (ed.), Languages of Cape York. Australian Institute of Aboriginal Studies, Canberra: 7-49.

Hockett, C.F. 1955. A Manual of Phonology (IJAL Monographs 11). Indiana University, Bloomington.

Ladefoged, P. 1971. Preliminaries to Linguistic Phonetics. University of Chicago Press, Chicago.

Li, F-K. 1965. The Tai and the Kam-Sui languages. Lingua 14: 148-79.

Merlingen, W. 1977. Artikulation und Phonematik des H. Verband der wissenschaftlichen Gesellschaften Österreichs, Vienna.

Pike, K.L. 1943. Phonetics. University of Michigan Press, Ann Arbor.

Roberts, A.H. 1965. A Statistical Linguistic Analysis of American English. Mouton, The Hague.

Singh, S. and Black, J.W. 1966. A study of twenty-six intervocalic consonants as spoken and recognized by four language groups. Journal of the Acoustical Society of America 39: 372-87.

Strevens, P. 1960. Spectra of fricative noise in human speech. Language and Speech 3: 32-49.

Wang, M.D. and Bilger, R.C. 1973. Consonant confusions in noise: a study of perceptual features. Journal of the Acoustical Society of America 54: 1248-66.

4

Nasals

4.1 Introduction

Unlike most of the types of segments which are the topics of chapters in this volume, nasals have been the subject of a good earlier survey. In fact, the study by Ferguson (1963) on nasals has served in many ways as the model of an article on universals of segment types. Ferguson's article provided a major part of the stimulus for the organization of a conference devoted to nasals and nasalization (Ferguson, Hyman and Ohala 1975). For this reason, this chapter will largely take the form of a discussion of the various "assumptions about nasals" put forward by Ferguson, checking them against the data in UPSID to provide the quantification which is lacking in Ferguson's article and is only partially provided by Crothers (1975) working from an early version of the Stanford Phonology Archive. However, before this discussion, some summary information on the types of nasal consonants included in the UPSID data file will be presented.

4.2 Types of nasals

There are 1057 nasals in the file, of which the great majority, 934 or 88.4%, are simple plain voiced nasals. There are a further 50 nasals which are plain voiced but have distinctive length or a secondary articulation. Only 36 or 3.4% are voiceless, a number almost equaled by the laryngealized nasals (34 or 3.2%). There are also 3 breathy voiced nasals reported (from Hindi-Urdu, 016, and !Xũ, 918). The distribution of nasals by place of articulation is given in Table 4.1. (A similar convention to that used in other chapters is used for nasals in the dental/alveolar region, that is, /"n"/ indicates a nasal whose exact place (dental or alveolar) is unspecified in the source, and /*n/ represents the total class of dental and alveolar nasals.)

Table 4.1 Nasal segments in UPSID

Place		No. of simple plain voiced nasals		No. of other nasals		Total	
Dental	n̪	55		10		65	
"Dent/Alv"	"n"	155	316	23	40	178	356
Alveolar	n	106		7		113	
Bilabial	m		299		47		346
Velar	ŋ		167		23		190
Palatal	ɲ		107		11		108
Retroflex	ɳ		20		1		21
Palato-alveolar	n̠		17		0		17
Labial-velar	m͡ŋ		6		1		7
Labio-dental	ɱ		1		0		1
Dental-palatal	n̪͡ɲ		1		0		1

Evidently, nasals in the dental/alveolar area are the most common, but bilabials are also very frequent. Although velar nasals are far from rare, they are much less frequent than velar stops: for example there are 283 UPSID languages with /k/ but only 167 with /ŋ/. On the other hand, palatal nasals are more common than might be expected from comparison with stop frequencies: there are 107 languages with /ɲ/ but only 41 with /c/. Note that no example of a phonemic uvular nasal is reported from the UPSID languages (38 languages have /q/). Of course, pharyngeal and glottal places of articulation are ruled out for nasals because of articulatory constraints.

Among the relatively small number of nasals that are not simple plain voiced ones, there seem to be three reliable patterns. The first is that there is a preferential association between bilabial place and voicelessness: of the 36 voiceless nasals, 11 are bilabial. This is a greater proportion than is found at other places of articulation. For example, compare the ratio of languages with voiceless nasals to those with plain voiced nasals at the bilabial place, 11/299 (.037), with the comparable ratio among combined dental/alveolar nasals, 8/305 (.026). The other two observations relate to secondary articulations: palatalization is associated more with bilabial place of articulation than with other places, whereas labialization is associated with velar place of articulation. Of 10 voiced nasals with palatalization, 6 are bilabial; of 10 voiced nasals with labialization, 7 are velar. In proportion to the number of plain voiced nasals these are far more frequent than either secondary articulation is with dental and alveolar nasals. The ratio of palatalized bilabial nasals to plain voiced bilabials is .020, whereas the ratio of palatalized dental/alveolar nasals to plain dental/alveolar nasals is .003. The ratio of labialized velar nasals to plain velar nasals is .042, but the ratio of labialized dental/alveolar nasals to plain dental/alveolar nasals is only .003. Labialization is also most commonly combined with velar place of articulation in other segment types, such as stops and fricatives, but palatalization is not especially associated with bilabial place in other segment types.

4.3 Ferguson's "Assumptions about nasals": primary nasal consonants

We now turn to a discussion of the proposals for universals about nasals put forward by Ferguson. He suggests that "every language has at least one primary nasal consonant (PNC) in its inventory". By a PNC, Ferguson means a phoneme of which the most characteristic allophone is a voiced nasal continuant. As he recognizes, there are several languages that do not have any such consonant, but their number is small. Hockett (1955) had already drawn attention to some of these, and others have been pointed out in the literature (Thompson and Thompson 1972; Le Saout 1973; Bentick 1975). In UPSID there are 10 languages without any primary nasal consonants, 4 of which have no phonemic nasal or nasalized segments of any kind. These 4 are Rotokas (625), Quileute (732), Puget Sound (734), and Mura (802). Of these, two have very small inventories altogether, and the other two are from the Northwest Coast area of North America - the area from which the first exceptions to this generalization were reported. The remaining 6 languages without nasals have prenasalized stops or nasalized vowels: Kpelle (103), Barasano (832) and Tucano (834) each have a series of 6 nasalized vowels, Hakka (502) has prenasalized stops /ᵐb, "ⁿd", ᵑg/, and Apinaye (809) and Siriono (829) have both a series of prenasalized stops and a series of nasalized vowels. Nasal consonant phones occur in this latter group of languages, as well as in several of the other languages without primary nasal phonemes referred to in the literature.

Although there are exceptions, it remains true that the very great majority of languages do have one or more nasals - almost 97% of the UPSID sample. None of the UPSID languages has more than 6 PNC's; this is the same number as the maximum number of place contrasts for stops (see Chapter 2). The number of languages with various numbers of PNC's is shown in Table 4.2. Since only plain voiced nasals are counted here, this is essentially equivalent to a tabulation of the number of place contrasts for nasals.

Table 4.2 Number of PNC's in UPSID languages

Number of PNC's	Number of languages	% of sample
0	10	3.2%
1	7	2.2%
2	101	31.9%
3	95	30.0%
4	83	26.2%
5	14	4.4%
6	7	2.2%

Ferguson's second suggestion is that if a language has only one PNC it will be an apical nasal, i.e. one with a dental or alveolar place of articulation. This class of segments is represented here by /*n/. Of the 7 languages listed in UPSID as having only one nasal, 5 do indeed have /*n/, namely Tlingit (701), Chipewyan (703), Wichita (755), Yuchi (757) and S. Nambiquara (816). Taoripi (623), with /m/, is an exception, as is Mixtec (728) with /ŋ/ (although this segment is arguably a surface derivative and Mixtec could be another language with no basic nasals). Although Ferguson's claim about languages with only one nasal is thus true of the majority of relevant UPSID languages, it is perhaps more important to stress that having only one nasal is an aberrant pattern. Languages with only one nasal are rare, even rarer than languages with no nasals (7 vs 10). Moreover, most (13 of 17) of the languages with either one or no nasals are American languages. The relatively frequent deficiency of nasals within the American languages seems to indicate somewhat of an areal and/or genetic trait which makes this group of languages stand out from the rest of the world's languages. However, too much should not be made of this as a characteristic of American languages, as there are another 76 in UPSID which have 2 or more nasals in their inventory. This is about 85% of this group, compared with about 98% of the non-American languages in UPSID - a smaller percentage but still an overwhelming majority.

Ferguson's claim can be interpreted in a slightly different sense, namely, that every language with any nasals has an /*n/. Exceptions to this claim are certainly rare. They include Taoripi and Mixtec, mentioned above, as well as Wapishana (822), which has bilabial and palato-alveolar nasals /m, n̠ /. All other languages in UPSID with any nasals have an /*n/, and there are 13 with both dental and alveolar nasals. In other words, 302 or 96% of the languages in the sample have /*n/.

Ferguson's third suggestion is that a language with 2 PNC's will have an /m/. All of the languages except Wapishana with 2 PNC's have a bilabial and one of the members of /*n/. Specifically, 21 are reported with /m, n̪/, 31 with /m, n/ and 48 with /m, "n"/. Out of the total of 101 languages with 2 PNC's, 28 also have one or more nasal vowels, and 15 have additional nasal segments which have a difference in phonation type or length or secondary articulation. Apart from the usual plain voiced nasals, 8 have laryngealized nasals, and 2 of these have voiceless nasals; one language has breathy voiced nasals. In 6 cases there are length contrasts among the nasals. In Finnish (053) a long velar nasal appears as well as long and short /m, n̪/. This segment is found as the "weak" alternant of /ŋk/ in consonant gradation (Austerlitz 1967: 24) and is a rather marginal member of the phoneme inventory; consequently it could be maintained that the primary nasal consonants in Finnish are only the bilabial and dental ones. The relationship between primary and secondary nasals is a subject that will be returned to later.

If Ferguson's third claim is interpreted as implying that all languages with at least 2 PNC's have an /m/, then there is only one marginal exception in UPSID. All of the languages with from 2 to 6 PNC's have /m/ except Irish (001), but this exception is more a result of definitional criteria than anything else. Irish has a contrasting pair of bilabial nasals with differing secondary articulations - palatalized opposed to labialized and velarized. It has no plain bilabial nasal, and because of this it violates this interpretation of Ferguson's generalization.

Crothers (1975) conflates Ferguson's first three observations into a single general rule, namely, "nearly all languages have contrasting labial and dental nasals" [presumably, dental or alveolar is intended]. Almost 94% of the UPSID languages (297 out of 317) have both /m/ and /*n/ in accord with this rule.

Ferguson does not extend his generalizations of this type beyond a second PNC. However, it is evident that the most usual third nasal is velar, 65 of the 95 languages with 3 PNC's having /m, *n, ŋ/, i.e. 68.4% of this group. However, there is a very strong minor pattern which includes a palatal or palato-alveolar nasal instead of a velar one, there being 27 languages representative of this pattern, or 28.4%. The greater frequency of /ŋ/ is more evident in the UPSID sample than in the sample used by Crothers, where /ŋ/ and /ɲ/ are somewhat closer to equal frequency. Of the remaining languages, two, Pashto (014) and Telugu (902), have a retroflex nasal, and Irish (001) has no bilabial PNC but has both palatal and velar nasals. However, this language is perhaps best regarded as a language with 4 PNC's, including /m/, for the reasons outlined above.

In the spirit of Ferguson's observations, we may add that a language with 4 PNC's has a palatal nasal. In a very large majority of cases, 75 of 83 or about 90%, the inventory of nasals in a language with 4 PNC's consists of /m, *n, *ɲ, ŋ/ (palato-alveolar and "pre-palatal" nasals are treated as members of the same class as /ɲ/ and the class is designated by /*ɲ/). The only reasonably common alternative is /m, *n, ṇ, ŋ/, with a retroflex in place of the palatal. Five languages have this pattern.

Of the 14 languages with 5 PNC's, all have /m, ŋ/. Five contrast dental and alveolar nasals, but there is no common overall pattern, with the fifth nasal being either retroflex (3 cases) or palatal (2 cases). Four languages, all Niger-Kordofanian, have labial-velar nasals as part of the set /m, *n, ɲ, ŋ, m͡ŋ/. Four languages have /m, *n, ṇ, *ɲ, ŋ/, with a retroflex nasal. Teke (127) is reported with a contrast of bilabial and labiodental nasals, /m, ɱ/, as well as /n, ɲ, ŋ/. It is the only language with a labiodental nasal in the UPSID file.

The languages with 6 PNC's are essentially uniform, having /m, n̪, n, ṇ, ɲ, ŋ/ as their system, apart from Iai (422) which has /m͡ŋ/ but no contrast between dental and alveolar. It is noteworthy that 11 of the 13 languages in the sample with both dental and alveolar nasals are languages with 5 or 6 PNC's and that 10 of these are Australian languages. It is valid to observe that only languages with a large number of nasals contrast dental and alveolar places, but also important to note the genetic bias in the distribution. Australian languages typically have more nasals than languages of other families; of the 19 Australian languages in UPSID, 11 have 5 or 6 nasals. Less than 3% of the languages in UPSID have more than 4 nasals but the percentage of Australian languages with that many is 57.9%.

4.4 Primary nasals and obstruents

The remaining observations by Ferguson relate to the connection between primary nasal consonants and other types of segments, specifically obstruents and secondary nasal consonants. He suggests that the number of PNC's in any language is never greater than the number of obstruents. There are no counterexamples to this claim in UPSID. In the majority of languages, plain voiced nasals are found at a subset of the places at which obstruents occur. In other words, the presence of a nasal at a given place usually implies the presence of an obstruent (specifically a plosive or affricate) at the same place of articulation. A frequent discrepancy is that obstruents occur at palato-alveolar place but the closest nasal is a palatal. This is close enough to be considered a matching place.

In 6 languages, Ewe (114), Efik (119), Songhai (200), Javanese (409), Chamorro (416), and Auca (818), /ɲ/ occurs but there is no palatal or palato-alveolar obstruent. But these 6 languages are the only exceptions to the stronger claim that PNC's may only occur if there is at least one obstruent with the same or similar place of articulation. That all the exceptions to this claim concern palatal nasals may indicate that there is some factor favoring palatal nasals such that they do not need the support of a obstruent at the same place. In this connection, it may be noted that a voiced nasal is the most common strictly palatal consonant after the palatal approximant /j/.

4.5 Secondary nasal consonants

Ferguson classifies nasal consonants other than plain voiced nasals as secondary nasal consonants (SNC's). This class includes nasals with a secondary articulation, or with an unusual phonation type as well as pre- or post-nasalized obstruents. He suggests that no language has SNC's unless it also has one or more PNC's, and that the number of SNC's in any language is never greater than the number of PNC's. Of the languages which have any secondary nasals of any kind, a relatively large proportion violate Fergusons's assumption, but this occurs most often because they may have more than one type of secondary nasal. An example is Lakkia (401) which has 3 PNC's /m, "n", ŋ/ but has 3 voiceless nasals plus voiced velars with palatalization and labialization for a total of 5 SNC's. It seems more valid to interpret this suggestion as applying separately to each of the types of secondary nasals, and for this reason the discussion will be organized to deal with each type of secondary nasal separately.

Other phonation types

Nasals with unusual phonation types, that is, voiceless, laryngealized or breathy voiced nasals, do not occur unless a plain voiced counterpart occurs in the language. With few exceptions, if there is a series of any of these types of SNC's it will have a member corresponding to each of the nasals of the plain voiced series (PNC's). The number of such SNC's thus is never greater in any one series than the number of PNC's but is often equal. A language with two such series thus usually has more SNC's than PNC's. The UPSID examples are Sedang (304), Sui (403), Klamath (707), and Otomi (716). These languages have both voiceless and laryngealized series of nasals which together add up to more than the number of PNC's. !Xũ (918) has laryngealized and breathy voiced bilabial nasals, but has plain voiced nasals at bilabial, alveolar and velar places. No language in UPSID has more nasals in any one series with an unusual phonation type than it has plain voiced nasals.

Nasals with secondary articulation

The general frequency of nasals with secondary articulations was briefly discussed in section 4.2 above. Within a given language, there are two general constraints on the occurrence of such nasals: no nasal with a secondary articulation occurs unless a simple nasal occurs at the same place of articulation, and none occurs unless consonants of another type also occur with the same secondary articulation and in the same place of articulation. For example, $/m^j/$ does not occur unless /m/ occurs, and a segment such as $/p^j/$ or $/b^j/$ also occurs. There are 16 languages in the sample which are relevant to these claims of which 14 conform to both. The other 2 languages each violate one of them only. !Xũ (918) has a pharyngealized velar nasal, but no other pharyngealized consonants, although it has a series of pharyngealized vowels. Irish (001) has the appropriate other secondarily-articulated consonants but has no simple /m/ although both $/m^j/$ and $/m^w/$ occur. The interpretation of the Irish system is complicated because of the pervasive nature of the morphophonemic distinction between "palatal" and "velar" variants of consonants which coincides poorly with a phonetic characterization of the segments. Only at the bilabial place of articulation are both variants produced with differing secondary articulations.

Long nasals

Similar conditions apply to distinctively long nasals as apply to those with secondary articulations. In the 13 languages with long nasals, a matching short nasal occurs with each long nasal, except for the case of /ŋ:/ in Finnish (053), discussed in section 4.3 above. There are, however, 3 languages where one or more long nasals occur but matching long consonants of other types are lacking. These are Chuvash (060), Ocaina (805) and !Xũ (918). (Chuvash does have distinctively long approximants but has no long bilabial consonants apart from /mː/.) Despite the exceptions, there is a very significant association between length in the nasal system and length in other consonant subinventories. For example, there are 11 languages with /mː/ and 9 languages with either /pː/ or /bː/ or both. In these two small groups, 8 languages are the same, i.e. have both /mː/ and a long bilabial plosive. The probability that segments of this type would co-occur if they were randomly distributed is about .0001. Applying this to our sample means that we would expect about one language in 900 to have this co-occurrence, instead of the observed frequency of about 1 in 40.

Because long consonants of all types are fairly rare in occurrence, it is not really possible to assign a direction to the association with long nasals. What we can observe is simply that the sort of phonetic and distributional facts which argue for interpretation of length as a property of unitary phonemes tend to be common to several types of segments in any relevant language.

For each of the types of SNC's considered above, the fact that languages have an equal or larger number of PNC's than they have in any one series of SNC's follows from the condition that a matching simple voiced nasal at the same place of articulation is presupposed by the presence of any SNC.

Prenasalized obstruents

There are 19 languages in UPSID with prenasalized segments. Such segments are all voiced obstruents. There are 66 prenasalized plosives, 7 affricates, and 3 fricatives. (There is one language, Aranda (362), with a series of nasally-released stops.) The languages with prenasalized obstruents would provide rather a large percentage of exceptions to the claim that languages do not have more SNC's than PNC's, since 10 of them have more prenasalized obstruents than PNC's. However, it seems more appropriate to relate prenasalized obstruents to the other obstruent series of the language, rather than considering them in relation to the nasals. There are several reasons for this. First, there are languages such as Hakka (502), Apinaye (809) and Siriono (829) which have no PNC's but do have a prenasalized plosive series. These 3 languages also lack a plain voiced plosive series; in a sense the prenasalized stops take its place. Secondly, there are languages which have both a series of PNC's and a prenasalized stop series in place of a simple voiced series of stops. Besides lacking a simple voiced obstruent series, such languages may have prenasalized obstruents at places where there is no simple nasal but where there is a voiceless obstruent. Examples include Washkuk (602), which has PNC's at bilabial, alveolar and palatal places but has no velar nasal. It has prenasalized voiced plosives including the velars /ŋ, ŋʷ/ and voiceless plosives, including /k, kʷ/, but no plain voiced plosives. Similarly, Ngizim (269) has 3 nasals but 5 prenasalized plosives, having velar and labialized velar prenasalized plosives but no velar nasal. Paez (804) also has 3 PNC's none of which is velar, whereas its prenasalized plosive series includes a velar. Ngizim and Paez have no plain voiced stops, but they have voiceless stops at places matching their prenasalized obstruents. The third type of example is provided by Sara (217), which has PNC's, voiced plosives and prenasalized plosives, but it has no velar PNC while there are velars in the plosive series.

Because of the pattern of exceptions to Ferguson's suggestion concerning SNC's, even in the modified form advanced here, prenasalized obstruents should be excluded from the definition of SNC's. They are instead subject to the generalization that a prenasalized obstruent does not occur unless an obstruent of the same class (plosive, affricate, fricative) occurs without prenasalization at the same (or similar) place of articulation. That is, /ᵐb/ does not occur unless, say, /p/ occurs in the same language. There are only 2 languages which violate this generalization. Washkuk (602) has /ᵐb/ and /ᵐbʷ/ among its prenasalized stops but has no other bilabial stops, although it does have bilabial fricatives /ɸ/ and /ɸʷ/. Sara (217) has a prenasalized palatal stop, but no simple palatal stop; however it does have a palato-alveolar affricate /dʒ/. All other cases conform; in fact, the more typical language with prenasalized stops or affricates has one at each place where a stop or affricate of another kind occurs. It is not unusual to find languages which have full matching series of voiced plosives, prenasalized obstruents and PNC's, such as Gbeya (129), Yulu (216), and Alawa (354), and languages with full matching series of PNC's and prenasalized stops but no voiced stops, such as Nambakaengo (626) and Kaliai (421).

Nasalized clicks

Ferguson included nasalized clicks among the secondary nasal consonants. A nasal escape of air can accompany any click production, and the nasal component can be either voiced or voiceless. Nasalized clicks are found as part of a set of click series and do not appear to be related to the number or nature of the system of true nasals in the languages concerned. Languages with clicks in their inventory seem to include nasalized ones among them; all 3 UPSID languages with clicks, Zulu (126), Nama (913) and !Xũ (918), have one or more series of nasalized clicks.

4.6 Restated generalizations about nasals

The observations concerning nasals above can be rephrased into an updated series of generalizations. Following each statement the number of conforming cases is given before the slash, and the number of relevant cases is given after the slash. These numbers may refer to segments or to languages, depending on the form of the statement. The percentage of cases which conform to each generalization is then given.

(i) If a segment is a nasal, it is voiced. 984/1057 93.1%.

(ii) A palatalized nasal is likely to be bilabial. 6/12 50.0%.

(iii) A labialized nasal is likely to be velar. 7/11 63.6%.

(iv) A voiceless nasal is more likely to have a bilabial place of articulation than any other place. 11/36 30.6%.

(v) Most languages have at least one nasal. 307/317 96.8%.

(vi) A language with any nasals has /*n/. 304/307 99.0%.

(vii) The presence of /m/ in a language implies the presence of /*n/. 297/299 99.3%.

(viii) The presence of either /ŋ/ or /*ɲ/ in a language implies the presence of both /m/ and /*n/. 197/200 98.5%.

(ix) The presence of both /n̪/ and /n/ in a language implies the presence of both /m/ and /ŋ/. 12/13 92.3%.

(x) The presence of a nasal at any given place of articulation implies the presence of an obstruent at a similar place. (Number of counterexamples not counted.)

(xi) The presence of a voiceless, laryngealized or breathy voiced nasal implies the presence of a plain voiced nasal with the same place of articulation. 73/73 100%.

(xii) The presence of a nasal with a secondary articulation implies the presence of a simple nasal at the same place of articulation. 24/26 92.3%.

(xiii) The presence of a nasal with a secondary articulation implies the presence of at least one other consonant of another type at the same place of articulation and with the same secondary articulation. 25/26 96.2%.

(xiv) The presence of a prenasalized obstruent implies the presence of a simple obstruent of the same class at a similar place of articulation. 73/76 96.1%.

4.7 Explanations for nasal patterns

Linguists are generally more successful at observing facts of the kind represented by (i) - (xiv) above than in explaining them, but explanation is obviously the more important goal. An important start has been made by Ohala (1975) toward developing explanations for nasal sound patterns where these may have a phonetic basis, but there is much that remains to be done. We will briefly review what seems to be the current state of research.

It is often assumed that the more distinctive speech sounds are those that will be used more frequently in the world's languages, since this will achieve the most successful transmission of a message. Some of the patterns of occurrence of nasals may be accounted for on the basis of ideas of this kind.

In the first place, the fact that so many languages have any nasals at all fits well with the fact that nasals have been shown to be highly distinctive. That is, they are rarely subject to confusion with other types of consonants and are reliably identified as nasals. (Some relevant studies are Miller and Nicely 1955; Singh and Black 1966; Shepard 1972; Goldstein 1977.) The distinctiveness of nasals as a class means that there is value in incorporating such sounds into any language, and that they are likely to be retained over time. Plentiful evidence is available from historical phonology that nasals are among the most stable of sounds diachronically.

It is less easy to argue on grounds of distinctiveness for the presence of multiple nasals in a language; although nasals as a class are distinct, they are prone to confusion within the class. Malécot (1956) and Nord (1976) are among those who have shown that nasals with different places of articulation are poorly distinguished in terms of the nasal murmur itself (as opposed to in terms of the transitions to adjoining vowels). Nonetheless to have up to 4 nasals in a single language is a common occurrence. As long as there are clear vowel transitions, this is perhaps not so surprising, but lack of distinctiveness conspires with articulatory convenience in limiting the contrastiveness of nasals in consonant clusters in most languages, where they are required to be homorganic (Greenberg 1978: 253).

There are some indications in favor of a perceptual basis to the hierarchy of preferred places of articulation for nasals, which runs in descending order of popularity: dental/alveolar, bilabial, velar, palatal. Although phonetic and perceptual studies have generally excluded palatal nasals from the inventory of sounds studied, there is some evidence for the relative reliability of identification of /m, n, ɲ/. Zee (1981) found that /n/ is most likely to be correctly identified, while House (1957) found that /ɲ/ is more likely to be misidentified as one of the other nasals. More specifically, Zee reports that /ɲ/ is especially likely to be identified as /n/ after /i/, whereas Malécot agrees with House that /m/ is most likely to be identified as /n/ before /i/. Zee also finds that after /i/ or /e/, /m/ is likely to be heard as /n/. These various reports indicate that there is more chance for misperceptions, perhaps aided by coarticulation effects in real speech, to favor /n/ at the expense of other nasals, and for /ɲ/ to be less favored than either /m/ or /n/. These data should be used with some caution as they may reflect the native language habits of the subjects used in the experiments, rather than more universal human perceptual proclivities. However, they do suggest that the most widely occurring nasals are the most reliably identified ones.

As for the fact that nasals are rarely voiceless, Ohala (1975) has pointed out both that voiceless nasals can barely be distinguished from each other on the basis of their noise spectrum, and that in languages which have voiceless nasals, there is a voiced portion before the vowel begins and it is this portion which makes them recognizable. It seems that, if voiceless nasals are developed in a language, they must either be lost through indistinctness, or have their voicing restored to them in time.

Other patterns, such as those involving the secondary articulations, or the relationships between nasals and obstruents, are likely to be related to wider issues concerning the exploitation of possible phonetic contrasts that go beyond a consideration of nasal consonants in isolation.

References

Austerlitz, R. 1967. The distributional identification of Finnish morphophonemes. _Language_ 43: 20-33.

Bentick, J. 1975. Le niaboua, langue sans consonnes nasales. _Annales de l'Université d'Abidjan, Série H, Linguistique_ 8: 5-14.

Crothers, J. 1975. Nasal consonant systems. In C.A. Ferguson, L.M. Hyman, and J.J. Hyman (eds.), _Nasálfest_. Stanford University, Stanford: 153-66.

Ferguson, C.A. 1963. Assumptions about nasals: a sample study in phonological universals. In J.H. Greenberg (ed.) _Universals of Language_. M.I.T. Press, Cambridge: 53-60.

Ferguson, C.A., Hyman, L.M. and Ohala, J.J. (eds.) 1975. _Nasálfest_ (Papers from a symposium on nasals and nasalization). Stanford University, Stanford.

Goldstein, L. 1977. Bias and asymmetry in speech perception. _UCLA Working Papers in Phonetics_ 39: 62-87.

Greenberg, J.H. 1978. Some generalizations concerning initial and final consonant clusters. In J.H. Greenberg et al. (eds.), _Universals of Human Language, Vol. 2, Phonology_. Stanford University Press, Stanford: 243-79.

Hockett, C.F. 1955. _A Manual of Phonology_ (IJAL Monographs 11). Indiana University, Bloomington.

House, A.S. 1957. Analog studies of nasal consonants. _Journal of Speech and Hearing Disorders_ 22: 190-204.

Le Saout, J. 1973. Langues sans consonnes nasales. _Annales de l'Université d'Abidjan, Série H, Linguistique_ 6: 179-205.

Malécot, A. 1956. Acoustic cues for nasal consonants: an experimental study involving tape-splicing techniques. _Language_ 32: 274-84.

Miller, G. and Nicely, P. 1955. An analysis of perceptual confusions among English consonants. _Journal of the Acoustical Society of America_ 27: 338-52.

Nord, L. 1976. Perceptual experiments with nasals. _Speech Transmission Laboratory, Quarterly Status and Progress Report_ (Royal Institute of Technology, Stockholm) 2-3: 5-8.

Ohala, J.J. 1975. Phonetic explanations for nasal sound patterns. In C.A. Ferguson, L.M. Hyman, and J.J. Hyman (eds.), _Nasálfest_. Stanford University, Stanford: 289-316.

Shepard, R.N. 1972. Psychological representation of speech sounds. In E.E. David and P.B. Denes (eds.) _Human Communication: A Unified View_. McGraw-Hill, New York: 67-113.

Singh, S. and Black, J.W. 1966. A study of twenty-six intervocalic consonants as spoken and recognized by four language groups. _Journal of the Acoustical Society of America_ 39: 372-87.

Thompson, L.C. and Thompson, M.T. 1972. Language universals, nasals and the Northwest Coast. In M.E. Smith (ed.), _Studies in Linguistics in Honor of George Trager_. Mouton, The Hague: 441-56.

Zee, E. 1981. Effect of vowel quality on perception of post-vocalic nasal consonants in noise. _Journal of Phonetics_ 9: 35-48.

5

Liquids

5.1 Introduction

For reasons to do with both acoustic similarities and common phonological patterning, laterals and r-sounds have been grouped together as "liquids" in phonetic tradition. Although the similarities involve principally the voiced non-fricative segments concerned (Goschel 1972; Bhat 1974), the term liquid in this paper will be applied to all lateral segments except lateral clicks and to all sounds that are included in the somewhat heterogeneous class of r-sounds. The core membership of this latter class consists of apical and uvular trills, taps and flaps.[1] Added to this core are a variety of fricative and approximant sounds which seem acoustically or articulatorily similar, or which are related by diachronic processes (Lindau-Webb 1980).

5.2 Overall frequency of liquids

Using the definition above, almost all languages in the UPSID sample of 317 languages have at least one liquid, that is 95.9% of them do. Most languages, that is 72.6%, have more than one liquid. Details of the distribution are given in Table 5.1. The patterns found for systems of each size will be analyzed in Section 5.5 below, following an examination of the occurrence of particular types of liquids. As far as the two major classes of liquids are concerned, some 81.4% of languages have one or more lateral segments, whereas 76.0% have one or more r-sounds. The total number of laterals occurring in the surveyed languages is much greater than the difference between these percentages would suggest, since there are more languages with greater numbers of laterals. In fact, about 57% of the liquids reported are laterals.

Liquids

Table 5.1 Number of liquids in UPSID languages

No. of liquids	No. of languages	Percent in survey
0	13	4.1%
1	74	23.3%
2	130	41.0%
3	46	14.5%
4	29	9.1%
5	14	4.4%
6	8	2.5%
7	2	0.6%
10	1	0.3%

5.3 Laterals

Types of laterals

The laterals which occur may be grouped under four broad headings: lateral approximants, taps/flaps, fricatives, and affricates. The occurrence of these types is summarized in Tables 5.2 - 5.5 where frequencies are expressed in terms of the percentage of the total number of laterals counted in the survey (418). Approximant lateral types are shown in Table 5.2. Plain voiced approximant laterals are by far the most common type of lateral. Other types of approximant laterals are rare and only occur in inventories in which a plain type appears.

Table 5.2 Approximant lateral types

	Number	Percent of laterals
Plain voiced	313	74.7%
Plain voiceless	11	2.6%
Laryngealized voiced	8	1.9%
Breathy voiced	1	0.2%
	---	-----
	333	79.7%

There may be some doubt as to whether linguists have consistently reported on the distinction between voiceless approximant laterals and voiceless fricative laterals, but the distinction is an important one to attempt to maintain. Unlike voiceless approximants, voiceless lateral fricatives are reported in inventories that contain no voiced lateral approximant (Tlingit, 701, Nootka, 730, Puget Sound Salish, 734, Chukchi, 908, Kabardian, 911) so there may be an important distributional difference between the two types of sounds. Moreover, lateral fricatives are quite likely to have affricate allophones, as in Zulu (126), Tolowa (704), Hupa (705), Nez Perce (706), Totonac (713), and Alabama (759). Voiceless lateral approximants do not seem to vary in this way.

Lateral taps and flaps are reported fairly rarely. The numbers are given in Table 5.3. There is reason to believe that segments of this type may be more frequent than the reports indicate. Few phonetic manuals mention their occurrence and there is some evidence (of an anecdotal nature) that field linguists often have difficulty in recognising them for what they are. In such cases lateral taps/flaps are likely to be reported as r-sounds (this is perhaps so in Tiwa, 740) or as approximant laterals (as perhaps has happened in Zoque, 711).

Table 5.3 Lateral taps and flaps

	Number	Percent of laterals
Plain voiced	9	2.2%
Laryngealized voiced	1	0.2%
	---	-----
	10	2.4%

The few flaps reported are all voiced. Lateral fricatives, on the other hand, are far more likely to be voiceless than voiced, as Table 5.4 shows.

Table 5.4 Lateral fricative types

	Number	Percent of laterals
Plain voiceless	34	8.1%
Plain voiced	9	2.2%
Ejective voiceless	2	0.5%
	---	----
	45	10.8%

Two languages in the survey have a voiced lateral fricative without a corresponding voiceless fricative. In Kanakuru (270) /lʒ/ only occurs "in a few words" and there is an approximant /l/, but in Pashto (014) a "prepalatal" fricative lateral is the only lateral. These examples show that it would be unsound to propose that voiced fricative laterals only occur with voiceless fricative laterals. Nonetheless, voiced lateral fricatives are distinctly rare. As noted in chapter 3, lateral fricatives are even more likely to be voiceless than fricatives of other types.

The ejective lateral fricatives reported (in Tlingit 701, Yuchi 757) are restricted to languages with glottalic consonants of other types and in both cases a non-ejective voiceless lateral fricative also occurs. Ejective laterals are far more likely to be affricates than fricatives, but one language in the survey, Tlingit 701, has both /"ɬ'"/ and /"t̪ɬ'"/ in its inventory. This language also lacks a "normal" voiced lateral approximant. Table 5.5 reports the types of lateral affricates in the survey.

Table 5.5 Lateral affricates

	Number	Percent of laterals
Ejective voiceless	14	3.3%
Plain voiceless	9	2.2%
Plain voiced	4	1.0%
Aspirated voiceless	2	0.5%
	---	----
	29	6.9%

A lateral affricate is almost always voiceless. It has a very high probability of being ejective and, in fact, is the only segment type so far reported with such a high probability of being ejective. The ejective lateral affricates only occur in languages which have a non-ejective lateral fricative or affricate (or both).

Places of articulation for laterals

Laterals are almost all articulated with the tip or blade of the tongue, but it is not possible to be very much more specific than that. Due to inadequacy of data, no attempt was made in UPSID to distinguish between apical and laminal articulations, and, in a very large number of instances, it is not possible to determine if a segment is dental or alveolar in place of articulation. A very large number of laterals is thus classified as "unspecified dental or alveolar". The data on place of articulation is given in Table 5.6 (percentages add to more than 100 because of rounding).

Table 5.6 Primary and secondary places of articulation for laterals

	Primary place of articulation							
	Dental	"Dental/ Alveolar"	Alveolar	Palato-alveolar	Retrof.	Palatal	Velar	Alveolar-velar ?
No secondary artic.	31	178	132	8	28	15	1	3
Pal'lzed	3	1	5	0	0	0	0	0
Velarized	0	7	3	0	0	1	0	0
Phar'gzed	0	1	1	0	0	0	0	0
	---	---	---	---	---	---	---	---
Totals	34	187	141	8	28	16	1	3
% of lat.	8.1%	44.7%	33.7%	1.9%	6.7%	3.8%	0.2%	0.7%

About 87% of all laterals are produced in the dental/alveolar region. Probably alveolar laterals are more frequent than dentals, but this cannot be determined with certainty from the available data. Retroflex laterals are the next most frequent and, of course, these too are tip or blade articulations. Laterals made with the body of the tongue are comparatively unusual. Among them, palatals are most frequent. Velar laterals are extremely rare -- only one example appears in the survey, in Yagaria (609). A few other cases are known from other languages, including the New Guinea languages Melpa, Mid-Waghi and Kanite (Ladefoged, Cochran and Disner 1977) and the Chadic language Kotoko (Paul Newman, personal communication). The 3 complex lateral segments reported to have both velar and dental/alveolar articulations are all somewhat obscurely described. All 3 are voiceless and fricative or affricate, being interpreted as /xɬ/, /kɬ/ (Ashuslay, 814) and /kɬ'/ (Zulu, 126). Apart from this rather dubious instance, there are no significant interactions between lateral manners and places of articulations. All types of laterals are predominantly dental or alveolar, and at all places the most common type of lateral is a plain voiced lateral approximant.

The preference for tip or blade articulations for laterals is presumably related to the greater opportunity to provide a free air passage behind the front closure if the body of the tongue is not involved in the articulation. Tongue-body laterals are probably more subject to processes resulting in their diachronic loss, as for example in the phenomenon known as "yeismo" in Spanish, which has transformed the palatal lateral /ʎ/ into a palatal approximant /j/ in many dialects (Guitarte 1971).

Summary statements on lateral segments

The observations above on lateral segments suggest that the following substantive generalizations can be made. After each statement, the number of conforming cases in the inventory is given before the number of potentially relevant cases, together with a calculation of the percentage of cases which conform.

(i) A lateral segment is most likely to be articulated with tongue tip or blade. 392/418 93.8%.

(ii) A lateral segment is most likely to be voiced. 347/418 83.0%.

(iii) A lateral segment is most likely to be an approximant. 333/418 79.7%.

(iv) A fricative lateral is most likely to be voiceless. 36/45 80.0%.

(v) A voiceless lateral is likely to be fricative. 36/72 50.0%.

(vi) An ejective lateral is most likely to be an affricate. 14/16 87.5%.

(vii) A lateral affricate is likely to be ejective. 14/29 48.3%.

It should be noted that (iv) and (v) are independent observations. The explanation for (iv) is likely to be related to the greater salience of voiceless fricatives in general, compared to their voiced counterparts (Goldstein 1977). The explanation for (v) is likely to be related to the greater salience of voiceless fricatives over voiceless approximants, added to the fact that the only places favored for affricates in general are palatal and palato-alveolar, which are disfavored places for laterals. There may, however, also be a special reason why diachronic processes act to retain few voiced lateral fricatives or voiceless lateral approximants, that is, these sounds are difficult to distinguish from non-lateral counterparts (e.g. [ɮ] --> [ʒ]; [l̥] --> [h]).

5.4 R-sounds

Types of r-sounds

The sources used to compile UPSID fail to specify the manner of articulation of segments represented by /r/ in 34 instances or 10.8% of the 316 r-sounds. These will be droppped from consideration in the analysis of the types of r-sounds below. It should be remembered that ignorance of how this group of sounds should be distributed into the various classes below adds a measure of uncertainty to some of the conclusions reached in this section.

Of the remaining 282 r-sounds, the largest number are reported as trills.[2] The data is reported in Table 5.7.

Table 5.7 Trills by phonation type

	Number	Percent of r-sounds
Plain voiced	130	46.1%
Plain voiceless	3	1.1%
Laryngealized voiced	1	0.4%
	---	-----
	134	47.5%

Obviously, trills are overwhelmingly voiced. The same is true of the next most frequent class of r-sound, consisting of taps and flaps. All reported taps/flaps are voiced, with only 3 being other than plain. The numbers are given in Table 5.8. Although fewer taps/flaps are reported than trills, the difference is less than the number of r-sounds with unspecified manner and hence it is not possible to conclude which of these types of r-sounds is actually most common in the languages of the world. In any case, trills and taps/flaps are closely related sound types (often both appear as allophones of the same phoneme) both of which involve an interruption of the flow of air through the oral cavity. It may be observed that about 86% of those r-sounds with specified manner are "interrupted".[3]

Table 5.8 Taps/flaps by manner

	Number	Percent of r-sounds
Plain voiced	104	36.9%
Plain voiceless	2	0.7%
Laryngealized voiced	1	0.4%
Voiced fricated	1	0.4%
	---	-----
	108	38.3%

The numbers of continuant r-sounds are shown in Table 5.9. As with other types of r-sounds, voicing is obviously the norm. Note that the fricatives included in the class of r-sounds are those non-sibilants made with the tongue tip or blade (apart from the dental /θ/ and /ð/). Despite the transcriptional convention which suggests that a voiced uvular fricative (/ʁ/) is an r-sound of some kind, it is not considered to be one here. A voiceless uvular fricative (/χ/) is never considered to be an r-sound, and, in general, uvular fricatives seem to be most closely connected with velar fricatives. For those interested, there are 16 voiced uvular fricatives in UPSID languages.

Table 5.9 Continuant r-sounds

	Number	Percent of r-sounds
Voiced approximant	28	9.9%
Voiced fricative	8	2.8%
Voiceless fricative	2	0.7%
	---	-----
	38	13.5%

Substantially more approximants are reported than fricatives. However there is considerable room for doubting the validity of the reporting of fricative r's. The criteria for reporting a sound as "some kind of r" rather than, say, as a voiced retroflex sibilant /ẓ/ are obscure and may not reflect a phonetic difference between /ẓ/ and /ɹ̌/, but instead be based on phonotactic considerations or other non-phonetic characteristics (including orthographic convention).

Places of articulation for r-sounds

As with laterals, there is a considerable number of instances where the place of articulation is only known to be in the dental/alveolar region somewhere. The tabulation for places of articulation for all of the 316 r-sounds in UPSID in Table 5.10 thus includes an unspecified dental/alveolar column. Of the 34 r-sounds with an unspecified manner, 27 also fall into this underspecified place category. However, unlike with laterals, it can be stated that the most common place of articulation for an r-sound is alveolar. There is a larger number of alveolar r-sounds (141) than any other category. Note that there are only a few r-sounds reported as dental, only about one fourteenth as many as those specified as alveolar, so that even if all the unspecified place segments were in fact dental, there would still be fewer dental than alveolar r-sounds. And, of course, the unspecified category is far more likely to be correctly divided in something approaching the ratio of the segments with known dental or alveolar place of articulation, i.e. in about a 1:14 ratio.

Table 5.10 Place of articulation, all r-sounds

	Primary place of articulation					
	Dental	"Dental/ alveolar"	Alveolar	Palato-alveolar	Retroflex	Uvular
No secondary articulation	9	118	135	2	38	3
Palatalized	1	3	4	0	0	0
Velarized	0	1	1	0	0	0
Pharyngealized	0	0	1	0	0	0
	---	---	---	---	---	---
Totals	10	122	141	2	38	3
Percent	3.2%	38.6%	44.6%	0.6%	12.0%	0.9%

The only other reasonably frequently occurring place for r-sounds is retroflex. Uvulars are quite rare (and mainly restricted to prestige dialects of Western European languages). Uvular trills are included in the survey from French (010), German (004) and Batak (413) and a uvular approximant occurs in Eastern Armenian (022). Other places are largely ruled out by definition.

Interaction between place and manner

There is an important interaction between place and manner which can be seen from Table 5.11, juxtaposing frequency of alveolar and retroflex types of r′s sorted by manners. (The unspecified dental/alveolar category has a distribution by manner similar to the alveolars.)

Table 5.11 Interaction of place and manner in r-sounds

		Alveolar		Retroflex	
		Number	Percent	Number	Percent
Interrupted:	trills	62	44.9%	5	13.9%
	taps/flaps	62	44.9%	11	30.6%
Continuant:	approximants	11	8.0%	15	41.7%
	fricatives	3	2.2%	5	13.9%

Liquids

Whereas an r-sound with an alveolar place is one of the interrupted types (trill/tap/flap) in almost 90% of cases, retroflex r-sounds are most commonly found as approximants in the languages surveyed and, relative to alveolars, are very rare as trills but more common as fricatives. Within the approximant class, 15 of 28 instances are reported as retroflex.[4]

Summary statements on r-sounds

The analysis in the preceding section suggests that the following substantive generalizations about r-sounds can be made:

(i) An r-sound is most likely to be voiced. 308/316 97.5%.

(ii) An r-sound is most likely to be dental or alveolar. 273/316 86.4%.

(iii) An r-sound is most likely to be interrupted. 244/282 86.5%.

(iv) A retroflex r-sound is likely to be a continuant. 20/38 52.6%.

(v) An approximant r-sound is likely to be retroflex. 15/28 53.6%.

(vi) A fricative r-sound is likely to be retroflex. 5/10 50.0%.

The explanation for (i) probably needs to be different for different types of r-sounds. Tap/flap durations are very short and connected speech is mostly voiced: the voicing of taps/flaps may result from an inability to switch back and forth from voicing to lack of voicing quickly enough. Approximants are predominantly voiced (see chapter 6), probably because voiceless approximants are poorly distinguished from each other and tend to fall together as the undifferentiated voiceless vowel /h/. However, there seems to be no equivalent reason for voiceless trills to be so rare. Trills generally have two or three contacts at a rate of vibration of about 28Hz (Ladefoged, Cochran and Disner 1977) requiring a substantial duration (on the order of 100 msec). They have some similarity in production to obstruents, which are preferentially voiceless (about 60% of stops are voiceless). But perhaps there is some factor in the aerodynamic conditions required for trilling which leads to the preference for voicing because of the associated reduction in air-flow.

5.5 Structure of liquid systems

Languages in the survey have up to 6 laterals and up to 4 r-sounds, although it is most typical to have only one of each. The number of languages with the various numbers of liquids are given in Table 5.12. About 31% of the languages have 2 or more laterals, but only 19% have as many r-sounds. Of the 230 languages with 2 or more liquids, 96 have more laterals than r-sounds, whereas only 23 have more r-sounds than laterals. The remainder have equal numbers of the 2 major types of liquids.

Table 5.12 Numbers of laterals and r-sounds per language

No. of laterals	0	1	2	3	4	5	6
No. of languages	58	157	63	23	9	3	3
Percent	18.3%	49.5%	19.9%	7.3%	2.8%	0.9%	0.9%
No. of r-sounds	0	1	2	3	4		
No. of languages	74	183	51	8	1		
Percent	23.3%	57.7%	16.1%	2.5%	0.3%		

Languages with one liquid (74, 23.3%)

In view of the greater overall frequency of laterals, it is rather surprising that languages having one liquid are more likely to have an r-sound (42) rather than a lateral (32), with the most frequent type of r-sound in these languages reported as a voiced flap (28 cases). However, in a number of cases, both lateral and non-lateral allophones occur, e.g. in Nasioi (624) the flap /ɾ/ occurs as a lateral before /u/ or /o/, in Barasano (832) the alveolar flap /ɾ/ has flapped nasal and lateral allophones, with lateral flaps occurring before central and back vowels and [ɾ] before front vowels and in all word-final environments. Similar allophonic variation is found in Tucano (834) but in this language it is a preceding central or back vowel which conditions the occurrence of the lateral allophone. Apinaye (809), Japanese (071), !Xũ (918) and perhaps Bribri (801) are among other languages with lateral allophones of a flapped r-sound. Korean (070), Dan (106) and Zande (130) are among languages with flapped r-sounds as allophones of a lateral phoneme. It is likely that other cases of fluctuation between lateral and nonlateral liquids are concealed in some of the less detailed descriptions. These fluctuations appear, not unexpectedly, to be more frequent in languages with only one liquid.

The most frequent lateral reported as sole liquid is a voiced dental or alveolar lateral approximant (28 of 32 cases). The only exceptions are the alveolar lateral flaps of Luvale (125) and Zande (130), the retroflex lateral flap of Papago (736) and the velar lateral approximant of Yagaria (609). The only approximants reported as sole liquids are laterals; r-sounds as sole liquids are almost always reported as flaps.

Liquids

Languages with 2 liquids (130, 41.0%)

The most typical language has 2 liquids, usually one lateral and one r-sound. Table 5.13 shows how 2-liquid systems break down.

Table 5.13 Systems with 2 liquids

	Number of languages	Percent of languages with 2 liquids	Percent of languages in sample
1 lateral, 1 r-sound	108	83.1%	34.1%
2 laterals	18	13.8%	5.7%
2 r-sounds	3	2.3%	0.9%

The usual system consists of a trill or tap/flap and a lateral approximant, these being the most common varieties of liquids. The systems with 2 laterals or 2 r-sounds do not contrast them by place of articulation but by manner, voicing or secondary articulation or some combination of these. The most frequent system of 2 laterals has a plain voiced lateral approximant and a voiceless lateral (13 of 28 cases). S. Nambiquara (816) has plain and laryngealized voiced retroflex lateral flaps, with non-lateral allophones reported for /ɺ/. Greenlandic (900) is also among the languages with flapped r-sounds as allophones of /l/ (Mase and Rischel 1971); it also has a long voiceless lateral fricative.

Languages with 3 liquids (46, 14.5%)

The structure of systems with 3 liquids is outlined in Table 5.14.

Table 5.14 Systems with 3 liquids

	Number of languages	Percent of languages with 3 liquids	Percent of languages in sample
2 laterals, 1 r-sound	23	50.0%	7.3%
1 lateral 2 r-sounds	17	37.0%	5.4%
3 laterals	6	13.0%	1.9%

A system with 2 laterals is somewhat more common than one with 2 non-laterals. The 2-lateral systems are about evenly divided between those with a contrast of place (dental/alveolar vs. palatal or retroflex) and those with a contrast of voicing, manner or secondary articulation between their laterals. No cases are reported in which the laterals contrast in both place and another feature. Languages with 2 r-sounds are more likely to contrast them in manner (12 out of 17) than on any other dimension (e.g. trill vs. tap/flap). In 7 cases there is a difference in the primary place of articulation (usually alveolar vs. retroflex) and in 5 of these this contrast is in addition to a manner difference. The systems with 3 laterals usually contain a contrast of voicing (5 out of 6) with one or two voiceless fricatives or affricates (including ejectives). These systems are only reported from American languages, predominantly from the Northwestern coastal region of the North American continent (5 of 6). Nootka (730) has 3 voiceless laterals /ɬ, tɬ, tɬ'/. Note that the 3-liquid systems in the survey do not include any in which all of the liquids are r-sounds.

Languages with 4 liquids (29, 9.1%)

The structure of systems with 4 liquids is shown in Table 5.15. A clear majority of these systems (19 of 29) consist of an equal number of lateral and nonlateral liquids.

Table 5.15 Systems with 4 liquids

	Number of languages	Percent of languages with 4 liquids	Percent of languages in sample
2 laterals, 2 r-sounds	19	65.5%	6.0%
3 laterals, 1 r-sound	6	20.7%	1.9%
1 lateral, 3 r-sounds	2	6.9%	0.6%
4 laterals	2	6.9%	0.6%

Of these, 7 languages have laterals that contrast in place of articulation alone; the remainder contrast laterals by manner, voicing or secondary articulations. Five languages contrast their 2 r-sounds by place of articulation but in 4 of these cases there is also a contrast of manner. In total, 12 of the 19 languages contrast their r-sounds by manner.

Liquids

Of those languages with 3 laterals, 2 contrast plain voiced lateral approximants at 3 different places of articulation. The remaining 5 contrast their laterals by voicing and/or manner differences and include at least 2 fricative or affricate laterals. The 2 languages with 3 r-sounds are both unusual. E. Armenian (022) is reported with an alveolar trill, a retroflex fricative and a uvular fricative beside a dental lateral, i.e. /r, ɹ̣̌, ʁ, l̪/. Malagasy (410) has /r, l/ plus voiced and voiceless "trilled retroflex affricates". The 4-lateral systems contrast their laterals by manner and voicing, not by place. Note again, no systems occur with all their liquids nonlateral.

Languages with 5 liquids (14, 4.4%)

The structure of systems with 5 liquids is shown in Table 5.16. The most typical of these systems consists of 3 laterals contrasted by place and 2 r-sounds differing in manner. This kind of system is principally represented by Australian languages (5 of 6 cases); Alawa (354) with alveolar, palato-alveolar and retroflex voiced lateral approximants, an alveolar trill and a retroflex approximant, i.e. /l, l̠, ḷ, r, ɹ/, is a representative example.

Table 5.16 Systems with 5 liquids

	Number of languages	Percent of languages with 5 liquids	Percent of languages in sample
3 laterals, 2 r-sounds	9	64.3%	2.8%
2 laterals, 3 r-sounds	1	7.1%	0.3%
4 laterals, 1 r-sound	2	14.3%	0.6%
5 laterals	2	14.3%	0.6%

On the other hand, Ngizim (269), one of the languages with 3 laterals and 2 r-sounds, and all the languages with 4 or 5 laterals in a 5-liquid system contrast their laterals by voicing and manner differences.

Systems with 6 or more liquids (11, 3.5%)

The structure of systems with 6 or more liquids is shown in Table 5.17.

Table 5.17 Systems with 6 or more liquids

	Number of languages	Percent of languages in sample
4 laterals, 2 r-sounds	3	0.9%
3 laterals, 3 r-sounds	2	0.6%
5 laterals, 1 r-sound	1	0.3%
6 laterals	2	0.6%
4 laterals, 3 r-sounds	2	0.6%
6 laterals 4 r-sounds	1	0.3%

Just as with the systems with 5 liquids, the laterals tend either to differ by place (Diyari, 367, Aranda, 362) or by manner and voicing (Sedang, 304, Chipewyan, 703, Haida, 700, Kwakw'ala, 731). There is however, one language, Diegueño (743), which includes intersecting contrasts of both place and voicing/manner, having the 4 laterals /l, l̠, ɬ, ɬ̠/. The largest number of laterals reported in the survey is 6. The 7-liquid languages are 2 Australian languages (Kariera-Ngarluma, 363, Arabana-Wanganura, 366) which contrast laterals at 4 different places of articulation, trills at 2 places and also have a retroflex approximant. Irish (001) is the language with 10 liquids, having voiceless counterparts to its voiced alveolar liquids that have morphophonologically specialized functions. Because of its voiceless r-sounds Irish is the only language in the sample with 4 r-sounds.

5.6 Generalizations on the structure of liquid systems

The languages in UPSID show up to 4 contrasts between places of articulation for laterals and up to 6 contrasts of manner and voicing for laterals. They show up to 3 contrasts of place for r-sounds and up to 3 contrasts of manner. These are likely to be the maxima for these contrasts. Although laterals are reported at 6 major places of articulation, no language is known to contrast palato-alveolar and palatal laterals, and velar laterals are so rare that for them to occur with laterals at 3 other places of articulation would simply be improbable [5] (Ladefoged, Cochran and Disner 1977 report dental, alveolar and velar lateral approximants co-occurring in Melpa). There has been relatively little work done on phonetic differences between laterals (but see Bladon 1979; Davey, Maddieson and Moshi 1982), so it is not clear if the failure to exploit all the places of articulation in one language could be attributed to a lack of phonetic distinctiveness. As there are no languages reported with over 6 laterals or over 3 r-sounds (apart from Irish), these automatically set the maxima for the other contrasts mentioned above.

The most commonly found systems containing one to 6 liquids are reviewed in Table 5.18. These patterns suggest that an inventory of liquids is generally expanded by adding more laterals before adding more r-sounds.

Table 5.18 Common structures of liquid inventories

No. of liquids	Most common structure	No./ total	Percent of cases
1	1 r-sound	42/74	56.8%
2	1 lateral, 1 r-sound	109/130	83.8%
3	2 laterals, 1 r-sound	23/46	50.0%
4	2 laterals, 2 r-sounds	19/29	65.5%
5	3 laterals, 2 r-sounds	9/14	64.3%
6	4 laterals, 2 r-sounds	3/8	37.5%

Several other generalizations concerning the structure of liquid systems also suggest themselves and are presented below.

(i) A language with two or more liquids is most likely to have at least one lateral. 227/230 98.7%.

(ii) A language with two or more liquids is most likely to include a lateral/nonlateral contrast between them. 198/230 86.1%.

(iii) A language with one or more laterals usually has a voiced lateral approximant. 255/258 98.8%.

(iv) A language with two or more laterals contrasts them either in place or in manner and voicing but not both. 97/101 96.0%.

(v) A language with two or more r-sounds is unlikely to restrict their contrast to place of articulation. 55/60 91.7%.

(vi) A liquid with both lateral and r-sound allophones is most likely to be the only liquid in the language. 8/10.

(vii) A language most often has two liquids (usually one lateral and one r-sound). 109/317 34.4%.

Although approximant laterals are the most common type of lateral, the probability of (iii) being true is significantly higher than their overall frequency as a percentage of all laterals (79.7%) would suggest. The two observations (iv) and (v) draw attention to a quite marked difference between laterals and r-sounds in the way that the systems are elaborated. The data is incomplete on point (vi) so no percentage is expressed. However, only two counterexamples are known from among the languages in the survey.

5.7 Conclusion

The survey of liquids in UPSID has revealed patterns of occurrence of different types of liquids which may be taken as reliable. These patterns concern both the overall frequency of particular sound types and their relation to the inventory in which they occur. Although such observations have an intrinsic interest of their own, their main value is to suggest avenues of investigation in diachronic phonology, articulatory phonetics or speech perception designed to seek the explanation for these patterns. Research on liquids in these fields seems to be a neglected area.

Notes

1. Provision to distinguish between taps and flaps was made in the variables employed in UPSID, but the sources used do not seem to distinguish them reliably. They have therefore been treated here as a single group. For more discussion of the use of these terms see Ladefoged (1971) and Elugbe (1978).
2. Ladefoged, Cochran and Disner (1977) claim that "very few languages have any trills at all." The data collected for UPSID suggest either that trills are not in fact particularly rare or that very many erroneous reports of trills occur in the literature.
3. Including voiceless and voiced "trilled retroflex affricates" reported in Malagasy (410) but not included in the totals given in Tables 5.7 and 5.8.
4. There may be some reporting bias reflected in this finding. A somewhat retracted articulation of approximant /r/ is labelled "retroflex" in some analyses of English (e.g. Kenyon 1926). This may have led to a predisposition to label any approximant "r" as retroflex among English-speaking linguists.
5. If the one instance of a velar lateral and the 4 instances of laterals at 4 places of articulation in UPSID are taken as indications of the frequency of such occurrences, then the probability that both would occur in the same language might be estimated at less than .00004 (i.e. in fewer than one language in 400,000).

References

Bhat, D.N.S. 1974. The phonology of liquid consonants. Working Papers in Language Universals (Stanford University) 16: 73-104.

Bladon, R.A.W. 1979. The production of laterals: some acoustic properties and their physiological implications. In H. and P. Hollien (eds.), Current Issues in the Phonetic Sciences (Amsterdam Studies in the Theory and History of Linguistic Science, Series 4, Current Issues in Linguistic Theory 9). John Benjamins, Amsterdam: 501-8.

Davey, A., Maddieson, I. and Moshi, L. 1982. Liquids in Chaga. UCLA Working Papers in Phonetics 54: 93-108.

Elugbe, B.O. 1978. On the wider application of the term "tap". Journal of Phonetics 6: 133-9.

Goldstein, L. 1977. Perceptual salience of stressed syllables. UCLA Working Papers in Phonetics 39: 37-60.

Goschel, J. 1972. Artikulation und Distribution der sogenannten Liquida r in den europäischen Sprachen. Indogermanische Forschungen 76: 84-126.

Guitarte, G.L. 1971. Notas para la historia del yeismo. Sprache und Geschichte: Festschrift für Harri Meier zum 65 Geburtstag. Fink, Munich: 179-98.

Kenyon, J.S. 1926. Some notes on American r. American Speech 1: 329-39.

Ladefoged, P. 1971. Preliminaries to Linguistic Phonetics. University of Chicago Press, Chicago.

Ladefoged, P., Cochran, A. and Disner, S. 1977. Laterals and trills. Journal of the International Phonetic Association 7: 46-54.

Lindau-Webb, M. 1980. The story of r. UCLA Working Papers in Phonetics 51: 114-19.

Mase, H. and Rischel, J. 1971. A study of consonant quantity in West Greenlandic. Annual Report of the Institute of Phonetics, University of Copenhagen 5: 175-247.

6

Vocoid approximants

6.1 Introduction

Approximants are consonantal sounds produced with a relatively unimpeded flow of air through the mouth. The constriction is not narrow enough to produce local turbulence, though cavity friction may be heard if the segment is voiceless (Catford 1977). Apart from those approximants which have a lateral escape or belong to the family of r-sounds, the only frequently-occurring approximants in the world's languages are those which have vocoid characteristics (Pike 1943). They are often known as "semi-vowels". This chapter examines the frequency of such sounds as phonemic units in the UPSID sample and discusses certain co-occurrence restrictions which relate to their role in phoneme inventories.

In the UPSID file, vocoid approximants have been coded as consonants if they don't alternate with syllabic vocoid pronunciations and share distributional properties with other consonants. Over 90% of the surveyed languages have one or more such segments.

6.2 Frequency of vocoid approximants

The great majority of languages, 86.1%, have a voiced palatal approximant /j/ or a closely similar segment, such as /ɩ̯/ in Khasi (302). Substantially fewer languages, 75.7%, have a voiced labial-velar approximant /w/ or a closely similar segment. The frequency of these segments and their co-occurrence is shown in Table 6.1. The occurrence of /w/ is associated with the occurrence of /j/. From the independently calculated frequencies of /w/ and /j/, they would be expected to occur together in only 65.2% of the languages, not the 71.3% shown in Table 6.1. If these two segments were independently distributed, then there would be 31 or 32 languages in the survey with /w/ but no /j/, rather than the 14 actually found.

Table 6.1 Distribution of /j/ and /w/ in UPSID languages

	With /j/	No /j/
With /w/	226 (71.3%)	14 (4.4%)
No /w/	47 (14.8%)	30 (9.5%)

In the UPSID data, therefore, the occurrence of /w/ usually implies the occurrence of /j/ in the same language. However, the association of /w/ and /j/ is not as strong in UPSID as that found by Stephens and Justeson (1979) in the materials collected for the Stanford Phonology Archive. In these materials /w/ occurs without /j/ in only 1% of the languages surveyed, as against over 4% in the UPSID languages. Stephens and Justeson also report substantially lower overall frequencies of both /w/ and /j/, with the percentage of languages having these segments about 15% lower in each case. It is not clear if these differences arise from the different selection of languages in the two surveys or from the application of different criteria for phonemic status of approximants. Nonetheless their claim that there is a statistically significant tendency for /w/ to occur only if /j/ also occurs is confirmed by our data (significance from χ^2 better than .001).

Other vocoid approximants are comparatively rare. They may be divided into two groups - those which are modified variants of /j/ and /w/ and those which have different places of articulation. Those in the second group include the labial-palatal approximant /ɥ/ (4 instances) and the velar approximant /ɣ̭/ (5 instances). These occur in less than 2% of the languages surveyed. They are not found in modified form in any of the UPSID languages. Palatal approximants occur voiceless, laryngealized and nasalized. Labial-velar approximants occur voiceless and laryngealized. The frequency of modified segments of these types is given in Table 6.2. Laryngealized approximants /j̰/ and /w̰/ occur with approximately equal frequency and are restricted to languages which have other glottalic or glottalized segments in their inventories and have plain voiced /j/ or /w/. Greenberg (1970) suggested that /j̰/ fills the place of an anticipated palatal implosive in languages with an implosive series and a palatal place of articulation. This issue is discussed in some detail in Chapter 7 where it is concluded that there does not seem to be support for it in the available data. A diachronic source of this kind for /j̰/ would predict that it would be more frequent than /w̰/, for which no parallel source is proposed. Only 5 of the 13 instances of /j̰/ in the survey occur in the kind of inventory that would appear to support Greenberg's suggestion. There is a much stronger association between the occurrence of /j̰/ and of /w̰/; in 12 cases /w̰/ and /j̰/ occur together. In other words, there is only one exception to the statement that the presence of /w̰/ implies the presence of /j̰/.

Table 6.2 Frequency of modified /j/ and /w/

Segment	No.	Percent of languages
/j̥/	7	2.2%
/j̰/	13	4.1%
/j̃/	3	0.9%
/ʍ/	11	3.5%
/w̰/	12	3.8%

The voiceless approximants /j̥/ and /ʍ/ differ fairly markedly in frequency, /ʍ/ being 1.7 times more frequent than /j̥/. This is particularly surprising when considered in comparison to the relative frequency of their voiced counterparts. The diachronic source of these voiceless segments is likely to be similar in both cases - documented instances seem to arise predominantly from a cluster of a voiceless obstruent and the voiced approximant, or from labialized or palatalized voiceless obstruents (which may be equivalent to a source in a cluster). Thus (one source of) /ʍ/ in Hupa (705) is from Proto-Athabaskan */ʃʷ/ (Huld 1980), Middle English /ʍ/ is derived from Old English /xʷ/, and */ʍ/ in early Northern Tai is derived from Proto-Tai */xʷ/ (Li 1977). They are likely to exit from inventories in a variety of ways, including vocalization (as in the widespread merger of */ʍ/ with /w/ in many varieties of Modern English), collapse into an undifferentiated voiceless vowel phoneme /h/ (as in the special development of */ʍ/ in English before /u/ and /o/ in words such as "who", "whoop"[1], "whole"), or fricativization (as in the idiolectal /ç/ for the initial segments /hj/ = [j̥j] in English words such as "huge", "human" etc.; compare the change of earlier German /w/ into /v/).

The relative frequency of /j̥/ and /ʍ/ suggests that there may be some factor which favors the development of /ʍ/ over /j̥/ or favors the loss of /j̥/ more than /ʍ/. It is probably the case that a true voiceless palatal approximant is poorly distinguishable from /h/, which occurs in most languages, and hence is likely to collapse together with it. If, on the other hand, /j̥/ is articulated more forcefully to preserve the distinction it would become a palatal fricative. A voiceless labial-velar approximant may survive better because its two strictures produce two cavities with resonances which are rather close to each other in frequency and hence reinforce each other (cf. Ohala and Lorentz 1977).

6.3 Approximants and related vowels

The approximants /j/ and /w/ are closely related to the high vowels /i/ and /u/ respectively. The vast majority of languages have both these vowels, but there are more cases in which /u/ is missing than /i/ - in fact, /u/ is the most frequently missing of the major peripheral vowels (see chapters 8 and 9). The greater frequency of /i/ is undoubtedly a predictor of the greater frequency of /j/. However, for both /j/ and /w/ there are a few languages which have the approximant but lack the corresponding vowel. The numbers are given in Table 6.3.

Table 6. 3 Common approximants occurring without cognate vowels

	No. of languages	% of sample
/j/ but no /i/	8	2.5%
/w/ but no /u/	23	7.3%

There are about 3 times as many cases of /w/ occurring without /u/ as of /j/ occurring without /i/. Disner in Chapter 9 suggests that the systems without /u/ may be regarded as falling into two principal classes: those with a "compensating" vowel which is high or back or rounded but not all three (such as /ɨ/, /ɯ/, /ʉ/ etc) and those which simply have a gap (and whose highest back vowel is usually /o/). This is suggestive of a variety of possible sources for /w/ and may predict that the class of /w/ segments in languages may vary phonetically through a greater range than /j/.

The less frequently occurring approximants /ɥ/ and /ɣ̭/ were also investigated in relation to the corresponding vowels, in this case /y/ and /ɯ/ respectively. The numbers are given in Table 6.4. These suggest that /ɥ/ is most likely to occur if /y/ also occurs in the inventory, but that there is no such dependence of /ɣ/ on the occurrence of /ɯ/. However since these numbers are so small no great reliance should be placed on these indications.

Table 6.4 Other approximants and vowels

	No. of languages
/ɥ/ and /y/	3
/ɥ/ but no /y/	1
/ɣ/ and /ɯ/	1
/ɣ/ but no /ɯ/	4

6.4 Approximants and related consonants

/j/ and palatalized consonants

True palatalized consonants, that is, ones with a palatal secondary articulation usually perceptible because of a /j/-like offglide, occur in about 10% of the languages in the survey. Since desyllabification of high vowels is a major process creating both /j/ and palatalized consonants, it might be expected that palatalized consonants would occur only in languages with /j/ (cf. Bhat 1978). There are, however, 3 languages in the survey which have palatalized consonants but no /j/-phoneme. This is exactly the number that would be predicted if there was no association between these 2 classes of sounds. Of these 3, Ocaina (805) seems straightforward, but Muinane (806) has a voiced palatal fricative /ǰ/ with [j] as an allophone, and Ket (906) also has /ǰ/, albeit largely restricted to intervocalic positions. Thus a generalization stating that palatalized consonants occur in inventories containing /j/ or /ǰ/ would have only one exception.

/w/, labial-velar stops and labialized velars

As /w/ has two strictures of equal rank it falls into a class with other labial-velar consonants, especially /k͡p/ and /g͡b/ which are the most common labial-velar consonants after /w/. These labial-velar stops may vary a good deal in their initiation (Ladefoged 1968) but belong together by virtue of their shared place of articulation. The co-occurrences between /w/ and /k͡p, g͡b/ are shown in Table 6.5 below:

Table 6.5 Co-occurrence of /w/ and labial-velar stops

	No. of languages	% of sample
/w/, /k͡p/ and /g͡b/	19	5.9%
/w/ and /k͡p/	1	0.3%
/w/ and /g͡b/	2	0.6%
no /w/ but /k͡p/ and /g͡b/	1	0.3%

An assumption that there is no relation betweeen the occurrence of /w/ and /k͡p/ or /g͡b/ predicts that we should expect 16 cases of /w/ with /k͡p/ (20 actual) and 16 or 17 cases of /w/ with /g͡b/ (21 actual). The observed numbers suggest that there is a tendency for /k͡p/, /g͡b/ to occur in systems with /w/ in preference to those lacking /w/. The one exception, Kpelle (103), is also unusual in another way that is described below.

There is an obvious similarity between labialized consonants and /w/, and there is a historically similar source for both types of sounds in desyllabification of /u/ in many instances. We might therefore expect labialized consonants to occur preferentially in languages which have /w/. By far the most frequent labialized consonant types are labialized velar stops (cf. Ohala and Lorentz 1977). We will therefore use them as archetypes of labialized consonants. The co-occurrences of /w/ with /kʷ/ are shown in Table 6.6 (/gʷ/ only occurs if /kʷ/ occurs, so is not separately listed).

Table 6.6 /w/ and labialized velar stops

	No. of languages	% of sample
/w/ and /kʷ/	35	11.0%
no /w/ but /kʷ/	5	1.6%

Random co-occurrence of /w/ and /kʷ/ would predict that there would be 30 languages in the sample which contained both of these segments. The observed number (35) suggests that there is a weak tendency for /kʷ/ to be more likely to occur in languages which have /w/. The exceptions to the trend in UPSID are Mixtec (728), Guarani (828), Wantoat (615), Chipewyan (703), and Kpelle (103). In Chipewyan the labialized velars have a rather marginally contrastive status, since they are largely restricted to occurrence before back rounded vowels where plain velars do not occur. Kpelle is unusual in being the only language in the survey which has both labial-velar and labialized velar stops; and it also lacks /w/!

6.5 Other approximants

In addition to the 4 most common approximants /j, w, ɥ, ɣ̑/ discussed above, it may be noted that 6 languages (1.9%) have a bilabial approximant /β̑/ and 6 have a labio-dental approximant /ʋ/. The remaining approximants in UPSID are classified as liquids and are discussed in Chapter 5.

6.6 Summary

Most languages have /j/ and /w/, with /j/ being more frequent. There is a strong tendency for the presence of /w/ to imply the presence of /j/ in the same language. The greater frequency of /j/ is parallel to the greater frequency of /i/ than /u/, but these facts are not directly related since /j/ may occur without /i/ and /w/ without /u/. Modified varieties of /j/ and /w/ only occur in languages with the plain voiced counterparts. There is some association between the occurrence of palatalized consonants and /j/ and between labial-velar stops and labialized velars (and other labialized consonants) and /w/.

Notes

1. This word now frequently receives a spelling pronunciation, with initial /w/ or even /ʍ/ supplanting the historically derived /h/.

References

Bhat, D.N.S. 1978. A general study of palatalization. In J.H. Greenberg et al. (eds.), Universals of Human Language, Vol. 2, Phonology. Stanford University Press, Stanford: 47-92.

Catford, J.C. 1977. Fundamental Issues in Phonetics. Indiana University Press, Bloomington.

Greenberg, J.H. 1970. Some generalizations concerning glottalic consonants, especially implosives. International Journal of American Linguistics 36: 123-45.

Huld, M. 1980. Tone in Proto-Athabaskan. Unpublished paper. Dept. of Classics, UCLA.

Ladefoged, P. 1968. A Phonetic Study of West African Languages. Cambridge University Press, London.

Li, F-K. 1977. A Handbook of Comparative Tai. University of Hawaii Press, Honolulu.

Ohala, J.J. and Lorentz, J. 1977. The story of [w]: an exercise in the phonetic explanation for sound patterns. Proceedings of the Third Annual Meeting, Berkeley Linguistic Society: 577-99.

Pike, K.L. 1943. Phonetics. University of Michigan Press, Ann Arbor.

Stephens, L.D. and Justeson, J.S. 1979. Some generalizations concerning glides. In D.I. Malsch et al. (eds.), Proceedings of the Eighth Annual Meeting of the Western Conference on Linguistics. Linguistic Research Inc, Carbondale and Edmonton: 151-64.

7

Glottalic and laryngealized consonants

7.1 Introduction

This chapter presents the results of a survey of the occurrence of glottalic consonants and other "glottalized" consonant segments in our sample of the world's languages, and relates their occurrence to the rest of the segments in the phonological inventories of the languages. It draws substantially on a previous survey of the same data by Fordyce (1980).

In an important earlier study, Greenberg (1970) discussed the distribution of glottalic consonants cross-linguistically and language-internally. Although there has been considerable subsequent work addressing Greenberg's claims, much of it either suggests specific counter-examples (e.g. Campbell 1973; Pinkerton 1980) or brings little additional data to bear on the general validity of his conclusions (e.g. Hamp 1970; Javkin 1977). Greenberg's main claims are summarized in the sentence "injectives [i.e. implosives] tend to have front articulation, ejectives to have back articulation". Greenberg acknowledges that these conclusions were partly anticipated by Haudricourt (1950) and independently discovered by Wang (1968).

Our goal is to determine whether these place of articulation preference hierarchies for implosives and ejectives can be substantiated and to discover other distributional patterns relating to glottalic and glottalized segments in the UPSID data. The possible phonetic motivations for the patterns found will also be discussed. Greenberg's generalizations were based on a survey of languages for which data was available rather than on a carefully structured sample and it is possible that his findings reflect accidental biases in the selection of languages examined. In using the UPSID sample we hope to avoid the likelihood of such a bias.

7.2 Glottalic and laryngealized sounds

It may be useful to offer some definitions of the classes of sounds which are the subject of this chapter. They are any segments produced with the glottalic airstream mechanism (i.e. ejectives and implosives) as well as "glottalized" segments where the glottal constriction does not serve as the airstream initiator (i.e. preglottalized and laryngealized consonants). Only those sounds articulated using the glottalic airstream mechanism will be referred to as glottalic. Pulmonic or velaric "glottalized" sounds will generally be referred to as laryngealized. Ejectives are those sounds produced by raising the larynx with the glottis closed; with a constriction in the oral cavity, air is compressed in the space enclosed between the oral constriction and the glottal closure. The oral occlusion or constriction is subsequently released with outward airflow. Implosives, on the other hand, are articulated by lowering of the larynx. In an idealized case, air enclosed between an oral occlusion and the laryngeal constriction is rarefied, and air flows in through the mouth when the oral closure is released. However, the glottis is usually not closed, but rather the vocal folds are allowed to vibrate through leakage of pulmonic air into the oral cavity (see Catford 1939). Thus ejectives tend to be unvoiced while implosives tend to be voiced.

Moreover, as noted by Ladefoged (1968), Pinkerton (1980) and others, "implosives" do not always entail inward oral air flow upon release even when the larynx lowering gesture is present. The distinction between truly imploded consonants and those which are preglottalized or laryngealized with minimal or zero implosion has been difficult to maintain in UPSID. These sounds are frequently not distinguished in the literature, but where the airstream initiator of the most typical allophone is known to be or may be other than glottalic, the sound is classified in UPSID as laryngealized. As both Ladefoged (1968) and Greenberg (1970) conclude, the potential phonological contrast of these differing types is not realized in any of the languages known to them directly or through the literature (nor in any included in UPSID).

It should be noted that the variables available for coding glottalic and laryngealized segments in UPSID limit the description of segments in certain phonetically plausible ways. Thus, ejectives must be specified as either ejective stop (glottalic egressive stops), ejective affricate (glottalic egressive affricates), or ejective fricative (glottalic egressive fricatives). The presumedly phonetically impossible ejective approximant, for instance, is therefore excluded a priori by the coding mechanism. Likewise, implosives may only be coded as implosive stops. The phonetically implausible implosive affricate, fricative or approximant is therefore excluded.[1] On the other hand, the UPSID variable "laryngealized" is not part of the set of mutually exclusive manners of articulation. Instead it reflects the possible and actual occurrences of preglottalized or laryngealized stops, affricates, fricatives, approximants, and vowels. Thus as Greenberg (1970:2) states, "the phonological opposition in individual languages between ejectives and injectives applies effectively only to obstruents"; other types of segments may be laryngealized but do not exhibit an ejective/implosive contrast.

Ejectives are the most widespread of the various types of segments being considered in this chapter, both from the genetic and geographical points of view. Although ejective systems are found in several of the world's major language families, by far the greatest number of languages with ejectives appear to be from the Americas. Two thirds (35 of 52) of the languages with ejectives in UPSID are in the Amerindian family - and most (30) of these are from North America. Almost 60% of the 51 Northern Amerindian languages in UPSID contain ejective systems. Only 4 of these languages also exhibit implosives or voiced laryngealized plosives. The particularly frequent occurrence of ejectives in this group of languages has been commented on before (e.g. Sherzer 1973), but the comprehensive nature of the UPSID sample allows this fact to be placed in its proper relief. These languages have an important property which sets them apart from the remainder of the language families of the world. Nine of the remaining languages with ejectives are in the Afro-Asiatic family, 3 are Nilo-Saharan, 3 are Caucasian, and there is one in each of the Indo-European, Niger-Kordofanian and Khoisan families. Ejectives are not known to occur outside of these major language families, although it is quite likely that they may occur in the Austro-Asiatic and/or Austro-Tai families, since voiced "glottalized" stops (implosive, preglottalized or laryngealized) are found there (e.g. in Vietnamese, 303; Sedang, 304; and Sui, 403).

As Greenberg (1970:2) notes, "the typical ejective obstruent is unvoiced". We find no exceptions to this in the languages surveyed, although phoneticians of the caliber of Catford and Pike have suggested that voiced ejectives are possible speech sounds. However, pre-voiced ejectives are reported in one language in the survey, !Xũ (918). This language has the most complex consonantal system of any of the languages in UPSID, including six series of stops apart from 48 click consonants. One of the stop series is described as consisting of voiced ejectives by Snyman (1969), but his description sounds as if there is necessarily a phonetic sequence of voicing preceding ejection in these segments. He says:

> what actually happens is that the vocal cords are activated by pulmonary air and they produce a voiced unemitted sound which we represent [ʖ]. (Both the nasal and oral passages are closed.) The unemitted sound [ʖ] is swiftly followed by the articulation of the ejected sound ... In close sequence [ʖ] and ... [the ejected sound] is perceived as a vocalized sound.

Thus, as far as is known, voiced ejectives, i.e. ejectives in which voicing continues through the stricture for the consonant, do not in fact occur in human languages. In "normal" ejectives, the available evidence shows that voicing begins very promptly on release of the glottal closure. Lindau (1982) shows this for ejective stops in Hausa and Navaho.

Implosives and their close relatives, voiced laryngealized plosives, are found in fewer of the major language families and are more limited geographically than ejectives. Most such systems (29 of 41) are to be found on the African continent. The distribution of implosives thus also has a strong areal concentration, but it is one which cuts across 3 major language families, Niger-Kordofanian (10 languages), Nilo-Saharan (10 languages), and Afro-Asiatic (9 languages). The largest number among the remaining languages are Amerindian languages (6), but there are a few languages from Austro-Asiatic (3), Austro-Tai (3), and Sino-Tibetan (1).

Laryngealized sonorants (nasals, liquids, and central approximants) are found in most language families mentioned above but not elsewhere. They too are most common in Amerindian languages.

7.3 Ejectives

Of the 317 languages in UPSID, 52 contain ejectives, making ejectives the most common of the glottalic or laryngealized segments. Twelve of these languages also exhibit implosive stops and 15 also exhibit some laryngealized stops, fricatives, sonorants, and/or vowels.

The most frequently occurring type of ejective is an ejective stop; there are twice as many ejective stops as ejective affricates in the data file - 188 to 94. Ejective fricatives are considerably rarer; only 20 are recorded in UPSID. Naturally, ejective stops have been the topic of more discussion than the other types of ejectives.

Ejective stops

Haudricourt (1950) suggested that ejective stops exhibit a strong preference for back articulations. Greenberg (1970) supported this claim mainly because he found that "a gap in the class of ejectives at the bilabial point of articulation is found in a number of world areas". Javkin (1977) made the implied hierarchy for ejective stops more explicit, formulating it as follows: "...[a language] will only have labial ejectives if it has alveolar and velar; it will only have alveolar if it has velar." (In this quote, "alveolar" refers to either dental or alveolar; as in other chapters we will use an asterisk before a phonetic symbol to designate the class of dentals and alveolars jointly.) Javkin counted the ejective stops in the Stanford Phonology Archive and saw the numbers as being generally confirmatory. The count is reproduced below as Table 7.1.

Table 7.1 Ejective Stops in the Stanford Phonology Archive

Labial	Dental/alveolar	Palatal	Velar	Uvular
26	29	7	31	15

There are relatively small differences in the numbers of ejectives reported at the 3 major places of articulation, but Javkin notes that the implicational hierarchy he has set up holds within the languages concerned. Javkin further notes that palatals and uvulars do not maintain the tendency to prefer a further back articulation over a further front one "since these places of articulation tend to disfavor stops". Indeed, as Javkin suggests, the relative disfavoring of palatals and uvulars is not restricted to glottalic consonants (see chapter 2 in this volume for details concerning non-glottalic stop distributions and Gamkrelidze 1978).

The frequency count of ejective stops in UPSID is given in Table 7.2. Plain velar ejective stops are no more frequent than plain dental or alveolar ones, there being 49 instances of each. However, because there are 3 languages (Nez Perce, 706, Pomo, 742, Wappo, 760) with both a dental and an alveolar ejective stop and one language (Kwakw'ala, 731) with no plain velar but with a labialized velar, there are four more languages with an ejective stop at the velar place than languages with one at the dental and alveolar places considered together (50 vs. 46). One language, Hupa (705), has /*tʼ/ but no /kʼ/ (it does have /qʼ/). A tendency to prefer velar place for ejective stops can be seen in the fact that presence of /*tʼ/ implies the presence of /kʼ/; it is significant that the 5 languages which have only one place of articulation for their ejective stops all have velars.

Table 7.2 Ejective stops in UPSID

	Labial	Dent/alv	Palatal	Velar	Uvular
Plain	33	49	7	49	19
Labialized	-	-	-	18	8
Palatalized	-	-	*	2	-
Prevoiced	1	1	-	1	-
	---	---	---	---	---
Total	34	50	7	70	27

What is far more salient is that both velar and dental/alveolar places are preferred to bilabial. There are significantly fewer occurrences of /p'/ than of either /k'/ or /*t'/. No language has /p'/ that does not have a velar, whereas 17 languages have /k'/ but no /p'/. Of the 11 languages with only two places of articulation for their ejective stops, 10 have /*t', k'/ (the exceptional case is Berta, 218, with /p', k'/). Thus the UPSID sample shows principally that bilabial place is disfavored for ejective stops. This is reminiscent of the findings with respect to voiceless plosives, which are also disfavored at the bilabial place, although there is some evidence that the tendency to avoid /p'/ is stronger than the tendency to avoid /p/. This raises the question of whether both of these patterns should be explained in the same way. This question will be taken up again below.

Uvular ejectives are relatively common. We may show this by comparing the ratio of uvular ejective stops to velar ejective stops, .39, with the ratio of plain voiceless uvular plosives to voiceless velar plosives, which is only .13. Their frequency is largely the result of the coincidence of two areal tendencies, use of the uvular place of articulation, and presence of ejectives, in North American languages. Of course, uvular ejectives are also consistent with a preference for back places for ejectives. The frequency of palatal ejective stops, on the other hand, is not disproportionate but is comparable to the proportion of plosives at the palatal place.

Only one type of secondary articulation is at all frequent with ejective stops, and that is labialization with velar or uvular ejectives. More will be said about secondary articulation below.

The detailed structure of ejective stop systems in the languages surveyed is shown in Table 7.3. Dental and alveolar stops have been pooled together, except in those languages where both occur. The presence of labialized ejective stops is indicated in a parenthetical comment unless they occur at a place where there is no corresponding plain ejective stop.

Table 7.3 Number of places of articulation for ejective stops

	Ejective stop inventory	Number of languages	
1 ejective stop	k'	5	(2 also with kʷ', 1 also has kʲ')
2 ejective stops	*t' k'	10	(3 also have kʷ')
	p' k'	1	
3 ejective stops	p' *t' k'	15	(4 also have kʷ')
	t' k' q'	1	
	t' c' q'	1	
4 ejective stops	p' *t' k' q'	10	(7 also have kʷ', qʷ')
	p' *t' c' k'	2	
	*t' c' k' q'	1	(also has kʷ', kʷ')
	p' t' t' k'	1	
5 ejective stops	p' t' c' k' q'	2	
	p' t' c' kʷ' q'	1	(has qʷ' but not k')
	p' t' t' k' q'	2	

Table 7.3 shows that the most commonly encountered set of ejective stops contains one at each of the most common places at which stops of any kind occur (bilabial, dental or alveolar, and velar). Frequently, these are the same places at which the language has other types of stops (glottal place is not considered in these cases). An example of this pattern is the stop system of Eastern Armenian (022):

p	t	k
pʰ	tʰ	kʰ
p'	t'	k'

or Tzeltal (712), whose stop system is as follows:

p	t	
		kʰ
b	d	g
p'	t'	k'

The only other reasonably common ejective stop systems are those containing either 2 ejective stops - dental or alveolar and velar - or 4 ejective stops - labial, dental or alveolar, velar, and uvular. Typical of one type of ejective stop system with only 2 places of articulation is Itonama (800) whose stop inventory is as follows:

p	t	k
	t^j	
b	d	
	t'	k'

Here there is no bilabial ejective even though the language has other types of stops at the bilabial place. Such languages are the crucial ones in establishing that there is a specific tendency to avoid bilabial ejective stops (cf. Haida, 700, below). The other main type of system is one in which there are other deficiencies among bilabial segments - several of the Semitic and Athabaskan languages lack a bilabial stop in another series as well as a bilabial ejective.

If there are 4 or 5 ejective stops, there is usually one at the uvular place: this is so for 16 of the 19 languages concerned. Again, there are usually stops in other series at the same places of articulation. Quileute (732) is representative of stop systems with 4 ejective stops:

p	t	k	q
		k^w	q^w
b	d	(g)	
p'	t'	k'	q'
		k^{w}'	q^{w}'

All the languages with ejective stops at 5 places of articulation include those stops found in the common 4-place inventory. An example is Jaqaru (820):

p	t	c	k	q
p^h	t^h	c^h	k^h	q^h
p'	t'	c'	k'	q'

Thus an inventory of ejective stops is usually built up this way: if there is one, it is velar; a second ejective is dental or alveolar; a third is bilabial; a fourth is uvular. A small minority of languages deviate from this pattern but the great majority conform (45 out of 52).

A few of the languages which are exceptions to this pattern suggest that it may sometimes be appropriate to recognize a single series of "glottalic" stops whose members may be phonetically diverse. An example is K'ekchi (714), which has three ejective stops at alveolar, velar and uvular places. It lacks a bilabial ejective, but has a laryngealized voiced bilabial stop. There are no other members of a voiced laryngealized series. Hence there is one "glottalic" consonant corresponding in place to each of the plain voiceless plosives. The K'ekchi stop inventory is:

Glottalic and laryngealized consonants

p	t	k	q
	t'	k'	q'
ɓ			

The comparative background to this situation in K'ekchi has been investigated by Pinkerton (1980), who examined the phonetic nature of corresponding segments in K'ekchi and 4 other languages in the Quichean group of Mayan languages. Among these 5 languages, ejectives, voiced and voiceless implosives, and voiced laryngealized stops interchange (and, for the bilabials only, even plain voiced stops are involved). The correspondences are shown in Table 7.4.

Table 7.4 Correspondences in 5 Quichean languages

K'ekchi	b̰/b	t'	k'	q' (varies with $q^<$)
Pocomchi	$p^<$	$t^<$	k'	$q^<$
Cakchiquel	b̰/b	t'	k'	$q^<$
Quiche	ɓ	t'	k'	$q^<$
Tzutujil	ɓ	ɗ	k'	$q^<$

Another exceptional language is Berta (218), a language with 2 ejective stops, one bilabial and the other velar:

b	"d"	g
p'		k'
	"ɗ"	

The general pattern leads us to expect a dental/alveolar ejective. This dental/alveolar slot is filled by a glottalic consonant, but it is a voiced implosive, and this implosive stands alone in Berta. Thus the "deficient" ejective series and the isolated alveolar implosive between them create a full series of glottalic stops, with a counterpart to the plain voiced stops of the language at each place. Among other languages which could be analyzed as having a single series of "glottalic" stops even though they are phonetically heterogeneous are Ik (208) and Hausa (266). In the case of Hausa, Carnochan (1951) has pointed to phonotactic constraints that apply to all consonants with a "glottalic" component (including /ʔ/).

A second class of exceptions is illustrated by Hupa (705), which seems at first glance particularly deviant in having 3 ejective stops but neither a velar nor a bilabial. Hupa is the only language with /c'/ and /q'/ that does not also have /p'/ and /*t'/ in its inventory.

Hupa stop system:

t	c	q
t^h	c^h	q^h
t'	c'	q'

In this language the ejective stop system shares the same unusual places of articulation as the voiceless plain and the voiceless aspirated stop series. If Hupa had the "normal" bilabial, alveolar and velar ejectives, it would be an exception to the general rule that languages have stops of different series at the same places of articulation (see Chapter 2). Specifically, this means that ejectives should be expected to occur only at places where non-glottalic stops occur. Thus, although there is a hierarchy of preferences for place of articulation for ejectives, it is outranked by the rule governing the relationship between places for plain stops and ejectives. In other words, as Fordyce (1980) stressed, phonological hierarchies may themselves be hierarchically arranged. Because Hupa conforms to the more important rule, it comes to violate the place hierarchy for ejectives considered by itself.

The importance of the connection between these rules can also be appreciated from an examination of Haida (700). For a language with 4 ejective stops, Haida has an unusual set - dental, palatal, velar, and uvular. It does not have an ejective at the bilabial place, although it does have plain voiceless and aspirated stops which are bilabial. However, there is no sense in which the palatal ejective stop has supplanted the more usual bilabial one. The palatal is not unexpected because Haida is conforming to the rule that ejective stops occur where there are also plain stops. Palatal ejectives are not common largely because palatal stops in general are not common. As noted above, this language constitutes part of the evidence for the conclusion that bilabial ejective stops are disfavored over dental/alveolar or velar ones.

Haida stop inventory:

p	"t"	c	k	q
			k^w	q^w
p^h	"t^h"	c^h	k^h	q^h
			k^{wh}	q^{wh}
	"t'"	c'	k'	q'
			$k^{w'}$	$q^{w'}$

The Wappo (760) system of 4 ejective stops, although it lacks a uvular one, is not an exception to the ejective place of articulation hierarchy.

It contains an unusual contrast between dental and alveolar ejective stops, but the same place contrast is also found among the plain voiceless stops. Here again the occurrence of an unusual ejective series can be attributed to the precedence established by the plain stop series in the language.

Two of the languages with 5 ejective stops, Nez Perce (706) and Pomo (742), also have both dental and alveolar stops, but there is no violation of the place of articulation preference hierarchy for ejective stops, which does not specify what a fifth member should be. The ejectives match the places of articulation found for the voiceless plosives in both of these languages, with the exception of Nez Perce /q'/ which appears despite the absence of /q/. The uvular place of articulation in Nez Perce is, however, represented by the affricate /qχ/, whereas there are no palatal or palato-alveolar obstruents of any kind. Given the rest of the Nez Perce system, an ejective at the uvular place of articulation is quite natural - certainly more so than a palatal one, for example.

On the other hand, the 4-ejective stop systems of Kefa (264) and Maidu (708) contain palatal ejectives rather than the more common uvular ejectives. However, these languages lack any stops in the uvular position:

Kefa stop inventory:

p	t	c	k
b	d	ɟ	g
p'	t'	c'	k'

Maidu stop inventory:

pʰ	tʰ	cʰ	kʰ
p'	t'	c'	k'
ɓ	ɗ		

The Maidu case is interesting since the plosives whose places of articulation are matched are aspirated ones rather than the voiceless unaspirated ones found in the other languages discussed here. Thus we may state more generally that an ejective usually occurs only if a plosive occurs at the same place. This rule is not limited to a particular type of plosives.

Ejective affricates and fricatives

Ejective affricates and fricatives have more limited occurrence than ejective stops. Forty languages in UPSID (12.6%) contain ejective affricates. In all but one of these languages, ejective stops occur as well. The exception is Iraqw (260) which does, however, have implosives.

Thus ejective affricates occur only in those systems containing glottalic stops (almost exclusively ejectives). The most commonly occurring ejective affricates are the sibilants /*ts'/ and /tʃ'/ and the lateral affricate /*tɬ'/. The figures are given in Table 7.5.

Table 7.5 Ejective affricates in UPSID

	tθ'	*tɬ'	*ts'	tʃ'	ṭṣ'	cç'	kx'	kɬ'
Simple	1	13	34	35	3	1	1	1
Labialized	0	0	1	1	0	0	1	0
Prevoiced	0	0	1	1	0	0	0	0
	---	---	---	---	---	---	---	---
Totals	1	13	36	37	3	1	2	1

Every language with any ejective affricates has at least one of the common sibilant types, /*ts'/ and /tʃ'/. Seven languages have only /tʃ'/, 5 have only /*ts'/, and 11 have both /*ts'/ and /tʃ'/ but no other ejective affricates. The remainder contain one or both of these sibilant ejective affricates plus one other, most frequently the lateral /*tɬ'/. Concerning /tʃ'/, Greenberg (1970: 17) commented that "for the palatal region in particular, it appears that the optimal ejective is the alveopalatal [affricate] rather than a stop". He goes on to observe that among non-glottalic obstruents, affricates are preferred over plosives in this articulatory region, and adds that the preference for affricates is even stronger in the case of ejective obstruents. In fact, Greenberg found "no example of an ejective palatal stop" in his sample. However, they not only do occur, but occur with a contrasting affricate. Of the 7 languages in UPSID with a palatal ejective stop, 5 also have a palato-alveolar or palatal ejective affricate. Nonetheless, Greenberg's observation may have some validity. While there are 5 times as many languages with /tʃ'/ than with /c'/, among the plain pulmonic obstruents there are only 3.4 times as many occurrences of /tʃ/ as /c/.

With regard to ejective fricatives, Greenberg noted that they are "relatively infrequent and always imply the presence of some ejectives with abrupt onset". In the UPSID languages, ejective fricatives imply ejective stops without exception. Most commonly they imply ejective affricates as well, but exceptions do occur. Ten UPSID languages contain ejective fricatives (3.2%); only 3 of these do not contain ejective affricates. The ejective fricatives reported in the survey are given in Table 7.6.

Table 7.6 Ejective fricatives in UPSID

	ɸ'	f'	*s'	ʃ'	ʂ'	ç'	x'	χ'	ɬ'
Simple	1	1	8	4	1	1	1	2	2
Labialized	0	0	0	0	0	0	1	1	0
	---	---	---	---	---	---	---	---	---
Total	1	1	8	4	1	1	2	3	2

Only /s'/ and /ʃ'/ occur in systems not containing ejective affricates. They are also the only ejective fricatives which occur without other ejective fricatives in the same language. Note that, among pulmonic fricatives, /f/ is almost as frequent as /ʃ/, but the ejective /f'/ is quite rare. Again, a labial place appears disfavored for an ejective.

Secondary articulations with ejectives

Labialization is the only secondary articulation which is at all common with ejective segments. It occurs most often with ejective stops: 18 languages in the survey have labialized ejective stops. Among the stops it only occurs with velars and uvulars (see Tables 7.2 and 7.3). Labialized uvulars only occur if there is a labialized velar in the language, but both these types are unusually common. Well over a third of the languages with plain velar or uvular ejective stops also have their labialized counterparts. Compare this with the fact that only about 13% of the languages with the plosive /k/ have the labialized counterpart /kʷ/. The apparent increase in labialization for velars and uvulars is probably due to areal factors. Most labialized ejective stops are in North American languages, where distinctive labialization of velars and uvulars frequently applies to several manners of consonants in the same language. Except for Kwakw'ala (731), with /kʷ'/ but no /k'/, these labialized ejectives never occur unless the plain counterpart also appears. In addition to /kʷ'/, Hausa (266) has a palatalized velar ejective stop. Labialization also occurs occasionally with certain ejective affricates and fricatives. The only occurrences of labialized ejective affricates are in Lak (912), which has /tsʷ'/ and /tʃʷ'/. The only labialized ejective fricatives are those found in Tlingit (701), which has /xʷ'/ and /χʷ'/.

7.4 Voiceless laryngealized segments

Voiceless laryngealized segments are somewhat related to ejectives. They have a glottal stricture simultaneous with the oral stricture, but this is not used as initiator of an airstream. Three languages in the survey have a set of voiceless laryngealized segments, Korean (070), Ashuslay (814), and Siona (833). The first two have /p̰, t̰, k̰, t̰ʃ/ in common. Hausa (266) has the voiceless laryngealized fricative /s̰/, which also occurs in both Korean and Siona. This set of segments in Korean, usually called "fortis" or "tense" obstruents, has been quite extensively studied, and several studies agree that they are produced with a narrow glottal aperture (e.g. Kim 1970), although there is also evidence that there is accompanying tension in the supraglottal structures (Kim 1965; Dart 1984). Hausa speakers vary considerably in their production of /s̰/. This segment is sometimes pronounced as an ejective fricative and it may also occur as an ejective affricate [ts’], as well as occurring as a pulmonic fricative with a glottal constriction. No other voiceless laryngealized fricative is reported, although S. Nambiquara (816) has a rather obscure segment which is described as a laryngealized /h/.

7.5 Implosives and voiced laryngealized plosives

As noted earlier, the only kind of glottalic ingressive segments reported are stops, that is, implosives. Thirty-two (10.1%) of the languages of the UPSID contain implosives. They are all voiced apart from the two segments /p˂/ and /t˂/ in Igbo (116). There are a further 10 languages which have voiced laryngealized plosives, making a total of 42 (13.2%). Since voiced implosives and voiced laryngealized plosives have often been discussed together, have not always been distinguished, and do not contrast we will discuss them together in this section. We will use the notation /ʔb/ to represent both /ɓ/ and /b̰/, etc., including when quoting from other authors. Greenberg (1970) used the term "injective" to cover both these segment types. Following Haudricourt (1950) and Wang (1968), he noted that "injectives tend to have front articulation". He goes on to suggest that

> if a language has one injective, it is /ʔb/; if two, they are /ʔb/ and /ʔd/ (the most common pattern); if three, they are /ʔb/, /ʔd/, and /ʔɟ/ (the latter a palatal stop, often replaced, however, by [the laryngealized approximant] /j̰/); and, if four, they are /ʔb/, /ʔd/, /ʔɟ/, and /ʔg/.

The general preference for front articulations was borne out in a count of the Stanford Phonology Archive by Javkin (1977). Table 7.7 gives the count of voiced implosives and voiced laryngealized plosives in the languages of UPSID, which shows a similar pattern for these stops at the different places of articulation.

Table 7.7 Voiced implosives and voiced laryngealized plosives in UPSID

	Labial	Dental/Alveolar	Retroflex	Palatal	Velar	Uvular
Vd. implosive	30	29	0	7	5	1
Vd. laryng'd.	9	7	1	0	0	0
	---	---	---	---	---	---
	39	36	1	7	5	1

These counts suggest that a correction might need to be made to the implicational hierarchy posited by Greenberg. In fact he notes himself that "there are a few languages whose sole injective is /ʔd/". The fact that /ʔb/ and /ʔd/ are essentially equally frequent, and that either may occur as the sole implosive in an inventory suggests that the hierarchy is blind to the distinction between labial and alveolar implosives.

The structure of the systems of implosives and laryngealized plosives is given in Table 7.8.

Table 7.8 Implosives and voiced laryngealized plosives in UPSID

Number of terms	Implosive/laryngealized plosive inventory	Number of languages	
1	ʔb	5	(1 also has p˂, t˂)
	ʔd	2	
	ʔḍ	1	
2	ʔb ʔd	25	
3	ʔb ʔd ʔɟ	4	
	ʔb ʔd ʔg	1	
4	ʔb ʔd ʔɟ ʔg	3	
	ʔb ʔd ʔɟ ʔɢ	1	

Of the languages with only one of this class of segments, 5 have /ʔb/ (Kpelle, 103, Igbo, 116, and Zulu, 126, have /ɓ/; Lakkia, 401, and K'ekchi, 714, have /b̰/). Berta (218) and Kullo (262) have /ɗ/ alone. Somali (258) has /ḍ̰/. The number of cases is small, so any interpretation of the results should be cautious. However, the systems with a single term here are varied, unlike ejective stops where a single term is always /k'/. The suggested revision of the hierarchical relationships of place in this case would go as follows: the presence of /ʔb/ implies the presence of /ʔd/ or of no other implosives, /ʔd/ implies the presence of /ʔb/ or of no other implosives, while /ʔɟ/ implies the presence of both /ʔb/ and /ʔd/, and /ʔg/ implies the presence of /ʔb/, /ʔd/, and /ʔɟ/.

As Greenberg observed, the system with two terms, one bilabial and one dental or alveolar, is the most common. In fact it is the only common system. All 25 languages with this inventory have velar stops in other stop series. This is quite strong evidence that the velar place is disfavored for voiced implosives and for voiced laryngealized plosives. An example of such a system is that of Doayo (128):

p	t	k	k͡p
b	d	g	g͡b
ɓ	ɗ		

A 3-term system also generally avoids use of the velar place of articulation, having members at the bilabial, dental or alveolar, and palatal places. An example of such a system is Yulu (216):

p	t	c	k	k͡p
b	d		g	g͡b
ɓ	ɗ	ʄ		

As in Yulu, so also in the other 3 languages concerned (Kadugli, 102, Angas, 267, Ngizim, 269) there is at least one plosive with a palatal place of articulation in the inventory. One language, Hamer (265), stands apart from the others with 3 implosive terms. It has them at bilabial, alveolar and velar places. Despite the presence of palatal plosives it does not have a palatal implosive. This language is discussed further below.

Three of the four 4-term systems contain /ʔb, *ʔd, ʔɟ, ʔg/. An example is Nyangi (207):

p	t	c	k
ɓ	ɗ	ʄ	ɠ

The other two languages concerned, Swahili (124) and Maasai (204), do not have palatal plosives in their inventories, although they do have palato-alveolar affricates. The unusual 4-term language is Ik (208), which has /ɓ, ɗ, ʄ, ʛ/, that is, it has a uvular rather than a velar fourth term. This is despite the fact that the language has no other reported uvular segments and does have velar plosives.

All 9 of the languages in UPSID with more than two implosives or voiced laryngealized plosives are from Africa. They are drawn from 3 different major language families, Niger-Kordofanian, Nilo-Saharan, and Afro-Asiatic. It follows also that the only languages using the palatal and velar places for segments of this type are African languages. Despite the small number of cases, this seems to be an important areal trend.

Glottalic and laryngealized consonants

We do not find evidence to support Greenberg's suggestion that languages often have /j̰/, a laryngealized palatal approximant, in place of /ʔɟ/. The most obvious candidate language in our sample to test this claim is Hamer (265), since it has both palatal plosives and an implosive series which lacks a palatal member. The Hamer stop inventory is:

p	t	c	k
b	d	ɟ	g
		k'	
ɓ	ɗ		ɠ

However Hamer does not have /j̰/ despite the obvious "gap" at the palatal place of articulation in the implosive series to which it could correspond. The segment /j̰/ does occur in 5 of the 25 languages with the two-term system /ʔb, ʔd/, but in all but one of these it occurs as part of a set of laryngealized continuants including at least /w̰/. Only in Hausa (266) could a case be made for considering /j̰/ as complementing a gap in the stop system. Moreover, in Hausa /j̰/ is historically derived from "palatalized" occurrences of /ɗ/. But Hausa is a special case. It does not outweigh the fact that most (28 of 33) languages with a series of implosives or voiced laryngealized stops but with no palatal member of the series lack /j̰/, or that most (8 of 13) languages with /j̰/ lack any implosives or voiced laryngealized plosives. It is true that no language in the survey has both /ʔɟ/ and /j̰/ which might be evidence for the suppletion of /ʔɟ/ by /j̰/. However, given the low frequency of these segment types only one co-occurrence of /ʔɟ/ and /j̰/ could be expected in a sample 3 times the size of the UPSID sample even if the occurrences of the two types were unrestricted. We therefore conclude that the suggestion that /j̰/ takes the place of /ʔɟ/ is unfounded. For discussion of /j̰/ in relation to other approximants see Chapter 6.

Retraction of dental/alveolar implosives

Both Greenberg (1970) and Haudricourt (1950) noted that an implosive corresponding to a non-implosive dental/alveolar is often retroflexed or, at least, articulated further back than the non-implosive. In UPSID a retroflex implosive or laryngealized voiced plosive occurs in only one language, Somali (258), in which the plain plosives are dental. Two other languages, Tama (210) and Yulu (216) have dental plosive /t̪, d̪/ but alveolar implosive /ɗ/. Apart from these instances, there is insufficient phonetic detail in most of the UPSID sources to determine if implosives are typically articulated with a further back contact than other stops made with the tongue tip and blade. A study of voiced alveolar plosives and implosives in Shona using dynamic palatography (Hardcastle and Brasington 1978) did find a more retracted contact (with a smaller area) for the implosive relative to the plosive for the speaker studied.

Voiceless implosives

Overwhelmingly, implosives are voiced. However voiceless implosives do occur. Only one language in UPSID, Igbo (116), has any voiceless implosives. Ladefoged et al. (1976) demonstrate that both voiced and voiceless bilabial implosives occur in the Owerri dialect of Igbo, so that /p˂/ is in contrast with /ɓ/. Igbo also has the voiceless alveolar implosive /t˂/. Pinkerton (1980) shows that the uvular ejective stop in K'ekchi (714) can vary allophonically with a voiceless uvular implosive, and in certain related Quichean languages the voiceless uvular implosive occurs as the normal case (see Table 7.4 above). Other examples of voiceless implosives are mentioned by Campbell (1973).

7.6 Languages with both ejective stops and implosives

Thirteen languages in UPSID contain both some ejectives and some implosives or voiced laryngealized plosives. Given the numbers of languages which have segments of these two classes, we would expect only 6 or 7 such languages in the sample if their occurrence was unassociated. The larger number suggests that these two classes of segments have a tendency to occur together in a language. One might also expect, given the differing place of articulation preferences for ejectives and implosives, that they would rarely occur at the same place of articulation. In several cases, however, they do. Zulu (126), Koma (220), Maidu (708) and Otomi (716) have both /p'/ and /ʔb/. Koma, Kullo (262), Maidu, Otomi, Mazahua (717), and Southern Nambiquara (816) have both /*t'/ and /*ʔd/. Hamer (265) has /k'/ and /ɠ/.

7.7 Laryngealized sonorants

The glottalic airstream mechanism is not used in the production of sonorant types of segments, but sonorants do occur laryngealized. As Greenberg (1970) noted, "the phonological opposition in individual languages between ejectives and injectives applies effectively only to obstruents, and is neutralized for sonants and semi-vowels". In other words, he regards laryngealized sonorants as counterparts in some way to the glottalic obstruents, although with a neutralization of the airstream contrast. There is evidence that glottalic obstruents and laryngealized sonorants are members of the same phonological class in at least some languages. For example, in Hausa any segment which is either glottalic or laryngealized may not co-occur with a different glottalic or laryngealized consonant in a word (Carnochan 1951). What is relevant here is that this rule disallows co-occurrence of the laryngealized sonorant /j̰/ with glottalic obstruents /k'/, /s̰/ etc.

Greenberg also noted that "there is quite surely no phonological contrast of voicing" for the laryngealized nasals and liquids, nor, we might add, for the laryngealized approximants and vowels. All segments of these classes in UPSID are reported as voiced. Moreover, in all cases a plain voiced counterpart also occurs in the inventory of a language if there is a laryngealized sonorant.

In general, laryngealized sonorants are found only in languages with glottalic stops. Nineteen of the 20 languages in UPSID which have laryngealized sonorants have ejective stops, implosives or voiced laryngealized plosives in their inventories. The exception is Tiddim Chin (513) with /l̰/ and /w̰/ but no other segments with a "glottalic" component. Within this group of sounds, laryngealized nasals and vocoid approximants are a little more frequent than laryngealized liquids, as Table 7.9 shows.

Table 7.9 Laryngealized nasals, liquids and approximants in UPSID

m̰	*n̰	ɲ̰	ŋ̰	"*r̰"	*l̰	j̰	w̰
14	14	3	3	5	8	13	14

The distribution of laryngealized nasals can be seen to be parallel to that of voiced "glottalized" stops in that both bilabial and dental/alveolar places are more common than back articulations, but yet are not between themselves in hierarchical relation. In most cases (13 of 17 languages concerned) /m̰/ and /*n̰/ occur together just as /ʔb/ and /*ʔd/ occur together. However, note that among plain voiced nasals bilabial and dental/alveolar places are also the most common and the velar place is less common (see Chapter 4). Hence it is not certain if the prevalence of /m̰/ and /n̰/ among laryngealized nasals should be attributed to their laryngealized nature or to their simply being nasals.

The laryngealized approximants /j̰/ and /w̰/ usually occur together (12 of 16 languages concerned). There are 5 languages with a laryngealized trill, tap or flap (collected in the table under the symbol /"*r̰"/). One language, Wapishana (822), has a laryngealized voiced retroflex fricative, /ẓ̰/.

7.8 Diachronic implications

Greenberg (1970: 23) suggests that "it is possible to derive the general diachronic hypothesis that at least one source of injectives might be a sound shift from voiced plain to voiced implosive stops". This is based on his observation that languages with implosives tend to lack corresponding non-implosive voiced stops. Greenberg also suggests that loss or addition of implosives should follow the place of articulation preference hierarchy for implosives discussed above. One reasonable prediction to read into his diachronic suggestions is that implosives at the same place of articulation as voiced plosives should be rather rare. This, however, is not the finding of our survey. As noted above, languages with implosives most commonly also have voiced plosives corresponding to each implosive. In a very few cases, such as Swahili (124), where there is no voiced plosive series, it does appear that the source of the implosives may be from an earlier voiced plosive series (Guthrie 1967-70). But even this case is unclear because it is conceivable that Swahili has merged a voiced plosive series with an implosive series; Stewart (1972) has found reasons to posit Proto-Bantu implosives in addition to voiced plosives. The failure to confirm Greenberg's prediction does not completely refute the diachronic hypothesis, since in the languages that do not conform to the prediction there may also have been a shift in another stop series to replace the former plain voiced series, or the original voiced plosive series may have split into plosive and implosive sets. However, it does weaken the evidence for positing voiced plosives as the straightforward source of implosives.

7.9 Phonetic explanations for the structure of glottalic systems

A phonetic explanation for Greenberg's (1970) place of articulation hierarchies of ejectives and implosives has been offered by several linguists, including Greenberg himself. Recall that some weakening of the preference hierarchies posited by Greenberg has been suggested. For ejectives, although a velar place of articulation is common, it is only marginally more common than a dental/alveolar one; however, both these places are preferred to a bilabial one. For implosives, etc., bilabial and dental/alveolar places of articulation are equally common, and both are preferred to velar.

Javkin (1977) clarified the role played by Boyle's Law in explaining implosive and ejective distributions, correcting a misinterpretation by Greenberg. Javkin (1977) noted that the claim that back articulations confer an advantage in compressing air in the supraglottal chamber (for ejectives) and front articulations confer an advantage in rarefying air (for implosives) cannot be entirely correct. This is because it takes the same effort to produce either compression or rarefaction in a chamber of a given size. What matters is the proportional change in the size of the chamber. Javkin's model suggests that the ability to change the volume of the chamber is proportionally greater for a velar closure than for a bilabial, dental or alveolar closure. That is, the same amount of raising or lowering of the larynx will have a greater effect on the volume of air between a velar closure and a glottal closure than if the oral closure is further forward. If articulatory efficiency were the explanation for the difference in the place preferences for ejectives and implosives, and there were nothing else to consider, then both types of sounds would show a preference for back articulation. It is possible to maintain this kind of explanation for the preference for velar ejectives, providing some overriding factor can be found to explain why implosives do not share the preference for back articulations. Javkin suggests that this factor is voicing.

As noted above, implosive segments are almost invariably voiced. If we grant, for the time being, that voicing is an essential part of their nature, then anything that facilitates voicing will be favored. In a voiced segment some volume of pulmonic air must flow into the oral cavity. The absolute volume by which the oral cavity is expanded must be greater than this volume of pulmonic air or there will be no rarefaction, hence no implosion. A chamber created by a back oral closure may not permit expansion by the required absolute volume, whereas one further forward may allow greater absolute expansion through adjustments of tongue position and oral cavity walls. Such oral cavity expansion has been shown to be normal in voiced plosives in several studies of English (e.g. Kent & Moll 1969; Smith 1971; Bell-Berti 1975; Westbury 1983), and Lindau (1982) specifically argues that the achievement of an even or rising amplitude of voicing throughout the closure may be a major part of the "target" in production of an implosive. Lindau compares the bilabial implosive and plosive in the Niger-Kordofanian language Degema and finds that whereas the amplitude of voicing actually increases during the closure for the implosive, during the plosive the amplitude of voicing tends to decay and the periods become irregular. Of course, some air can flow through the glottis without any cavity expansion being required. Again, the further forward the oral closure is formed, the less the intraoral air pressure increases for a given volume of transglottal air flow.

No measurements have been done to confirm the occurrence of oral cavity expansion by tongue movement, jaw lowering or use of the cheeks in production of implosives, although Hardcastle and Brasington (1978) show a pattern in the occlusion for an alveolar implosive in Shona which is consistent with some cavity expansion by tongue lowering. Nonetheless, the theory that such expansion occurs is plausible and appealing. In addition to accounting for a preference for bilabial implosives, it also suggests why the patterns for voiced laryngealized plosives are similar to those for true implosives. For, as Greenberg (1970) and Ladefoged (1968) have noted, "implosives" do not always entail inward air flow upon release. In some languages (e.g. Hausa, 266) some speakers use implosives while others use laryngealized stops. If implosion, especially the contribution of the lowering of the larynx to oral cavity expansion facilitating transglottal air flow, is predominantly a mechanism employed in the more general aim of achieving salient voicing in the production of a stop, then actual achievement of inward oral air flow is a minor part of the target. This means that the cavity expansion need only equal, not exceed, the volume of transglottal air flow.

Note that we are not suggesting that plain voiced plosives are likely to become implosives (pace Greenberg) as speakers endeavor to sustain voicing through the duration of the oral closure. Instead it seems more likely that, given a contrast between voiced stops of two different types in a language, a tactic for enhancing the contrast between them by implosion and emphasized voicing is exploited. In this view, implosives and voiced laryngealized plosives would be expected to co-occur with plain voiced plosives, as they do. Because the cavity expansion possibilities are greatest when there is a front articulation, not only is a front articulation preferred when the target is to achieve enhanced voicing, but also when the target is for an "ordinary" degree of voicing, since if the oral cavity is not expanded, voicing will cease when the oral air pressure reaches equilibrium with the subglottal air pressure. Hence place preferences for voiced implosives and for voiced plosives are similar (see Chapter 2). The disfavored velar implosives, if they arose, would tend to fall together with voiced velar plosives, since it would be difficult to maintain a distinction between them on the basis of differences in their voicing characteristics.

On the other hand, since production of voiceless plosives has nothing to do with rarefaction of air in a closed chamber, we would expect place preferences for ejective stops and voiceless plosives to differ, as they do. A small chamber confers no advantage in producing voiceless plosives, hence no preference for a velar place is found. Instead, dental or alveolar plosives are most common, perhaps because the tongue tip/blade is the most mobile of all the articulators. Note that this view predicts that *voiceless* implosives should show the same preferences for back articulations as ejectives, rather than those found for voiced implosives, since the preference for front articulation in voiced implosives is attributed to the intention to achieve voicing. The data in UPSID is insufficient to deal with this question. The one language with voiceless implosives, Igbo (116), looks like a counterexample since it has them at bilabial and alveolar places, and not at the velar place, but note that several of the Mayan languages cited in Table 7.4 have uvular implosives which are voiceless.

7.10 *Summary of generalizations*

In this section we recapitulate the most important observations about glottalic and laryngealized consonants discussed in this chapter. After each statement, a fraction is given which represents the number of cases which conform with the statement over the number of relevant cases. The percentage of conforming cases is also given. Note that some of the statements are made about segments and some are made about languages.

(i) An ejective segment is voiceless. 309/312 99.0%.

(ii) An ejective segment is likely to be a stop. 188/312 60.3%.

(iii) If a language has /p'/ it also has /*t'/. 33/34 97.1%.

(iv) If a language has /*t'/ it also has /k'/. 45/46 97.8%.

(v) If a language has only one ejective stop, it is /k'/. 5/5 100%.

(vi) If a language has /c'/ or /q'/ it also has /p'/, /*t'/ and /k'/. 15/19. 78.9%.

(vii) If a language has /q^{w}'/ it also has /q'/ and /k^{w}'/. 8/8 100%.

(viii) If a language has /k^{w}'/ it also has /k'/. 17/18 94.4%.

(ix) If a language has ejective affricates it also has ejective stops. 39/40 97.5%.

(x) An ejective affricate segment is usually sibilant. 70/88 79.5%.

(xi) If a language has any ejective fricatives, at least one of them is sibilant. 10/10 100%.

(xii) An implosive segment is voiced. 72/74 97.3%.

(xiii) A language with any implosives or laryngealized voiced stops has /ʔb/ and /ʔd/. 36/42 85.7%.

(xiv) If a language has /ʔg/ it has /ʔɟ/. 3/4 75.0%.

(xv) Laryngealized sonorants are voiced. 74/74 100%.

(xvi) If a laryngealized sonorant segment occurs, the plain voiced counterpart occurs in the same language. 74/74 100%.

(xvii) If a language has any laryngealized sonorants it also has glottalic or laryngealized stops. 19/20 95.0%.

Notes

1. Hoard (1978) reports, as secondary allophones of the ejective affricates /ts'/ and /tɬ'/, the voiced implosive counterparts [ɗz] and [ɗɮ] in the Tsimshian language Gitksan (not included in UPSID). From the description provided it is not clear if these voiced alternates of the voiceless ejective affricates are actually imploded or not. However, since they contrast phonetically with corresponding plain voiced affricates in certain environments, it is probable that their articulation is, if not implosive, at least accompanied by laryngeal constriction. Still, the particular allophone characterizable as "most typical" for these segments (i.e., that which would be coded by UPSID) is in both cases the voiceless ejective affricate and hence it is still true that no phonemic voiced implosive affricate segment is known to occur. A similar analysis is presumably maintainable in regard to the voiced palatal implosives of Fula and Serer (also not in UPSID) which are slightly affricated (Ladefoged, personal communication).

References

Bell-Berti, F. 1975. Control of pharyngeal cavity size for English voiced and voiceless stops. Journal of the Accoustical Society of America 57: 456-64.

Campbell, L. 1973. On glottalic consonants. International Journal of American Linguistics 39: 44-6.

Carnochan, J. 1951. Glottalization in Hausa. Transactions of the Philological Society 1951: 78-109.

Catford, J. 1939. On the classification of stop consonants. Le Maître Phonétique, 3rd series, 65: 2-5.

Dart, S. 1984. Testing an aerodynamic model with measured data from Korean. UCLA Working Papers in Phonetics 59: 1-17.

Fordyce, J.F. 1980. On the nature of glottalic and laryngealized consonant and vowel systems. UCLA Working Papers in Phonetics 50: 120-54.

Gamkrelidze, T.V. 1978. On the correlation of stops and fricatives in a phonological system. In J. H. Greenberg et al. (eds.), Universals of Human Language, Vol. 2, Phonology. Stanford: Stanford University Press.
Greenberg, J.H. 1970. Some generalizations concerning glottalic consonants, especially implosives. International Journal of American Linguistics 36: 123-45.
Guthrie, M. 1967-70. Comparative Bantu. Gregg, Farnborough.
Hamp, E. 1970. Maya-Chipaya and the typology of labials. Papers from the Sixth Regional Meeting, Chicago Linguistic Society: 20-2.
Hardcastle, W.J. and Brasington, R.W.P. 1978. Experimental study of implosive and voiced egressive stops in Shona: an interim report. Work in Progress (Phonetics Laboratory, University of Reading) 2: 66-97.
Haudricourt, A-G. 1950. Les consonnes préglottalisées en Indochine. Bulletin de la Société Linguistique de Paris 46: 172-82.
Hoard, J.E. 1978. Obstruent voicing in Gitksan: some implications for distinctive feature theory. In E-D. Cook and J. Kaye (eds.), Linguistic Studies of Native Canada. University of British Columbia Press, Vancouver.
Javkin, H. 1977. Towards a phonetic explanation for universal preferences in implosives and ejectives. Proceedings of the Berkeley Linguistics Society 3: 559-65.
Kent, R.D. and Moll, K.L. 1969. Vocal tract characteristics of the stop cognates. Journal of the Acoustical Society of America 46: 1549-55.
Kim, C-W. 1965. On the autonomy of the tensity feature in stop classification (with special reference to Korean stops). Word 21: 339-59.
Kim, C-W. 1970. A theory of aspiration. Phonetica 21: 107-16.
Ladefoged, P. 1968. A Phonetic Study of West African Languages. Cambridge University Press, Cambridge.
Ladefoged, P., Williamson, K., Elugbe, B. and Uwalaka, A.A. 1976. The stops of Owerri Igbo. Studies in African Linguistics, Supplement 6: 147-64.
Lindau, M. 1982. Phonetic differences in glottalic consonants. UCLA Working Papers in Phonetics 54: 66-77.
Pinkerton, S. 1980. Quichean (Mayan) glottalized and non-glottalized stops: a phonetic study with implications for phonological universals. Report of the Phonology Laboratory (University of California, Berkeley) 5: 106-13
Sherzer, J. 1973. Areal linguistics in North America. In T.A. Sebeok (ed.) Current Trends in Linguistics, Vol. 10, Linguistics in North America. Mouton, The Hague: 749-95.
Smith, T.S. 1971. A Phonetic Study of the Function of the Extrinsic Tongue Muscles (UCLA Working Papers in Phonetics 18). University of California, Los Angeles.
Snyman, J.W. 1969. An Introduction to the !Xũ (!Kung) Language. A.A. Balkema, Cape Town.
Stewart, J.M. 1972. "Implosives" in Proto-Bantu. Paper presented at the Tenth West African Languages Congress, Legon, Ghana.
Wang, W.S-Y. 1968. The basis of speech. Project on Linguistic Analysis Reports, second series, No. 4. University of California, Berkeley.
Westbury, J. 1983. Enlargement of the supraglottal cavity and its relation to stop consonant voicing. Journal of the Acoustical Society of America 73: 1322-36.

8

Vowels

8.1 Introduction

Vowels are discussed in two chapters in this book. In the present chapter we will deal with questions of which vowels are most frequent in the world's languages and how many vowels are typically found. A brief discussion of diphthongs is also included. In the following chapter, contributed by Sandra F. Disner, the focus is on the structure of vowel systems.

8.2 Types of vowels

The entire UPSID database contains entries for 2549 monophthongal vowels, that is, a mean of fractionally over 8 for each language. In addition there are 83 diphthongal segments included, making a total of 2632 vocalic segments. In the following sections, we will describe the most frequent types of vowels and comment on some of the implications.

The three conventional parameters for vowel description are those of vowel height, backness, and lip-rounding. In the UPSID data file, vowels are classified as having one of five different heights, high, higher mid, mid, lower mid, or low. Vowels described as being mid may in fact lie between higher and lower mid positions, or they may have simply been transcribed or labeled as mid vowels without any further specification in the source consulted for the language in question. In either case, such vowels are distinguished notationally from higher mid vowels by being enclosed in double quote marks, i.e. /e/, /ø/, and /o/ represent higher mid vowels, but /"e"/, /"ø"/, and /"o"/ represent mid vowels. We will also use the term "in the mid range" to cover the three height positions higher mid, mid, and lower mid as a group. Within each height category, further classification is made with the use of a variable called "nonperipheral"; for example /ɩ/ differs from /i/ in that it is nonperipheral. The UPSID variables permit vowels to be classified on the front/back dimension as being front, central, or back. Again, finer differences can be represented by defining a vowel as nonperipheral. Only two lip positions, unrounded or rounded, are provided for in UPSID.

In terms of these three basic parameters of vowel quality, our survey provides few surprises. It largely supports the findings of previous studies of vowel inventories such as those of Hockett (1955), Sedlak (1969) and Crothers (1978). It is, however, wider in scope and is able to add more reliable quantification. The total of 2549 monophthongal vowels is broken down according to these parameters in Table 8.1.

Table 8.1 Broad classification of types of vowels in UPSID

	Front		Central		Back		
	Unround	Round	Unround	Round	Unround	Round	Totals
High	452	29	55	10	31	417	994
Mid range	425	32	100	8	19	448	1032
Low	81	0	392	1	13	36	523
Totals	958	61	547	19	63	901	2549
	1019		566		964		

We may make the following observations. Vowels in the mid range are a little more common than high vowels, namely 1032 to 994, or 40.5% of the sample to 39.0%. Low vowels are substantially less common, amounting to only 20.5%. There are slightly more front vowels than back vowels, namely 1019 to 964, or 40.0% of the population compared with 37.8%. Central vowels are considerably less common, amounting only to 22.2%. Unrounded vowels are considerably more frequent than rounded vowels, namely 1569 to 981 or 61.5% to 38.5%.[1]

There are some interesting asymmetries when the interactions of the three basic parameters are looked at. Front vowels are usually unrounded (94.0%), back vowels usually rounded (93.5%). Low vowels are usually central (75.1%) and central vowels are usually low (69.4%). High front vowels are more frequent than high back vowels. In the mid range, vowels are more commonly back than front if the lip position is unmarked (i.e. unrounded if front, rounded if back), but front rounded vowels are more frequently found than back unrounded. Nonback low vowels are extremely unlikely to be rounded (only one case in 474).

The most common individual vowel qualities reported are given in Table 8.2. This table lists those vowels which are found to occur in at least 30% of the languages in the survey. The number of languages shown here is the number which have the given vowel quality either long or short; for example, 290 is the number of languages out of the UPSID sample of 317 that have one or both of /i/ and /i:/. Recall that /"o"/ and /"e"/ may not be reliably distinct from other vowels in the mid range.

Table 8.2 Most common vowel qualities

Vowel	Number of languages	Percent
High and low vowels		
/i/	290	91.5%
/a/	279	88.0%
/u/	266	83.9%
Vowels in the mid range		
/"o"/	139	43.8%
/"e"/	118	37.2%
/ɛ/	118	37.2%
/o/	109	34.4%
/e/	100	31.5%
/ɔ/	99	31.2%

The 3 vowels at the corners of the conventional vowel triangle, /i, a, u/, are the most widespread, but note that there are 24 fewer languages with /u/ than with /i/. These three vowels might be expected to be equally favored, because they each lie at an acoustic extreme. The low vowel /a/ has the highest first formant, /i/ and /u/ have the lowest first formant but /i/ has the highest second (and third) formant, whereas /u/ has the lowest second formant. However, a contributory factor to the relative disfavoring of /u/ may be the lower amplitude typical of /u/. In the higher part of the mid range, note that there are substantially more cases of back /o/ and /"o"/ than of the front vowels /e/ and /"e"/, but among lower mid vowels /ɛ/ is a little more common than /ɔ/. The within-language asymmetries that contribute to these differences are analyzed further in Chapter 9.

8.3 Number of vowels per language

The smallest number of phonemic vowels in any of the UPSID languages is 3 and the largest is 24. The modal number is, unsurprisingly, 5. The number of languages with a given number of simple vowels is shown in Table 8.3.

Table 8.3 Number of languages with given number of vowels

No. of vowels	No. of languages	Percent
3	18	5.7%
4	15	4.7%
5	68	21.5%
6	43	13.6%
7	34	10.7%
8	24	7.6%
9	28	8.8%
10	16	5.0%
11	11	3.4%
12	18	5.7%
13	4	1.3%
14	7	2.2%
15	8	2.5%
16	10	3.2%
17 and over	13	4.1%

Some languages have been analyzed in the linguistic literature as having fewer than three phonemic vowels. The best known are Kabardian (911) and Abaza (Allen 1965; Anderson 1978). However, more conservative analyses of these languages can be defended in which less of the contrast between syllables is attributed to the consonants. This approach results in an analysis in which they have only three vowels - it is clear that these are languages with a small number of vowel contrasts under any analysis. As noted in Chapter 1, we do not find that having a small number of vowels in general predicts a large number of consonant contrasts, although this is a feature of the Kabardian inventory which has been commented on a great deal. Note that languages with 3 vowels also include Mura (802) with only 8 consonants, Gugu-Yalanji (364) with only 13 consonants and Alabama (759) with only 14.

8.4 Distinctive vowel qualities

Many languages have several series of vowels, for example, short and long vowels, oral and nasalized vowels, plain voiced and laryngealized vowels. In the greater number of such cases, the vowels in one series can be matched with vowels that are similar in quality in other series, so the number of vowel phonemes is greater than the number of different vowel qualities in the languages concerned. A simple example of this is a language such as Mazatec (727) which has oral vowels /i, ɛ, a, o/ and nasalized vowels /ĩ, ɛ̃, ã, õ/. While there are 8 phonemic vowels here, there are only 4 vowel qualities involved. In other languages there may be qualities in one series which do not occur outside that series. An example is Zande (130) which has /ẽ, õ/ but not /e, o/. In such a language the total number of vowel qualities may be larger than the number found in any one given series. The count of vowel qualities in the UPSID languages is given in Table 8.4.

Table 8.4 Number of vowel qualities

No. of vowel qualities	No. of languages	Percent of languages
3	17	5.4%
4	27	8.5%
5	98	30.9%
6	60	18.9%
7	47	14.8%
8	17	5.4%
9	25	7.9%
10	15	4.7%
11	2	0.6%
12	5	1.6%
13	2	0.6%
14	0	0.0%
15	2	0.6%

In certain respects the number of distinctive vowel qualities in a language provides a more appropriate measure for comparing vowel systems than does the total number of vocalic phonemes. This is because the number of vowel qualities indicates how greatly the most basic parameters of vowel contrast (height, backness, rounding) are being used. No language in UPSID has less than 3 vowel qualities. The most common number, found in almost a third of the languages, is 5. Almost two-thirds of the languages have between 5 and 7 vowel qualities, although up to 10 is still relatively common. The two languages with the largest number of vowel qualities in UPSID are the two Germanic languages in the survey, German (004) and Norwegian (006), which have 15. Contrasts of a large number of vowel qualities seem disproportionately common in Indo-European languages - of the 11 languages with more than 10 vowel qualities, 5 are Indo-European. Almost 24% of the Indo-European languages included in UPSID have over 10 vowel qualities, whereas only 3.5% of the total sample have that many.

8.5 Properties of vowel series

The tabulation in Table 8.4 shows the numbers of vowel qualities that are found in one or more of the series of vowels that a language may have. In this section we will discuss the properties that distinguish vowel series from each other. The most important of these are length and nasalization.

Length

Vowel length contrasts (short vs. long, or short vs. overshort) are only recorded as phonemic in UPSID if they are linked to vowel quality differences. In other words, if all the vowel qualities found in a language participate in a length contrast, length is treated as a suprasegmental feature or as resulting from a juxtaposition of simple vowels rather than as a property of individual phonemes. There are three types of situations where vowel length is represented in the phoneme inventory. In some languages the long and short vowel sets do not overlap in quality; such a case is Kurdish (015) with a 9-vowel inventory consisting of the following:

short			long		
ɩ	ɨ	ʊ	iː		uː
	"ə"		"eː"		"oː"
				aː	

In such a case, length could have been treated as predictable from vowel quality. More commonly, some vowels in each set have the same quality, as in Tonkawa (752) with /u, uː/ and /a, aː/ pairs but with short /ɩ, ɛ, ɔ/

versus long /i:, e:, o:/. Tonkawa is thus considered a language with 8 vowel qualities and 10 vowel phonemes. An alternative analysis of the language might say that the quality differences were predictable from length, which would result in this being treated as a language with a 5-vowel system. But here as in other areas, UPSID has preferred to keep possibly redundant phonetic information in the data.

The third situation in which length is represented is where the qualities of the longer vowels are a subset of the qualities of the shorter vowels or vice versa, as, for example, in Atayal (407) with 5 short vowels /i, ɛ, a, ɔ, u/ and 2 long vowels /i:, u:/, or Yurak (056) with 5 short vowels /i, e, a, o, u/ and 3 overshort vowels /ĭ, ă, ŭ/. These two languages have 5 vowel qualities but 7 and 8 vowel phonemes respectively. In all three situations outlined here, the property of length (or shortness) only applies to vowels of certain qualities in the inventory, hence it is considered to be inherent in the phoneme. With contrastive length defined in this way, there are 62 languages in the sample with length contrasts, or 19.6%.

The probability of length being part of the vowel system increases with the number of vowel quality contrasts. No language with 3 vowel qualities includes length, only 14.1% of the languages with 4-6 vowel qualities have some inherent length differences, whereas 24.7% of languages with 7-9 vowel qualities have length, and 53.8% of languages with 10 or more vowel qualities have length. We may speculate that there are two diachronic factors responsible for this trend; languages with an originally suprasegmental vowel length contrast may begin to add quality differences to the quantitative difference (probably the case in Tonkawa, as in Navaho, 702, Arabic, 250, Telugu, 902, etc.), and languages with large numbers of qualitatively distinct vowels may begin to recruit length differences to additionally distinguish them (there are no clear cases of this in UPSID but compare the ongoing lengthening of /æ/ in English, perhaps to distinguish it from /ɛ/). In either case the outcome is the same - the use of combinations of durational and qualitative differences to mutually reinforce the distinctiveness of vowel contrasts.

Among the major vowel qualities there are some important asymmetries concerning length. We may summarize the most important of these as follows: a higher-mid vowel is more likely to be long than a lower-mid vowel; a low vowel which is either front or back is more likely to be long than a low central vowel; a front rounded vowel is more likely to be long than a front unrounded vowel. Table 8.5 gives the "length ratio" of selected vowel qualities, calculated by expressing the number of long vowels as a proportion of the number of languages with vowels of the given quality whether long or short (as in Table 8.1).

Table 8.5 Length ratios of common vowel qualities

	Front		Back	
Mid vowels				
	e:/e	.280	o:/o	.284
	"e:"/"e"	.088	"o:"/"o"	.098
	ɛ:/ɛ	.103	ɔ:/ɔ	.090
Low vowels				
	æ:/æ	.256	ɑ:/ɑ	.318
		a:/a	.129	
Selected other vowels				
	i:/i	.151	u:/u	.146
	y:/y	.238		
	œ:/œ	.400		

The higher mid long vowels /e:/ and /o:/ are far more likely to appear in a language without corresponding short vowels of the same quality than any of the other vowels examined. In 18% of the languages with the vowel quality /e(:)/ and 19.6% of the languages with the vowel quality /o(:)/ the vowel only occurs long. For comparison, this figure is 6.6% for the vowel quality /i(:)/, 4.9% for /u(:)/ and 2.9% for /a(:)/. This suggests that mid vowels tend to be raised when lengthened and/or lowered when shortened, giving rise to associations between height and length. A well-known diachronic example of this occurred in Late Latin (Griffiths 1966), and the subsequent loss of length contrasts left Italian with the 4 mid vowels /e, ɛ, o, ɔ/ in place of Classical Latin /e:, e, o:, o/. This illustrates one specific direction the qualitative reinforcement of quantity differences referred to in the previous paragraph can take.

Nasalization

Vowel nasalization is more common than inherent vowel length in the UPSID languages, 71 languages or 22.4% of the sample having a contrast of oral and nasalized vowels. There is again a tendency for this feature to be more likely to occur in languages with a larger number of vowel quality contrasts but the trend is less pronounced than with length: 21.2% of languages with 4-6 vowel qualities have contrastive nasalization, 22.5% of languages with 7-9 vowel qualities have it, but 53.8% of languages with 10 or more vowel qualities have it. This distribution arises in part because vowels with nasalization sometimes have different qualities from their closest oral counterpart; for example the 3 nasalized vowels of Burmese (509) are reported as /ɪ̃, æ̃, ɷ̃/ but the closest counterparts among the 8 oral vowels are given as /i, a, u/. Thus Burmese arrives at a total of 11 vowel qualities. However, such cases are relatively rare; only 4 of the 14 languages with 10 or more vowel qualities that have nasalized vowels include any vowel qualities that are found in the nasalized set alone. These are Dan (106), Zande (130) and Sara (217) as well as Burmese. These 4 languages amount to only 15.4% of the 26 languages with 10 or more vowel qualities.

By far the most common nasalized vowels are the 3 vowels whose oral counterparts are also most common. There are 59 languages with /ĩ/ or its long counterpart, 58 with /ã(:)/ and 55 with /ũ(:)/. These frequencies are representative of a general pattern: nasalized vowel frequency is generally correlated with the frequency of the oral equivalent. The number of occurrences of a given nasalized vowel is about one-fifth the number of the oral counterpart. However, there is one salient exception to this pattern among the more common vowel qualities, and that is the higher mid vowel /ẽ/. Only 11 languages have /ẽ(:)/ whereas 22 have /ɛ̃(:)/. There is no similar discrepancy between higher and lower mid back rounded vowels, in fact 21 languages have /õ(:)/ whereas only 19 have /ɔ̃(:)/. Lowering of mid (and high) vowels diachronically and allophonically has been frequently commented on (e.g. Foley 1975; Wright 1980) but no asymmetry between front and back vowels appears to have been mentioned before. A possible interpretation of the difference between front and back mid vowels would be that the lowering process leads to a greater lowering of front vowels than of back vowels in the mid range under nasalization. This could cause /ẽ/ and /ɛ̃/ to merge as /ɛ̃/. Wright (1980) showed how the acoustic effect of nasalization was perceived as a lowering of vowel height in mid vowels but his analyses of the perceptual distance between oral and nasal equivalents of a set of vowels do not explain the asymmetry found in the UPSID data. If anything, they suggest that there is a greater perceived lowering of back vowels under nasalization than of front vowels.

Among less frequent vowel qualities there may also be a significant exception to the usual pattern. On the basis of the usual ratio of oral to nasalized vowels, 4 or 5 nasalized high front rounded vowels would have been anticipated to occur in the survey. But there are no occurrences of /ỹ/ (or /Ỹ/). Since other front rounded vowels and unrounded high front vowels occur nasalized with the expected frequency it is not clear why the combination of rounding and nasalization does not occur with high front position.

Other properties of vowel sets

The other properties which establish sets of vowels in some of the languages in UPSID are pharyngealization, laryngealization and breathy voice. There are 5 languages with contrastive sets of pharyngealized vowels: Evenki (067), Neo-Aramaic (255), Hamer (265), Lak (912) and !Xũ (918). !Xũ also has vowel sets resulting from contrasts of nasalization and length. The intersection of these features with the pharyngealization contrast produces 8 vowel sets. Two languages are analyzed as having contrastively laryngealized vowels, Sedang (304) and S. Nambiquara (816). In the latter language, nasalization intersects with laryngealization to produce 4 sets of vowels. Two languages have contrastive voiceless vowels, Ik (208) and Dafla (508), and one language has breathy vowels, Tamang (507). The source consulted for this language treats the breathiness as an inherent part of a set of contrasting tones rather than localizing it in the vowel. But the two "breathy tones" have the same pitch shapes as the two plain tones, therefore Tamang is regarded here as a language with just two tones and a segmental contrast of breathiness.

The instances of these various properties are too few to encourage very much generalization, although it should be noted that no language has a set of these "marked" vowels which contains more contrasts than is found in the set of plain voiced vowels. In this respect these features appear more like nasalization than like length.

In the languages with laryngealized, voiceless or breathy vowels, the vowels in these sets have the same qualities as vowels which are found in the plain voiced vowel set. But in a number of cases pharyngealized vowels are more centralized than the closest non-pharyngealized vowel. For example, Evenki has /u/ but /ʊˤ/, Hamer has /i, e, ɑ, o, u/ but /ɩˤ, "eˤ", ɐˤ, ɔˤ, ʊˤ/, and Lak has /i, a, u/ but /"eˤ", æˤ, "oˤ"/. These variations in vowel quality are reminiscent of the qualitative differences between sets of vowels in vowel harmony languages whose harmony is based on variable pharynx width (tongue root advancement). Among languages of this type in UPSID are Akan (115, see Lindau 1979), Igbo (116) and Luo (205, see Jacobson 1978).[2] In the vowel harmony languages there does not seem to be a strong percept of pharyngeal constriction for the vowels in the set with narrow pharynx. Instead, the vowels in the two sets are usually well-distinguished auditorily by the basic parameters of vowel quality, and they have been represented in UPSID on this basis. The languages with contrastive pharyngealization may help to throw some light on the origin of vowel harmony. Pharyngealization is not a harmonizing property in these languages, but the nature of the vowel shifts observed does suggest that pharyngeal width differences may be causally involved in creation of the quality differences in vowel harmony, rather than merely co-occurring with them. It has been suggested that the origin of vowel harmony lies in consonant voicing differences, and voiced consonants (at least the obstruents among them) typically are produced with a wider pharynx (see, for example, Perkell 1969).

8.6 Diphthongs

Relatively few languages are considered to have phonologically unitary diphthongs under the criteria used in UPSID (for further details on these see Chapter 10). Obviously a much larger number of languages permit sequences of juxtaposed vocalic segments which might be considered phonetically to be diphthongs, or have diphthongal sounds which arise allophonically. Because diphthongs are so frequently derived in this way rather than being underlying segments, UPSID does not provide a good basis for analysis of the phonetic patterns in diphthongs. Nonetheless, we offer the following brief comments on the diphthongs that do occur. There are a total of 83 diphthongal segments recorded in UPSID from 23 different languages. Fully 22 of these 83 diphthongs are from a single language, !Xũ (918). This language has 4 sets of diphthongs: plain oral, plain nasalized, pharyngealized oral, and pharyngealized nasalized (cf. the 8 sets of monophthongal vowels it has). Of the other languages with diphthongs, 2 (Kurdish, 015, and Acoma, 749) have 8 each, one (Dani, 613) has 5, 2 (Hindi-Urdu, 016, and Yagaria, 609) have 4. There are a further 5 languages with 3 diphthongs, 3 languages with 2 and 8 languages with one diphthong.

The diphthongal segments reported are rather heterogeneous and do not show much clear patterning. The only ones recorded which are at all common, i.e. occur in more than 2 languages, are those shown in Table 8.6. Though the numbers are small, this table seems to indicate that diphthongs that begin or end with a high vowel element are preferred over those which lack such an element. This cannot be explained as being the result of an attempt to maximize the distinctiveness of the diphthongs, since diphthongs with short trajectories through the vowel space, such as /ei/, /ie/ and /ou/, are found among the more common types as readily as those with a large trajectory through this space, such as /ai/, /au/ and /ui/.

Table 8.6 Common diphthongs

/ei/	6	(also Burmese, 509, with /ẽĩ/ but not /ei/)
/ai/	5	(plus 2 languages with /ae/)
/au/	5	(plus 2 languages with /ao/)
/ou/	4	(also Burmese, 509, with /õũ/ but not /ou/)
/ui/	4	
/io/	4	(including Evenki with /io:/)
/ie/	3	
/oi/	3	

8.7 Summary

The principal conclusions reached in this chapter can be summarized as follows. Front vowels are usually unrounded, back vowels are usually rounded, low vowels are usually central and central vowels are usually low. All languages have at least 3 phonemic vowels. Nearly all languages have /i, a, u/, but among these the vowel /u/ is more often absent than /i/ or /a/. The most common number of vowel phonemes in a language is 5, and the most common number of distinctive vowel qualities in a language is also 5. Contrastive length is associated with an increase in the number of distinctive vowel qualities in an inventory. The higher mid vowels /e/ and /o/ are more likely to appear long without a short counterpart than lower mid vowels. Among nasalized vowels, /ɛ̃/ is comparatively rare. No language has more vowels in a secondary set than it has in its primary set, where secondary means vowels with nasalization, pharyngealization or an unusual phonation type, and primary means that set of vowels with normal voicing and no secondary articulation which has the most members (in some languages this is a set of long vowels). Diphthongs show a preference for including a high vowel element.

Notes

1. Note that the percentages are almost exactly what would obtain if all languages had the 5 vowel system provided for by the Roman alphabet, /i, e, a, o, u/. This system has 40% high vowels, 40% mid vowels, 20% low vowels; 40% front vowels, 40% back vowels, 20% central vowels; 60% unrounded vowels, 40% rounded vowels.
2. A similar basis for vowel harmony, under the name of "register", has also been suggested for some Austro-Asiatic languages (Gregerson 1976).

References

Allen, W.S. 1965. On one-vowel systems. Lingua 13: 111-24.
Anderson, S.R. 1978. Syllables, segments and the Northwest Caucasian languages. In A. Bell and J.B. Hooper (eds.), Syllables and Segments. North-Holland, Amsterdam: 47-58.
Crothers, J. 1978. Typology and universals of vowel systems. In J.H. Greenberg et al. (eds.), Universals of Human Language, Vol. 2, Phonology. Stanford University Press, Stanford: 93-152.
Foley, J. 1975. Nasalization as a universal phonological process. In C.A. Ferguson, L.M. Hyman and J.J. Ohala (eds.), Nasálfest. Stanford University, Stanford: 197-212.
Gregerson, K.J. 1976. Tongue-root and register in Mon-Khmer. In P. Jenner, L. Thompson and S. Starosta (eds.), Austro-Asiatic Studies, Vol. 1. University of Hawaii Press, Honolulu.
Griffiths, T.G. 1966. The Italian Language. Faber, London.
Hockett, C.F. 1955. A Manual of Phonology (IJAL Memoir 11). Indiana University, Bloomington.
Jacobson, L.C. 1978. DhoLuo Vowel Harmony (UCLA Working Papers in Phonetics 43). University of California, Los Angeles.
Lindau, M. 1979. The feature expanded. Journal of Phonetics 7: 163-76.
Perkell, J.S. 1969. Physiology of Speech Production: Results and Implications of a Quantitative Cineradiographic Study. M.I.T. Press, Cambridge, Massachusetts.
Sedlak, P. 1969. Typological considerations of vowel quality systems. Working Papers in Language Universals (Stanford University) 1: 1-40.
Wright, J. 1980. The behavior of nasalized vowels in the perceptual vowel space. Report of the Phonology Laboratory (University of California, Berkeley) 5: 127-63.

9

Insights on vowel spacing [1]

9.1 Introduction

This chapter presents the results of an analysis of the vowel systems of the 317 languages in the UCLA Phonological Segment Inventory Database (UPSID). It shows that deviations from the patterns predicted by a theory which proposes that vowels are dispersed in the available phonetic space are relatively infrequent and, for the most part, confined to matters of small scale, falling into a few definable classes. It will be argued that in most of these deviations from the predicted patterns there is nonetheless evidence that vowels tend toward a balanced and wide dispersion in the available phonetic space.

9.2 Preliminaries

A few basic vowel inventories and a few basic configurations show up time and again in natural languages, while other, no more complex patterns are rare or totally absent. The most prevalent patterns seem to be the so-called "triangular" systems, particularly those of average size, and notably the 5-vowel systems. For example, over a quarter of the 209 languages in the Stanford Phonology Archive have a triangular 5-vowel system consisting of /i, ɛ, a, ɔ, u/, while less than 5% have any of the other 5-vowel configurations; the "square" 4-vowel and 6-vowel systems combined total less than 10% (Crothers 1978).

Several attempts to explain these patterns invoke a principle of vowel dispersion, proposed in slightly differing versions by Liljencrants and Lindblom (1972), Lindblom (1975), Terbeek (1977), and Maddieson (1977).[2] This principle holds that vowels tend to be evenly distributed in the available phonetic space and also widely distributed, within the limitations of the particular system. The proposed models for vowel dispersion predict an optimal arrangement for any given number of vowels in the system; such theoretical systems may then be compared with the vowel systems of natural languages.

Just such a comparison is the starting point for the present study. The vowel systems of 317 languages are examined for symmetry and dispersion. We take note of those systems in which the vowels are not evenly or widely distributed in the available space, and seek to determine whether these vowel configurations can nevertheless be accounted for in a principled way. There may, for example, be straightforward historical or phonetic explanations for these "defective" vowel systems. If, however, there remain a substantial number of vowel systems which seem to obey no apparent rule, we should perhaps reconsider the notion of dispersion. It may be the case that vowel spacing is not at all a principled matter, and the success of, say, the Liljencrants and Lindblom model in predicting the balance of the vowel systems may prove to be merely coincidental.[3]

Note that the existence of at least some defective vowel systems in natural languages does not automatically rule out a dispersion theory. The claims made by a dispersion theory may be essentially correct, but languages could nonetheless undergo processes which produce defective vowel systems, e.g. vowel mergers, shifts, etc. If this is the case then we should expect to see evidence of pressure to "correct" the vowel spacing by compensatory shifts. This understanding of the interaction of vowel dispersion and other processes predicts that vowel systems, studied synchronically, should include those which, although well-spaced, show compensation or rotation of the vowels. Some of the ways in which defective vowel systems could assume configurations that are basically consistent with the dispersion hypothesis as understood here are illustrated below.

Three possibilities are illustrated in Figure 9.1. The first, 9.1 (a), shows a system with a gap, represented by [], in the high back region, but with a back mid vowel higher in the phonetic space than the corresponding front mid vowel. The system appears "skewed" and gives the appearance that one vowel has been attracted to a higher position to compensate for the presence of a gap. The second, 9.1 (b), illustrates another possibility, in which the entire system is rotated with respect to the typical, unmarked configuration for a vowel system of a particular size (here, a 5-vowel system), thereby achieving maximal dispersion with a slightly different orientation. The third, 9.1 (c), illustrates a defective system that is complemented with a vowel of unexpected quality in the vicinity of the gap. This, too, serves to balance the system to a certain degree.

(a) (b) (c)

i [] ɨ [] u

o ɩ o [] ø o

ɛ

ɛ

a a a

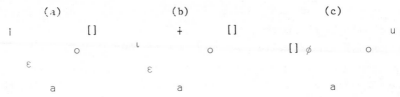

Figure 9.1 "Defective" vowel systems

However, not all conceivable defective systems are open to interpretation as basically consistent with a theory of dispersion in the phonetic space. For example, there may be skewed systems in which the vowel adjacent to the gap is farther away from it than would be expected from comparison with the paired vowel, as in Figure 9.2 (a). Or there may be systems in which a vowel of unexpected quality is located well away from the vicinity of the gap, increasing the imbalance even more, e.g. 9.2 (b), Also, there may be systems such as 9.2 (c) which are not open to interpretation as making any compensation for the imbalance in the system. These "stationary" systems simply contain a gap.

(a) (b) (c)

i [] i y u i []

e e [] e o

ɔ

a a a

Figure 9.2 Unbalanced vowel systems

These systems appear to be counter-examples to a theory of maximal dispersion. However, such cases as 9.2 (c) are ambiguous in that the vowels might well be phonetically underspecified representations of the vowels in the systems in Figure 9.1 (a) or (c). Whether or not the vowels of a particular language are represented in sufficient phonetic detail in UPSID depends greatly on the phonetic judgments and transcription methods of the field linguist. Some linguists report the auditory quality of vowels in the narrowest detail, while others simply rely on the commonest vowel symbols, often those available on any typewriter, to make all the necessary distinctions.[4] Unfortunately, while a vowel system reported as /i, e, a, o, u/ may be faithfully representing a perfectly balanced system, it may also be concealing a wealth of unreported phonetic detail.

The typology of deviations described above establishes that the question of the essential correctness of vowel dispersion hypotheses can be addressed by a study of thé frequency with which different types of apparent exceptions to it appear. The next section discusses how a study of this topic was carried out.

9.3 Method

Data

The UPSID sample of 317 languages was tested for vowel dispersion. The descriptive sources were carefully examined for any details which might possibly shed light on the true phonetic quality of the vowels under study, and the maximum available detail which could be represented in the coding scheme was retained.

The vowel phonemes in UPSID are represented on a height scale with 5 basic values (high, higher mid, mid, lower mid, low). In this chapter mid and higher mid vowels are usually transcribed with the same symbols, but where it is necessary to distinguish between them mid vowels are shown by symbols in quotes, e.g. /"e"/ vs. /e/. Two additional heights, "lowered high" and "raised low", are also recognized. The vowels are also categorized on a backness scale with 3 values (front, central, back), and on a rounding scale with 2 values (rounded, unrounded). Additional dimensions pertaining to length, nasalization, phonation characteristics (laryngealization, breathiness), and other features (r-coloration, lip compression) were recorded in the archive, but for purposes of clarity and simplicity these distinctions are not discussed in the present chapter.

The vowels will be discussed in terms of a distinction between "peripheral" and "interior" vowels. (Note that this distinction is not the same as that represented by the variable "peripheral" in the UPSID database; see Chapter 10.) The "peripheral" vowels are the front unrounded, back rounded, and low vowels, all of which lie along the margins of the available phonetic space. It should be noted, however, that the high central vowels, although they occupy one of the margins of the phonetic space, do not fall within the peripheral category; this more restrictive definition of peripherality is justified on phonological grounds, as the high central vowels tend not to pattern with the true peripheral vowels in natural languages, and they are also less common than other peripheral vowels. Thus, high central /ɨ/ and /ʉ/, along with the remaining phonetically centralized vowels, constitute the set of "interior" vowels.

Identifying "defective" vowel systems

A basic characteristic of all maximally dispersed vowel systems is that there are no unbalanced gaps in the primary (peripheral) vowel system. A language with a gap is defined as one which fails to utilize a particular region of the vowel space, while fitting one or more vowels into each of the remaining regions. We tested the 317 languages to identify those which contained gaps in the peripheral vowel system.

The test examined whether the 5 major regions along the periphery of the vowel space, high front, high back, mid front, mid back, and low central, were filled with at least one vowel. A high or mid region may, however, be left empty without being considered a gap so long as no other peripheral vowel in the system has a similar value on the height scale. This qualification ensures that balanced 3-vowel systems /i, a, u/ or /e, a, o/ will not be classed as defective. Put more formally, this test requires that any vowel which is [α high, β back] be matched by at least one [α high, - β back] vowel in the high and mid regions of the vowel space. There must also be at least one [+ low] vowel in the system.

It should be emphasized that this is a very weak test of dispersion, designed simply to find out whether the framework of the vowel system, that is, the major peripheral subdivisions of the vowel space, fulfills the requirements of wide and even distribution in the available space. There are many other possible violations of the dispersion theory, unevenly distributed interior vowels, multiple vowels in a single major subdivision of the vowel space, and the like, which are not detected by this particular test procedure. Future investigations will have to address these more subtle violations. For the present, however, our test will show whether or not the basic requirements of vowel dispersion are met in the languages of our sample.

The various formulations of the dispersion model differ in predicting a more or less wide spacing of the vowels in the available phonetic space. Although we will not be able to resolve the question of whether maximal or merely adequate dispersion is the correct formulation of this principle, our results may be suggestive. Vowel systems which lack one or more of the "point vowels" /i/, /a/ (or /ɑ/), and /u/, that is, those vowels with the most extreme values for height and backness, are not exploiting the vowel space to the maximum. Therefore, such systems are perhaps better explained by a theory of adequate, rather than maximal, dispersion. We should not, in any event, allow our test procedure to impose expectations of maximal dispersion by classifying such systems as defective. This calls for an exception: namely, those vowel systems which lack all high vowels or all low vowels, but are otherwise balanced, should not be classed as defective systems. This exception only affects a small number of languages. Only 2 of the 317 languages were found to lack low vowels. The Cheremis (051) system is centered rather high in the vowel space, although it does count among its 8 non-low vowels the lower mid interior vowel /ʌ/. Tagalog (414), on the other hand, has a 3-vowel system /ɩ, ə, ɷ/ that is somewhat compressed: it descends no lower than the mid vowel /ə/, and its remaining two points fall somewhat short of maximally high /i/ and /u/.[5] This compression suggests that the Tagalog vowel system is, indeed, only adequately dispersed in the available space. Three other languages, Squamish (733), Alabama (759), and Amuesha (824), lack high vowels. All of these have a basic 3-vowel system, /e, a, o/, which is centered rather low in the vowel space, with two higher mid vowels, but no high or lowered high vowels. Squamish also has /ə/ in the center of the vowel space. For these languages, and for Cheremis, which are compressed along one edge of the vowel space only, acoustic measurements are needed to determine whether near-maximal, or only adequate, dispersion is in effect.

9.4 Analysis of defective systems

Only 43 languages (13.6% of the sample) were found to have vowel systems with at least one major gap. These will be discussed below under various headings.

Four-vowel systems

The test procedure does not classify vowel systems in the same way as the dispersion models. One particular configuration of vowels which is classified as "defective" by our criteria is, in fact, fully in accordance with both the Liljencrants and Lindblom model and Lindblom's later refinement of it. This is the 4-vowel system /i, ɛ, a, u/. In this case the basic /i, a, u/ system has been expanded by a single vowel, and the one first chosen is the front vowel /ɛ/. (The corresponding back vowel /ɔ/ is not predicted to appear until the inventory has reached at least 5 vowels.)

By our procedure all 4-vowel systems with one mid vowel are regarded as defective. This classification seems justified since these systems are in any case rare. There are 6 such cases. Of these, Shasta (746), Paez (804), and Moxo (827) have the inventory predicted by Liljencrants and Lindblom,

/i, ɛ, a, u /. Bardi (357) has a 4-vowel system in which the single mid vowel is the back rounded vowel /o/, contrary to that prediction. Two other languages resemble the predicted system, but are rather more symmetrical in the distribution of their 4 vowels. Wichita (755) has a back vowel /ɒ/ in place of /a/, yielding a system with 2 back and 2 front vowels. Cayapa (803), a Paezan language quite closely related to Paez, has /i, ɛ, ɑ, ɷ/. Rather than occupying their expected positions in the vowel space, both the back vowels are closer to the gap in the lower mid region where /ɔ/ might be expected. In this way the vowels are rather equally spaced. Certain other 4-vowel languages are analyzed as having two gaps in their peripheral vowel system. These are discussed in a later section.

Frequency of missing vowels

Crothers (1978: 106), reporting on the Stanford Archive languages, notes that the missing vowels are "generally /e/, /u/, or /o/, never /i/". And though he formulates the near universal that "all languages have /i, a, u/" (p. 115), the counterexamples and borderline cases that he reports all have to do with deviations from an expected high back rounded vowel. This, he notes, reflects the /a/ > /i/ > /u/ hierarchy observed by both Greenberg (1966) and Jakobson (1941). (> can be read as "is presupposed by".)

Our own frequency count of the missing vowels in UPSID confirms that the high front and the low central vowels are less likely to be missing than the high back rounded vowel, i.e. /a/ and /i/ > /u/. It further shows that the high back vowel is more likely to be absent in natural languages than either the front or the back mid vowels, i.e. /e/ and /o/ > /u/. Almost half of the 35 languages which lack a single vowel lack /u/; 9 others lack /e/, 7 lack /o/, and 2 lack /a/. The implied ranking is therefore:

$$\begin{Bmatrix} \text{i} \\ \text{a} \end{Bmatrix} > \begin{Bmatrix} \text{e} \\ \text{o} \end{Bmatrix} > \text{u}$$

rather than the /a/ > /i/ > /u/ > /e/ > /o/ which is generally assumed. This fact does not seem to have been commented on in the literature, and it may have implications that bear on such ideas as markedness and the choice between maximal and adequate dispersion.

In addition to the languages which lack a single vowel, 6 lack more than one vowel. The most common pattern (5 languages) involves a missing high back vowel and mid front vowel, creating a double gap of positive slope as shown in Figure 9.3 (a). None of the languages exhibits a gap of negative slope due to the lack of a high front vowel and a mid back vowel, as in Figure 9.3 (b). Vertical gaps are also rare: only one language lacks back high and mid vowels, as in Figure 9.3 (c). (Recall that languages which lack both front and back high vowels or both front and back mid vowels are exempted from the "defective" category.)

(a)		(b)		(c)	
i	[]	[]	u	i	[]
[]	o	e	[]	e	[]
a		a		a	

Figure 9.3 Languages with 2 major gaps

The defective languages demonstrate that vowel systems occasionally <u>do</u> avoid certain regions of the space. These systems will be discussed below in terms of the typology discussed in Section 9.2 above.

Stationary systems

Leaving aside the matter of ambiguity of transcription, our investigation reveals that 9 or perhaps 10 languages fall under the category of "stationary" systems, that is, systems which have a gap that they do not appear to compensate for in any way. All of these happen to be 3 or 4-vowel systems, although larger systems can be stationary just as well. In these systems all the vowels are peripheral vowels of the most common types, and the systems are otherwise balanced, with no evidence of skewing from the front to the back. Clear examples of such stationary systems are Klamath (707), which has the vowel system /i, "e", a, "o"/, and Bardi (357), Shasta (746), Paez (804) and Moxo (827), which, as mentioned above, lack a mid vowel. The Campa (825) system is similar to Klamath, except that the mid vowels are reported as being "mid close", i.e. higher mid. Tacana (812) is recorded in UPSID as having the same system as Klamath (although the back vowel is recorded in one source as /u/ rather than /o/). In Hupa (705), the basic system is a not-fully-peripheral /e, o, a/. However, /ɩ/ occurs in the language as a surface segment. Depending on the status accorded to this anomalous segment, the language may or may not be viewed as having a gap in the high back region of the vowel space. Mura (802) has a 3-vowel system /i, a, o/. This could be classed as doubly defective by our test, with /i/ implying a missing /u/ and /o/ implying a missing /e/. However, there is no evidence in the source to indicate whether the transcription reflects phonetic reality or orthographic convention. The system could be a rotated system such as /i˃, o, æ/, which is maximally dispersed in the vowel space. Seneca (754) might well be added to this group of languages. It has an /u/

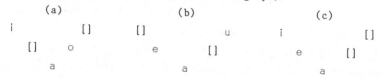

vowel which occurs only rarely; if this is considered as a gap, there is no evidence that it is being compensated for in the vowel system. This language is discussed further below.

As we have mentioned, genuine stationary systems constitute a counterexample to the theory of maximal dispersion. However, we cannot dismiss the possibility that certain important phonetic details have been obscured by a broad phonetic transcription in the examples above. Therefore, a theory of dispersion cannot be disproven with this set of potential counterexamples. Definitive evidence against such a theory will have to be sought in the form of systems with unevenly spaced vowels (systems that have been rotated into asymmetrical patterns), rather than in systems which appear not to have compensated for the gap at all.

Complementary vowels

Some of the languages in our inventory have defective systems that are complemented by a single vowel of unexpected phonetic quality which shares some of the features of the missing vowel. Vowel systems of this sort can be classed into 3 major types, namely, those in which the complementary vowel is (i) a central vowel (9 languages), (ii) a front rounded or back unrounded vowel (13 languages), or (iii) a peripheral vowel similar to the missing vowel but lacking a counterpart of equal height and opposite rounding elsewhere in the vowel system (6 languages). Stated more formally, if the missing vowel is [α high, β back, γ low, δ round], then the complementary vowel is:

$$\text{(i)}\ \begin{bmatrix} \alpha\ \text{high} \\ +\ \text{central} \end{bmatrix}, \quad \text{(ii)}\ \begin{bmatrix} \alpha\ \text{high} \\ \beta\ \text{back} \\ -\beta\ \text{round} \end{bmatrix} \quad \text{or} \quad \text{(iii)}\ \begin{bmatrix} -\alpha\ \text{high or}\ -\ \text{low} \\ \beta\ \text{back} \end{bmatrix}$$

We will discuss each of these types in turn.

Vowels of unexpected backness ([α high, + central])

Two principal patterns of this type are found: /ə/ for an expected missing mid or low vowel (e.g. in Tagalog, 414, Changchow, 503, and Acoma, 749), or /ɨ/ for an expected missing high vowel (e.g. for missing /u/ in Abipon, 815). There are several other languages with a missing mid or low vowel. Margi (268) has /ɛ/ but mostly in loanwords; /ə/ and /o/ are the only truly native mid vowels. Bashkir (063) has no /"e"/, but the system is complemented in several alternate ways. In addition to /ə/ there is /ø/, and there is also evidence of compensation in the peripheral system. In

Cheremis (051), /ə/ offsets a missing low vowel, but there is also evidence of compensation. Among languages with a missing high vowel Cofan (836) is very similar to Abipon, but with evidence of compensation as well. These 3 languages are discussed further below. In Chacobo (811), in addition to a missing high back vowel, a front mid vowel is also lacking. There is no central vowel to offset the latter. This double gap may perhaps be better explained as a rotation of the entire system.

Vowels of unexpected lip position ([α high, β back, -β round])

Systems of this type fit into the "defective" category somewhat more marginally than the previous type. On a formant chart with F1 and F2 as the axes, the front rounded vowels and the back unrounded vowels are more centralized than their front unrounded and back rounded counterparts, but less so than the true central vowels /ə/ and /ɨ/. Crothers nevertheless classes these centralized vowels together with the true central vowels, and does not regard any such "interior" vowels as fulfilling the requirements for maximal dispersion of the system. Liljencrants and Lindblom take no stand on the status of the front rounded and back unrounded vowels; their model is not designed to generate this particular set of vowels.[6]

Thirteen defective systems in our sample have a vowel with the same height and backness as the missing peripheral vowel, but with the opposite rounding. Only in Bashkir (063) and Khalaj (064) are the complementary vowels (/ø/ in each case) embedded in a series (/y, ø, ɤ/ for Bashkir; /y, ø/ for Khalaj). In the remaining 11 cases the vowel complementing the peripheral system is the only front rounded or back unrounded vowel in the language. This fact suggests that the front rounded and back unrounded vowels do not show up casually in the vowel system. Moreover, in examples such as Gilyak (909), with /ø/ for a missing /e/, and Island Carib (823), with /ɤ/ for a missing /o/, the complementary role of the mid interior vowel is underscored by the lack of a high interior vowel such as /y/ or /ɯ/ in the system. In most languages with front rounded or back unrounded vowels the system "builds down" from /y/ to /ø/ to /ɤ/, or from /ɯ/ to /ɤ/ to /ʌ/, such that the lower vowel implies the presence of the higher. The isolated /ø/ and /ɤ/ of Gilyak and Island Carib are therefore quite unusual. Their isolation suggests that they do not represent an incipient interior vowel system, but instead are likely to be closely associated with the gap in the mid peripheral region.

In 10 languages all gaps are complemented by a single front rounded vowel or back unrounded vowel. There are 3 languages with /ɯ/ for a missing high back rounded vowel: Japanese (071), Nunggubuyu (353), and Alawa (354). Nimboran (604) has /ɯ/ and /ɤ/ for missing high and mid back rounded vowels. The complementation in Island Carib and Gilyak has been mentioned in the previous paragraph. In Bashkir and Khalaj, mentioned above, the complementary vowels form part of a front rounded system; both have /ø/ for a missing mid front unrounded vowel. In Jaqaru (820) the native vowel system is /i, a, ɯ/, though an additional vowel /ɛ/ appears in a limited number of loanwords (this vowel is excluded from the UPSID inventory). In Ocaina (805), in addition to complementation by /ɯ/, there is evidence of compensation in the peripheral vowel system (see below).

In another 3 languages, Adzera (419), Nez Perce (706) and Amahuaca (810), only one of two gaps in the peripheral vowel system is complemented. All of these examples involve a double gap of positive slope (missing /e, u/) rather than the other possibility, a gap of negative slope (missing /i, o/). In each case, the gap where /u/ is expected is complemented by /ɯ/, while the gap where /e/ is expected remains uncomplemented. It is rather surprising that the complementary vowel in these double-gap systems is always the high back vowel /ɯ/ rather than the front mid vowel /ø/. Such preferential treatment of the high back region of the vowel space is quite unexpected in view of the fact that defective vowel systems are far more likely to be lacking a high back vowel than a front mid vowel. We might well expect a greater number of /ɯ/'s overall, due to the frequent absence of /u/; what is surprising is the complementation of /u/ instead of the complementation of /e/ in systems which lack both. Still, in Amahuaca and Nez Perce the gap where /e/ is expected is somewhat offset by compensation in the high front region. In addition, Nez Perce has a peripheral vowel of unexpected height in the low front region. Adzera, however, shows no evidence of such compensation; there is simply a gap in the mid front region.

It is somewhat surprising to note the predominance of /ɯ/ over other complementary interior vowels (/y, ø, e, ɤ, ʌ/). While this fact obviously relates to the frequent absence of /u/, the latter might just as well go uncompensated, or else be compensated by some other vowel or by rotation of the system as a whole. Moreover, while we might expect the presence of /ɯ/ to presuppose the presence of /u/, just as, in general, /y/ presupposes /i/, this is not true in the relatively large number of vowel systems in which /ɯ/ stands alone. (No defective vowel system has a complementary /y/ in place of missing /i/.)

An investigation of the acoustic, perceptual, and auditory quality of the vowel /ɯ/ suggests that this vowel is in fact quite centralized, verging on the quality of central /ɨ/. For example, Ward's (1938) auditory analysis of Bamum /ɯ/ places this vowel well away from cardinal /u/, half-way between the central and back regions of the phonetic chart. Hombert (personal communication) has conducted a perceptual test on speakers of 3 Bamileke languages, Banjoun, Fe?Fe?, and Bangangte in which synthetic vowels were presented to the subjects, and the formant frequencies which corresponded to "acceptable" vowels in their languages were noted. For the /ɯ/ in these languages the mean acceptable F1 was 260 Hz., and F2 was 1391 Hz.; this corresponds to a high and almost central vowel. Papçun (1976) plotted the vowels of Spanish and Japanese in a normalized acoustic space. Spanish has a rounded /u/ and Japanese an unrounded /ɯ/. He found that the difference between these high back vowels lies mainly in F2, which is approximately 725 Hz. for the Spanish vowel but 1275 Hz. for the Japanese vowel, corresponding to a considerably centralized location in the acoustic space. The vowel /ɯ/ thus appears to be similar to the vowel /ɨ/. If we combine the 9 vowel systems complemented by /ɯ/ with the 3 complemented by /ɨ/ into a single category, we find that these 12 cases constitute the majority of cases of complementation in our sample; complementation by any of the remaining interior vowels /y, ø, ɤ, ɘ/ occurs in only 10 languages. The high interior region seems to be a favored area for complementary vowels. The significance of this fact is not readily apparent, and merits further perceptual and acoustic study. It may be the case that the corner of the vowel space in which the high back vowel /u/ is to be found is simply smaller, in perceptual terms, than we might otherwise expect, and hence /ɨ/, /ʉ/ and /ɯ/ are closer to each other perceptually than the acoustic facts suggest.

Vowels of unexpected height ([−α high or −γ low; β back])

This category is reserved for those vowel systems with two peripheral vowels instead of one in a region vertically adjacent to the gap in the system. Here the complementary vowel is distinguished from other peripheral vowels by its unexpected quality. In the case of non-low vowels we shall define the complementary vowel as the one which lacks a counterpart of equal height and opposite rounding elsewhere in the vowel system (e.g. the vowel /o/ in a system such as /i, ε, a, ɔ, o/). In the case of low vowels, the complementary vowel is always the non-central vowel, i.e. the low vowel that is not /a/. The precise location of the gap in the system may be inferred from the height of the matching vowel of opposite backness and rounding. Thus, a missing high back vowel matched by /ɩ/ will be considered a missing /ɷ/.

While many patterns of complementation are possible, only 3 occur in our sample. Kunimaipa (620) has a high back /ɷ/ for a missing mid back vowel. Navaho (702) and Nootka (730) have a higher mid back /o/ for a missing high back vowel. The Nootka case is discussed further below. Taishan (501), Nez Perce (706), and Ket (906) have a raised low front /æ/ for a missing mid front vowel. There is no instance of a peripheral vowel of unexpected quality which is several levels of vowel height away from the gap it complements. The additional vowels appear in the immediately adjacent vertical sector of the vowel space in all but one of these languages. Kunimaipa has /ɷ/ complementing a gap at /o/ (it has the front vowel /e/); Taishan, Nez Perce, and Ket all have /æ/ complementing a gap at /ε/ (each of these languages has the back vowel /ɔ/); Nootka and Navaho have /o(:)/ complementing a gap at /ɷ/ or /u/ (cf. Nootka /ɩ/ and Navaho /i:/). Only in the long vowel set in Navaho is the complementary vowel /o:/ one step further removed from the gap (specifically identified as a missing /u:/ by our criteria), that is, the complementary vowel is not /ɷ:/. Note that the short vowel system of Navaho appears as a "stationary" system, since front /ε/ is matched by back /ɔ/.

The vowel systems in which a single vowel of unexpected quality complements a gap in the peripheral system constitute the major portion (28 of 43, or about 65%) of the defective vowel systems in our sample. We have seen, for example, systems lacking a high back vowel being complemented by a high central vowel /ɨ/, a higher mid back vowel /o/, or a high back unrounded vowel /ɯ/. Similarly, systems lacking a mid front vowel were found to be complemented by /ə/ or /æ/ or /ø/, rather than by any more remote segment. The common denominator among almost all 31 of the complementary vowels in our sample is that they bear a close phonetic resemblance to the expected vowel. Due to this fact, the systems containing such complementary vowels are "not excessively deviant" from the predicted, fully-dispersed vowel system. We may assert that they obey some sort of dispersion rule although one whose requirements are obviously weaker than maximal dispersion.

Complementary vowels with additional adjustments

We have seen that a few of the systems with complementary vowels seem to be striving for a greater degree of dispersion in the vowel space. Not only is there a complementary vowel near the site of the expected vowel, but the system is skewed such that one or more of the remaining vowels is found closer to this gap than we would otherwise expect, based on the height of the matching vowel(s). For example, the Gilyak (909) system, lacking a mid front vowel, is complemented by the nonperipheral vowel /ø/; moreover, both the high front /ɩ/ and the low /æ/ are unexpectedly close to the gap. That is, lowered high /ɩ/ appears rather than /i/ and raised high fronted /æ/ appears rather than /a/. In the Cofan (836) system, which lacks a high back vowel, the gap is flanked on two sides by a complementary /ɨ/ and by a higher than expected /o/ (as evidenced by the imbalance in the mid vowels, lower mid /ɛ/ vs. mid /o/). Rather than occupying their expected locations, these vowels seem to position themselves closer to the gap. Ocaina (805) lacks a high back rounded vowel, but has complementary /ɯ/ and it also has /o/ in proximity. Bashkir (063) lacks a mid front unrounded vowel, but has complementary /ø/ and /ə/ and it also has a raised /æ/ in proximity.

Again we must consider the possibility of underspecification of the phonetic vowel quality. Some of the authors undoubtedly have chosen a broader system of phonetic transcription than others, thus possibly obscuring some evidence of rotation of the vowel system. We therefore cannot rule out the possibility that some other cases of vowel system complementation in our sample are accompanied by some compensation in the peripheral vowel system.

Compensation in the peripheral vowel system

Most of the defective vowel systems that we have examined thus far have fallen into two basic categories: ones in which there is either no evidence of any compensation for the gap in the system (stationary systems), and ones in which there is a single vowel of unexpected quality in the system, either a non-peripheral vowel, or a peripheral vowel of unexpected height, which may be regarded as complementary (complemented systems). We have, however, noted a few cases of complemented vowel systems whose remaining peripheral vowels are displaced toward the gap as well; these systems thereby achieve an even greater degree of compensation. A number of other languages in our sample lack a complementary vowel but nevertheless show evidence of such displacement, even to the point of rotating the entire system.

Compensations involving a single vowel

Vowel systems of this sort are very similar to vowel systems with a complementary peripheral vowel of unexpected height. In both cases there is a vowel in the system which is found closer to the gap than we would otherwise expect, based on the height of the closest corresponding vowel at the opposite end of the backness scale. The crucial difference, of course, is that in the latter systems this vowel shares its region with another peripheral vowel, while in the former it is alone in its region of the vowel space. In both Ocaina (805) and Cofan (836), discussed in the preceding section, there is an /o/ which is higher than the corresponding front vowel /ɛ/, thus compensating for the missing high back vowel to some degree. Bashkir (063), which lacks a mid front vowel, also shows evidence of compensation. In these examples the vowel system is also complemented by vowels of unexpected lip position. Five other systems lack a complementary vowel, but otherwise follow the Ocaina pattern. Malagasy (410) lacks a high back vowel, but has /o/ in proximity to the gap, as evidenced by the imbalance of /"e"/ and /o/. Mazatec (727) lacks a high back vowel, but has /o/ in proximity, as evidenced by the imbalance of /ɛ/ and /o/. Cheremis (051) lacks a low central vowel, but has /ɛ/ in proximity, as evidenced by the imbalance of /ɛ/ and /o/. Amahuaca (810) lacks a mid front vowel, but has /ɩ/ in proximity, as evidenced by the imbalance of high vowels /ɩ/ and /ɯ/. Wichita (755) lacks a mid back vowel but has /ɒ/ (rather than /a/) in proximity.

Compensations involving multiple vowels

Vowel systems with displacements at more than one point in the peripheral system show an even greater tendency toward dispersion in the vowel space. In the extreme case, most or all of the vowels in the language show a displacement from the expected values (/i, u/ for high vowels, /e, o/ for mid vowels, and /a/ for low vowels) in the direction of the gap; this may be considered a rotation of the entire system. Such a systematic displacement may well result in a maximally dispersed vowel system, which is oriented along a slightly different axis from that of most other vowel systems.

In Gilyak (909), discussed above, two of the peripheral vowels, /ɩ/ and /æ/, show evidence of displacement toward a gap in the front mid region of the system. Other cases of multiple displacement are rather uncommon, although in Cayapa (803) the vowel system as a whole appears to be compensating for a gap in the mid back region. The high back vowel /ɷ/ is lower than its front counterpart /i/, and the low vowel /ɑ/ is further back than the expected /a/. The quality of the mid front vowel is reported as /ɛ/, and though there is no mid back vowel against which to test its height, we may perhaps infer (from the use of the symbol /ɛ/, rather than the unmarked /e/) that it is lower than expected, backing up the displacement of the low vowel. From what appears to be an anchor point at /i/, the vowels of Cayapa are displaced from their expected values according to the pattern in Figure 9.4.

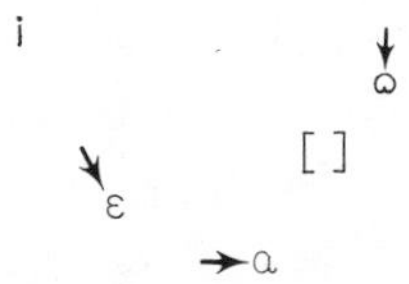

Figure 9.4 Cayapa vowels

The resulting dispersion is very nearly maximal, in spite of the absence of one phonological category.

When a gap occurs in the peripheral vowel system, some or all of the remaining peripheral vowels are often found to be displaced in the direction of the gap, regardless of whether the gap is otherwise offset by a vowel of unexpected quality elsewhere in the system. The displacement may be interpreted as a means of establishing a wider and more even dispersion of the peripheral vowels, in spite of the gap. Ten of the languages in our sample (23% of the defective systems) show evidence of some such compensation in the peripheral vowel system. However, only 2 of these languages, or possibly 3, extend the compensation beyond a single vowel. This is largely due to the fact, noted above, that most of the defective vowel systems in our sample are lacking a high back vowel; in these systems only one peripheral vowel, the mid back rounded vowel, verges on the gap. Now, we would naturally expect that vowel(s) adjacent to any gap would show a greater shift in vowel quality than the vowels further away, which, if anything, need only make subtle adjustments to those adjustments which have preceded them. For most gaps, then, we can expect to find evidence of a few displacements. However, in the case of systems lacking a high back vowel, it is far less likely that the peripheral vowel on the far side of the gap (the high front vowel) would be affected from so great a distance across the upper boundary of the vowel space. Therefore, displacement of a single vowel might provide an adequate degree of dispersion for these languages.

Unevenly spaced vowel systems

The languages discussed thus far do not exhaust the list of defective vowel systems in our sample. Vowels in the remaining systems appear to be distributed unevenly in the phonetic space, contrary to the predictions of any dispersion theory. As we have stated, vowel systems of this sort are the only ones which can validly be used to disprove a dispersion theory, for stationary systems, although they run counter to the predictions of such a theory, are indistinguishable from dispersed systems that merely lack adequately reported phonetic detail.

Two languages, Hopi (738) and Auca (818), constitute the clearest examples of unevenly spaced systems in our sample. They share a number of characteristics, notably a gap in the high back region and an apparent displacement of the remaining vowels away from this gap. A similar phenomenon may be found in Nootka (730), but the phonetic interpretation of the data is subject to question. Seneca (754) is another language that might be considered in this class.

Voegelin (1956: 24) commented on Hopi: "So far as vowel placements are concerned, Hopi is extraordinarily asymmetrical." The analysis of Hopi in UPSID assumes the vowel inventory /i, ø, æ, a, ɤ/ plus the diphthong /ou/. The diphthong /ou/ could be regarded as a peripheral back vowel displaced toward the gap at /u/. Similarly, /æ/, a front vowel of unexpected height adjacent to the gap in the mid front region, verges close upon the low central vowel /a/, with no accommodation on the part of the latter. There are, however, indications that the peripheral system is actually more dispersed than this analysis would lead us to believe. Although Voegelin classifies it as central, the vowel /a/ of the Mesa dialect of Hopi is, according to Whorf, "as in calm". This suggests a back, or at least a back-central quality, which is as expected if an adequate separation is to be maintained between the two low vowels, and, simultaneously, if the separation between the backmost low vowel and the mid back vowel is not to become too great. An alternative analysis would view all of these displacements together as consequences of a compensation for the missing high back vowel, in other words, a near-complete rotation of the peripheral system. According to such an analysis, the peripheral vowels of the defective Hopi system are systematically displaced from the expected /i, e, a, o/ to the existing /i, æ, ɑ, ou/ as the presence of the gap (at /u/) draws the vowels successively toward the gap in a counterclockwise pattern.

If the displacements described above are indeed accurate, the net result is that the Hopi system achieves a considerable degree of dispersion with a nearly "square" peripheral vowel system plus two interior mid vowels (/ø, ɤ/). Such an "hourglass" pattern may in a sense be more fully dispersed than the system with 6 peripheral vowels predicted by the dispersion models.

The Auca system is described as /i, e, æ, a, o/. The /e/ is said to range from [ɩ] to [ɛ], and the /o/ from [o] to [u] and inward to [ɯ]. No further phonetic detail is provided for /i/, /æ/ or /a/. The unexpectedly high range of the mid vowel /o/ is suggestive of compensation for a missing back vowel, but the juxtaposition of vowels /i, e, æ, a/, well away from the gap at /u/, is surprising and unique among the systems in our sample. As for Nootka (Tseshaht), whether or not this system is actually defective is subject to some dispute. The source consulted on this language, Sapir and Swadesh (1939), suggests that Nootka has a gap in the high back region of the vowel space. One interpretation of their descriptions is that the language has a low vowel /ɑ/ that is displaced toward, rather than away from, the unexpected vowel /o/. A relatively high position for /o/ is indicated by the authors' statement that /o/ and /o:/ "have the tongue position of the vowel of coat and the lip position of hoot" (p. 13.). This gives a Nootka system consisting of /i, ɛ, ɑ, ɔ, o/. However, the source also compares the phonetic quality of the Nootka vowel /o/ to that in put, and long /o:/ to that in food, just as /i/ is compared with pit and /i:/ with feed. On the basis of these phonetic descriptions, it may be that the Nootka system is not defective at all, since they suggest the system contains a high back vowel after all.

If Seneca is considered to have a gap at /u/ (/u/ is rare), then it is surprising that the back vowel /"o"/ seems to be less high than the front vowel /e/. However, this may be a case where, rather than a failure of a gap to draw a vowel toward it in the back vowel region, there is instead a pressure to raise /e/ in the front. This is because there is also the vowel /æ/ in the front vowel set, making a vowel inventory which consists of /i, e, æ, a, "o", (u)/.

9.5 Conclusions

The great majority of vowel systems in our sample assume configurations which are predictable from a theory of vowel dispersion, considered in the light of some basic facts about the overall number of vowels, their degree of peripherality, and the like. At first glance there appear to be 43 languages which are exceptions to the notion of vowel dispersion, in that one or more of the 5 major regions of the vowel space remain unfilled. However, some measure of dispersion is in force even in many of these "defective" systems. As a result, these systems maintain a degree of balance in spite of the obvious gap.

The defective systems may be classed into 3 major categories. Nine of these 43 languages simply tolerate the gap in the system, showing no evidence of any compensatory shifts (although such shifts may in fact be present and merely overlooked in the broad phonological accounts). Some 2 to 4 of the languages with major gaps show a displacement of the remaining vowels away from the gap, resulting in an even more uneven distribution of the vowels. The great majority of the defective systems, at least 30 languages, tend toward a balanced distribution of vowels in the available space, either by complementation with a vowel of unexpected quality or by a displacement toward the gap of some or all vowels in the system.

Thus the number of obvious exceptions to a vowel dispersion hypothesis in the whole of the UPSID data is extremely small. About 86% of the languages have vowel systems that are built on a basic framework of evenly dispersed peripheral vowels. About another 10% approach this specification. This strongly indicates that a vowel dispersion theory correctly captures a principle governing the distribution of vowels in natural languages.

Notes

1. This chapter was contributed by Sandra Ferrari Disner.
2. The formulations differ somewhat in the degree of dispersion they propose, but no attempt will be made in this paper to choose between them. Except for the absence of vowels at the extreme corners of the vowel space, the data is unsuited for this task. For the most part, we can only look at <u>areas</u> within the phonetic vowel space and label the general arrangements according to which areas are filled. In order to investigate whether specific <u>points</u> in the space are filled, we would need acoustic measurements drawn from a large number of speakers of each language (see Disner 1980).
3. For example, the apparent success of such a model might be attributable to heavy emphasis on a few language areas in the sample utilized by Liljencrants and Lindblom, or to a bias in the sources in favor of reporting apparently balanced vowel systems when adequate phonetic detail is lacking.
4. Considerable energy was expended to seek out whatever phonetic detail was available in the sources, regardless of the authors' transcriptions. Cross-references were checked, footnotes examined, and a good deal of reading between the lines was done in hopes of adding some detail to the reported phonetic quality. Skewed vowel systems provide us with particularly valuable information on the phonetic quality of the vowels in question. A linguist who is little concerned

with phonetic detail, or who does all his transcriptions on the typewriter, may well report pairs of vowels such as [e, ɔ] simply as /e, o/. However, it is extremely unlikely that a pair of vowels reported as skewed (e.g. /e, ɔ/) is actually balanced (/e, o/). Here there is little doubt that the front vowel is higher than the back, i.e. that the front vowel is closer to the /i/ region than the back vowel is to the /u/ region. We can therefore draw firmer conclusions about the degree of vowel dispersion in the phonetic space from these skewed systems. We should, on the other hand, refrain from drawing too-firm conclusions from balanced pairs of vowels.

5. The Stanford archive notes that /e/ and /o/ occur in a great many loanwords in the dialect of educated Manila speakers. These have been excluded from the UPSID inventory, since we have chosen to represent a more conservative dialect of the language.
6. It is not clear to what extent we can consider systems with such vowels to be defective. Certain configurations of peripheral and nonperipheral vowels may, in fact, be _more_ dispersed in the vowel space than the corresponding peripheral systems.

References

Crothers, J. 1978. Typology and universals of vowel systems. In J.H. Greenberg et al. (eds.), _Universals of Human Language, Vol. 1: Theory and Methodology_. Stanford University Press, Stanford: 93-152.

Disner, S.F. 1980. Evaluation of vowel normalization procedures. _Journal of the Acoustical Society of America_ 67: 253-61.

Greenberg, J.H. 1966. _Language Universals, with Special Reference to Feature Hierarchies_. Mouton, The Hague.

Jakobson, R. 1941. Kindersprache, Aphasie, und allgemeine Lautgesetze. Reprinted in _Selected Writings I_. Mouton, The Hague: 328-401.

Liljencrants, J. and Lindblom, B. 1972. Numerical similation of vowel quality systems: the role of perceptual contrast. _Language_ 48: 839-62.

Lindblom, B. 1975. Experiments in sound structure. Paper read at the Eighth International Congress of Phonetic Sciences, Leeds.

Maddieson, I. 1977. Tone loans: a question concerning tone spacing and a method of answering it. _UCLA Working Papers in Phonetics_ 36: 49-83.

Papçun, G. 1976. How may vowel systems differ? _UCLA Working Papers in Phonetics_ 31: 38-46.

Sapir, E. and Swadesh, M. 1939. _Nootka Texts_. Linguistic Society of America, Philadelphia.

Terbeek, D. 1977. Some constraints on the principle of maximum perceptual contrast between vowels. _Proceedings of the Thirteenth Regional Meeting of the Chicago Linguistic Society_: 640-50.

Voegelin, C.F. 1956. Phonemicizing for dialect study, with reference to Hopi. _Language_ 32: 116-35.

Ward, I.C. 1938. The phonetic structure of Bamum. _Bulletin of the School of Oriental and African Studies_ 9: 423-38.

10

The design of the UCLA Phonological Segment Inventory Database (UPSID)

10.1 Introduction

As remarked in the preface to this volume, the discovery of generalizations concerning the content and structure of phonological inventories has been a significant objective of recent work in linguistics. UPSID is designed as a tool for research into these questions, providing uniform data from a properly balanced sample of an adequate number of languages for statistically reliable conclusions to be reached. It differs in some major ways from the Stanford Phonology Archive (SPA) compiled at Stanford University, although this archive served as a model for our work. Stanford's plan was more ambitious than the plan for UPSID, but Stanford's team found that they had to limit the size of their language sample as their work progressed. The final report includes information on the phonologies of 196 languages. A principal reason for exclusion was the scarcity of adequately detailed phonological descriptions. The variability in detail of the sources which were used also necessarily produced entries which vary in their completeness--from those which cover little more than a list of phonemes to those which are able to include a lot of allophonic details and information on phonological alternations. Thus, for retrieval of certain information, the true sample size is smaller than 196 languages. With each reduction, the likelihood that the sample is no longer representative and properly balanced increases. With Stanford's experience in mind, UPSID was designed to be narrower in the scope of information about each language entered, but to be more comprehensive in the number of languages covered. Users of SPA have also commented that there is a certain inflexibility inherent in the format chosen for data entry. This is basically a text-oriented system (for some description, see Vihman 1974).

For example, each segment is entered as an alphabetic character (p, b, m, etc.) or string (l-retroflex, epsilon, o-open-long-nasalized, etc), followed by a rather open-ended set of features attributed to the segment (e.g. obstruent, bilabial, voiceless, etc.), plus comments from the source and so on. With this format, retrieval of essentially numerical data is not the most readily achieved operation, and manipulation of the data can be complex and cumbersome. Stanford's aim was to maximize "accountability" i.e. limiting their information to that available in the source grammar. This sometimes results in essentially the same segment receiving different descriptions in different languages. In designing UPSID, we have aimed to maximize the ease and flexibility with which numerical data can be manipulated, and have decided that the compilers may on occasion need to adopt a more active role in interpreting the source to guarantee a consistent treatment of similar sounds. We also differ somewhat from SPA on the principles that should govern selection of languages, e.g. in rejecting the number of speakers as a criterion for inclusion (or exclusion) of a language. Nonetheless we have profited greatly from the example of SPA, and from the excellent hard work that went into its compilation, by using the final report as a secondary source of data. The following sections describe the plan of UPSID.

10.2 Selection of languages for UPSID

The ideal sample for purposes of statistical evaluation is a random sample, drawn from the total population under study. In the case of language data, the "population" is all the world's extant languages. It is impossible to draw a random sample from this population for two reasons. First, there are areas of the world about whose languages we have no data or wholly inadequate data. Second, a "language" is not a clearly demarcated object. The common criterion of "mutual comprehensibility" used to define linguistic similarity yields a gradient, and besides, is often not reflexive in its characteristics (cf. Ladefoged et al. 1972: 65-8). Thus, unlike a population of, say, registered voters, it is not possible to enumerate and individualize the members of the population. Hence, no basis exists for drawing a random sample.

A proper sample of languages must therefore be constructed by some other sampling procedure. The chosen one is a variety of quota sample (in fact, the usual linguistic sampling procedure is to draw a quota sample based on typological, genetic or areal groupings). The principle on which

UPSID is based is to select one and only one language from each moderately distant genetic grouping, so that the selected languages represent in proper proportion the internal genetic diversity of various groupings. The obvious difficulties in the way of such a scheme are the lack of sound genetic classifications in certain areas (e.g. South America, New Guinea), the difficulty of comparing genetic distances in different language families, and lack of requisite data from some known groups. The advantages of this procedure are that it precludes, in principle, selection of data which represents arguably the same language in several varieties (unlike SPA which includes, for example, both Moroccan and Egyptian dialects of Arabic, and Maltese); also it directs a principled search for the data to fulfill the quota design and avoids undue reliance on descriptions that happen to be at hand (the "bibliographic convenience" factor mentioned by Bell 1978). A genetic basis for the sample is selected in preference to any other since it is the only classification which is, in principle, not arbitrarily determined by the criteria chosen for the classification, but instead aims to represent real historical relationships. In addition, it is appropriately independent of the phonological characteristics of which it is desired to find the frequencies. Note that the phonological uniqueness of a language is not a basis for inclusion. Because each language included is relatively distinct genetically from all others in the sample, each represents the outcome of the opportunity for independent operation of historical processes. Similarities between languages in the sample are therefore not due solely to the effect of shared historical origin. As noted before, the number of speakers is considered a quite inappropriate basis for including (or excluding) a language. The size of extant populations of speakers of languages is an accident of political and social history that is quite irrelevant to questions relating to the structure of human languages.

No thorough-going attempt to determine a single criterion for the degree of genetic separation required for inclusion of a language has been made. The procedure has been to assemble the most comprehensive and accurate genetic classifications available and to produce, by synthesis of several classifications where necessary, an overall classification for each of 11 major groupings of languages, plus several smaller groups. Intermediate levels of classification were then sampled to select the languages for inclusion in UPSID. The density of this sampling might be thought of as representing an intention to include no pair of languages which had not developed within their own independent speech communities for at least some 1000-1500 years, but to include one language from within each group of languages which shared a closer history than that. The 11 major groupings, plus an "others" category, are shown in Table 10.1, together with the number of languages included in UPSID from each and the range of identification numbers assigned to each grouping.

Table 10.1 Language families in UPSID

Language family	Identification numbers	No. of languages included
Indo-European	000-049	21
Ural-Altaic	050-099	22
Niger-Kordofanian	100-199	31
Nilo-Saharan	200-249	21
Afro-Asiatic	250-299	21
Austro-Asiatic	300-349	6
Australian	350-399	19
Austro-Tai	400-499	25
Sino-Tibetan	500-599	18
Indo-Pacific	600-699	27
Amerindian	700-899	89
Others (Dravidian, Caucasian, Khoisan, Eskimo-Aleut, etc.)	900-999	18

An example might help to clarify the process. The existence of a Nilo-Saharan language family was proposed by Greenberg (1966). A composite classification was drawn up using Greenberg (1966, 1971), Tucker and Bryan (1956, 1966), Bender (1976) and other minor sources. This included 10 major groupings of languages whose relationship to each other is clearly relatively remote. Seven of these (Songhai, Saharan, Maban, Fur, Berta, Kunama and Koman) were judged to have relatively little internal diversity and hence were represented by one language each. (The Saharan group consists of 4 languages whose diversity might be sufficient to merit more than one representative.) An eighth group, Gumuz, is insufficiently known and no phonological data is available. This leaves two groupings with considerable internal diversity, Eastern Sudanic and Central Sudanic, consisting of 11 and 7 sub-groupings respectively. In one subgroup, namely the Nilotic subgroup of Eastern Sudanic, the degree of internal genetic diversity justified inclusion of a language of each of the Western, Eastern and Southern branches. The target was therefore 13 Eastern Sudanic languages. Data from 11 were actually obtained, as two groupings were found to lack adequate data. Only 3 of the targeted 7 Central Sudanic languages were included; in this case partly because sources known to exist were unavailable to us. Thus an ideal figure of 28 languages to represent all of Nilo-Saharan is reflected with some imperfection in a total of 21 actually sampled, a 75% "response rate".

In certain instances, notably the Southern Ameridian groups of languages and the Indo-Pacific family, it proved much more difficult to obtain complete classifications and to resolve conflicting groupings. In these instances it is not really possible to assess how adequately the whole family has been sampled. However, an educated guess is that overall the present sample contains between 70-80% of the languages that it should include in order to completely fulfill its design specifications. An alphabetized list and a classified list (with only a skeleton classification) of the languages included are given in Appendix A. In these lists, languages included in the SPA are indicated by (S). The sources examined for the phonological data are also listed in this appendix. In some cases these have only been consulted indirectly via Stanford's report.

10.3 Determining the inventories

For each language a list of phonologically contrastive segments was drawn up. This procedure presupposes that such an analysis represents significant and interesting facts about a language. We do not propose to take space to argue for this proposition here - merely to point out that in practice nearly all linguists use such an analysis. Our own view goes further than some in asserting that the phonological segments can (and should) be characterized by certain phonetic attributes. Linguists who believe that phonology is necessarily involved with purely abstract constructs will part company with us at this point. (However, since such abstractions cannot be compared, they presumably are not interested in the kind of language universal properties this archive is designed to investigate.)

Determining the phonological inventory for each language involves two principal aspects, determining how many contrastive units there are and determining what phonetic characteristics should be attributed to each one. The first aspect concerns defining what is meant by contrast and resolving questions about the unity or otherwise of "suspect" complex phonetic events, such as affricates, geminated consonants, prenasalized stops, etc., and diphthongs. These are all open to interpretation as unitary segments or as sequences of some simpler segments in the language.

For our purposes "contrasts" are sound differences capable of distinguishing lexemes or morphemes in the language involved, given that data on factors that principally concern phonological properties themselves, such as stress placement, syllabification, boundaries (word, morpheme, etc.), and so on, can be used to predict variants but that diacritical features, arbitrary rule types, morpheme classes, etc., cannot be so used. These principles are applied to evaluate critically the information in the source, and consequently the resulting analysis may differ from the phonological inventory assumed in the source.

The suspect consonantal units/clusters have been examined as carefully as the available information permits in order to determine their status as units or sequences. If, for example, they can be split by a morpheme boundary or form a part of a more general set of permitted clusters, including for example non-homorganic clusters, they are treated as sequences. If, on the other hand, there are no similar clusters to those that would be created by a sequence interpretation, this is taken as favoring a unit interpretation.

Analysis of phonetic diphthongs is one of the most problematical areas. A phonetic diphthong might have one of 3 phonological interpretations: (1) as a phonemic unit, (2) as a vowel and a consonant in sequence (in either order), or (3) as two vowels in sequence. The first interpretation is chosen for the Khoisan language !Xũ (918), which is analyzed as having a relatively large number of diphthongs among its phonemes. Their phonological unity is indicated by the fact that they have the same distributional patterns as the simple vowels with respect to syllables and tones. In this language, if [au] was analyzed as /aw/ and [oa] as /wa/, and so on, it would introduce syllable-final consonants and syllable-initial clusters to a language that otherwise lacks them. The second interpretation is chosen for Standard Thai (400). Thai has a set of syllable-final consonants (nasals) before which both long and short simple vowels can occur with any of the 5 tone patterns of the language. When the phonetic diphthongs, which always end with an [i] or [u]-like vocoid, are analyzed as vowel + approximant consonant they fit in with the pattern established by these other syllable-final sonorant consonants (Gandour 1975). The third interpretation is chosen for a language such as Hawaiian (424), in which phonetic diphthongs have traditionally been viewed as resulting from juxtaposition of separate vowels. All vowels can occur in sequence with each other, sequences with /w/ are distinct from vowel plus /u/, and vowels in a diphthongal sequence that are contiguous with a like vowel coalesce (e.g. /ia/ + /a/ --> [ia]). All of these points argue for the analysis of these diphthongs as consisting of two independent vowels. Overall, relatively few languages are judged to have unit diphthongs.

In addition to the above considerations, certain types of contrasts have been interpreted as suprasegmental, i.e. as not relevant to setting up an inventory of phonological segments. These have included, by definition, tone and stress phenomena. Nasalization and properties involved in vowel harmony systems have always been treated as segmental. Length, however, has been treated as suprasegmental if it applies to a whole class of segments, such as all vowels. Otherwise it is treated as a segmental property: for example, Yay (402) has long and short low vowels /a, a:/ but the other vowels do not contrast in length. So there is considered to be no basis in this language for regarding length as suprasegmental; it is an attribute of a particular segment only.

The remaining issue concerning the size of the inventory of segments has to do with inclusion or exclusion of segments with more or less marginal status. Certain segments which occur only, say, in interjections or in foreign words that are clearly not established as loans have been excluded from the inventory altogether. In other instances, segments which might from certain points of view be considered marginal are included without any indication of a distinctive status. This would be the case, for example, for segments which are restricted to loanwords if the loans appear to be fully assimilated in the language concerned. Efforts have been made to reach decisions on straightforward inclusion or exclusion in the great majority of cases. However, in a minority of instances a third option has been taken. That is to include the segments but to indicate the nature of their marginal status by a value of a special variable. The details of this option are discussed below in section 10.4.

Each segment that is judged to deserve inclusion in the inventory for a given language is represented by a phonetic specification. In determining the phonetic properties to be attributed to each segment, an allophone which could be considered the most representative was identified. Wherever sufficient information was available, this selection was based on 3 principal considerations: (1) which allophone has the widest distribution (i.e. appears in the widest range of and/or most frequently occurring environments); (2) which allophone most appropriately represents the phonetic range of variation of all allophones; (3) which allophone is the one from which other allophones can be most simply and naturally derived. There are cases in which answers to these questions produce conflicting results; in these cases an attempt was made to resolve the conflict by considering how badly overall the conditions would be violated if the answer given by, say, consideration (2) was preferred over that given by (1), and to select the answer which did least violence to all 3 considerations taken together.

The degree of phonetic detail aimed at in the segment specifications is one that is approximately equal to that attained by the traditional 3-term label of phonetics, specifying voicing, place and manner for consonants, height, frontness and lip-position for vowels, plus additional labels required for features such as secondary articulations, etc. The set of coding variables to represent the required phonetic attributes is discussed in full below. Overall, the effort was to design a set of variables which was as little prone to errors of interpretation and as little likely to generate impressions of explicitness when unjustified as could reasonably be accommodated within practical limits of convenience and economy. The variable set is designed so that there is a minimum of appeal to redundancy to interpret their meaning. It was also designed to accommodate some of the major indeterminacies found in the phonological sources consulted. However, the database cannot be used without danger of misinterpretation unless the system of coding variables is fully understood. Moreover, the design of the variable set forces certain choices to be made when entering data, and at the same time limits the phonetic distinctions which may be drawn. For these reasons, it is recommended that the following section be read carefully by those who are interested in obtaining the clearest understanding of the results of UPSID represented in the preceding chapters.

10.4 Indices and variables

Each segment in the actual UPSID database is represented as a separate record in the form of a (notional) 80-column card image. The first 7 columns are devoted to identifying indices, 10-70 contain variables for phonetic attributes, 80 contains the ANOMALY feature. Each of the variables referring to phonetic attributes takes a value of 1 or 0, with 1 indicating that the allophone chosen to represent the segment possesses the attribute named and 0 indicating that it lacks the attribute. (There are a few minor exceptions to this rule which are explained below.) In the exposition which follows, each variable is referenced by its (notional) column location, given a definition and followed by the form of the variable name in the actual computer database (parenthesized and in capitals). For convenience, the variables are grouped into classes. Notes and comments on the use of the variables are interspersed where appropriate.

Indices

1-4. Language identification number (LANGNO). This number serves to identify the language to which a segment belongs. It consists of 3 digits, the first and sometimes second of which indicates affiliation to one of the major groupings used as the genetic basis of the sampling (see Table 10.1).

5-7. Segment identification number (SEGNO). Each segment within a language is numbered sequentially. The combination of LANGNO and SEGNO thus identifies one and only one record in the data base.

Alphanumeric segment code

8-9. Segment code (SEGCODE). For convenience in assembling the data base, a mainly alphabetic code was devised to represent commonly occurring segments. Variable values were then generated from this code. As these symbols have a useful mnemonic function, they have been left in the file.

Variables indicating place of articulation

All consonants except /h/ and /ɦ/ are specified for at least one place of articulation. Places are listed in the conventional front to back sequence. Double articulations are indicated by specifying two places of articulation, but secondary articulations are indicated by use of a separate set of variables. /h/ and /ɦ/, having place determined by environment, do not receive any place specification.

10. Bilabial (BILABIAL).

11. Labiodental (LABODENT).

12. Dental (DENTAL). This variable has the value 1 for true dental consonants. Specific indication that a segment is dental must be provided in the source, for example if it says "the tongue touches the teeth" or "/t̪/ is like French t, not English t". The description "dental" is often

applied to a segment which is more accurately described as alveolar, hence, unless such added evidence is available, segments that are merely called dental are not assumed to be true dentals.

13. Unspecified dental or alveolar (UNSPDENT). Segments simply indicated by transcriptions using /t, d, s/ etc. may be either dental or alveolar. In order not to falsify the data, this variable is used to indicate such segments with an incompletely specified place of articulation. Segments described simply as "dentals" are also included here.

14. Alveolar (ALVEOLAR).

15. Palato-alveolar (PALATALV). Palato-alveolar and alveo-palatal are not distinguished.

16. Retroflex (RETROFLX).

17. Palatal (PALATAL).

18. Velar (VELAR).

19. Uvular (UVULAR).

20. Pharyngeal (PHARYNGL).

21. Glottal (GLOTTAL). This variable is only used for glottal stops; the characterization of /h/ as a "glottal fricative" is rejected.

Variables indicating manner of articulation

Conventional phonetic labels, such as "plosive", "click", "vowel" generally combine information on aperture and airstream. This set of variables does likewise. All segments, except /h/ and /ɦ/, must receive the value 1 for least one of these; rarely, a segment may have the value 1 for more than one, e.g. a fricative trill.

22. Plosive (PLOSIVE). Pulmonic egressive stops, including glottal stops, receive the value 1 for this variable. Note that nasals are not considered to be stops of any sort.

23. Implosive (IMPLOSIV). Glottalic ingressive stops, whether voiced or voiceless, have the value 1 for this variable.

24. Ejective stop (EJECTSTP).

25. Click (CLICK). Non-affricated clicks have the value 1 for this variable.

26. Fricative (FRICATIV). Pulmonic egressive fricatives have the value 1 for this variable. Note that /h/ and /ɦ/ are not considered fricatives.

27. Ejective fricative (EJECTFRC).

28. Affricate (AFFRICAT). Pulmonic egressive affricates have the value 1 for this variable.

29. Ejective affricate (EJECTAFF).

30. Affricated click (AFFCLICK).

31. Unspecified "r-sound" (UNSPECR). This variable takes the value 1 for segments which are simply identified as some kind of "r-sound" (e.g. by being transcribed /r/ or called a "vibrant") but which cannot be further classified as a trill, tap, flap, approximant, etc.

32. Tap (TAP).

33. Flap (FLAP).

34. Trill (TRILL).

35. Approximant (APPROXMT). This variable has the value 1 for all consonants produced with open approximation, e.g. "semi-vowels", r-glides, nonfricative laterals, etc.

36. Nasal (NASAL). Nasal consonants (with complete oral closure) receive the value 1 for this variable. Nasalized segments, including consonants with nasal onsets, are identified by a different variable (see 45 below).

37. Simple vowel (SIMPVOWL). Monophthongal vowels have the value 1 for this variable. A segment which is not identified as either a simple vowel or a diphthong (38 below) is thereby classified as a consonant.

38. Diphthong (DIFTHONG). This variable takes the value 1 for unit diphthongs. Phonetic diphthongs which are phonologically analyzed as the result of a juxtaposition of simple vowels or a vowel and an approximant are, of course, not units but sequences and their components will be entered as separate phonemes.

Other consonant features

39. Lateral (LATERAL). This variable takes the value 1 for all lateral segments, e.g. it indicates lateral release in lateral affricates.

40. Sibilant (SIBILANT). This variable serves to identify the class of sibilants within the fricative/affricate group. In many languages this phonetic property is functionally redundant as place of articulation will distinguish the same class. However, it has occasional distinctive function in differentiating between fricatives and/or affricates with similar place of articulation but distinct acoustic characteristics (e.g. /s̪/ vs. /θ/).

Secondary articulations

41. Labialized (LABLZED).

42. Palatalized (PALTLZED). This variable takes the value 1 only for true palatalized consonants, i.e. those with a secondary palatal articulation. Thus a segment /c/ which occurs in a language as part of a "palatalized"

series of stops /p^j, t^j/ etc., will not be coded with this feature. Instead it will be reported as a palatal stop.

43. Velarized (VELRZED). This variable only takes the value 1 for true velarized segments. This value was also used to characterize vowels with velar stricture, reported in Siriono (829).

44. Pharyngealized (PHARGZED). Unlike the preceding secondary articulation variables, which usually only have the value 1 for consonants, this variable takes the value 1 equally for consonants and vowels.

45. Nasalized (NASLZED). This variable takes the value 1 for nasalized consonants and vowels, i.e. those with simultaneous nasal and oral escape. It is also used to characterize prenasalized stops (when these are clearly units). Thus the value 1 for this variable in combination with the value 1 for any stop variable (except click or affricated click) indicates a nasal onset to the stop.

46. Nasal release (NASRELSE). Takes the value 1 for postnasalized segments only.

Vowel features

All simple vowels are specified by a value of 1 on one vowel height, one vowel backness and one lip position variable. They may also have the value 1 for other variables to indicate other distinctions. Diphthong segments are specified by assigning the value 1 to all the vowel quality variables needed to describe both their beginning and end points. A set of diphthong variables, discussed below, indicates the order of conflicting specifications.

47. High (HIGH).

48. Higher mid (HIGHMID).

49. Mid (MID). This variable is used with systematic ambiguity for both those vowels which are indicated as "mid" without further particularization and those which are true mid vowels (i.e. lie between higher mid and lower mid on a height scale).

50. Lower mid (LOWMID). Note that /ɛ/ and /ɔ/ are considered lower mid vowels, not low vowels.

51. Low (LOW).

52. Front (FRONT).

53. Central (CENTRAL). Note that /a/ in most languages is considered a central vowel, not a back vowel.

54. Back (BACK).

55. Nonperipheral (NONPERIF). This variable takes the value 1 for "laxed" noncentral vowels which are produced away from the periphery of the vowel space, for example, /ɩ/ and /ω/. It may on occasion serve a mainly diacritical function where other features fail to distinguish vowels.
56. Rounded (ROUNDED).
57. Unrounded (UNROUNDD).
58. Lip-compressed (LIPCOMP). This variable takes the value 1 for "labial" vowels that are produced with vertical compression of the lips but no drawing in and forward of the corners of the mouth ("rounding").
59. R-colored (RCOLORED). This variable takes the value 1 for retroflexed or r-colored vowels.

Diphthong variables
The 3 variables for characterizing movement in diphthongs differ from most other variables in the inventory, which indicate only presence or absence of the attribute named by the variable. For diphthong variables a zero value may indicate a specific property of a diphthong, namely movement in the opposite direction to that indicated by the variable name. Also, unlike most of the variables, they require reference to the values of other variables for their interpretation. Their function is to indicate which value precedes when conflicting specifications of vowel height, backness or lip position are given to a single segment. This method of coding diphthongs was adopted in order to avoid a very large number of variables.
60. Backing (BACKING). This variable takes the value 1 when the end point of a diphthong is more back than the beginning, as in /iə/, /eu/, /əu/ etc. It takes the value 0 when the end point is either more front than or has the same degree of backness as the beginning, as in /oi/, /ae/, /ou/, etc. Note that only 3 degrees of backness are considered (front, central, back).
61. Lowering (LOWERING). This variable takes the value 1 for diphthongs that have an end point lower than their beginning, such as /iə/, /ea/, etc. It takes the value 0 when the endpoint is higher than or equal to the beginning on the 5-point vowel height scale used in UPSID, for example /oi/, /ou/, /ai/ etc.
62. Rounding (ROUNDING). This variable takes the value 1 when the endpoint of a diphthong is rounded but the beginning is unrounded, as in /eu/, /ao/, etc. It takes the value 0 when the endpoint is unrounded or both the beginning and endpoints are rounded, as in /oi/, /ai/ or /ou/.

Note that a pair of diphthongs such as /oi/ and /io/ receive the same values on the vowel variables. This will involve having conflicting values for height, backness and rounded; they will be specified as being both high and mid, front and back, rounded and unrounded. The diphthong features interpret these conflicts. Thus /oi/ will have the value 0 for all 3 diphthong variables since there is no backing, lowering or rounding movement in this diphthong. Yet because the segment has conflicting values, there must be movement; it has to be in the opposite direction from the variable names, i.e. fronting, raising and unrounding. On the other hand, /io/ receives the value 1 for all diphthong features indicating that the mid portion of the diphthong follows the high portion, the back portion follows the front portion and the rounded portion follows the unrounded portion.

Variables for phonation types, etc.

63. Voiceless (VOICELES). This variable takes the value 1 for all segments in which the vocal cords do not vibrate. The segment /h/ has the value 1 for this variable but for no others.

64. Voiced (VOICED). This variable takes the value 1 for all segments in which the vocal cords vibrate, whether as "regular" voicing or in some other mode (creaky, breathy etc.). The segment /ɦ/ has the value 1 for this variable, but for no others.

65. Aspirated (ASPIRATD). This variable takes the value 1 for all voiceless aspirated segments. So-called "voiced aspirates" do not have the value 1 for this feature, but instead for the variable "breathy".

66. Laryngealized (creaky, glottalized) (LARYNGD). This variable takes the value 1 for all segments with a laryngeal constriction in which that constriction is not serving as an airstream initiator or primary place of articulation. Thus, "glottalized" consonants, laryngealized vowels, etc. have value 1 for this variable. Various distinctions which have been made in the literature between "pre-glottalized", "postglottalized", "creaky" etc. were judged to be inconsistently applied and hence it was decided not to represent such distinctions in the inventory. Some inaccuracies regarding the distinction between a segment which is glottalized and one with a glottalic airstream (an implosive or ejective) have undoubtedly remained.

67. Long (LONG). This variable takes the value 1 for contrastively long vowels or geminate consonants which are single units but are not generated

as part of a general series of such long segments either from a suprasegmental length feature or because adjacent identical segments occur. (See "overshort" below.)

68. Breathy (voiced aspirated, murmured) (BREATHY). This variable takes the value 1 for all segments characterized by breathiness.

69. Overshort (OVERSHORT). In certain languages, the basic series of vowels is longer than a subset which may occur contrastively short. The variable "overshort" takes the value 1 for such contrastively short segments.

70. Preaspirated (PREASPRT).

The anomaly variable

80. Anomaly (ANOMALY). This variable indicates segments with a somewhat doubtful or marginal status in an inventory, but with sufficient claim to be included that they were not simply eliminated from consideration. Unlike the variables related to phonetic attributes, "anomaly" may take values greater than 1. A value of 0 indicates a segment is a normal full member of the inventory of the language. The other values have the meanings described below:

1 - Indicates a segment of extremely low frequency (e.g. it only occurs in a handful of words or certain morphological markers, but these are well entrenched parts of the language).

2 - Indicates a segment that occurs only in foreign words or unassimilated loans but these are frequent enough to consider including the segment in the inventory.

3 - Indicates a segment which is posited in underlying forms to account for some phonological patternings but which is neutralized in surface forms. (Very rarely used.)

4 - Indicates a segment which is treated as phonemic in UPSID but which may be regarded as derived from other underlying segments. (Very rarely used.)

5 - Indicates a segment which although apparently a genuine member of the inventory, is described in particularly obscure or contradictory fashion (e.g. a segment in Ashuslay, 814, described as simultaneously a (velar) stop and a lateral).

The values 3 and 4 were provided in order to provide an escape from unresolved questions concerning membership of inventories. In practice, very little use has been made of these indications as a resolution has been achieved in nearly all cases.

10.5 Using UPSID

As readers may be interested in the practicalities of working with UPSID, a brief description of its use is included as a final section of this chapter. UPSID consists of 9957 records of the form described in section 10.4. These constitute a SAS (Statistical Analysis System) file on a resident disk pack at UCLA's Central Computing facility. SAS (SAS Institute Inc. 1982) is a powerful and flexible data manipulation and statistical analysis system. It conveniently permits selection of subsets of records, computation of language-by-language totals or frequency counts on the complete data set, creation of new variables for special purposes and many other operations to be performed. Of course, it will also straightforwardly print out the information in the file. The phonemic charts in the data section of this book have been compiled from a printout of the information on each language.

Without duplicating procedural information, which is more properly sought in the SAS manual, an example of the use of UPSID will be given. This, it is hoped, will help to clarify the conceptual steps involved in obtaining answers from the database.

Suppose that one wishes to use the UPSID data to check the hypothesis that no nasal consonant appears in a language unless a stop occurs at the same place of articulation. As a first step it is necessary to define more precisely what is intended by the terms such as "stop", "nasal", "place of articulation" in this hypothesis and then to translate this into the appropriate set of UPSID variable values. Let us assume that what is intended by "stops" are plosives and central affricates, but not lateral affricates, implosives, ejectives, clicks etc., and "nasals" are voiced nasal consonants. Let us also assume that "place of articulation" refers to the usual set of primary places of articulations, that double articulations count as separate "places" but that secondary articulations will not be taken into account (e.g. /k/ and /kʷ/ will both count as velar).

The data to be selected for examination from the main file is now clear. It includes any segment meeting one of the following specifications: (i) it has the value 1 for the variable "plosive"; (ii) it has the value 1 for the variable "affricate" and the value 0 for "lateral"; (iii) it has the value 1 for the variables "nasal" and "voiced". All other segments can be excluded and all variables except for "nasal" and those relating to places of articulation can be dropped from the new, more compact, data file which is to be tested. Among places of articulation, pharyngeal and glottal can also be dropped as nasals cannot be produced at these places.

Now, we may restate the hypothesis as it relates to this reduced data set. The question to be answered is: for each segment with a given language number and the value 1 for "nasal", is there a segment with a matching language number, matching values for the place of articulation features and the value 0 for the variable "nasal"?

There are a number of ways one might proceed in order to obtain the answer to this question, but one simple way is to create an index which represents in a single number the information that one is interested in. There are 10 relevant place of articulation variables, plus one double articulation (labial-velar) that is found in nasals. Since labial-velars are to be counted separately, a new "labial-velar" variable can be generated and the original values for "labial" and "velar" set to 0 for labial-velar segments. Next, 11 additional variables, one for each place at which nasals occur, can be generated and set to some conveniently large value, say 10, for every segment which is a nasal at the given place. The value 1 can then be changed to 0 for the original place variables for all the nasals, leaving only the stops and affricates with non-zero values for these variables. One can then sum the totals for each variable on a language-by-language basis. This will produce a single line of data for each language in which each non-zero value for an original place of articulation variable indicates that a plosive or affricate appears at that place in the language and non-zero values for the new nasal place variables indicate that a nasal occurs at that place.

One can now add the summed value for each original place variable and the corresponding nasal place variable for each language. This will produce a two-digit number which indicates whether or not each nasal is matched by a plosive at the same place. Any nasals remaining unmatched will be indicated by a value of 10 (or a multiple of 10) for the relevant nasal place variable. These cases can easily be listed and their frequency, distribution by place, etc., examined. For example, a language with the inventory of stops, affricates and nasals shown below would have the value 12 (1 nasal, 2 plosives) at the bilabial and dental places of articulation and the value 24 (2 nasals, 4 plosives) at the velar place of articulation:

p b	t d	tʃ		k g	kʷ gʷ
m	n		ɲ	ŋ	ŋʷ

The palatal nasal place variable would have the value 10, indicating that there was no palatal plosive or affricate matching the palatal nasal. This language would then contain an exception to the hypothesis under investigation. The hypothesis could be modified so that a palatal nasal was considered to be matched by a palato-alveolar affricate and the modified hypothesis tested by adding the values for the original "palato-alveolar" and "palatal" variables together for each record to produce a more broadly defined palatal variable. This would produce an index value of 11 (1 nasal, 1 affricate) and no exception to the hypothesis.

References

Bell, A. 1978. Language samples. In J.H. Greenberg et al. (eds.), Universals of Human Language, Vol. 1, Method and Theory. Stanford University Press, Stanford, California: 123-56.

Bender, M.L. 1976. Nilo-Saharan overview. In M.L. Bender (ed.), The Non-Semitic Languages of Ethiopia (Monograph 5, Committee on Ethiopian Studies, African Studies Center). Michigan State University, East Lansing: 439-83.

Ferguson, C.A. 1963. Some assumptions about nasals. In J.H. Greenberg (ed.), Universals of Language. MIT Press, Cambridge: 42-7.

Gandour, J. 1975. On the representation of tone in Siamese. In J.G. Harris and J.R. Chamberlain (eds.), Studies in Tai Linguistics in Honor of William J. Gedney. Central Institute of English Language, Bangkok: 170-95.

Greenberg, J.H. 1966. The Languages of Africa. Indiana University Press, Bloomington.

Greenberg, J.H. 1970. Some generalizations concerning glottalic consonants, especially implosives. International Journal of American Linguistics 36: 123-45.

Greenberg, J.H. 1971. Nilo-Saharan and Meroitic. In T. Sebeok (ed.), Current Trends in Linguistics, Vol. 7, Sub-Saharan Africa. Mouton, The Hague: 421-42.

Hurford, J.R. 1977. The significance of linguistic generalizations. Language 53: 574-620.

Hyman, L.M. 1977. On the nature of linguistic stress. In L.M. Hyman (ed.), Studies in Stress and Accent (Southern California Occasional Papers in Linguistics 4). University of Southern California, Los Angeles: 37-82.

Jakobson, R. and Halle, M. 1956. Phonology and Phonetics. (Part 1 of) Fundamentals of Language. Mouton, The Hague: 3-51.

Ladefoged, P. 1971. Preliminaries to Linguistic Phonetics. University of Chicago Press, Chicago and London.

Ladefoged, P., Glick, P. and Criper, C. 1972. Language in Uganda. Oxford University Press, London.

SAS Institute Inc. 1982. SAS User's Guide, 1982 Edition: Basics. SAS Institute Inc, Cary, North Carolina.

Trubetskoy, N. 1939. Grundzüge der Phonologie (Travaux du Cercle Linguistique de Prague 9). Prague.

Tucker, A.N. and Bryan, M.A. 1956. The Non-Bantu Languages of Northeast Africa (Handbook of African Languages, Part 3). Oxford University Press for International African Institute, London.

Tucker, A.N. and Bryan, M.A. 1966. Linguistic Analyses: The Non-Bantu Languages of Northeastern Africa. Oxford University Press for International African Institute, London.

Vihman, M.M. 1974. Excerpts from the Phonology Archive coding manual. Working Papers on Language Universals (Stanford University) 15: 141-53.

Appendix A: Language lists and bibliography of data sources

The languages included in the UPSID sample are listed below, first according to a genetic classification, and secondly in alphabetical order. The genetic listing enables a quick check to be made on which languages are included from a given family. The genetic classification provided is intended only as an outline. Main subfamilies that are not listed have no representative in UPSID. In a few cases the affiliation of a language is uncertain (e.g. Cofan, 836). For convenience, the large Amerindian family has been divided on a geographical basis. The alphabetical listing enables a check to be made for inclusion of a particular language. The language names are those used throughout the book, but in some cases a cross-reference from an alternative name is given to assist in tracking down a given language. In both lists the language name is followed by the language identification number. These numbers are assigned mainly on a genetic basis (see Chapter 10). Note that, because of late additions and deletions to the sample, the sequence of numbers within a genetic group is not always continuous. The phonemic charts in this book are presented in the order of these identification numbers. The alphabetical list also serves as the key to the data sources consulted for each language. These sources are identified by author and date; the full references may be found in the bibliography of sources which forms the third part of this appendix. A language included in the Stanford Phonology Archive (SPA) is indicated by S after the language name in both lists. It may be assumed that the SPA report was consulted in determining the inventory for that language. For most of these languages, the sources used by SPA have also been directly consulted, and, for a few, additional or different sources were used. The remaining languages were analyzed solely at UCLA.

1. Genetic listing of languages and outline classification

Indo-European (000-049)

Greek:	Greek 000 S
Celtic:	Irish 001 S, Breton 002 S
Germanic:	German 004 S, Norwegian 006 S
Baltic:	Lithuanian 007 S
Slavic:	Russian 008 S, Bulgarian 009 S
Romance:	French 010 S, Spanish 011 S, Romanian 012 S
Iranian:	Farsi 013 S, Pashto 014 S, Kurdish 015
Indic:	Hindi-Urdu 016 S, Bengali 017 S, Kashmiri 018 S, Punjabi 019 S, Sinhalese 020 S
Albanian:	Albanian 021 S
Armenian:	Eastern Armenian 022 S

Ural-Altaic (050-099)

Finno-Ugric:	Ostyak 050 S, Cheremis 051 S, Komi 052 S, Finnish 053 S, Hungarian 054 S, Lappish 055
Samoyed:	Yurak 056 S, Tavgy 057
Turkic:	Osmanli (Turkish) 058 S, Azerbaijani 059 S, Chuvash 060 S, Yakut 061 S, Kirghiz 062 S, Bashkir 063, Khalaj 064, Tuva 065.
Mongolian:	Mongolian 066 S
Tungus:	Evenki 067 S, Goldi 068, Manchu 069
Korean:	Korean 070 S
Japanese:	Japanese 071 S

<u>Niger-Kordofanian</u> (100-199)	
Kordofanian:	Katcha 100 S, Moro 101, Kadugli 102
Mande:	Kpelle 103 S, Bisa 104, Bambara 105, Dan 106
West Atlantic:	Wolof 107 S, Diola 108, Temne 109
Voltaic:	Dagbani 110 S, Senadi 111, Tampulma 112, Bariba 113
Kwa:	Ewe 114 S, Akan 115 S, Igbo 116 S, Gã 117 S
Togo Remnant:	Lelemi 118
Cross River:	Efik 119
Plateau:	Birom 120, Tarok (Yergam) 121, Amo 122
Bantoid:	Beembe 123 S, Swahili 124 S, Luvale 125 S, Zulu 126 S, Teke (Kukuya)127
Adamawa:	Doayo 128
Eastern:	Gbeya 129 S, Zande 130
<u>Nilo-Saharan</u> (200-249)	
Songhai:	Songhai 200 S
Saharan:	Kanuri 201 S
Maban:	Maba 202
Fur:	Fur 203
Eastern Sudanic:	Maasai 204 S, Luo 205 S, Nubian 206 S, Nyangi 207, Ik 208, Sebei 209, Tama 210, Temein 211, Nera 212, Tabi 213, Mursi 214
Central Sudanic:	Logbara 215 S, Yulu 216, Sara 217
Berta:	Berta 218
Kunama:	Kunama 219
Koman:	Koma 220
<u>Afro-Asiatic</u> (250-299)	
Semitic:	Arabic 250 S, Tigre 251 S, Amharic 252 S, Hebrew 253 S, Socotri 254, Neo-Aramaic 255
Berber:	Shilha 256 S, Tuareg 257
Cushitic:	Somali 258 S, Awiya 259 S, Iraqw 260 S, Beja 261
Omotic:	Kullo 262, Dizi 263, Kefa 264, Hamer 265
Chadic:	Hausa 266 S, Angas 267 S, Margi 268 S, Ngizim 269, Kanakuru 270
<u>Austro-Asiatic</u> (300-349)	
Munda:	Mundari 300 S, Kharia 301 S
Khasi:	Khasi 302 S
Vietmuong:	Vietnamese 303 S
Bahnaric:	Sedang 304 S
Khmer:	Khmer 306 S
<u>Australian</u> (350-399)	
Iwaidjan:	Maung 350 S
Bureran:	Burera 352
Tiwian:	Tiwi 351
Nunggubuyan:	Nunggubuyu 353 S
Maran:	Alawa 354 S
Daly:	Maranungku 355 S, Malakmalak 356
Nyulnyulan:	Bardi 357
Pama-Nyungan:	Wik-Munkan 358 S, Kunjen 359 S, Western Desert 360 S, Nyangumata 361 S, Aranda 362, Kariera-Ngarluma 363, Gugu-Yalanji 364, Mabuiag 365, Arabana-Wanganura 366, Diyari 367, Bandjalang 368

Austro-Tai (400-499)

Kam-Tai:	Standard Thai 400 S, Lakkia 401 S, Yay 402 S, Sui 403, Saek 404, Po-ai 405, Lungchow 406
Atayalic:	Atayal 407 S
West Indonesian:	Sundanese 408 S, Javanese 409 S, Malagasy 410 S, Cham 411 S, Malay 412 S, Batak 413 S
Philippine:	Tagalog 414 S, Sa'ban 415 S, Chamorro 416 S, Rukai 417
Formosan:	Tsou 418
N.E. New Guinea:	Adzera 419 S, Roro 420
New Britain:	Kaliai 421 S
Loyalty Is:	Iai 422 S
Polynesian:	Maori 423 S, Hawaiian 424 S

Sino-Tibetan (500-599)

Sinitic:	Mandarin 500 S, Taishan 501 S, Hakka 502 S, Changchow 503 S, Amoy 504, Fuchow 505, Kan 506
Himalayish:	Tamang 507
Mirish:	Dafla 508 S
Lolo-Burmese:	Burmese 509 S, Lahu 510 S
Kachin:	Jingpho 511
Kuki-Chin:	Ao 512, Tiddim Chin 513
Baric:	Garo 514 S, Boro 515
Karenic:	Karen 516 S
Miao-Yao:	Yao 517 S

Indo-Pacific (600-699)

Andamanese:	Andamanese 600
West New Guinea:	Asmat 601 S
North New Guinea:	Washkuk 602 S, Sentani 603 S, Nimboran 604, Iwam 605
South-East New Guinea:	Telefol 606 S
Central New Guinea:	Selepet 607 S, Gadsup 608 S, Yagaria 609, Kewa 610, Chuave 611, Pawaian 612, Dani 613, Wantoat 615, Daribi 616, Fasu 617
South New Guinea:	Suena 618
North-East New Guinea:	Dera 619
East New Guinea:	Kunimaipa 620 S, Yareba 621, Koiari 622, Taoripi 623
Bougainville:	Nasioi 624 S, Rotokas 625
Central Melanesian:	Nambakaengo 626

Amerindian I (Northern) (700-799)

Haida:	Haida 700 S
Tlingit:	Tlingit 701
Athapaskan:	Navaho 702 S, Chipewyan 703 S, Tolowa 704 S, Hupa 705 S
Northern Penutian:	Nez Perce 706 S, Klamath 707
California Penutian:	Maidu 708 S, Wintu 709
Mexican Penutian:	Chontal 710 S, Zoque 711 S, Tzeltal 712 S, Totonac 713 S, K'ekchi 714, Mixe 715
Oto-Manguean:	Otomi 716 S, Mazahua 717 S, Mazatec 727 S, Mixtec 728 S, Chatino 729
Wakashan:	Nootka 730 S, Kwakw'ala 731 S
Chemakuan:	Quileute 732
Salish:	Squamish 733 S, Puget Sound 734 S
Uto-Aztecan:	Papago 736 S, Luiseño 737 S, Hopi 738 S, Yaqui 739
Kiowa-Tanoan:	Tiwa (Picuris) 740 S

Hokan:	Karok 741 S, Pomo 742 S, Diegueño 743 S, Achumawi 744, Yana 745, Shasta 746
Tarascan:	Tarascan 747 S
Zuni:	Zuni 748 S
Keres:	Acoma 749
Macro-Algonkian:	Ojibwa 750 S, Delaware 751 S, Tonkawa 752, Wiyot 753
Macro-Siouan:	Seneca 754 S, Wichita 755 S, Dakota 756 S, Yuchi 757 S, Tunica 758 S, Alabama 759 S
Wappo:	Wappo 760

Amerindian II (Southern) (800-899)

Chibchan:	Itonama 800 S, Bribri 801, Mura 802
Paezan:	Cayapa 803 S, Paez 804 S
Witotoan:	Ocaina 805 S, Muinane 806
Carib:	Carib 807 S
Macro-Ge:	Apinaye 809 S
Pano-Tacanan:	Amahuaca 810 S, Chacobo 811 S, Tacana 812, Cashinahua 813
Mataco:	Ashuslay 814
Guaycuru:	Abipon 815
Nambiquara:	Southern Nambiquara 816
Zaparoan:	Arabela 817, Auca 818
Quechumaran:	Quechua 819 S, Jaqaru 820 S
Chon:	Gununa-Kena (Puelche) 821
Arawakan:	Wapishana 822 S, Island Carib 823 S, Amuesha 824 S, Campa 825 S, Guajiro 826 S, Moxo 827 S
Tupi:	Guarani 828 S, Siriono 829 S
Guahibo-Pamigua:	Guahibo 830
Tucanoan:	Ticuna 831 S, Barasano 832 S, Siona 833, Tucano 834
Jivaroan:	Jivaro 835 S, Cofan 836
Penutian:	Araucanian 837 S

Other Families (900-999)

Eskimo-Aleut:	Greenlandic 900 S, Aleut 901 S
Dravidian:	Telugu 902 S, Kota 903 S, Kurukh 904 S, Malayalam 905, Brahui 917
Paleo-Siberian:	Ket 906 S, Yukaghir 907 S, Chukchi 908 S, Gilyak 909 S
Caucasian:	Georgian 910 S, Kabardian 911 S, Lak 912 S
Khoisan:	Nama 913 S, !Xũ 918
Basque:	Basque 914 S
Burushaski:	Burushaski 915 S
Ainu:	Ainu 916 S

2. Alphabetic list of languages with key to sources

Abipon 815	Najlis (1966)
Achumawi 744	Olmsted (1964, 1966)
Acoma 749	Miller (1966)
Adzera 419 S	Holzknecht (1973)
Ainu 916 S	Simeon (1969)
Akan 115 S	Welmers (1946), Schachter and Fromkin (1968), Stewart (1967)
Alabama 759 S	Rand (1968)
Alawa 354 S	Sharpe (1972)
Albanian 021 S	Newmark (1957)

Aleut 901 S Bergsland (1956)
Amahuaca 810 S Osborn (1948)
Amharic 252 S Leslau (1968), Klingenheben (1966), Sumner (1957)
Amo 122 di Luzio (1972)
Amoy Chinese 504 [Hanyu Fangyan Gaiyao] (1960)
Amuesha 824 S Fast (1953)
Andamanese 600 Voegelin and Voegelin (1966), Radcliffe-Brown (1914)
Angas 267 S Burquest (1971)
Ao 512 Gowda (1972)
Apinaye 809 S Burgess and Ham (1968)
Arabana-Wanganura 366 Hercus (1973)
Arabela 817 Furne (1963)
Arabic 250 S Mitchell (1962), Tomiche (1964), Kennedy (1960)
Aranda 362 O'Grady, Voegelin and Voegelin (1966)
Araucanian 837 S Echeverria and Contreras (1965)
Armenian, Eastern 022 S Allen (1950)
Ashuslay 814 Stell (1972)
Asmat 601 S Voorhoeve (1965)
Atayal 407 S Egerod (1966)
Auca 818 Saint and Pike (1962)
Awiya 259 S Hetzron (1969)
Aymara, see Jaqaru
Azande, see Zande
Azerbaijani 059 S Householder (1965)
Bambara 105 Bird, Hutchinson and Kante (1977)
Bandjalang 368 Cunningham (1969)
Barasano 832 S Stolte and Stolte (1971)
Bardi 357 Metcalfe (1971)
Bariba 113 Welmers (1952)
Bashkir 063 Poppe (1964)
Basque 914 S N'diaye (1970)
Batak 413 S van der Tuuk (1971)
Beembe 123 S Jacquot (1962)
Beja 261 Hudson (1976)
Bengali 017 S Ferguson and Chowdhury (1960)
Berta 218 Triulzi, Dafallah and Bender (1976)
Birom 120 Wolff (1959)
Bisa 104 Naden (1973)
Boro 515 Bhat (1968)
Brahui 917 Emeneau (1937), De Armond (1975)
Breton 002 S Ternes (1970)
Bribri 801 Arroyo (1972)
Bulgarian 009 S Klagstad (1958), Aronson (1968)
Burera 352 Glasgow and Glasgow (1967)
Burmese 509 S Okell (1969)
Burushaski 915 S Morgenstierne (1945)
Campa 825 S Dirks (1953)
Carib 807 S Peasgood (1972), Hoff (1968)
Cashinahua 813 Kensinger (1963)
Cayapa 803 S Lindskoog and Brend (1962)
Chacobo 811 S Prost (1967)
Cham 411 S Blood (1967)
Chamorro 416 S Topping (1973,1969), Seiden (1960)
Changchow Chinese (Wu) 503 S Chao (1970)
Chasta Costa, see Tolowa
Chatino 729 Pride (1965)
Cheremis 051 S Ristinen (1960)

Chipewyan 703 S Li (1946, 1933, 1932)
Chontal 710 S Keller (1959)
Chuave 611 Thurman (1970)
Chukchi 908 S Skorik (1968,1961)
Chuvash 060 S Andreev (1966), Krueger (1961)
Cofan 836 Borman (1962)
Dafla 508 S Ray (1967)
Dagbani 110 S Wilson and Bendor-Samuel (1969)
Dakota 756 S Boas and Deloria (1939)
Dan 106 Béarth and Zemp (1967)
Dani 613 Bromley (1961), van der Stap (1966)
Daribi 616 MacDonald (1973)
Delaware 751 S Voegelin (1946)
Dera 619 Voorhoeve (1971)
Diegueño 743 S Langdon (1970)
Diola 108 Sapir (1965)
Diyari 367 Austin (1978)
Dizi 263 Allen (1976b)
Doayo 128 Wiering (1974)
Efik 119 Cook (1969)
Evenki 067 S Novikova (1960)
Ewe 114 S Berry (no date a), Stahlke (1971), Ladefoged (1968)
Fante, see Akan
Farsi 013 S Obolensky, Panah and Nouri (1963)
Fasu 617 Loeweke and May (1964)
Finnish 053 S Lehtinen (1964), Harms (1964)
French 010 S Sten (1963)
Fuchow Chinese 505 [Hanyu Fangyan Gaiyao] (1960)
Fur 203 Beaton (1968), Tucker and Bryan (1966)
Gã 117 S Berry (no date b), J.N.A. Nartey (p.c.)
Gadsup 608 S Frantz and Frantz (1966)
Garo 514 S Burling (1961)
Gbeya 129 S Samarin (1966)
Georgian 910 S Robins and Waterson (1952), Tschenkeli (1958), Vogt (1938, 1958)
German 004 S Moulton (1962), Philipp (1974)
Gilyak (Nivkh) 909 S Panfilov (1962, 1968)
Goldi 068 Avrorin (1968)
Greek 000 S Householder, Kazazis and Koutsoudas (1964)
Greenlandic 900 S Rischel (1974), Thalbitzer (1904), Kleinschmidt (1851)
Guahibo 830 Kondo and Kondo (1967)
Guajiro 826 S Holmer (1949)
Guarani 828 S Gregores and Suarez (1967), Uldall (1956), Lunt (1973)
Gugu-Yalanji 364 Oates and Oates (1964), Wurm (1972a), Oates (1964)
Gununa-Kena 821 Gerzenstein (1968)
Haida 700 S Sapir (1923)
Hakka Chinese 502 S Hashimoto (1973)
Hamer 265 Lydall (1976)
Hausa 266 S Hodge (1947), Kraft and Kraft (1973), Hodge and Umaru (1963)
Hawaiian 424 S Pukui and Elbert (1965)
Hebrew 253 S Chayen (1973), Cohen and Zafrani (1968)
Hindi-Urdu 016 S Kelkar (1968), Vermeer and Sharma (1966)
Hopi 738 S Whorf (1946), Voegelin (1956)
Huambisa, see Jivaro
Hungarian 054 S Kalman (1972), Banhidi, Jokay and Szabo (1965),

Hall (1938, 1944)
Hupa 705 S Woodward (1964), Golla (1970)
Iai 422 S Ozanne-Rivierre (1976), Tryon (1968)
Igbo 116 S Williamson (1969), Carnochan (1948), Swift, Ahaghota and Ugorji (1962)
Ignaciano, see Moxo
Ik 208 Heine (1975b)
Inuit, see Greenlandic
Iraqw 260 S Whiteley (1958)
Irish 001 S Mhac an Fhailigh (1968), Sommerfelt (1964)
Island Carib 823 S Taylor (1955)
Itonama 800 S Liccardi and Grimes (1968)
Iwam 605 Laycock (1965)
Japanese 071 S Bloch (1950), Martin (1952), Jorden (1963)
Jaqaru 820 S Hardman (1966)
Javanese 409 S Horne (1961)
Jingpho 511 Liu (1964)
Jivaro 835 S Beasley and Pike (1957)
Kabardian 911 S Kuipers (1960)
Kadugli 102 Abdalla (1973)
Kaliai 421 S Counts (1969)
Kan Chinese 506 [Hanyu Fangyan Gaiyao] (1960)
Kanakuru 270 Newman (1974)
Kanuri 201 S Lukas (1937)
Karen (Sgaw) 516 S Jones (1961)
Kariera-Ngarluma 363 O'Grady, Voegelin and Voegelin (1966), Wurm (1972a)
Karok 741 S Bright (1957)
Kashmiri 018 S Kelkar and Trisal (1964)
Katcha 100 S Stevenson (1957) Tucker and Bryan (1966)
Kefa 264 Fleming (1976)
K'ekchi 714 Haeseriju (1966), Freeze (1975)
Ket 906 S Dul'zon (1968), Krejnovich (1968a)
Kewa 610 Franklin and Franklin (1962)
Khalaj 064 Doerfer (1971)
Khalka, see Mongolian
Kharia 301 S Biligiri (1965), Pinnow (1959)
Khasi 302 S Rabel (1961)
Khmer 306 S Huffman (1970a, 1970b), Jacob (1968)
Kirghiz 062 S Herbert and Poppe (1963)
Klamath 707 Barker (1964)
Koiari 622 Dutton (1969)
Koma 220 Tucker and Bryan (1966)
Komi 052 S Lytkin (1966), Bubrikh (1949)
Korean 070 S Martin (1951), Cho (1967), Martin and Lee (1969)
Kota 903 S Emeneau (1944)
Kpelle 103 S Welmers (1962), Hyman (1973)
Kullo 262 Allen (1976a)
Kunama 219 Tucker and Bryan (1966)
Kunimaipa 620 S Pence (1966)
Kunjen 359 S Sommer (1969)
Kurdish 015 Abdulla and McCarus (1967)
Kurukh 904 S Pinnow (1964), Pfeiffer (1972)
Kwakw'ala 731 S S. R. Anderson (p.c.), Boas (1947) Grubb (1977)
Lahu 510 S Matisoff (1973)
Lak 912 S Murkelinskij (1967), Zhirkov (1955), Khaidakov (1966)
Lakkia 401 S Haudricourt (1967)
Lappish 055 Hasselbrink (1965)

Lelemi 118 Hoftmann (1971)
Lithuanian 007 S Senn (1966), Augustitis (1964), Ambrazas, et al. (1966)
Logbara 215 S Crazzolara (1960), Tucker and Bryan (1966)
Luiseño 737 S Malécot (1963), Bright (1965, 1968), Kroeber and Grace (1960)
Lungchow 406 Li (1977)
Luo 205 S Gregersen (1961)
Lushootseed, see Puget Sound Salish
Luvale 125 S Horton (1949)
Maasai 204 S Tucker and Mpaayei (1955), Tucker and Bryan (1966)
Maba 202 Tucker and Bryan (1966)
Mabuiag 365 Wurm (1972a)
Maidu 708 S Shipley (1956, 1964)
Malagasy 410 S Dahl (1952), Dyen (1971)
Malakmalak 356 Tryon (1974), Birk (1975)
Malay 412 S Verguin (1967), MacDonald and Soenyono (1967)
Malayalam 905 Kumari (1972), McAlpin (1975), Velayudhan (1971)
Manchu 069 Austin (1962)
Mandarin Chinese 500 S Dow (1972), Chao (1968), C-C. Cheng (1973)
Maori 423 S Biggs (1961), Hohepa (1967)
Maranungku 355 S Tryon (1970)
Margi 268 S Hoffmann (1963)
Maung 350 S Capell and Hinch (1970)
Mazahua 717 S Spotts (1953)
Mazatec 727 S Pike and Pike (1947)
Mixe (Totontepec) 715 Crawford (1963), Schoenhals and Schoenhals (1965)
Mixtec 728 S Hunter and Pike (1969)
Mongolian (Khalka) 066 S Hangin (1968), Street (1963), Luvšanvandan (1964)
Moro 101 Black (1971)
Moxo 827 S Ott and Ott (1967)
Muinane 806 Walton and Walton (1967)
Mundari 300 S Gumperz and Biligiri (1957)
Mura 802 Sheldon (1974)
Mursi 214 Turton and Bender (1976)
Nama 913 S Beach (1938), Ladefoged and Traill (1980)
Nambakaengo 626 Wurm (1972b)
Nambiquara, Southern 816 Price (1976)
Nasioi 624 S Hurd and Hurd (1966)
Navaho 702 S Sapir and Hoijer (1967)
Nenets, see Yurak
Neo-Aramaic 255 Garbell (1965)
Nera 212 Thompson (1976)
Nez Perce 706 S Aoki (1970, 1966)
Ngizim 269 Schuh (1972)
Nimboran 604 Anceaux (1965)
Nivkh, see Gilyak
Nootka (Tseshaht) 730 S Sapir and Swadesh (1939, 1955)
Norwegian 006 S Vanvik (1972)
Nubian (Mahas) 206 S Bell (1971)
Nunggubuyu 353 S Hughes and Leeding (1971)
Nyangi 207 Heine (1975a)
Nyangumata 361 S O'Grady (1964)
Ocaina 805 S Agnew and Pike (1957)
Ojibwa 750 S Bloomfield (1956)
Osmanli (Turkish) 058 S Swift (1963), Lees (1961)
Ostyak 050 S Gulya (1966)
Otomi 716 S Blight and Pike (1976)

Paez 804 S Gerdel (1973)
Papago 736 S Hale (1959), Saxton (1963), I. Maddieson (p.c.)
Pashto 014 S Shafeev (1964)
Pawaian 612 Trefry (1972)
Persian, see Farsi
Po-Ai 405 Li (1977)
Pomo 742 S Moshinsky (1974)
Puget Sound Salish 734 S Snyder (1968)
Punjabi 019 S Gill and Gleason (1963)
Quechua 819 S Bills, Vallejo and Troike (1969), Lastra (1968)
Quileute 732 Powell (1975)
Romanian 012 S Agard (1958), Ruhlen (1973)
Roro 420 Bluhme (1970), Davis (1974)
Rotokas 625 Firchow and Firchow (1969)
Rukai 417 Li (1973)
Russian 008 S Jones and Ward (1969), Halle (1959)
Sa'ban 415 S Clayre (1973)
Saek 404 Gedney (1970)
Sara 217 Caprile (1968), Thayer and Thayer (1971)
Sebei 209 Montgomery (1970)
Sedang 304 S Smith (1968)
Selepet 607 S McElhanon (1970)
Senadi 111 Welmers (1950)
Seneca 754 S Chafe (1967)
Sentani 603 S Cowan (1965)
Shasta 746 Silver (1964)
Shilha 256 S Applegate (1958)
Sinhalese 020 S Coates and da Silva (1960)
Siona 833 Wheeler and Wheeler (1962)
Siriono 829 S Priest (1968)
Socotri 254 Johnstone (1975), Leslau (1938)
Somali 258 S Armstrong (1934), Andrzejewsky (1955)
Songhai 200 S Prost (1956), Williamson (1967)
Spanish 011 S Navarro (1961), Harris (1969), Saporta and Contreras (1962)
Squamish 733 S Kuipers (1967)
Suena 618 Wilson (1969)
Sui 403 Li (1948)
Sundanese 408 S Van Syoc (1959), Robins (1953)
Swahili 124 S Polomé (1967)
Tabi 213 Tucker and Bryan (1966)
Tacana 812 Key (1968), Van Wynen and Van Wynen (1962)
Tagalog 414 S Bloomfield (1917), Schachter and Otanes (1972)
Tahaggart, see Tuareg
Taishan Chinese 501 S T.M. Cheng (1973)
Tama 210 Tucker and Bryan (1966)
Tamang 507 Mazaudon (1973)
Tampulma 112 Bergman, Gray and Gray (1969)
Taoripi 623 Brown (1973)
Tarascan 747 S Foster (1969)
Tarok 121 Robinson (1974)
Tavgy 057 Castrén (1966), Tereščenko (1966)
Teke (Kukuya) 127 Paulian (1975)
Telefol 606 S Healey (1964)
Telugu 902 S Lisker (1963), Krishnamurti (1961), Kelley (1963) Kostić et al (1977)
Temein 211 Tucker and Bryan (1966)

Temne 109	Dalby (1966), Wilson (1961)
Thai (Standard) 400 S	Abramson (1962), Noss (1954, 1964)
Ticuna 831 S	Anderson (1959), Anderson (1962)
Tiddim Chin 513	Henderson (1965)
Tigre 251 S	Palmer (1962)
Tiwa (Picuris) 740 S	Trager (1971)
Tiwi 351	Osborne (1974)
Tlingit 701	Story and Naish (1973), Swanton (1909)
Tolowa 704 S	Bright (1964)
Tonkawa 752	Hoijer (1972, 1949)
Totonac 713 S	Aschmann (1946)
Tseshaht, see Nootka	
Tsou 418	Tung (1964)
Tuareg 257	Prasse (1972)
Tucano 834	West and Welch (1967)
Tunica 758 S	Haas (1941)
Turkish, see Osmanli	
Tuva 065	Sat (1966)
Tzeltal 712 S	Kaufman (1971)
Vietnamese 303 S	Thompson (1965)
Wantoat 615	Davis (1969)
Wapishana 822 S	Tracy (1972)
Wappo 760	Sawyer (1965)
Washkuk 602 S	Kooyers, Kooyers and Bee (1971)
Western Desert 360 S	Douglas (1955, 1964)
Wichita 755 S	Garvin (1950), Rood (1975)
Wik-Munkan 358 S	Sayers and Godfrey (1964)
Wintu 709	Broadbent and Pitkin (1964)
Wiyot 753	Teeter (1964)
Wolof 107 S	Sauvageot (1965)
!Xũ 918	Snyman (1969, 1975)
Yagaria 609	Renck (1967, 1975)
Yakut 061 S	Krueger (1962), Böhtlingk (1964)
Yana 745	Sapir and Swadesh (1960)
Yao 517 S	Purnell (1965)
Yaqui 739	Johnson (1962), Crumrine (1961)
Yareba 621	Weimer and Weimer (1972)
Yay 402 S	Gedney (1965)
Yuchi 757 S	Crawford (1973), Ballard (1975)
Yukaghir 907 S	Krejnovich (1958, 1968b)
Yulu 216	Thayer (1969), Santandrea (1970)
Yurak 056 S	Hajdú (1963), Decsy (1966), Ristinen (1965, 1968)
Zande 130	Tucker and Hackett (1959)
Zoque 711 S	Wonderly (1951)
Zulu 126 S	Doke (1926, 1961)
Zuni 748 S	Newman (1965)

3. Bibliography of data sources

Abdalla, A.I. 1973. *Kadugli Language and Language Usage* (Salambi Prize Series 3). Khartoum University Press, Khartoum.

Abdulla, J. and McCarus, E.N. 1967. *Kurdish Basic Course - Dialect of Sulaimania, Iraq*. University of Michigan Press, Ann Arbor.

Abramson, A.S. 1962. *The Vowels and Tones of Standard Thai: Acoustical Measurements and Experiments* (IJAL 28/2 Part II, Indiana University Publications in Anthropology, Folklore and Linguistics 20). Indiana University, Bloomington.

Agard, F.B. 1958. *Structural Sketch of Rumanian* (Language monograph 26). Linguistic Society of America, Baltimore.

Agnew, A. and Pike, E.G. 1957. Phonemes of Ocaina (Huitoto). International Journal of American Linguistics 23: 24-7.
Allen, E.J. 1976a. Kullo. In M.L. Bender (ed.), The Non-Semitic Languages of Ethiopia. African Studies Center, Michigan State University, East Lansing: 324-50.
Allen, E.J. 1976b. Dizi. In M.L. Bender (ed.), The Non-Semitic Languages of Ethiopia. African Studies Center, Michigan State University, East Lansing: 377-92.
Allen, W.S. 1950. Notes on the phonetics of an Eastern Armenian speaker. Transactions of the Philological Society: 180-206.
Ambrazas, V., Vajtkavichjute, V., Valjatskene, A., Morkunas, K., Sabaljauskas, A., and Ul'vidas, K. 1966. Litovskij jazyk. In V.V. Vinogradov (ed.), Jazyki Narodov SSSR, Vol. 1. Nauka, Leningrad and Moscow: 500-27.
Anceaux, J.C. 1965. The Nimboran Language: Phonology and Morphology. Nijhoff, The Hague.
Anderson, D. 1962. Conversational Ticuna. Summer Institute of Linguistics, University of Oklahoma, Norman.
Anderson, L. 1959. Ticuna vowels: with special regard to the system of five tonemes. Publicacãos do Museu Nacional, Série Lingüistica Especial 1 (Museu Nacional, Rio de Janeiro): 76-119.
Andrzejewsky, B.W. 1955. The problem of vowel representation in the Isaaq dialect of Somali. Bulletin of the School of Oriental and African Studies 17: 567-80.
Andreev, I.A. 1966. Chuvashskij jazyk. In V.V. Vinogradov (ed.), Jazyki Narodov SSSR Vol. 2. Nauka, Leningrad and Moscow: 43-65.
Aoki, H. 1966. Nez Perce vowel harmony and Proto-Sahaptian vowels. Language 42: 759-67.
Aoki, H. 1970. Nez Perce Grammar. University of California Press, Berkeley and Los Angeles.
Applegate, J.R. 1958. An Outline of the Structure of Shilha. American Council of Learned Societies, New York.
Armstrong, L.E. 1934. The phonetic structure of Somali. Mitteilungen des Seminars für Orientalische Sprachen (Berlin) 37/3: 116-61.
Aronson, H.I. 1968. Bulgarian Inflectional Morphophonology. Mouton, The Hague.
Arroyo, V.M. 1972. Lenguas Indigenas Costarricenses, 2nd ed. Editorial Universitaria Centroamericana, San Jose, Costa Rica.
Aschmann, H.P. 1946. Totonaco phonemes. International Journal of American Linguistics 12: 34-43.
Augustitis, D. 1964. Das Litauische Phonationssystem. Sagner, Munich.
Austin, P.A. 1978. A Grammar of the Diyari Language of North-East South Australia. Ph. D. Thesis. Australian National University, Canberra.
Austin, W. 1962. The phonemics and morphophonemics of Manchu. In N. Poppe (ed.), American Studies in Altaic Linguistics (Indiana University Publications, Uralic and Altaic Series 13). Indiana University, Bloomington: 15-22.
Avrorin, V.A. 1968. Nanajski jazyk. In V.V. Vinogradov (ed.), Jazyki Narodov SSSR, Vol. 5. Nauka, Leningrad and Moscow: 5: 129-48.
Ballard, W.L. 1975. Aspects of Yuchi morphonology. In J.M. Crawford (ed.), Studies in Southeastern Indian Languages. University of Georgia Press, Athens, Georgia: 164-87.
Banhidi, Z., Jokay, A. and Szabo, D. 1965. Lehrbuch der Ungarischen Sprache. Publishing House for Textbooks, Budapest.
Barker, M.A.R. 1964. Klamath Grammar. University of California Press, Berkeley and Los Angeles.

Beach, D.M. 1938. The Phonetics of the Hottentot Language. Heffer, Cambridge.
Béarth, T. and Zemp, H. 1967. The phonology of Dan (Santa). Journal of African Languages 6: 9-29.
Beasley, D. and Pike, K.L. 1957. Notes on Huambisa phonemics. Lingua Posnaniensis 6: 1-8.
Beaton, A.C. 1968. A Grammar of the Fur Language (Linguistic Monograph Series 1). Sudan Research Unit, University of Khartoum, Khartoum.
Bell, H. 1971. The phonology of Nobiin Nubian. African Language Review 9: 115-39.
Bergman, R., Gray, I., and Gray, C. 1969. Collected Field Reports on the Phonology of Tampulma. Institute of African Studies, University of Ghana, Legon.
Bergsland, K. 1956. Some problems of Aleut phonology. In M. Halle (ed.), For Roman Jakobson. Mouton, The Hague: 38-43.
Berry, J. no date a. The Pronunciation of Ewe. Heffer, Cambridge.
Berry, J. no date b. The Pronunciation of Gã. Heffer, Cambridge.
Bhat, D.N.S. 1968. Boro Vocabulary. Deccan College, Poona.
Biggs, B. 1961. The structure of New Zealand Maori. Anthropological Linguistics 3/3: 1-54.
Biligiri, H.S. 1965. Kharia: Phonology, Grammar and Vocabulary. Deccan College, Poona.
Bills, G.D., Vallejo C., B. and Troike, R.C. 1969. An Introduction to Spoken Bolivian Quecha. University of Texas Press for Institute of Latin American Studies, Austin.
Bird, C., Hutchinson, J., and Kante, M. 1977. An Ka Bamanankan Kalan: Beginning Bambara. Indiana University Press, Bloomington.
Birk, D.B.W. 1975. The phonology of Malakmalak. Papers in Australian Linguistics 8 (Pacific Linguistics, Series A, 39): 59-78.
Black, Mr. and Mrs. K. 1971. The Moro Language: Grammar and Dictionary (Linguistic Monograph Series 6). Sudan Research Unit, University of Khartoum, Khartoum.
Blight, R.C. and Pike, E.V. 1976. The phonology of Tenango Otomi. International Journal of American Linguistics 42: 51-7.
Bloch, B. 1950. Studies in colloquial Japanese, IV: Phonemics. Language 26: 86-125.
Blood, D.L. 1967. Phonological units in Cham. Anthropological Linguistics 9: 15-32.
Bloomfield, L. 1917. Tagalog Texts with Grammatical Analysis (University of Illinois Studies in Language and Literature 3/2-3). University of Illinois, Urbana.
Bloomfield, L. 1956. Eastern Ojibwa. University of Michigan Press, Ann Arbor.
Bluhme, H. 1970. The phoneme system and its distribution in Roro. In S.A. Wurm and D.C. Laycock (eds.), Pacific Linguistic Studies in Honor of Arthur Capell (Pacific Linguistics, Series C, 13): 867-77.
Boas, F. 1947. Kwakiutl grammar. Transactions of the American Philosophical Society 37: 201-377.
Boas, F. and Deloria, E. 1939. Dakota Grammar (Memoirs of the National Academy of Sciences 23/2). Washington, D.C.
Böhtlingk, O. 1964. Uber die Sprache der Jakuten (reprint of Dr. A. Th. v. Middendorff's Reise in der äussersten Norden und Osten Sibiriens, Band III, St. Petersburg, 1851; Indiana University Publications, Uralic and Altaic Series 35). Indiana University, Bloomington.
Borman, M.B. 1962. Cofan phonemes. Studies in Ecuadorian Indian Languages 1. Summer Institute of Linguistics, University of Oklahoma, Norman: 45-9.

Bright, J.O. 1964. The phonology of Smith River Athapaskan (Tolowa). International Journal of American Linguistics 30: 101-7.
Bright, W. 1957. The Karok Language. University of California Press, Berkeley and Los Angeles.
Bright, W. 1965. Luiseño phonemics. International Journal of American Linguistics 31: 342-5.
Bright, W. 1968. A Luiseño Dictionary. University of California Press, Berkeley and Los Angeles.
Broadbent, S.M. and Pitkin, H. 1964. A comparison of Miwok and Wintu. In W. Bright (ed.), Studies in Californian Linguistics. University of California Press, Berkeley and Los Angeles: 19-45.
Bromley, H.M. 1961. The Phonology of Lower Grand Valley Dani (Verhandelingen van het Koninklijk Instituut voor Taal-, Land- en Volkenkunde 34). Nijhoff, The Hague.
Brown, A.H. 1973. The Eleman language family. In K. Franklin (ed.), The Linguistic Situation in the Gulf District and Adjacent Areas, Papua New Guinea (Pacific Linguistics, Series C, 26). Australian National University, Canberra: 279-375.
Bubrikh, D.V. 1949. Grammatika Literaturnogo Komi Jazyka. Leningrad State University, Leningrad.
Burgess, E. and Ham, P. 1968. Multilevel conditioning of phoneme variants in Apinaye. Linguistics 41: 5-18.
Burling, R. 1961. A Garo Grammar. Deccan College, Poona.
Burquest, D.A. 1971. A Preliminary Study of Angas Phonology. Institute of Linguistics, Zaria.
Capell, C. and Hinch, H.E. 1970. Maung Grammar. Mouton, The Hague.
Caprile, J-P. 1968. Essai de phonologie d'un parler mbay. Bulletin de la SELAF 8: 1-40.
Carnochan, J. 1948. A study on the phonology of an Igbo speaker. Bulletin of the School of Oriental and African Studies 22: 416-27.
Castrén, M.A. 1966. Grammatik der Samojedischen Sprachen (Indiana University Publications, Uralic and Altaic Series 53 [Reprint of 1854 edition, St. Petersburg]). Indiana University, Bloomington.
Chafe, W.L. 1967. Seneca Morphology and Dictionary. Smithsonian Institution, Washington, D.C.
Chao, Y-R. 1968. A Grammar of Spoken Chinese. University of California Press, Berkeley.
Chao, Y-R. 1970. The Changchow dialect. Journal of the American Oriental Society 90: 45-59.
Chayen, M.J. 1973. The Phonetics of Modern Hebrew. Mouton, The Hague.
Cheng, C-C. 1973. A Synchronic Phonology of Mandarin Chinese. Mouton, The Hague.
Cheng, T.M. 1973. The phonology of Taishan. Journal of Chinese Linguistics 1: 256-322.
Cho, S-B. 1967. A Phonological Study of Korean (Acta Universitatis Upsaliensis, Studia Uralica et Altaica Upsaliensia 2). Almqvist and Wiksells, Uppsala.
Clayre, I.F.C.S. 1973. The phonemes of Sa'ban: a language of Highland Borneo. Linguistics 100: 26-46.
Coates, W.A. and da Silva, M.W.S. 1960. The segmental phonemes of Sinhalese. University of Ceylon Review 18: 163-75.
Cohen, D. and Zafrani, H. 1968. Grammaire de l'Hébreu Vivant. Presses Universitaires de France, Paris.
Cook, T.L. 1969. The Pronunciation of Efik for Speakers of English. Indiana University, Bloomington.
Counts, D.R. 1969. A Grammar of Kaliai-Kove. University of Hawaii Press, Honolulu.

Cowan, H.K.J. 1965. Grammar of the Sentani Language (Verhandelingen van het Koninklijk Instituut voor Taal-, Land- en Volkenkunde 47). Nijhoff, The Hague.
Crawford, J.C. 1963. Totontepec Mixe Phonotagmemics. Summer Institute of Linguistics, University of Oklahoma, Norman.
Crawford, J.M. 1973. Yuchi phonology. International Journal of American Linguistics 39: 173-9.
Crazzolara, J.P. 1960. A Study of the Logbara (Ma'di) Language. Oxford University Press, London.
Crumrine, L.S. 1961. The Phonology of Arizona Yaqui (Anthropological Papers of the University of Arizona 5). University of Arizona, Tucson.
Cunningham, M.C. 1969. A Description of the Yugumbir Dialect of Bandjalang (University of Queensland Faculty of Arts Papers 1/8). University of Queensland Press, Brisbane.
Dahl, O.C. 1952. Etude de phonologie et de phonétique malagache. Norsk Tidsskrift for Sprogvidenskap 16: 148-200.
Dalby, D. 1966. Lexical analysis in Temne with an illustrative wordlist. Journal of West African Languages 3: 5-26.
Davis, D.R. 1969. The distinctive features of Wantoat phonemes. Linguistics 47: 5-17.
Davis, M.M. 1974. The dialects of the Roro language of Papua: a preliminary survey. Kivung 8: 3-22.
De Armond, R.C. 1975. Some rules of Brahui conjugation. In H.G. Schiffman and C.M. Eastman (eds.), Dravidian Phonological Systems. University of Washington Press, Seattle.
Decsy, G. 1966. Yurak Chrestomathy (Indiana University Publications, Uralic and Altaic Series 50). Indiana University, Bloomington.
Di Luzio, A. 1972. Preliminary description of the Amo language. Afrika und Ubersee 56: 3-60.
Dirks, S. 1953. Campa (Arawak) phonemes. International Journal of American Linguistics 19: 302-4.
Doerfer, G. 1971. Khalaj Materials (Indiana University Publications, Uralic and Altaic Series 115). Indiana University, Bloomington.
Doke, C.M. 1926. The phonetics of the Zulu language. Bantu Studies Special number.
Doke, C.M. 1961. Textbook of Zulu Grammar. Longmans, Cape Town.
Douglas, W.H. 1955. Phonology of the Australian aboriginal language spoken at Ooldea, South Australia, 1951-1952. Oceania 25: 216-29.
Douglas, W.H. 1964. An Introduction to the Western Desert Language (Oceania Linguistic Monographs 4, revised ed.). University of Sydney, Sydney.
Dow, F.D.M. 1972. An Outline of Mandarin Phonetics. Faculty of Asian Studies, Australian National University, Canberra.
Dul'zon, A.P. 1968. Ketskij Jazyk. Tomsk University, Tomsk.
Dutton, T.E. 1969. The Peopling of Central Papua (Pacific Linguistics, Series B, 9). Australian National University, Canberra.
Dyen, I. 1971. Malagasy. In T.A. Sebeok (ed.), Current Trends in Linguistics, Vol. 8, Linguistics in Oceania. Mouton, The Hague: 211-39.
Echeverria, M.S. and Contreras, H. 1965. Araucanian phonemics. International Journal of American Linguistics 31: 132-5.
Egerod, S. 1966. A statement on Atayal phonology. Artibus Asiae, Supplement 23: 120-30
Emeneau, M.B. 1937. Phonetic observations on the Brahui language. Bulletin of the School of Oriental Studies 8: 981-3.
Emeneau, M.B. 1944. Kota Texts, Vol. 1. University of California Press, Berkeley and Los Angeles.
Fast, P.W. 1953. Amuesha (Arawak) phonemes. International Journal of American Linguistics 19: 191-4.

Ferguson, C.A. and Chowdhury, M. 1960. The phonemes of Bengali. *Language* 36: 22-59.

Firchow, I. and Firchow, J. 1969. An abbreviated phoneme inventory. *Anthropological Linguistics* 11: 271-6.

Fleming, H.C. 1976. Kefa (Gonga) Languages. In M.L. Bender (ed.), *The Non-Semitic Languages of Ethiopia*. African Studies Center, Michigan State University, East Lansing: 351-76.

Foster, M.L. 1969. *The Tarascan Language*. University of California Press, Berkeley and Los Angeles.

Franklin, K. and Franklin, J. 1962. Kewa I: phonological asymmetry. *Anthropological Linguistics* 4/7: 29-37.

Frantz, C.I. and Frantz, M.E. 1966. Gadsup phoneme and toneme units. *Pacific Linguistics*, Series A, 7: 1-11.

Freeze, R.A. 1975. *A Fragment of an Early Kekchí Vocabulary* (University of Missouri Monographs in Anthropology 2). University of Missouri, Columbia.

Furne, R. 1963. Arabela phonemes and high-level phonology. *Studies in Peruvian Indian Languages 1*. Summer Institute of Linguistics, University of Oklahoma, Norman: 193-206.

Garbell, I. 1965. *The Jewish Neo-Aramaic Dialect of Peralan, Azerbaijan*. Mouton, The Hague.

Garvin, P.L. 1950. Wichita I: phonemics. *International Journal of American Linguistics* 16: 179-84.

Gedney, W.J. 1965. Yay, a Northern Tai language in North Vietnam. *Lingua* 14: 180-93.

Gedney, W.J. 1970. The Saek language of Nakhon Phanom province. *Journal of the Siam Society* 58: 67-87.

Gerdel, F. 1973. Paez phonemics. *Linguistics* 104: 28-48.

Gerzenstein, A. 1968. *Fonología de la lengua Gününa-küna* (Cuadernos de Linguistica Indigena 5). Centro de Estudios Linguisticos, University of Buenos Aires, Buenos Aires.

Gill, H.S. and Gleason, H.A. 1963. *A Reference Grammar of Panjabi*. Hartford Seminary Foundation, Hartford.

Glasgow, D. and Glasgow, K. 1967. The phonemes of Burera. *Papers in Australian Linguistics* 1 (Pacific Linguistics, Series A, 10): 1-14.

Golla, V.K. 1970. *Hupa Grammar*. Ph.D. Dissertation. University of California, Berkeley.

Gowda, K.S.G. 1972. *Ao-Naga Phonetic Reader*. Central Institute of Indian Languages, Mysore.

Gregersen, E.A. 1961. *Luo: A Grammar*. Ph. D. Dissertation. Yale University, New Haven.

Gregores, E. and Suarez, J.A. 1967. *A Description of Colloquial Guarani*. Mouton, The Hague.

Grubb, D.M. 1977. *A Practical Writing System and Short Dictionary of Kwakw'ala (Kwakiutl)*. National Museum of Man, Ottawa.

Gulya, J. 1966. *Eastern Ostyak Chrestomathy* (Indiana University Publications, Uralic and Altaic Series 51). Indiana University, Bloomington.

Gumperz, J.J. and Biligiri, H.S. 1957. Notes on the phonology of Mundari. *Indian Linguistics* 17: 6-15.

Haas, M.R. 1941. Tunica. *Handbook of American Indian Languages, Vol. 4*. Augustin, New York: 1-143.

Haeseriju, E.V. 1966. *Ensayo de la Gramática del K'ekchí*. Suquinay, Purulha.

Hajdú, P. 1963. *The Samoyed Peoples and Languages* (Indiana University Publications, Uralic and Altaic Series 14). Indiana University, Bloomington.

Hale, K. 1959. *A Papago Grammar*. Ph.D. Dissertation. Indiana University, Bloomington.
Hall, R.A. 1938. *An Analytical Grammar of the Hungarian Language* (Language Monograph 18). Linguistic Society of America, Philadelphia.
Hall, R.A. 1944. *Hungarian Grammar* (Language Monograph 21). Linguistic Society of America, Baltimore.
Halle, M. 1959. *The Sound Pattern of Russian*. Mouton, The Hague.
Hangin, J.G. 1968. *Basic Course in Mongolian* (Indiana University Publications, Uralic and Altaic Series 73). Indiana University, Bloomington.
(*Hanyu Fangyan Gaiyao*) 1960. [Outline of Chinese Dialects]. Wenzi Gaige Chubanshe, Beijing.
Hardman, M.J. 1966. *Jaqaru: Outline of Phonological and Morphological Structure*. Mouton, The Hague.
Harms, R.T. 1964. *Finnish Structural Sketch* (Indiana University Publications, Uralic and Altaic Series 42). Indiana University, Bloomington.
Harris, J.T. 1969. *Spanish Phonology*. MIT Press, Cambridge, Massachusetts.
Hashimoto, M.J. 1973. *The Hakka Dialect*. Cambridge University Press, Cambridge.
Hasselbrink, G. 1965. *Alternative Analyses of the Phonemic System in Central-South Lappish* (Indiana University Publications, Uralic and Altaic Series 49). Indiana University, Bloomington.
Haudricourt, A-G. 1967. La langue lakkia. *Bulletin de la Société de Linguistique de Paris* 62: 165-82.
Healey, A. 1964. *Telefol Phonology* (Pacific Linguistics, Series B, 3). Australian National University, Canberra.
Heine, B. 1975a. Tepes und Nyangi: zwei ostafrikanische Restsprachen. *Afrika und Ubersee* 58: 263-300.
Heine, B. 1975b. Ik - eine ostafrikanische Restsprache. *Afrika und Ubersee* 59: 31-56.
Henderson, E.J. 1965. *Tiddim Chin: A Descriptive Analysis of Two Texts*. Oxford University Press, London.
Herbert, R.J. and Poppe, N. 1963. *Kirghiz Manual* (Indiana University Publications, Uralic and Altaic Series 33). Indiana University, Bloomington.
Hercus, L.A. 1973. The prestopped nasal and lateral consonants in Arabana-Wanganura. *Anthropological Linguistics* 14: 293-305.
Hetzron, R. 1969. *The Verbal System of Southern Agaw*. University of California Press, Berkeley and Los Angeles.
Hodge, C.T. 1947. *An Outline of Hausa Grammar* (Language Dissertation 41). Linguistic Society of America, Baltimore.
Hodge, C.T. and Umaru, I. 1963. *Hausa Basic Course*. Foreign Service Institute, Washington D.C.
Hoff, B.J. 1968. *The Carib Language* (Verhandelingen van het Koninklijk Instituut voor Taal-, Land- en Volkenkunde 55). Nijhoff, The Hague.
Hoffmann, C. 1963. *A Grammar of the Margi Language*. Oxford University Press for International African Institute, London.
Hoftmann, H. 1971. *The Structure of the Lelemi Language*. Enzyklopädie, Leipzig.
Hohepa, P.W. 1967. *A Profile Generative Grammar of Maori* (IJAL Memoir 20, Indiana University Publications in Anthropology and Linguistics). Indiana University, Bloomington.
Hoijer, H. 1946. Tonkawa. In H. Hoijer (ed.), *Linguistic Structures of Native America*. Wenner-Gren Foundation, New York: 289-311.
Hoijer, H. 1949. *An Analytic Dictionary of the Tonkawa Language*. University of California Press, Berkeley and Los Angeles.

Hoijer, H. 1972. Tonkawa Texts. University of California Press, Berkeley and Los Angeles.
Holmer, N.M. 1949. Goajiro (Arawak) I: Phonology. International Journal of American Linguistics 14: 45-56.
Holzknecht, K.G. 1973. The phonemes of the Adzera language. Pacific Linguistics, Series A, 38: 1-11.
Horne, E.C. 1961. Beginning Javanese. Yale University Press, New Haven.
Horton, A.E. 1949. A grammar of Luvale. Witwatersrand University Press, Johannesburg.
Householder, F.W. 1965. Basic course in Azerbaijani (Indiana University Publications, Uralic and Altaic Series 45). Indiana University, Bloomington.
Householder, F.W., Kazazis, K. and Koutsoudas, A. 1964. Reference Grammar of Literary Dhimotiki (IJAL 30/2 Part II, Publications of the Indiana University Research Center in Anthropology, Folklore and Linguistics, 31). Indiana University, Bloomington.
Hudson, R.A. 1976. Beja. In M.L. Bender (ed.), The Non-Semitic Languages of Ethiopia. African Studies Center, Michigan State University, East Lansing: 97-132.
Huffman, F.E. 1970a. The Cambodian System of Writing and Beginning Reading. Yale University Press, New Haven.
Huffman, F.E. 1970b. Modern Spoken Cambodian. Yale University Press, New Haven.
Hughes, E.F. and Leeding, V.J. 1971. The phonemes of Nunggubuyu. Papers on the Languages of Australian Aboriginals (Australian Aboriginal Studies 38): 72-81.
Hunter, G.G. and Pike, E.V. 1969. The phonology and tone sandhi of Molinos Mixtec. Linguistics 47: 24-40.
Hurd, C. and Hurd, P. 1966. Nasioi Language Course. Department of Information and Extension Services, Port Moresby.
Hyman, L.M. 1973. Notes on the history of Southwestern Mande. Studies in African Linguistics 4: 183-96.
Jacob, J.M. 1968. Introduction to Cambodian. Oxford University Press, London.
Jacquot, A. 1962. Notes sur la phonologie du beembe (Congo). Journal of African Languages 1: 232-42.
Johnson, J.B. 1962. El Idioma Yaqui. Instituto Nacional de Antropología e Historia, Mexico.
Johnstone, T.M. 1975. The modern South Arabian languages. Afroasiatic Linguistics 1: 93-121.
Jones, D. and Ward, D. 1969. The Phonetics of Russian. Cambridge University Press, Cambridge.
Jones, R.B. 1961. Karen Linguistic Studies. University of California Press, Berkeley and Los Angeles.
Jorden, E.H. 1963. Beginning Japanese, Part I. Yale University Press, New Haven.
Kalman, B. 1972. Hungarian historical phonology. In L. Benko and S. Imre (eds.), The Hungarian Language. Mouton, The Hague.
Kaufman, T. 1971. Tzeltal Phonology and Morphology. University of California Press, Berkeley and Los Angeles.
Kelkar, A.R. 1968. Studies in Hindi-Urdu I: Introduction and Word Phonology. Postgraduate and Research Institute, Deccan College, Poona.
Kelkar, A.R. and Trisal, P.N. 1964. Kashmiri word phonology: a first sketch. Anthropological Linguistics 6/1: 13-22.
Keller, K.C. 1959. The phonemes of Chontal (Mayan). International Journal of American Linguistics 24: 44-53.

Kelley, G. 1963. Vowel phonemes and external vocalic sandhi in Telugu. Journal of the American Oriental Society 83: 67-73.
Kennedy, N.M. 1960. Problems of Americans in Mastering the Pronunciation of Egyptian Arabic. Center for Applied Linguistics, Washington, D.C.
Kensinger, K.M. 1963. The phonological hierarchy of Cashinahua. Studies in Peruvian Indian Languages 1. Summer Institute of Linguistics, University of Oklahoma, Norman: 207-17.
Key, M.R. 1968. Comparative Tacanan Phonology. Mouton, The Hague.
Khaidakov, S.M. 1966. Ocherki po Lakskoj Dialektologii. Nauka, Moscow.
Klagstad, H. 1958. The phonemic system of colloquial standard Bulgarian. Slavic and East European Journal 16: 42-54.
Kleinschmidt, S. 1851. Grammatik der Grönländischen Sprache. Reimer, Berlin.
Klingenheben, A. 1966. Deutsch-Amharischer Sprachführer. Harrassowitz, Wiesbaden.
Kondo, V. and Kondo, R. 1967. Guahibo phonemes. Phonemic Systems of Colombian Languages. Summer Institute of Linguistics, University of Oklahoma, Norman: 89-98.
Kooyers, O., Kooyers, M., and Bee, D. 1971. The phonemes of Washkuk (Kwoma). Te Reo 14: 36-41.
Kostić, D., Mitter, A., and Krishnamurti, B. 1977. A Short Outline of Telugu Phonetics. Indian Statistical Institute, Calcutta.
Kraft, C.H. and Kraft, M.G. 1973. Introductory Hausa. University of California Press, Berkeley.
Krejnovich, E.A. 1958. Jukagirskij jazyk. Academy of Sciences of the USSR, Moscow and Leningrad.
Krejnovich, E.A. 1968a. Ketskij jazyk. In V.V. Vinogradov (ed.), Jazyki Narodov SSSR, Vol. 5. Nauka, Leningrad and Moscow: 453-73.
Krejnovich, E.A. 1968b. Jukagirskij jazyk. In V.V. Vinogradov (ed.), Jazyki Narodov SSSR, Vol. 5. Nauka, Leningrad and Moscow: 435-52.
Krishnamurti, B. 1961. Telugu Verbal Bases. University of California Press, Berkeley and Los Angeles.
Kroeber, A.L. and Grace, G.W. 1960. The Sparkman Grammar of Luiseño. University of California Press, Berkeley and Los Angeles.
Krueger, J.R. 1961. Chuvash Manual (Indiana University Publications, Uralic and Altaic Series 7). Indiana University, Bloomington.
Krueger, J.R. 1962. Yakut Manual (Indiana University Publications, Uralic and Altaic Series 21). Indiana University, Bloomington.
Kuipers, A.H. 1960. Phoneme and Morpheme in Kabardian. Mouton, The Hague.
Kuipers, A.H. 1967. The Squamish Language. Mouton, The Hague.
Kumari, B.S. 1972. Malayalam Phonetic Reader. Central Institute of Indian Languages, Mysore.
Ladefoged, P. 1968. A Phonetic Study of West African Languages, 2nd ed. Cambridge University Press, Cambridge.
Ladefoged, P. and Traill, A. 1980. The phonetic inadequacy of phonological specifications of clicks. UCLA Working Papers in Phonetics 49: 1-27.
Langdon, M. 1970. A Grammar of Diegueño, Mesa Grande Dialect. University of California Press, Berkeley and Los Angeles.
Lastra, Y. 1968. Cochabamba Quechua Syntax. Mouton, The Hague.
Laycock, D.C. 1965. Three Upper Sepik phonologies. Oceanic Linguistics 4: 113-17.
Lees, R.B. 1961. The Phonology of Modern Standard Turkish. Indiana University, Bloomington.
Lehtinen, M. 1964. Basic Course in Finnish. Indiana University, Bloomington.
Leslau, W. 1938. Lexique Socotri. Klincksiek, Paris.

Leslau, W. 1968. Amharic Textbook. University of California Press, Berkeley.
Li, F-K. 1932. A list of Chipewyan stems. International Journal of American Linguistics 7: 122-51.
Li, F-K. 1933. Chipewyan consonants. Bulletin of the Institute of History and Philology, Academia Sinica Ts'ai Yuan P'ei Anniversary Volume, (Supplementary Volume 1): 429-67.
Li, F-K. 1946. Chipewyan. In H. Hoijer (ed.), Linguistic Structures of Native America. Wenner-Gren Foundation, New York: 394-423.
Li, F-K. 1948. The distribution of initials and tones in the Sui language. Language 24: 160-7.
Li, F-K. 1977. A Handbook of Comparative Tai. University of Hawaii Press, Honolulu.
Li, P.J-K. 1973. Rukai Structure (Special Publication 64). Institute of History and Philology, Academia Sinica, Taipei.
Liccardi, M. and Grimes, J. 1968. Itonama intonation and phonemes. Linguistics 38: 36-41.
Lindskoog, J.N. and Brend, J.M. 1962. Cayapa phonemics. Studies in Ecuadorian Indian Languages 1. Summer Institute of Linguistics, University of Oklahoma, Norman: 31-44.
Lisker, L. 1963. Introduction to Spoken Telugu. American Council of Learned Societies, New York.
Liu, L. 1964. Ching-p'o-yü Kai-k'uang. Chung Kuo Yu Wen 5: 407-17.
Loeweke, E. and May, J. 1964. The phonological hierarchy in Fasu. Anthropological Linguistics 7/5: 89-97.
Lukas, J. 1937. A Study of the Kanuri Language. Oxford University Press, London.
Lunt, H.G. 1973. Remarks on nasality: the case of Guarani. In S.R. Anderson (ed.), A Festschrift for Morris Halle. Holt, Rinehart and Winston, New York: 131-9.
Luvšanvandan, S. 1964. The Khalkha-Mongolian phonemic system. Acta Orientalia (Academiae Scientiarum Hungaricae) 17: 175-85.
Lydall, J. 1976. Hamer. In M.L. Bender (ed.), The Non-Semitic Languages of Ethiopia. African Studies Center, Michigan State University, East Lansing: 393-438.
Lytkin, V.I. 1966. Komi-Zyrjanskij jazyk. In V.V. Vinogradov (ed.), Jazyki Narodov SSSR, Vol.3. Nauka, Moscow and Leningrad: 281-99.
Malécot, A. 1963. Luiseño, a structural analysis I: Phonology. International Journal of American Linguistics 29: 89-95.
MacDonald, G.E. 1973. The Teberan Language Family. In K. Franklin (ed.), The Linguistic Situation in the Gulf District and Adjacent Areas, Papua New Guinea (Pacific Linguistics, Series C, 26): 113-48.
MacDonald, R.R. and Soenyono, D. 1967. Indonesian Reference Grammar. Georgetown University Press, Washington, D.C.
Martin, S.E. 1951. Korean Phonemics. Language 27: 519-33.
Martin, S.E. 1952. Morphophonemics of Standard Colloquial Japanese (Language Dissertation 47). Linguistic Society of America, Baltimore.
Martin, S.E. and Lee, Y-S.C. 1969. Beginning Korean. Yale University Press, New Haven.
Matisoff, J.A. 1973. The Grammar of Lahu. University of California Press, Berkeley and Los Angeles.
Mazaudon, M. 1973. Phonologie Tamang (Népal) (Collection "Tradition Orale" 4). SELAF, Paris.
McAlpin, D.W. 1975. The morphophonology of the Malayalam noun. In H.F. Schiffman and C. Easton (eds.), Dravidian Phonological Systems. University of Washington, Seattle: 206-23.

McElhanon, K.A. 1970. Selepet Phonology (Pacific Linguistics, Series B, 14). Australian National University, Canberra.
Metcalfe, C.D. 1971. A tentative statement of the Bardi aboriginal language. Papers on the Languages of Australian Aboriginals (Australian Aboriginal Studies 38): 82-92.
Mhac An Fhailigh, E. 1968. The Irish of Erris, Co. Mayo. Dublin Institute for Advanced Studies, Dublin.
Miller, W.R. 1966. Acoma Grammar and Texts. University of California Press, Berkeley and Los Angeles.
Mitchell, T.F. 1962. Colloquial Arabic. English Universities Press, London.
Montgomery, C. 1970. Problems in the development of an orthography for the Sebei language of Uganda. Journal of the Language Association of East Africa 1: 48-55.
Morgenstierne, G. 1945. Notes on Burushaski phonology. Norsk Tidsskrift for Sprogvidenskap 13: 61-95.
Moshinsky, J. 1974. A Grammar of Southeastern Pomo. University of California Press, Berkeley and Los Angeles.
Moulton, W.G. 1962. The Sounds of English and German. University of Chicago Press, Chicago.
Murkelinskij, G.B. 1967. Lakskij jazyk. In V.V. Vinogradov (ed.), Jazyki Narodov SSSR, Vol. 4. Nauka, Moscow and Leningrad: 489-507.
Naden, A.J. 1973. The Grammar of Bisa. Ph. D. Thesis. School of Oriental and African Studies, London University, London.
Najlis, E.L. 1966. Lengua Abipona I. Centro de Estudios Linguisticos, Universidad de Buenos Aires.
Navarro, T.T. 1961. Manual de Pronunciación Española, 10th ed. Consejo Superior de Investigaciones Cientificas, Madrid.
N'diaye, G. 1970. Structure du Dialecte Basque de Maya. Mouton, The Hague.
Newman, P. 1974. The Kanakuru Language. Cambridge University Press, Cambridge.
Newman, S. 1965. Zuni Grammar. University of New Mexico Press, Albuquerque.
Newmark, L. 1957. Structural Grammar of Albanian (IJAL 23/4 Part II, Indiana University Research Center in Anthropology, Folklore and Linguistics, Publication 4). Indiana University, Bloomington.
Noss, R.B. 1954. An Outline of Siamese Grammar. Ph. D. Dissertation. Yale University, New Haven.
Noss, R.B. 1964. Thai Reference Grammar. Foreign Service Institute, Washington, D.C.
Novikova, K.A. 1960. Ocherki Dialektov Evenskogo Jazyka: Ol'skij Govor 1. Academy of Sciences of the USSR, Moscow and Leningrad.
Oates, L.F. 1964. Distribution of phonemes and syllables in Gugu-Yalanji. Anthropological Linguistics 1: 23-6.
Oates, W. and Oates, L.F. 1964. Gugu-Yalanji and Wik-Munkan Language Studies (Occasional Papers in Aboriginal Studies 2). Australian Institute of Aboriginal Studies, Canberra.
Obolensky, S., Panah, K.Y., and Nouri, F.K. 1963. Persian Basic Course. Center for Applied Linguistics, Washington D.C.
O'Grady, G.N. 1964. Nyangumata Grammar (Oceania Linguistic Monographs 9). University of Sydney, Sydney.
O'Grady, G.N., Voegelin, C.F. and Voegelin, F.M. 1966. Phonological diversity. Languages of the World: Indo-Pacific Fascicle 6 (Anthropological Linguistics 8/2): 56-67.
Okell, J. 1969. A Reference Grammar of Colloquial Burmese. Oxford University Press, London.
Olmsted, D.L. 1964. A History of Palaihnihan Phonology. University of California Press, Berkeley and Los Angeles.

Olmsted, D.L. 1966. Achumawi Dictionary. University of California Press, Berkeley and Los Angeles.
Osborn, H. 1948. Amahuaca phonemes. International Journal of American Linguistics 14: 188-90.
Osborne, C.R. 1974. The Tiwi Language (Australian Aboriginal Studies 55). Australian Institute for Aboriginal Studies, Canberra.
Ott, W. and Ott, R. 1967. Phonemes of the Ignaciano language. Linguistics 35: 56-60.
Ozanne-Rivierre, F. 1976. Le Iaai, SELAF, Paris.
Palmer, F.R. 1962. The Morphology of the Tigre Noun. Oxford University Press, London.
Panfilov, V.Z. 1962. Grammatika Nivkhskogo Jazyka, I. Akademia Nauk, Moscow and Leningrad.
Panfilov, V.Z. 1968. Nivhskij jazyk. In V.V. Vinogradov (ed.), Jazyki Narodov SSSR, Vol. 5. Nauka, Moscow and Leningrad: 408-34.
Paulian, C. 1975. Le Kukya, Langue Teke du Congo (Bibliothèque de la SELAF 49-50). SELAF, Paris.
Peasgood, E.T. 1972. Carib phonology. In J.E. Grimes (ed.), Languages of the Guianas. Summer Institute of Linguistics, University of Oklahoma, Norman: 35-41.
Pence, A. 1966. Kunimaipa phonology: hierarchical levels. Pacific Linguistics, Series A, 7: 49-97.
Pfeiffer, M. 1972. Elements of Kurux Historical Phonology. E.J. Brill, Leiden.
Philipp, M. 1974. Phonologie des Deutschen. Kohlhammer, Stuttgart.
Pike, K.L. and Pike, E.V. 1947. Immediate constituents of Mazateco syllables. International Journal of American Linguistics 13: 78-91.
Pinnow, H-J. 1959. Versuch einer Historischen Lautlehre der Kharia-Sprache. Harrassowitz, Wiesbaden.
Pinnow, H-J. 1964. Bemerkungen zur Phonetik und Phonemik des Kurukh. Indo-Iranian Journal 8: 32-59.
Polomé, E.C. 1967. Swahili Language Handbook. Center for Applied Linguistics, Washington, D.C.
Poppe, N. 1964. Bashkir Manual (Indiana University Publications, Uralic and Altaic Series 36). Indiana University, Bloomington.
Powell, J.V. 1975. Proto-Chimakuan: Materials for a Reconstruction. Working Papers in Linguistics, University of Hawaii 7/2.
Prasse, K-G. 1972. Manuel de Grammaire Touarègue. Akademisk Forlag, Copenhagen.
Price, P.D. 1976. Southern Nambiquara phonology. International Journal of American Linguistics 42: 338-48.
Pride, K. 1965. Chatino Syntax. Summer Institute of Linguistics, University of Oklahoma, Norman.
Priest, P. 1968. Phonemes of the Siriono Language. Linguistics 41: 102-8.
Prost, A. 1956. La Langue Songay et ses Dialectes (Mémoires de l'Institut francais d'Afrique Noire 47). IFAN, Dakar.
Prost, G.R. 1967. Phonemes of the Chacobo language. Linguistics 35: 61-5.
Pukui, M.K. and Elbert, S.H. 1965. Hawaiian-English Dictionary, 6th ed. University of Hawaii Press, Honolulu.
Purnell, H.C. 1965. Phonology of a Yao Dialect. Hartford Seminary Foundation, Hartford.
Rabel, L. 1961. Khasi, a Language of Assam. Louisiana State University Press, Baton Rouge.
Radcliffe-Brown, A. 1914. Notes on the languages of the Andaman Islands. Anthropos 9: 36-52.
Rand, E. 1968. The structural phonology of Alabaman, a Muskogean language. International Journal of American Linguistics 34: 94-103.

Ray, P.S. 1967. Dafla phonology and morphology. Anthropological Linguistics 9: 9-14.
Renck, G.L. 1967. A tentative statement of the phonemes of Yagaria. Papers in New Guinea Linguistics 6 (Pacific Linguistics, Series A, 12): 19-48.
Renck, G.L. 1975. A Grammar of Yagaria (Pacific Linguistics, Series B, 40). Australian National University, Canberra.
Rischel, J. 1974. Topics in West Greenlandic Phonology. Akademisk Forlag, Copenhagen.
Ristinen, E.K. 1960. An East Cheremis Phonology (Indiana University Publications, Uralic and Altaic Series 1). Indiana University, Bloomington.
Ristinen, E.K. 1965. On the phonemes of Nenets. Ural-Altaische Jahrbücher 36: 154-64.
Ristinen, E.K. 1968. Problems concerning vowel length in Nenets. Ural-Altaische Jahrbücher 40: 22-44.
Robins, R.H. 1953. The phonology of the nasalized verbal forms in Sundanese. Bulletin of the School of Oriental and African Studies 15: 138-45.
Robins, R.H. and Waterson, N. 1952. Notes on the phonetics of the Georgian word. Bulletin of the School of Oriental and African Studies 15: 55-72.
Robinson, J.O.S. 1974. His and hers morphology: the strange case of the Tarok possessives. Studies in African Linguistics Supplement 6: 201-9.
Rood, D. 1975. The implications of Wichita phonology. Language 51: 315-37.
Ruhlen, M. 1973. Rumanian Phonology. Ph. D. Dissertation. Stanford University, Palo Alto.
Saint, R. and Pike, K.L. 1962. Auca phonemics. In B. Elson (ed.), Studies in Ecuadorian Indian Languages 1. Summer Institute of Linguistics, University of Oklahoma, Norman: 2-30.
Samarin, W.J. 1966. The Gbeya Language. University of California Press, Berkeley and Los Angeles.
Santandrea, S. 1970. Brief Grammar Outlines of the Yulu and Kara Languages (Museum Combonianum 25). Nigrizia, Bologna.
Sapir, E. 1923. The phonetics of Haida. International Journal of American Linguistics 3-4: 143-58.
Sapir, E. and Hoijer, H. 1967. The phonology and morphology of the Navaho language. University of California Press, Berkeley and Los Angeles.
Sapir, E. and Swadesh, M. 1939. Nootka Texts. Linguistic Society of America, Philadelphia.
Sapir, E. and Swadesh, M. 1955. Native accounts of Nootka ethnography (IJAL 21/4 Part II, Indiana University Publications in Anthropology, Folklore and Linguistics). Indiana University, Bloomington.
Sapir, E. and Swadesh, M. 1960. Yana Dictionary. University of California Press, Berkeley and Los Angeles.
Sapir, J.D. 1965. A Grammar of Diola-Fogny. Cambridge University Press, Cambridge.
Saporta, S. and Contreras, H. 1962. A Phonological Grammar of Spanish. University of Washington Press, Seattle.
Sastry, J.V. 1972. Telugu Phonetic Reader. Central Institute of Indian Languages, Mysore.
Sat, S.C. 1966. Tuvinskij jazyk. In V.V. Vinogradov (ed.), Jazyki Narodov SSSR, Vol 2. Nauka, Moscow and Leningrad: 387-402.
Sauvageot, S. 1965. Description Synchronique d'un Dialecte Wolof: le Parler du Dyolof (Mémoires de l'Institut Fondamental d'Afrique Noire 73). IFAN, Dakar.
Sawyer, J.O. 1965. English-Wappo Vocabulary. University of California Press, Berkeley and Los Angeles.

Saxton, D. 1963. Papago phonemes. International Journal of American Linguistics 29: 29-35.
Sayers, B. and Godfrey, M. 1964. Outline Description of the Alphabet and Grammar of a Dialect of Wik-Munkan, Spoken at Coen, North Queensland (Occasional Papers in Aboriginal Studies 2). Australian Institute of Aboriginal Studies, Canberra.
Schachter, P. and Fromkin, V.A. 1968. A Phonology of Akan:Akuapem,Asante, Fante (UCLA Working Papers in Phonetics 9). Phonetics Laboratory, University of California, Los Angeles.
Schachter, P. and Otanes, F.T. 1972. Tagalog Reference Grammar. University of California Press, Berkeley and Los Angeles.
Schoenhals, A. and Schoenhals, L.C. 1965. Vocabulario Mixe de Totontepec. Summer Institute of Linguistics, Mexico.
Schuh, R. 1972. Aspects of Ngizim Syntax. Ph. D. Dissertation. University of California, Los Angeles.
Seiden, W. 1960. Chamorro phonemes. Anthropological Linguistics 2/4: 6-33.
Senn, A. 1966. Handbuch der Litauischen Sprache, Band 1:Grammatik. Winter, Heidelberg.
Shafeev, D.A. 1964. A Short Grammatical Outline of Pashto (translated and edited by H.H. Paper). Indiana University, Bloomington.
Sharpe, M. 1972. Alawa Phonology and Grammar (Australian Aboriginal Studies 37). Australian Institute of Aboriginal Studies, Canberra.
Sheldon, S.N. 1974. Some morphophonemic and tone perturbation rules in Mura-Piraha'. International Journal of American Linguistics 40: 279-82.
Shipley, W.F. 1956. The phonemes of Northeastern Maidu. International Journal of American Linguistics 22: 233-7.
Shipley, W.F. 1964. Maidu Grammar. University of California Press, Berkeley and Los Angeles.
Silver, S. 1964. Shasta and Karok: a binary comparison. In W. Bright (ed.), Studies in California Linguistics. University of California Press, Berkeley and Los Angeles: 170-81.
Simeon, G. 1969. Hokkaido Ainu phonemics. Journal of the American Oriental Society 89: 751-7.
Skorik, P.I. 1961. Grammatika Chukotskogo Jazyka, 1. Akademia Nauk, Moscow and Leningrad.
Skorik, P.I. 1968. Chukotskij jazyk. In V.V. Vinogradov (ed.), Jazyki Narodov SSSR, Vol. 5. Nauka, Moscow and Leningrad: 248-70.
Smith, K.D. 1968. Laryngealization and de-laryngealization in Sedang phonemics. Linguistics 38: 52-69.
Snyder, W. 1968. Southern Puget Sound Salish: phonology and morphology. Sacramento Anthropology Society Papers 8: 2-22.
Snyman, J.W. 1969. An Introduction to the !Xũ Language. Balkema, Cape Town.
Snyman, J.W. 1975. Zu|'hõasi Fonologie en Woordeboek. Balkema, Cape Town.
Sommer, B.A. 1969. Kunjen Phonology: Synchronic and Diachronic (Pacific Linguistics, Series B, 11). Australian National University, Canberra.
Sommerfelt, A. 1964. Consonant clusters or single phonemes in Northern Irish? In D. Abercrombie, et al. (eds.), In Memory of Daniel Jones. Longmans, London: 368-73.
Spotts, H. 1953. Vowel harmony and consonant sequences in Mazahua (Otomi). International Journal of American Linguistics 19: 253-8.
Stahlke, H. 1971. Topics in Ewe phonology. Ph. D. Dissertation. University of California, Los Angeles.
Stell, N.N. 1972. Fonología de la lengua axɨuxɨaj (Cuadernos de Linguistica Indigena 8). Centro de Estudios Linguisticos, University of Buenos Aires, Buenos Aires.
Sten, H. 1963. Manuel de Phonétique Française. Munksgaard, Copenhagen.

Stevenson, R.C. 1957. A survey of the phonetics and grammatical structure of the Nuba mountain languages IV. Afrika und Ubersee 61: 27-65.
Stewart, J.M. 1967. Tongue root position in Akan vowel harmony. Phonetica 16: 185-204.
Stolte, J. and Stolte, N. 1971. A description of Northern Barasano phonology. Linguistics 75: 86-92.
Story, G.L. and Naish, C.M. 1973. Tlingit Verb Dictionary. Alaska Native Language Center, University of Alaska, Fairbanks.
Street, J.C. 1963. Khalkha Structure (Indiana University Publications, Uralic and Altaic Series 24). Indiana University, Bloomington.
Summer, C. 1957. Etude Expérimentale de L'Amharique Moderne. University College Press, Addis Ababa.
Swanton, J.R. 1909. Tlingit Myths and Texts (Bureau of American Ethnology Bulletin 39). Smithsonian Institution, Washington, D.C.
Swanton, J.R. 1911. Tlingit. In F. Boas (ed.), Handbook of American Indian Languages, Part 1 (Bureau of American Ethnology Bulletin 40). Smithsonian Institution, Washington, D.C.: 425-559.
Swift, L.B. 1963. A Reference Grammar of Modern Turkish (Indiana University Publications, Uralic and Altaic Series 19). Indiana University, Bloomington.
Swift, L.B., Ahaghota, A., and Ugorji, E. 1962. Igbo Basic Course. Foreign Service Institute, Washington, D.C.
Taylor, D. 1955. The phonemes of the Hopkins dialect of Island Carib. International Journal of American Linguistics 21: 233-41.
Teeter, K.V. 1964. The Wiyot Language. University of California Press, Berkeley and Los Angeles.
Tereščenko, N.M. 1966. Nganasanskij jazyk. In V.V. Vinogradov (ed.), Jazyki Narodov SSSR, Vol. 3. Nauka, Moscow and Leningrad: 438-57.
Ternes, E. 1970. Grammaire Structurale du Breton de l'Île de Groix. Winter, Heidelberg.
Thalbitzer, W. 1904. A Phonetical Study of the Eskimo Language (Meddelelser om grønland 31). Copenhagen.
Thayer, L.J. 1969. A Reconstructed History of the Chari Languages: Comparative Bonbo-Bagirmi-Sara Segmental Phonology with Evidence from Arabic Loanwords. Ph. D. Dissertation. University of Illinois, Urbana.
Thayer, L.J. and Thayer, J.E. 1971. Fifty Lessons in Sara-Ngambay. University of Indiana, Bloomington.
Thompson, E.D. 1976. Nera. In M.L. Bender (ed.), The Non-Semitic Languages of Ethiopia. African Studies Center, Michigan State University, East Lansing: 484-94.
Thompson, L.C. 1965. A Vietnamese Grammar. University of Washington Press, Seattle.
Thurman, R.C. 1970. Chuave phonemic statement. Ms.
Tomiche, N. 1964. Le Parler Arabe du Caire. Mouton, Paris and The Hague.
Topping, D.M. 1969. Spoken Chamorro. University of Hawaii Press, Honolulu.
Topping, D.M. 1973. Chamorro Reference Grammar. University of Hawaii Press, Honolulu.
Tracy, F.V. 1972. Wapishana phonology. In J.E. Grimes (ed.), Languages of the Guianas. Summer Institute of Linguistics, University of Oklahoma, Norman: 78-84.
Trager, F.H. 1971. The phonology of Picuris. International Journal of American Linguistics 37: 29-33.
Trefry, D. 1972. Phonological Considerations of Pawaian (Oceania Linguistic Monographs 15). University of Sydney, Sydney.
Triulzi, A., Dafallah, A.A., and Bender, M.L. 1976. Berta. In M.L. Bender (ed.), The Non-Semitic Languages of Ethiopia. African Studies Center, Michigan State University, East Lansing: 513-32.

Tryon, D.T. 1968. Iai Grammar (Pacific Linguistics, Series B, 8). Australian National University, Canberra.
Tryon, D.T. 1970. An Introduction to Maranungku (Northern Australia) (Pacific Linguistics, Series B, 15). Australian National University, Canberra.
Tryon, D.T. 1974. Daly Family Languages (Pacific Linguistics, Series C, 32). Australian National University, Canberra.
Tschenkeli, K. 1958. Einführung in die Georgische Sprache I. Amirani, Zurich.
Tucker, A.N. and Bryan, M.A. 1966. Linguistic Analyses: the Non-Bantu Languages of North-Eastern Africa. Oxford University Press for International African Institute, London.
Tucker, A.N. and Hackett, P.E. 1959. Le Groupe Linguistique Zande (Annales du Musée Royal de l'Afrique Centrale, Série in 8, Sciences Humaines, 22). Musée Royale de l'Afrique Centrale, Tervuren.
Tucker, A.N. and Mpaayei, J.T.O. 1955. A Maasai Grammar (Publications of the African Institute, Leyden, 2). Longmans, London.
Tung, T-H. 1964. A Descriptive Study of the Tsou Language, Formosa (Special Publication 48). Institute of History and Philology, Academia Sinica, Taipei.
Turton, D. and Bender, M.L. 1976. Mursi. In M.L. Bender (ed.), The Non-Semitic Languages of Ethiopia. African Studies Center, Michigan State University, East Lansing: 533-62.
Uldall, E. 1956. Guarani sound system. International Journal of American Linguistics 20: 341-2.
Van Der Stap, P.A.M. 1966. Outline of Dani Morphology (Verhandelingen van het Koninklijk Instituut voor Taal-, Land- en Volkenkunde 48). Nijhoff, The Hague.
Van Der Tuuk, H.N. 1971. A Grammar of Toba Batak. Nijhoff, The Hague.
Van Syoc, W.B. 1959. The Phonology and Morphology of the Sundanese Language. Ph. D. Dissertation. University of Michigan, Ann Arbor.
Vanvik, A. 1972. A phonetic-phonemic analysis of Standard Eastern Norwegian. Norwegian Journal of Linguistics 26: 119-64.
Van Wynen, D. and Van Wynen, M.G. 1962. Fonemas Tacana y Modelos de Acentuación (Notas Lingüísticas de Bolivia 6). Summer Institute of Linguistics, Cochabamba.
Velayudhan, S. 1971. Vowel Duration in Malayalam. The Dravidian Linguistic Association of India, Trivandrum.
Verguin, J. 1967. Le Malais: Essai d'Analyse Fonctionelle et Structurale . Mouton, Paris and The Hague.
Vermeer, H.J. and Sharma, A. 1966. Hindi-Lautlehre. Groos, Heidelberg.
Voegelin, C.F. 1946. Delaware: an Eastern Algonquian language. In H. Hoijer (ed.), Linguistic Structures of Native America. Wenner-Gren Foundation, New York, 130-57.
Voegelin, C.F. 1956. Phonemicizing for dialect study with reference to Hopi. Language 32: 116-35.
Voegelin, C.F. and Voegelin, F.M. 1966. [Andamanese]. Languages of the World: Indo-Pacific Fascicle 8 (Anthropological Linguistics 8/4): 10-13.
Vogt, H. 1938. Esquisse d'une grammaire du georgien moderne. Norsk Tidsskrift for Sprogvidenskap 9: 5-114.
Vogt, H. 1958. Structure phonémique du georgien. Norsk Tidsskrift for Sprogvidenskap 18: 5-90.
Voorhoeve, C.L. 1965. The Flamingo Bay Dialect of the Asmat Language. Smits, The Hague.
Voorhoeve, C.L. 1971. Miscellaneous notes on languages in West Irian, New Guinea. Papers in New Guinea Linguistics 14 (Pacific Linguistics, Series A, 28): 47-114.

Walton, J. and Walton, J. 1967. Phonemes of Muinane. Phonemic Systems of Colombian Languages. Summer Institute of Linguistics, University of Oklahoma, Norman: 37-47.
Weimer, H. and Weimer, N. 1972. Yareba phonemes. Te Reo 15: 52-7.
Welmers, W.E. 1946. A Descriptive Grammar of Fanti (Language Dissertation 39). Linguistic Society of America, Philadelphia.
Welmers, W.E. 1950. Notes on two languages of the Senufo group, I: Senadi. Language 26: 126-46.
Welmers, W.E. 1952. Notes on the structure of Bariba. Language 28: 82-103.
Welmers, W.E. 1962. The phonology of Kpelle. Journal of African Languages 1: 69-93.
West, B. and Welch, B. 1967. Phonemic system of Tucano. Phonemic systems of Colombian Languages. Summer Institute of Linguistics, University of Oklahoma, Norman: 11-24.
Wheeler, A. and Wheeler, M. 1962. Siona phonemics. Studies in Ecuadorian Indian Languages 1. Summer Institute of Linguistics, University of Oklahoma, Norman: 96-111.
Whiteley, W.H. 1958. A Short Description of Item Categories in Iraqw. East African Institute of Social Research, Kampala.
Whorf, B.L. 1946. The Hopi language, Toreva dialect. In H. Hoijer (ed.), Linguistic Structures of Native America. Wenner-Gren Foundation, New York: 158-83.
Wiering, E. 1974. The indicative verb in Doowa̰a̰yaayo. Linguistics 124: 33-56.
Williamson, K. 1967. Songhai Word List (Gao Dialect). Research Notes, Department of Linguistics and Nigerian Languages, University of Ibadan, 3: 1-34.
Williamson, K. 1969. Igbo. In E. Dunstan (ed.), Twelve Nigerian Languages Longmans, London, 85-96.
Wilson, D. 1969. Suena phonology. Papers in New Guinea Linguistics 9 (Pacific Linguistics, Series A, 18): 87-93.
Wilson, W.A.A. 1961. An Outline of the Temne Language. School of Oriental and African Studies, University of London, London.
Wilson, W.A.A. and Bendor-Samuel, J.T. 1969. The phonology of the nominal in Dagbani. Linguistics 52: 56-82.
Wolff, H. 1959. Subsystem typologies and area linguistics. Anthropological Linguistics 1/7: 1-88.
Wonderly, W.L. 1951. Zoque II: phonemes and morphophonemes. International Journal of American Linguistics 17: 105-23.
Woodward, M.F. 1964. Hupa phonemics. In W. Bright (ed.), Studies in California Linguistics. University of California Press, Berkeley and Los Angeles: 199-216.
Wurm, S. 1972a. Languages of Australia and Tasmania. Mouton, The Hague.
Wurm, S. 1972b. Notes on the indication of possession with nouns in Reef and Santa Cruz Islands languages. Papers in Linguistics of Melanesia 3 (Pacific Linguistics, Series A, 35): 85-113.
Zhirkov, L.I. 1955. Lakskij jazyk: fonetika i morfologija. Akademia Nauk, Moscow.

Appendix B: Phoneme charts and segment index for UPSID languages

The following pages contain charts showing the phoneme inventory of each of the carefully selected sample of 317 languages which comprise the UCLA Phonological Segment Inventory Database (UPSID). It also includes an index of each segment type which occurs in the database. This index is arranged according to the phonetic classification of the segments, and includes the number of languages with each given segment type and a list of the languages in which it occurs.

The phoneme charts and segment index make available to other users the basic data of UPSID. With these tools, much of the information in the database can be manipulated without the use of a computer. For example, the question "Does /g/ only occur in languages with /k/?" can be answered for the UPSID sample by using the index to find the list of languages with /g/ and then turning to each relevant chart to see if /k/ occurs, or cross-checking with the list of languages with /k/ in the index. More complex co-occurrences of segments can be examined more easily by a study of the charts.

Publishing the data in this form serves another purpose, that of making the interpretations of the phoneme inventories adopted in UPSID open to independent evaluation. Scholars may reach their own conclusions on the appropriateness of the inventory as it is represented in UPSID.

The charts

Consonants

The consonants of each language are represented by phonetic symbols located on a chart which is fully labeled for each place of articulation, secondary articulation, and manner of articulation which occurs in that language. Places of articulation are arranged along the top of the chart in a sequence from the front to the back of the oral cavity. These places correspond to those recognized in the list of variables used in the UPSID database (Chapter 10). The last place of articulation in this sequence is glottal. Note that /h/ is not considered to have a glottal place of articulation, but to have a variable place. It is placed after glottal. In addition to dental and alveolar places, an unspecified dental or alveolar column is included for those segments which are not precisely identified as being one or the other in the source used for the description of a given language. This column is labeled dental/alveolar.

Double articulations are listed after variable place in a front-to-back sequence determined by the more forward of the two articulations concerned. Secondary articulations are placed in the columns following the primary place. Nasalization, including pre- and post-nasalization, is considered a secondary articulation. It is listed first among them. Other secondary articulations follow in a sequence from the front to the back of the oral cavity, i.e. labialization is first, pharyngealization is last.

Manners of articulation are arranged down the chart in a sequence in which the primary arrangement is by decreasing degrees of stricture, with stops first and approximants last. Stops are followed by affricates, fricatives, nasals, taps, trills, and flaps, then approximants. Within stops, plosives precede ejective stops and implosives. The Khoisan languages Nama and !Xũ required special handling because of their large inventories of clicks. The clicks are placed on a separate chart. Sibilant affricates and fricatives follow nonsibilant ones, and lateral affricates and fricatives follow both. Lateral approximants precede central ones. A special category for segments which are simply identified as some kind of r-sound follows taps, trills and flaps.

Differences in phonation type are nested within this sequence in a way similar to the way that secondary articulations are nested within the sequence of primary places. However, the sequence of phonation types varies for different classes of consonants. For plosives, affricates and fricatives - which are more commonly voiceless - voiceless types are listed first. For nasals, trills, flaps and approximants - which are more commonly voiced - voiced types are listed first. More unusual phonation types follow the plain voiceless or voiced types, so that voiceless aspirated or laryngealized (glottalized) voiceless categories follow the plain voiceless, and breathy (murmured) or laryngealized voiced types follow the plain voiced. Ejective affricates or fricatives follow their pulmonic central or lateral counterparts.

Each phonemic consonant segment in the language is represented by a symbol placed at the intersection of the row and column defining its place and manner. The symbols used are orthodox I.P.A. symbols as far as possible. However, I.P.A. conventions have been supplemented in some cases, drawing on conventions used in Preliminaries to Linguistic Phonetics (P. Ladefoged, University of Chicago Press, 1971) and elsewhere in phonetic literature, or newly invented for the purpose. The result is a transcription system in which each symbol, meaning any distinct letter or combination of letter(s) and diacritic(s), uniquely represents one segment type. That is to say, each symbol corresponds to one and only one combination of values for the phonetic variables in the UPSID data file. In particular, it may be noted that unspecified dental/alveolar segments are distinguished from alveolar segments in transcription by the use of quote marks, e.g. /"t"/ vs. /t/. An r-sound of unspecified manner is represented by a doubled letter r; thus /rr/ represents an unspecified type of r-sound with alveolar place of articulation, and /"rr"/ represents an unspecified r-sound of undetermined dental or alveolar place of articulation.

Vowels

The vowels of each language are given below the consonant chart. The vowel charts are not fully labeled. Instead, the choice of symbols is left to provide more of the information on the nature of the vowels in question. However, labels are provided for those levels of the familiar dimension of vowel height that are represented in the given language, and the symbols are arranged in a left to right order which corresponds to a front-to-back dimension. The layout approximates a conventional vowel chart of triangular shape. Lip position is indicated entirely by choice of symbol. Where rounded and unrounded vowels occur with the same height and front/back positions the front unrounded vowel precedes the front rounded vowel and the back rounded vowel precedes the back unrounded vowel. The pair of symbols is separated by a comma. In many languages there are several separate series of vowels (short vs. long, oral vs. nasalized, etc.). These are given in separate arrangements, with the "plainest" series first.

Transcriptions for vowels are also based on I.P.A. conventions, apart from a few necessary additional distinctions. Overshort vowels are indicated with a superscript micron. Mid vowels which are not further distinguished as higher mid (half-close) or lower mid (half-open) are represented by letters enclosed in quote marks. The same letters without the quotes represent higher mid vowels. Thus /e/ is a higher mid front unrounded voiced vowel, /"e"/ is a similar vowel which is only described as mid (it might be in the middle of the mid range, or vary in quality within the mid range, or it might just be incompletely described). Since the vowels are not fully labeled on the charts a key to the vowel symbols and the diacritics which may be applied to them is given on page 204.

If a language has any diphthongs which are accepted as unit phonemes by the criteria used by UPSID, they are given to the right of the simple vowels. No attempt is made to label the diphthongs; they are simply represented by digraphs indicating approximate starting and ending points.

Segment index

Anomalous segments

Those segments in the inventory of a given language that are regarded as somewhat anomalous (though still worthy of being included in the inventory) are indicated by superscript numbers on the charts. These correspond to the non-zero values of the "anomaly" variable in the UPSID data file which are defined in Chapter 10.

Abbreviations of phonetic terms used on the charts

Some of the phonetic labels have had to be abbreviated to save space on the charts. Below is a listing of all the abbreviations used. Many are self-evident, but in the event that an abbreviation is unclear, its expansion can be found here.

Abbreviation	Expansion
affric, aff., af.	affricate
alv.	alveolar
approx., appr., app.	approximant
asp.	aspirated
cent., c.	central
cl., c.	click
eject.	ejective
fric.	fricative
labial-vel.	labial-velar
laryngd., laryng.	laryngealized
lat.	lateral
nas.	nasal
nonsib.	nonsibilant
palato-alv.	palato-alveolar
plos.	plosive
preasp.	preaspirated
rel.	release
sib.	sibilant
var.	variable
vel.	velar
vl.	voiceless
vd.	voiced
w.	with

The index

The index to segment types is divided into 10 major sections:

1. plosives
2. glottalic stops
3. clicks (including affricated clicks)
4. affricates (including ejective affricates)
5. fricatives (including ejective fricatives)
6. nasals
7. trills, taps, and flaps
8. approximants
9. vowels
10. diphthongs.

These sections separate segments into major manner classes. Within these sections, the sequence of segments is ordered in a way that is similar to the way the charts are arranged, except that, since the index is a list rather than a two-dimensional array, the values for manner and place features are nested into a single sequence. Within each section, place is given priority over manner with the following exceptions:

(a) ejectives precede implosives in section 2.

(b) affricated clicks follow plain clicks in section 3.

(c) ejective affricates and fricatives follow all the pulmonic types in sections 4 and 5.
(d) in section 7, trills precede taps, which precede flaps. Unspecified r-sounds are included at the end of this section.
(e) lateral segments are grouped together in the relevant sections, following segments with central articulation in sections 3, 4, 5 and 7, but preceding central segments in section 8. This arrangement juxtaposes the common types of flapped and approximant laterals in sections 7 and 8. Note that the arrangements specified in (b), (c), and (d) above take precedence over (e).

Voiceless segments of a given place are listed before voiced ones in sections 1, 2, 3, 4, and 5. Voiced ones precede voiceless ones of the same place in sections 6, 7, 8, 9, and 10. Other modifications of the phonation type are next most highly ranked, while secondary articulations (of place) are the most superficial criterion for sequencing. Thus, a voiceless aspirated alveolar plosive will precede any voiced alveolar plosives, and a palatalized voiceless aspirated alveolar plosive follows one with no secondary articulation but precedes a velarized one.

Vowels are arranged in three main classes: all front vowels are listed before all central vowels, which in turn precede all back vowels. Within each height/backness class (e.g. high front or lower mid back), unrounded vowels precede rounded vowels. This arrangement applies even for back vowels, where rounding is more common. Other modifications (such as nasalization, pharyngealization) form the most superficial level of vowel classification.

Diphthongs are arranged in the following way. First, the quality of the vowel recognized as their point of origin is used to arrange them in a similar way to that in which the simple vowels are arranged. Diphthongs starting with a high front unrounded vowel come first and so on. Those with the same starting point are then arranged on the basis of the vowel quality recognized for their ending point. The manner in which this is done can be understood by imagining an array of lines on the conventional vowel chart from the point of origin to the point of termination. The diphthongs are then sequenced in an "anticlockwise" manner with the closest to 12:00 o'clock as the starting point. Note that the transcriptional distinction between mid vowels (/"e"/, /"o"/ etc.) and higher mid vowels (/e/, /o/ etc.) is not maintained for diphthongs. No quote marks are used here.

Following each phonetic definition, a list of those languages in UPSID in which the defined segment occurs is given. The listing of language names is in the order in which identification numbers were assigned, which corresponds with a few exceptions to the order in which languages appear in the genetic listing given in Appendix A. If a segment is regarded as anomalous in a language, the language is listed at the end of the entry for the segment following a short keyword which describes the nature of the anomaly. The following are the keywords used in the index to correspond to the non-zero values of the "anomaly" variable in the UPSID data file.

Value of anomaly	Index keyword	Brief definition
1	RARE	Extremely low lexical frequency
2	LOAN	Occurs in unassimilated loans
3	?ABSTRACT	Posited underlying segment
4	?DERIVED	Segment possibly derivable from others
5	OBSCURE	Particularly vague or contradictory description.

Segment index

Vowel symbols and diacritics used on phoneme charts

	Front	Central	Back
High	i, y	ɨ, ʉ	u, ɯ
Lowered high	ɪ, Y	ɨ̞, ʉ̞	ʊ, ɯ̞
Higher mid	e, ø	ə, ɵ	o, ɤ
Mid	"e", "ø"	"ə", "ɵ"	"o", "ɤ"
Lower mid	ɛ, œ	ɜ,	ɔ, ʌ
Raised low	æ,	ɐ,	ɒ̝, ɑ̝
Low	a̟,	a,	ɒ, ɑ

Diacritics (exemplified with the vowel /a/):

/a:/	long
/ă/	overshort
/a̰/	laryngealized
/a̤/	breathy voiced
/ḁ/	voiceless
/ã/	nasalized
/aʳ/	retroflexed
/aˠ/	with velar stricture
/a̟/	fronted
/a̠/	retracted
/a̞/	lowered
/a̝/	raised
/aˤ/	pharyngealized

SEGMENT INDEX

1. PLOSIVES

Voiceless bilabial plosive /p/ 263 (-9)
Greek, German, Lithuanian, Russian, French, Spanish, Romanian, Pashto, Kurdish, Hindi-Urdu, Bengali, Kashmiri, Punjabi, Sinhalese, Albanian, E. Armenian, Ostyak, Cheremis, Komi, Finnish, Hungarian, Lappish, Yurak, Tavgy, Azerbaijani, Chuvash, Kirghiz, Bashkir, Khalaj, Tuva, Goldi, Korean, Japanese, Moro, Kadugli, Kpelle, Bisa, Bambara, Dan, Wolof, Diola, Temne, Dagbani, Senadi, Tampulma, Bariba, Igbo, Birom, Tarok, Amo, Beembe, Swahili, Luvale, Zulu, Teke, Doayo, Gbeya, Zande, Kanuri, Fur, Maasai, Luo, Nyangi, Ik, Sebei, Temein, Tabi, Mursi, Logbara, Yulu, Sara, Koma, Hebrew, Neo-Aramaic, Awiya, Iraqw, Kefa, Hamer, Angas, Margi, Ngizim, Kanakuru, Mundari, Kharia, Khasi, Sedang, Khmer, Maung, Tiwi, Burera, Nunggubuyu, Maranungku, Malakmalak, Bardi, Wik-Munkan, Kunjen, Western Desert, Nyangumata, Aranda, Kariera-Ngarluma, Gugu-Yalanji, Mabuiag, Arabana-Wanganura, Diyari, Standard Thai, Lakkia, Yay, Sui, Saek, Po-ai, Lungchow, Atayal, Sundanese, Javanese, Malagasy, Cham, Malay, Batak, Tagalog, Sa'ban, Chamorro, Rukai, Tsou, Roro, Kaliai, Iai, Maori, Hawaiian, Mandarin, Taishan, Hakka, Changchow, Amoy, Fuchow, Kan, Tamang, Dafla, Burmese, Lahu, Jingpho, Ao, Tiddim Chin, Garo, Boro, Karen, Yao, Andamanese, Asmat, Sentani, Nimboran, Iwam, Gadsup, Yagaria, Pawaian, Dani, Wantoat, Daribi, Fasu, Suena, Dera, Kunimaipa, Taoripi, Nasioi, Rotokas, Nambakaengo, Haida, Tlingit, Navaho, Chipewyan, Tolowa, Nez Perce, Wintu, Chontal, Zoque, Tzeltal, Totonac, K'ekchi, Mixe, Otomi, Mazahua, Chatino, Nootka, Quileute, Squamish, Puget Sound, Papago, Luiseño, Hopi, Yacqui, Tiwa, Karok, Pomo, Diegueño, Achumawi, Shasta, Tarascan, Zuni, Ojibwa, Delaware, Tonkawa, Wiyot, Dakota, Yuchi, Alabama, Wappo, Itonama, Bribri, Mura, Cayapa, Paez, Ocaina, Muinane, Carib, Apinaye, Amahuaca, Chacobo, Tacana, Cashinahua, Ashuslay, Abipon, S. Nambiquara, Arabela, Auca, Quechua, Jaqaru, Gununa-Kena, Amuesha, Campa, Guajiro, Moxo, Guarani, Siriono, Guahibo, Ticuna, Barasano, Siona, Tucano, Jivaro, Cofan, Araucanian, Greenlandic, Telugu, Kurukh, Malayalam, Yukaghir, Chukchi, Gilyak, Georgian, Nama, Basque, Burushaski, Ainu, Brahui, !Xũ, RARE Manchu, Island Carib; LOAN Yakut, Evenki, Lelemi, Amharic, Telefol, Mazatec, Mixtec.

Long voiceless bilabial plosive /p:/ 7
Punjabi, Finnish, Yakut, Japanese, Maranungku, Delaware, Lak.

Palatalized voiceless bilabial plosive /p^j/ 7 (-1)
Lithuanian, Russian, Yurak, Igbo, Nambakaengo, Amuesha; LOAN Cheremis.

Labialized voiceless bilabial plosive /p^w/ 1
Nambakaengo.

Voiceless aspirated bilabial plosive /p^h/ 82 (-4)
Breton, Norwegian, Bulgarian, Farsi, Hindi-Urdu, Bengali, Kashmiri, Punjabi, E. Armenian, Osmanli, Azerbaijani, Kirghiz, Korean, Ewe, Akan, Igbo, Gã, Beembe, Swahili, Zulu, Mundari, Kharia, Khasi, Sedang, Khmer, Kunjen, Standard Thai, Lakkia, Yay, Sui, Saek, Lungchow, Cham, Adzera, Mandarin, Taishan, Hakka, Changchow, Amoy, Fuchow, Kan, Tamang, Dafla, Burmese, Lahu, Jingpho, Tiddim Chin, Karen, Yao, Selepet, Daribi, Nambakaengo, Klamath, Maidu, Wintu, Otomi, Mazahua, Kwakw'ala, Tiwa, Yana, Tarascan, Acoma, Wiyot, Dakota, Yuchi, Tunica, S. Nambiquara,

Quechua, Jaqaru, Wapishana, Cofan, Kota, Gilyak, Georgian, Kabardian, Lak, Burushaski, !Xũ; RARE Haida; LOAN Mongolian, Po-ai, Telugu.

Long voiceless aspirated bilabial plosive /p^{h}:/ 1
Punjabi.

Labialized velarized voiceless aspirated bilabial plosive /p̴^{wh}/ 1
Irish.

Palatalized voiceless aspirated bilabial plosive /p^{jh}/ 3
Irish, Bulgarian, Igbo.

Voiceless preaspirated bilabial plosive /^{h}p/ 2 (-1)
Guajiro; OBSCURE Ojibwa.

Voiceless bilabial plosive with breathy release /$p^{ɦ}$/ 2
Javanese, Changchow.

Laryngealized voiceless bilabial plosive /p̰/ 3
Korean, Ashuslay, Siona.

Voiced bilabial plosive /b/ 198 (-11)
Greek, Breton, German, Norwegian, Lithuanian, Russian, Bulgarian, French, Romanian, Farsi, Pashto, Kurdish, Hindi-Urdu, Bengali, Kashmiri, Punjabi, Sinhalese, Albanian, Komi, Hungarian, Lappish, Tavgy, Osmanli, Yakut, Bashkir, Khalaj, Tuva, Mongolian, Evenki, Goldi, Manchu, Japanese, Katcha, Moro, Kadugli, Kpelle, Bisa, Bambara, Dan, Wolof, Diola, Temne, Dagbani, Tampulma, Bariba, Ewe, Akan, Igbo, Gã, Lelemi, Efik, Birom, Tarok, Amo, Teke, Doayo, Gbeya, Zande, Songhai, Kanuri, Maba, Fur, Luo, Nubian, Ik, Tama, Temein, Nera, Tabi, Mursi, Logbara, Yulu, Sara, Berta, Kunama, Koma, Tigre, Amharic, Hebrew, Socotri, Neo-Aramaic, Shilha, Tuareg, Somali, Awiya, Iraqw, Beja, Dizi, Kefa, Hamer, Hausa, Angas, Margi, Ngizim, Kanakuru, Mundari, Kharia, Khasi, Alawa, Mabuiag, Bandjalang, Standard Thai, Yay, Sui, Saek, Sundanese, Malagasy, Cham, Malay, Batak, Tagalog, Sa'ban, Chamorro, Rukai, Tsou, Adzera, Roro, Iai, Amoy, Dafla, Burmese, Lahu, Jingpho, Tiddim Chin, Garo, Boro, Yao, Andamanese, Nimboran, Telefol, Yagaria, Chuave, Suena, Dera, Kunimaipa, Yareba, Koiari, Nasioi, Tlingit, Klamath, Wintu, Tzeltal, Chontal, Otomi, Chatino, Kwakw'ala, Quileute, Puget Sound, Papago, Yacqui, Pomo, Yana, Acoma, Dakota, Yuchi, Alabama, Itonama, Bribri, Mura, Cayapa, Ocaina, Muinane, Carib, Tacana, Cashinahua, Auca, Gununa-Kena, Island Carib, Siriono, Guahibo, Ticuna, Barasano, Tucano, Cofan, Telugu, Kota, Kurukh, Malayalam, Ket, Yukaghir, Kabardian, Lak, Basque, Burushaski, Brahui, !Xũ; RARE Seneca; LOAN Finnish, Chuvash, Zoque, Mazatec, Tiwa, Tarascan, Tunica, Wappo, Moxo; OBSCURE Yurak.

Long voiced bilabial plosive /b:/ 5
Punjabi, Wolof, Arabic, Shilha, Somali.

Prenasalized voiced bilabial plosive /^{m}b/ 18 (-1)
Luvale, Gbeya, Yulu, Sara, Berta, Ngizim, Sedang, Alawa, Hakka, Washkuk, Selepet, Kewa, Wantoat, Nambakaengo, Paez, Apinaye, Siriono; RARE Kaliai.

Prenasalized labialized voiced bilabial plosive /$^{m}b^{w}$/ 2
Washkuk, Nambakaengo.

Nasally-released voiced bilabial plosive /b^{m}/ 1
Aranda.

Labialized voiced bilabial plosive /b^{w}/ 1
Irish.

Palatalized voiced bilabial plosive /b^{j}/ 6 (-1)
Irish, Lithuanian, Russian, Bulgarian, Igbo; OBSCURE Yurak.

Breathy voiced bilabial plosive /b̤/ 6 (-1)
Hindi-Urdu, Bengali, Igbo, Mundari, Kharia; LOAN Telugu.

Palatalized breathy voiced bilabial plosive /b̤^{j}/ 1
Igbo.

Laryngealized voiced bilabial plosive /b̰/ 9
Logbara, Ngizim, Sedang, Lakkia, Sui, Lungchow, K'ekchi, Otomi, Wapishana.

Voiceless dental plosive /t̪/ 72
Russian, French, Spanish, Kurdish, Hindi-Urdu, Sinhalese, Albanian, Finnish, Hungarian, Azerbaijani, Khalaj, Tuva, Manchu, Katcha, Moro, Kadugli, Temne, Gbeya, Ik, Tama, Temein, Tabi, Logbara, Yulu, Kunama, Arabic, Tigre, Neo-Aramaic, Tuareg, Beja, Mundari, Kharia, Tiwi, Nunggubuyu, Kunjen, Western Desert, Aranda, Kariera-Ngarluma, Arabana-Wanganura, Diyari, Standard Thai, Sundanese, Javanese, Malagasy, Rukai, Roro, Maori, Tamang, Garo, Yao, Nimboran, Nez Perce, Tzeltal, Mixe, Nootka, Squamish, Papago, Luiseño, Pomo, Diegueño, Alabama, Wappo, Gununa-Kena, Guarani, Siona, Araucanian, Greenlandic, Telugu, Malayalam, Georgian, Nama, Brahui.

Long voiceless dental plosive /t̪:/ 2
Finnish, Arabic.

Palatalized voiceless dental plosive /t̪^{j}/ 1
Russian.

Pharyngealized voiceless dental plosive /t̪^{ʕ}/ 2
Arabic, Tuareg.

Long pharyngealized voiceless dental plosive /t̪^{ʕ}:/ 1
Arabic.

Voiceless aspirated dental plosive /t̪^{h}/ 22
Irish, Norwegian, Farsi, Hindi-Urdu, Osmanli, Azerbaijani, Ewe, Gã, Somali, Mundari, Kharia, Kunjen, Standard Thai, Tamang, Yao, Selepet, Yana, Acoma, Guahibo, Kota, Georgian, Kabardian.

Voiceless dental plosive with breathy release /t̪^{ɦ}/ 1
Javanese.

Voiced dental plosive /d̪/ 53 (-3)
Irish, Norwegian, Russian, French, Farsi, Kurdish, Hindi-Urdu, Sinhalese, Albanian, Hungarian, Osmanli, Khalaj, Tuva, Manchu, Katcha, Kadugli, Ewe, Gbeya, Ik, Tama, Temein, Tabi, Logbara, Yulu, Kunama, Arabic, Tigre, Neo-Aramaic, Tuareg, Somali, Beja, Mundari, Kharia, Standard Thai, Malagasy, Rukai, Garo, Yao, Nimboran, Kunimaipa, Mixe,

Papago, Yana, Acoma, Gununa-Kena, Telugu, Kota, Malayalam, Kabardian, Brahui; LOAN Tzeltal, Wappo; ?DERIVED Finnish.

Long voiced dental plosive /d̪:/ 2
Arabic, Somali.

Prenasalized voiced dental plosive /ⁿd̪/ 2
Gbeya, Selepet.

Nasally-released voiced dental plosive /d̪ⁿ/ 1
Aranda.

Palatalized voiced dental plosive /d̪ʲ/ 1
Russian.

Pharyngealized voiced dental plosive /d̪ˤ/ 2
Arabic, Tuareg.

Long pharyngealized voiced dental plosive /d̪ˤ:/ 1
Arabic.

Breathy voiced dental plosive /d̪̤/ 3
Hindi-Urdu, Mundari, Kharia.

Laryngealized voiced dental plosive /d̪̰/ 1
Logbara.

Voiceless dental/alveolar plosive /"t"/ 135
Greek, German, Lithuanian, Romanian, Pashto, Bengali, Kashmiri, Punjabi, E. Armenian, Ostyak, Cheremis, Lappish, Yurak, Tavgy, Chuvash, Yakut, Kirghiz, Evenki, Goldi, Korean, Japanese, Wolof, Dagbani, Senadi, Igbo, Tarok, Beembe, Swahili, Luvale, Doayo, Songhai, Kanuri, Maba, Maasai, Nubian, Sebei, Nera, Mursi, Arabic, Amharic, Hebrew, Socotri, Shilha, Awiya, Kullo, Dizi, Kefa, Hausa, Khasi, Sedang, Khmer, Maranungku, Wik-Munkan, Gugu-Yalanji, Mabuiag, Lakkia, Yay, Sui, Po-ai, Lungchow, Atayal, Cham, Malay, Batak, Tagalog, Tsou, Kaliai, Iai, Mandarin, Taishan, Hakka, Changchow, Amoy, Fuchow, Kan, Dafla, Burmese, Lahu, Jingpho, Karen, Andamanese, Sentani, Telefol, Pawaian, Dani, Wantoat, Suena, Dera, Kunimaipa, Taoripi, Nasioi, Nambakaengo, Haida, Tlingit, Chipewyan, Tolowa, Chontal, Mazahua, Mazatec, Mixtec, Chatino, Tiwa, Karok, Shasta, Zuni, Delaware, Tonkawa, Wiyot, Seneca, Wichita, Dakota, Yuchi, Itonama, Bribri, Mura, Carib, Amahuaca, Ashuslay, Abipon, Arabela, Quechua, Island Carib, Guajiro, Siriono, Ticuna, Jivaro, Cofan, Aleut, Kurukh, Ket, Yukaghir, Chukchi, Gilyak, Basque, Burushaski.

Long voiceless dental/alveolar plosive /"t:"/ 7
Punjabi, Yakut, Japanese, Shilha, Maranungku, Delaware, Lak.

Labialized voiceless dental/alveolar plosive /"tʷ"/ 1
Nambakaengo.

Palatalized voiceless dental/alveolar plosive /"tʲ"/ 8 (-2)
Lithuanian, Yurak, Chuvash, Nambakaengo, Itonama, Ket; LOAN Cheremis; ?DERIVED Songhai.

Pharyngealized voiceless dental/alveolar plosive /"tˤ"/ 1
Shilha.

Voiceless aspirated dental/alveolar plosive /"t^h"/ 48 (-2)
Breton, Bulgarian, Bengali, Kashmiri, Punjabi, E. Armenian, Kirghiz, Mongolian, Korean, Akan, Igbo, Beembe, Swahili, Khasi, Sedang, Khmer, Lakkia, Yay, Lungchow, Cham, Adzera, Mandarin, Taishan, Hakka, Amoy, Fuchow, Kan, Burmese, Lahu, Jingpho, Karen, Nambakaengo, Haida, Tolowa, Mazahua, Kwakw'ala, Tiwa, Wiyot, Wichita, Dakota, S. Nambiquara, Quechua, Cofan, Gilyak, Lak, Burushaski; LOAN Irish, Po-ai.

Long voiceless aspirated dental/alveolar plosive /"t^h:"/ 1
Punjabi.

Palatalized voiceless aspirated dental/alveolar plosive /"t^{jh}"/ 1
Bulgarian.

Velarized voiceless aspirated dental/alveolar plosive /"$ŧ^h$"/ 1
Chipewyan.

Preaspirated voiceless dental/alveolar plosive /"^ht"/ 1
Guajiro.

Voiceless dental/alveolar plosive with breathy release /"$t^ɦ$"/ 1
Changchow.

Laryngealized voiceless dental/alveolar plosive /"$\underset{\sim}{t}$"/ 2
Korean, Ashuslay.

Voiced dental/alveolar plosive /"d"/ 77 (-5)
Greek, Breton, German, Lithuanian, Bulgarian, Romanian, Pashto, Bengali, Kashmiri, Punjabi, Lappish, Tavgy, Yakut, Mongolian, Evenki, Japanese, Wolof, Dagbani, Senadi, Akan, Igbo, Tarok, Doayo, Songhai, Kanuri, Maba, Nubian, Nera, Mursi, Berta, Amharic, Hebrew, Socotri, Shilha, Kullo, Kefa, Hausa, Khasi, Kariera-Ngarluma, Mabuiag, Yay, Sui, Cham, Malay, Batak, Tagalog, Adzera, Iai, Amoy, Dafla, Burmese, Lahu, Jingpho, Andamanese, Sentani, Suena, Dera, Tlingit, Chatino, Yuchi, Itonama, Bribri, Carib, Island Carib, Ticuna, Cofan, Kurukh, Ket, Yukaghir, Lak, Basque, Burushaski; RARE Chontal; LOAN Irish, Chuvash, Telefol, Tiwa.

Long voiced dental/alveolar plosive /"d:"/ 3
Punjabi, Arabic, Shilha.

Prenasalized voiced dental/alveolar plosive /"nd"/ 9
Luvale, Yulu, Berta, Sedang, Hakka, Wantoat, Nambakaengo, Mazatec, Siriono.

Long prenasalized voiced dental/alveolar plosive /"nd:"/ 1 (-1)
RARE Kaliai.

Prenasalized labialized voiced dental/alveolar plosive /"$^nd^w$"/ 1
Nambakaengo.

Palatalized voiced dental/alveolar plosive /"d^j"/ 4 (-1)
Lithuanian, Bulgarian, Ket; ?DERIVED Songhai.

Pharyngealized voiced dental/alveolar plosive /"$d^ʕ$"/ 1
Shilha.

Breathy voiced dental/alveolar plosive /"d̤"/ 3 (-1)
Bengali, Igbo; LOAN Telugu.

Laryngealized voiced dental/alveolar plosive /"d̰"/ 3
Sedang, Sui, Lungchow.

Voiceless alveolar plosive /t/ 102 (-1)
Komi, Bashkir, Katcha, Kadugli, Kpelle, Bisa, Bambara, Dan, Diola, Temne, Tampulma, Bariba, Lelemi, Efik, Birom, Amo, Zulu, Teke, Zande, Fur, Luo, Nyangi, Temein, Sara, Koma, Iraqw, Hamer, Angas, Margi, Ngizim, Kanakuru, Vietnamese, Maung, Tiwi, Burera, Nunggubuyu, Malakmalak, Bardi, Kunjen, Western Desert, Nyangumata, Aranda, Arabana-Wanganura, Diyari, Saek, Javanese, Sa'ban, Chamorro, Ao, Tiddim Chin, Boro, Asmat, Washkuk, Iwam, Gadsup, Yagaria, Kewa, Chuave, Daribi, Fasu, Yareba, Koiari, Rotokas, Navaho, Hupa, Nez Perce, Wintu, Zoque, Totonac, K'ekchi, Otomi, Quileute, Puget Sound, Hopi, Yacqui, Pomo, Diegueño, Achumawi, Tarascan, Ojibwa, Wappo, Cayapa, Paez, Muinane, Apinaye, Chacobo, Tacana, Cashinahua, S. Nambiquara, Auca, Jaqaru, Amuesha, Campa, Moxo, Guahibo, Barasano, Tucano, Araucanian, Ainu, Brahui, !Xũ; OBSCURE Ojibwa.

Palatalized voiceless alveolar plosive /t^{j}/ 3
Nyangumata, Paez, Ocaina.

Voiceless aspirated alveolar plosive /t^{h}/ 19
Zulu, Vietnamese, Kunjen, Saek, Changchow, Tiddim Chin, Daribi, Navaho, Hupa, Klamath, Maidu, Wintu, Otomi, Tarascan, Tunica, Jaqaru, Wapishana, Kota, !Xũ.

Voiceless alveolar plosive with breathy release /$t^{ɦ}$/ 1
Javanese.

Voiced alveolar plosive /d/ 65 (-5)
Komi, Bashkir, Katcha, Kadugli, Kpelle, Bisa, Bambara, Dan, Diola, Temne, Tampulma, Bariba, Gã, Efik, Birom, Amo, Teke, Zande, Fur, Luo, Temein, Sara, Koma, Iraqw, Hamer, Angas, Margi, Kanakuru, Alawa, Diyari, Bandjalang, Saek, Sundanese, Sa'ban, Chamorro, Tiddim Chin, Boro, Gadsup, Chuave, Yareba, Koiari, Klamath, Wintu, Otomi, Kwakw'ala, Quileute, Puget Sound, Pomo, Cayapa, Muinane, Tacana, Cashinahua, Auca, Wapishana, Guahibo, Barasano, Tucano, Kota, Brahui, !Xũ; LOAN Zoque, Yacqui, Tarascan, Tunica, Moxo.

Prenasalized voiced alveolar plosive /^{n}d/ 7
Sara, Ngizim, Alawa, Washkuk, Kewa, Paez, Apinaye.

Prenasalized palatalized voiced alveolar plosive /$^{n}d^{j}$/ 1
Paez.

Nasally-released alveolar plosive /d^{n}/ 1
Aranda.

Palatalized voiced alveolar plosive /d^{j}/ 1
Ocaina.

Velarized voiced alveolar plosive /d̴/ 1
!Xũ.

Laryngealized voiced alveolar plosive /d̰/ 3
Ngizim, Otomi, Wapishana.

Voiceless palato-alveolar plosive /t̠/ 7
Nunggubuyu, Malakmalak, Bardi, Wik-Munkan, Aranda, Cayapa, Campa.

Voiced palato-alveolar plosive /d̠/ 2
Alawa, Cayapa.

Prenasalized voiced palato-alveolar plosive /ⁿd̠/ 1
Alawa.

Nasally-released voiced palato-alveolar plosive /d̠ⁿ/ 1
Aranda.

Voiceless retroflex plosive /ṭ/ 28 (-1)
Pashto, Hindi-Urdu, Bengali, Kashmiri, Punjabi, Sinhalese, Moro, Maba, Beja, Mundari, Kharia, Maung, Nunggubuyu, Bardi, Western Desert, Nyangumata, Aranda, Kariera-Ngarluma, Arabana-Wanganura, Diyari, Cham, Rukai, Iai, Telugu, Kurukh, Malayalam, Burushaski; ?DERIVED Tiwi.

Long voiceless retroflex plosive /ṭ:/ 1
Punjabi.

Laryngealized voiceless retroflex plosive /ṭ̰/ 1
Siona.

Voiceless aspirated retroflex plosive /ṭʰ/ 10 (-1)
Norwegian, Hindi-Urdu, Bengali, Kashmiri, Punjabi, Kharia, Cham, Kota, Burushaski; LOAN Telugu.

Long voiceless aspirated retroflex plosive /ṭʰ:/ 1
Punjabi.

Voiced retroflex plosive /ḍ/ 23
Norwegian, Pashto, Hindi-Urdu, Bengali, Kashmiri, Punjabi, Sinhalese, Lelemi, Maba, Awiya, Beja, Mundari, Kharia, Alawa, Diyari, Rukai, Iai, Papago, Telugu, Kota, Kurukh, Malayalam, Burushaski.

Long voiced retroflex plosive /ḍ:/ 1
Punjabi.

Prenasalized voiced retroflex plosive /ⁿ̣ḍ/ 1
Alawa.

Nasally-released voiced retroflex plosive /ḍⁿ̣/ 1
Aranda.

Breathy voiced retroflex plosive /ḍ̤/ 5 (-1)
Hindi-Urdu, Bengali, Mundari, Kharia; LOAN Telugu.

Laryngealized voiced retroflex plosive /ḍ̰/ 1
Somali.

Long laryngealized voiced retroflex plosive /ḍ̰:/ 1
Somali.

Voiceless palatal plosive /c/ 41 (-2)
Ostyak, Komi, Tavgy, Azerbaijani, Katcha, Kadugli, Wolof, Diola, Senadi, Tampulma, Birom, Nyangi, Sebei, Tabi, Mursi, Yulu, Hamer, Angas, Margi, Ngizim, Vietnamese, Burera, Kunjen, Kariera-Ngarluma, Gugu-Yalanji, Arabana-Wanganura, Diyari, Yay, Cham, Malay, Yao, Kewa, Haida, Hupa, Muinane, Jaqaru, Kurukh, Gilyak, Basque; RARE Karen, OBSCURE Cofan.

Voiceless aspirated palatal plosive /cʰ/ 16 (-3)
Breton, Azerbaijani, Kunjen, Yay, Cham, Yao, Haida, Hupa, Klamath, Maidu, Kwakw'ala, Acoma, Jaqaru; RARE Karen; LOAN Osmanli; OBSCURE Cofan.

Voiced palatal plosive /ɟ/ 31 (-2)
Breton, Komi, Tavgy, Katcha, Wolof, Diola, Senadi, Tampulma, Birom, Maba, Tama, Temein, Tabi, Mursi, Tuareg, Hamer, Angas, Margi, Ngizim, Sundanese, Malay, Yao, Klamath, Kwakw'ala, Acoma, Muinane, Kurukh, Yukaghir, Basque; LOAN Osmanli; OBSCURE Cofan.

Long voiced palatal plosive /ɟː/ 1
Ngizim.

Prenasalized voiced palatal plosive /ᶮɟ/ 3
Yulu, Sara, Apinaye.

Voiceless velar plosive /k/ 283 (-3)
Greek, German, Lithuanian, Russian, French, Spanish, Romanian, Pashto, Kurdish, Hindi-Urdu, Bengali, Kashmiri, Punjabi, Sinhalese, Albanian, E. Armenian, Ostyak, Cheremis, Komi, Finnish, Hungarian, Lappish, Yurak, Tavgy, Chuvash, Yakut, Bashkir, Khalaj, Tuva, Evenki, Goldi, Manchu, Korean, Japanese, Katcha, Moro, Kadugli, Kpelle, Bisa, Bambara, Dan, Wolof, Diola, Temne, Dagbani, Senadi, Tampulma, Bariba, Igbo, Lelemi, Efik, Birom, Tarok, Amo, Swahili, Luvale, Zulu, Teke, Doayo, Gbeya, Zande, Songhai, Kanuri, Maba, Fur, Maasai, Luo, Nubian, Nyangi, Ik, Sebei, Tama, Temein, Nera, Tabi, Mursi, Logbara, Yulu, Sara, Kunama, Koma, Arabic, Amharic, Tigre, Hebrew, Socotri, Neo-Aramaic, Shilha, Tuareg, Awiya, Iraqw, Beja, Kullo, Dizi, Kefa, Hausa, Angas, Margi, Ngizim, Kanakuru, Mundari, Kharia, Khasi, Vietnamese, Sedang, Khmer, Maung, Tiwi, Burera, Nunggubuyu, Maranungku, Malakmalak, Bardi, Wik-Munkan, Kunjen, Western Desert, Nyangumata, Aranda, Kariera-Ngarluma, Gugu-Yalanji, Mabuiag, Arabana-Wanganura, Diyari, Standard Thai, Lakkia, Yay, Sui, Saek, Po-ai, Lungchow, Atayal, Sundanese, Javanese, Malagasy, Cham, Malay, Batak, Tagalog, Chamorro, Rukai, Tsou, Roro, Kaliai, Iai, Maori, Hawaiian, Mandarin, Taishan, Hakka, Changchow, Amoy, Fuchow, Kan, Tamang, Dafla, Burmese, Lahu, Jingpho, Ao, Tiddim Chin, Garo, Boro, Karen, Yao, Andamanese, Asmat, Washkuk, Sentani, Nimboran, Iwam, Telefol, Gadsup, Yagaria, Chuave, Pawaian, Dani, Wantoat, Daribi, Fasu, Suena, Dera, Kunimaipa, Yareba, Koiari, Taoripi, Nasioi, Rotokas, Nambakaengo, Haida, Tlingit, Navaho, Chipewyan, Tolowa, Nez Perce, Wintu, Chontal, Zoque, Totonac, K'ekchi, Mixe, Otomi, Mazahua, Mazatec, Mixtec, Chatino, Nootka, Quileute, Puget Sound, Papago, Luiseño, Hopi, Yacqui, Tiwa, Karok, Pomo, Diegueño, Achumawi, Shasta, Tarascan, Ojibwa, Delaware, Tonkawa, Wiyot, Seneca, Wichita, Dakota, Yuchi, Alabama, Wappo, Itonama, Bribri, Mura, Cayapa, Paez, Ocaina, Muinane, Carib, Apinaye, Amahuaca, Chacobo, Tacana, Cashinahua, Ashuslay, Abipon, S. Nambiquara, Arabela, Auca, Quechua, Jaqaru, Gununa-Kena, Amuesha, Campa, Guajiro, Moxo, Guarani, Siriono, Guahibo, Ticuna, Barasano, Siona, Tucano, Jivaro, Cofan, Araucanian,

Greenlandic, Aleut, Telugu, Kurukh, Malayalam, Ket, Yukaghir, Chukchi,
Gilyak, Georgian, Nama, Basque, Burushaski, Ainu, Brahui, !Xũ; RARE
Squamish, Island Carib; LOAN Azerbaijani.

ong voiceless velar plosive /k:/ 9
 Punjabi, Finnish, Yakut, Japanese, Arabic, Shilha, Maranungku, Delaware,
 Lak.

abialized voiceless velar plosive /kʷ/ 38 (-1)
 Kpelle, Igbo, Amharic, Awiya, Iraqw, Beja, Hausa, Ngizim, Lakkia,
 Taishan, Washkuk, Telefol, Dani, Wantoat, Nambakaengo, Haida, Tlingit,
 Chipewyan, Tolowa, Mazahua, Mixtec, Nootka, Quileute, Squamish, Puget
 Sound, Luiseño, Hopi, Tiwa, Diegueño, Tarascan, Tonkawa, Wiyot, Wichita,
 S. Nambiquara, Guarani, Ticuna, Siona; ?DERIVED Otomi.

ong labialized voiceless velar plosive /kʷ:/ 1
 Lak.

alatalized voiceless velar plosive /kʲ/ 5
 Lithuanian, Russian, Hausa, Nambakaengo, Siriono.

haryngealized voiceless velar plosive /kˤ/ 1
 Shilha.

oiceless aspirated velar plosive /kʰ/ 79 (-3)
 Irish, Breton, Norwegian, Bulgarian, Farsi, Hindi-Urdu, Bengali,
 Kashmiri, Punjabi, E. Armenian, Osmanli, Azerbaijani, Korean, Ewe, Akan,
 Igbo, Gã, Beembe, Swahili, Zulu, Somali, Mundari, Kharia, Khasi, Sedang,
 Khmer, Kunjen, Standard Thai, Lakkia, Yay, Saek, Lungchow, Cham, Adzera,
 Mandarin, Taishan, Hakka, Changchow, Amoy, Fuchow, Kan, Tamang, Burmese,
 Lahu, Jingpho, Karen, Yao, Selepet, Daribi, Nambakaengo, Haida, Navaho,
 Klamath, Maidu, Tzeltal, Otomi, Mazahua, Yana, Tarascan, Acoma, Wiyot,
 Wichita, Dakota, Yuchi, Tunica, S. Nambiquara, Quechua, Jaqaru,
 Wapishana, Cofan, Kota, Gilyak, Georgian, Lak, Burushaski, !Xũ; LOAN
 Mongolian, Po-ai, Telugu.

ong voiceless aspirated velar plosive /kʰ:/ 1
 Punjabi.

abialized voiceless aspirated velar plosive /kʷʰ/ 14 (-1)
 Igbo, Lakkia, Taishan, Haida, Mazahua, Kwakw'ala, Tarascan, Zuni, Wiyot,
 Wichita, S. Nambiquara, Kabardian, Lak; RARE Navaho.

alatalized voiceless aspirated velar plosive /kʲʰ/ 4
 Irish, Bulgarian, Lakkia, Kabardian.

reaspirated voiceless velar plosive /ʰk/ 2 (-1)
 Guajiro; OBSCURE Ojibwa.

oiceless velar plosive with breathy release /kʱ/ 2
 Javanese, Changchow.

aryngealized voiceless velar plosive /k̰/ 3
 Korean, Ashuslay, Siona.

Voiced velar plosive /g/ 175 (-14)
Greek, Irish, Breton, German, Norwegian, Lithuanian, Russian, Bulgarian, French, Romanian, Farsi, Pashto, Kurdish, Hindi-Urdu, Bengali, Kashmiri, Punjabi, Sinhalese, Albanian, Komi, Hungarian, Lappish, Tavgy, Osmanli, Yakut, Bashkir, Khalaj, Tuva, Mongolian, Evenki, Goldi, Manchu, Katcha, Moro, Kadugli, Kpelle, Bisa, Bambara, Dan, Diola, Temne, Dagbani, Senadi, Tampulma, Bariba, Ewe, Akan, Igbo, Gã, Lelemi, Birom, Tarok, Amo, Teke, Doayo, Gbeya, Zande, Songhai, Kanuri, Maba, Fur, Luo, Nubian, Ik, Tama, Temein, Nera, Tabi, Mursi, Logbara, Yulu, Sara, Berta, Kunama, Koma, Tigre, Amharic, Hebrew, Socotri, Neo-Aramaic, Shilha, Tuareg, Somali, Awiya, Iraqw, Beja, Kullo, Dizi, Kefa, Hamer, Hausa, Angas, Margi, Ngizim, Kanakuru, Mundari, Kharia, Alawa, Mabuiag, Bandjalang, Sundanese, Malagasy, Malay, Batak, Tagalog, Chamorro, Rukai, Adzera, Iai, Amoy, Dafla, Burmese, Lahu, Jingpho, Tiddim Chin, Garo, Boro, Yao, Andamanese, Nimboran, Yagaria, Kewa, Chuave, Suena, Dera, Kunimaipa, Yareba, Koiari, Rotokas, Tlingit, Klamath, Mixe, Otomi, Mazahua, Chatino, Papago, Yana, Acoma, Yuchi, Bribri, Mura, Cayapa, Ocaina, Muinane, Carib, Auca, Wapishana, Island Carib, Ticuna, Barasano, Tucano, Cofan, Telugu, Kota, Kurukh, Yukaghir, Lak, Basque, Burushaski, Brahui, !Xũ; RARE Puget Sound; LOAN Finnish, Chuvash, Sa'ban, Telefol, Zoque, Tzeltal, Quileute, Yacqui, Tiwa, Tarascan, Tunica, Wappo; ?DERIVED Japanese.

Long voiced velar plosive /gː/ 4
Punjabi, Arabic, Shilha, Somali.

Prenasalized voiced velar plosive /ᵑg/ 18 (-1)
Luvale, Gbeya, Yulu, Sara, Berta, Ngizim, Sedang, Alawa, Hakka, Washkuk, Selepet, Wantoat, Nambakaengo, Mazatec, Paez, Apinaye, Siriono; RARE Kaliai.

Labialized prenasalized voiced velar plosive /ᵑgʷ/ 4
Ngizim, Washkuk, Wantoat, Nambakaengo.

Nasally-released voiced velar plosive /gᵑ/ 1
Aranda.

Labialized voiced velar plosive /gʷ/ 14 (-1)
Kpelle, Igbo, Amharic, Awiya, Iraqw, Beja, Hausa, Ngizim, Tlingit, Mazahua, Kwakw'ala, Puget Sound, Kabardian; ?DERIVED Otomi.

Palatalized voiced velar plosive /gʲ/ 5
Irish, Lithuanian, Bulgarian, Hausa, Kabardian.

Breathy voiced velar plosive /g̤/ 7 (-1)
Hindi-Urdu, Bengali, Igbo, Mundari, Kharia, !Xũ; LOAN Telugu.

Labialized breathy voiced velar plosive /g̤ʷ/ 1
Igbo.

Voiceless uvular plosive /q/ 38 (-2)
Kurdish, Kirghiz, Arabic, Neo-Aramaic, Tuareg, Awiya, Iraqw, Hamer, Sui, Atayal, Lahu, Haida, Tlingit, Hupa, Wintu, Totonac, K'ekchi, Nootka, Quileute, Squamish, Puget Sound, Luiseño, Hopi, Pomo, Achumawi, Abipon, Quechua, Jaqaru, Gununa-Kena, Greenlandic, Aleut, Ket, Yukaghir, Chukchi, Gilyak, Burushaski; RARE Diegueño; LOAN Hindi-Urdu.

Labialized voiceless uvular plosive /q^w/ 9 (-1)
Awiya, Iraqw, Haida, Tlingit, Quileute, Squamish, Puget Sound, Luiseño; LOAN Nootka.

Long labialized voiceless uvular plosive /q^w:/ 1
Lak.

Voiceless aspirated uvular plosive /q^h/ 11
Kirghiz, Sui, Lahu, Haida, Klamath, Kwakw'ala, Quechua, Jaqaru, Gilyak, Lak, Burushaski.

Labialized voiceless aspirated uvular plosive /q^{wh}/ 3
Haida, Kwakw'ala, Lak.

Voiced uvular plosive /ɢ/ 8
Farsi, Somali, Awiya, Kunimaipa, Tlingit, Klamath, Kwakw'ala, Lak.

Long voiced uvular plosive /ɢ:/ 1
Somali.

Labialized voiced uvular plosive /$ɢ^w$/ 4
Awiya, Tlingit, Kwakw'ala, Lak.

Voiced pharyngeal plosive /*ʕ/ 1
Iraqw.

Glottal plosive /ʔ/ 146 (-11)
Farsi, Kurdish, Yurak, Tavgy, Wolof, Kanuri, Maba, Luo, Tabi, Logbara, Berta, Koma, Arabic, Tigre, Hebrew, Socotri, Neo-Aramaic, Somali, Iraqw, Beja, Kullo, Kefa, Hausa, Margi, Khasi, Vietnamese, Sedang, Khmer, Wik-Munkan, Standard Thai, Lakkia, Yay, Sui, Saek, Po-ai, Lungchow, Atayal, Sundanese, Javanese, Cham, Tagalog, Sa'ban, Chamorro, Rukai, Tsou, Adzera, Roro, Hawaiian, Changchow, Amoy, Burmese, Jingpho, Ao, Tiddim Chin, Garo, Karen, Yao, Washkuk, Gadsup, Yagaria, Dani, Nasioi, Haida, Tlingit, Chipewyan, Tolowa, Hupa, Nez Perce, Klamath, Wintu, Chontal, Zoque, Tzeltal, Totonac, K'ekchi, Mixe, Otomi, Mazahua, Mazatec, Mixtec, Chatino, Nootka, Kwakw'ala, Quileute, Squamish, Puget Sound, Papago, Luiseño, Hopi, Yacqui, Tiwa, Karok, Pomo, Diegueño, Achumawi, Yana, Shasta, Zuni, Acoma, Ojibwa, Tonkawa, Wiyot, Seneca, Wichita, Yuchi, Tunica, Wappo, Itonama, Mura, Cayapa, Paez, Ocaina, Muinane, Apinaye, Chacobo, Tacana, Ashuslay, S. Nambiquara, Gununa-Kena, Wapishana, Amuesha, Guajiro, Moxo, Guarani, Ticuna, Siona, Tucano, Cofan, Kurukh, Ket, Chukchi, Kabardian, Lak, Nama, Brahui; RARE Temne, Gbeya, Lahu, Tarascan, Jivaro; LOAN Hindi-Urdu, Osmanli, Bashkir; ?DERIVED Mundari, Navaho, Carib.

Long glottal plosive /ʔ:/ 1
Arabic.

Labialized glottal plosive /$ʔ^w$/ 1
Kabardian.

Pharyngealized glottal plosive /$ʔ^ʕ$/ 1
Nootka.

Voiceless labial-velar plosive /k͡p/ 18

Kpelle, Dan, Dagbani, Senadi, Tampulma, Bariba, Ewe, Gã, Lelemi, Efik, Birom, Tarok, Amo, Doayo, Gbeya, Zande, Logbara, Yulu.

Voiced labial-velar plosive /g͡b/ 19
Kpelle, Dan, Temne, Dagbani, Senadi, Tampulma, Bariba, Ewe, Gã, Lelemi, Birom, Tarok, Amo, Doayo, Gbeya, Zande, Logbara, Yulu, Iai.

Prenasalized voiced labial-velar plosive /ᵐ͡ᵑg͡b/ 1
Gbeya.

Voiceless dental-palatal plosive /t̪͡c/ 1
Maung.

2. GLOTTALIC STOPS
(Note that 'voiced ejectives' in !Xũ are prevoiced, the release is voiceless.)

Voiceless bilabial ejective stop /p'/ 33 (-1)
E. Armenian, Zulu, Berta, Koma, Kefa, Tlingit, Nez Perce, Klamath, Maidu, Wintu, Chontal, Tzeltal, Otomi, Nootka, Kwakw'ala, Quileute, Squamish, Puget Sound, Tiwa, Pomo, Yana, Shasta, Acoma, Dakota, Wappo, S. Nambiquara, Quechua, Jaqaru, Gununa-Kena, Georgian, Kabardian, Lak; LOAN Amharic.

Voiced bilabial ejective stop /b'/ 1
!Xũ.

Voiceless dental ejective stop /t̪'/ 11
Nez Perce, Tzeltal, Nootka, Squamish, Pomo, Yana, Acoma, Wappo, Gununa-Kena, Georgian, Kabardian.

Voiceless dental/alveolar ejective stop /"t'"/ 21
E. Armenian, Tigre, Amharic, Socotri, Kullo, Dizi, Kefa, Haida, Tlingit, Chipewyan, Tolowa, Chontal, Mazahua, Kwakw'ala, Tiwa, Shasta, Dakota, Yuchi, Itonama, Quechua, Lak.

Voiceless alveolar ejective stop /t'/ 17
Zulu, Koma, Navaho, Hupa, Nez Perce, Klamath, Maidu, Wintu, K'ekchi, Otomi, Quileute, Puget Sound, Pomo, Wappo, S. Nambiquara, Jaqaru, !Xũ.

Voiced alveolar ejective stop /d'/ 1
!Xũ.

Voiceless palatal ejective stop /c'/ 7
Haida, Hupa, Klamath, Maidu, Kwakw'ala, Acoma, Jaqaru.

Voiceless velar ejective stop /k'/ 49 (-1)
E. Armenian, Zulu, Ik, Berta, Koma, Tigre, Amharic, Socotri, Kullo, Dizi, Kefa, Hamer, Hausa, Haida, Tlingit, Navaho, Chipewyan, Tolowa, Nez Perce, Klamath, Maidu, Wintu, Chontal, Tzeltal, K'ekchi, Otomi, Mazahua, Nootka, Quileute, Puget Sound, Tiwa, Pomo, Yana, Shasta, Zuni, Acoma, Wichita, Dakota, Yuchi, Wappo, Itonama, S. Nambiquara, Quechua, Jaqaru, Gununa-Kena, Georgian, Lak, !Xũ; RARE Squamish.

Labialized voiceless velar ejective stop /kʷ'/ 18 (-2)
Amharic, Hausa, Haida, Tlingit, Chipewyan, Tolowa, Mazahua, Nootka, Kwakw'ala, Quileute, Squamish, Puget Sound, Zuni, S. Nambiquara, Kabardian, Lak; RARE Tiwa; ?DERIVED Otomi.

Palatalized voiceless velar ejective stop /kʲ'/ 2
Hausa, Kabardian.

Voiced velar ejective stop /ɡ'/ 1
!Xũ.

Voiceless uvular ejective stop /q'/ 19 (-1)
Kefa, Haida, Tlingit, Hupa, Nez Perce, Klamath, Wintu, K'ekchi, Kwakw'ala, Quileute, Squamish, Puget Sound, Pomo, Quechua, Jaqaru, Georgian, Kabardian, Lak; LOAN Nootka.

Labialized voiceless uvular ejective stop /qʷ'/ 8
Haida, Tlingit, Nootka, Quileute, Squamish, Puget Sound, Kabardian, Lak.

Voiceless bilabial implosive /p˂/ 1
Igbo.

Voiced bilabial implosive /ɓ/ 30 (-1)
Katcha, Kadugli, Kpelle, Dan, Igbo, Tarok, Swahili, Zulu, Doayo, Gbeya, Maasai, Nyangi, Ik, Tama, Mursi, Yulu, Sara, Koma, Hamer, Hausa, Angas, Margi, Kanakuru, Vietnamese, Khmer, Karen, Maidu, Mazahua, S. Nambiquara; RARE Iraqw.

Voiced dental implosive /ɗ̪/ 3
Kadugli, Gbeya, Ik.

Voiced dental/alveolar implosive /"ɗ"/ 13
Katcha, Tarok, Swahili, Doayo, Maasai, Mursi, Yulu, Berta, Kullo, Hausa, Karen, Mazahua, S. Nambiquara.

Voiceless alveolar implosive /t˂/ 1
Igbo.

Voiced alveolar implosive /ɗ/ 13 (-1)
Dan, Nyangi, Tama, Sara, Koma, Hamer, Angas, Margi, Kanakuru, Vietnamese, Khmer, Maidu; RARE Iraqw.

Voiced palatal implosive /ʄ/ 7
Kadugli, Swahili, Maasai, Nyangi, Ik, Yulu, Angas.

Voiced velar implosive /ɠ/ 5
Swahili, Maasai, Nyangi, Ik, Hamer.

Voiced uvular implosive /ɢ˂/ 1
Ik.

3. CLICKS

(Including affricated clicks. Note that clicks may be affricated in two ways. The front release may be affricated or the back (velar) release may be affricated. UPSID refers only to the former as affricated clicks. A fricated release of the back closure is referred to as velarization of the click.)

Voiceless alveolar click /ǂ/ 2
Nama, !Xũ.

Segment index

Velarized voiceless alveolar click /ǂ̴/ 1
!Xũ.

Voiceless aspirated alveolar click /ǂʰ/ 1
!Xũ.

Nasalized voiceless aspirated alveolar click /ŋ̊ǂʰ/ 2
Nama, !Xũ.

Velarized voiceless aspirated alveolar click /ǂ̴ʰ/ 1
Nama.

Glottalized nasalized voiceless alveolar click /ŋ̊ǂˀ/ 2
Nama, !Xũ.

Glottalized velarized voiceless alveolar click /ǂ̴ˀ/ 1
!Xũ.

Voiced alveolar click /gǂ/ 1
!Xũ.

Nasalized voiced alveolar click /ŋǂ/ 2
Nama, !Xũ.

Velarized voiced alveolar click /gǂ̴/ 1
!Xũ.

Breathy voiced alveolar click /g̤ǂ/ 1
!Xũ.

Nasalized breathy voiced alveolar click /ŋ̤ǂ/ 1
!Xũ.

Glottalized velarized voiced alveolar click /gǂ̴ˀ/ 1
!Xũ.

Voiceless palato-alveolar click /ǂ̠/ 2
Zulu, Nama.

Nasalized voiceless aspirated palato-alveolar click /ŋ̊ǂ̠ʰ/ 1
Nama.

Velarized voiceless aspirated palato-alveolar click /ǂ̠ʰ/ 1
Nama.

Glottalized nasalized voiceless palato-alveolar click /ŋ̊ǂ̠ˀ/ 1
Nama.

Nasalized voiced palato-alveolar click /ŋǂ̠/ 1
Nama.

Voiceless palatal click /ʗ/ 1
!Xũ.

Velarized voiceless palatal click /ʗ̴/ 1
!Xũ.

Voiceless aspirated palatal click /ʗʰ/ 1
!Xũ.

Nasalized voiceless aspirated palatal click /ŋ̊ʗʰ/ 1
!Xũ.

Glottalized nasalized voiceless palatal click /ŋ̊ʗˀ/ 1
!Xũ.

Glottalized nasalized velarized voiceless palatal click /ŋ̊ʗ̴ˀ/ 1
!Xũ.

Voiced palatal click /gʗ/ 1
!Xũ.

Nasalized voiced palatal click /ŋʗ/ 1
!Xũ.

Velarized voiced palatal click /gʗ/ 1
!Xũ.

Breathy voiced palatal click /g̤ʗ/ 1
!Xũ.

Glottalized velarized voiced palatal click /gʗ̴ˀ/ 1
!Xũ.

Nasalized breathy voiced palatal click /ŋ̤ʗ/ 1
!Xũ.

Voiceless dental affricated click /ǀ̠ˢ/ 2
Nama, !Xũ.

Velarized voiceless dental affricated click /ǀ̴̠ˢ/ 1
!Xũ.

Voiceless aspirated dental affricated click /ǀ̠ˢʰ/ 1
!Xũ.

Nasalized voiceless aspirated dental affricated click /ŋ̊ǀ̠ˢʰ/ 2
Nama, Xũ.

Velarized voiceless aspirated dental affricated click /ǀ̴̠ʰ/ 1
Nama.

Glottalized nasalized voiceless dental affricated click /ŋ̊ǀ̠ˢˀ/ 1
Nama, !Xũ.

Glottalized nasalized velarized voiceless dental affricated click /ŋ̊ǀ̴̠ˢˀ/ 1
!Xũ.

Voiced dental affricated click /gǀ̠ˢ/ 1
!Xũ.

Velarized voiced dental affricated click /gǂ̪ˢ/ 1
!Xũ.

Nasalized voiced dental affricated click /ŋǂ̪ˢ/ 2
Nama, !Xũ.

Glottalized velarized voiced dental affricated click /gǂ̪ˢˀ/ 1
!Xũ.

Nasalized breathy voiced dental affricated click /ŋ̤ǂ̪ˢ/ 1
!Xũ.

Breathy voiced dental affricated click /g̤ǂ̪ˢ/ 1
!Xũ.

Voiceless alveolar affricated click /ǂˢ/ 1
Zulu.

Voiceless palatal lateral affricated click /ʖ^ʎ/ 1
!Xũ.

Velarized voiceless palatal lateral affricated click /ʖ^ʎ/ 1
!Xũ.

Voiceless aspirated palatal lateral affricated click /ʖ^ʎh/ 1
!Xũ.

Glottalized nasalized voiceless palatal lateral affricated click /ŋ̊ʖ^ʎ/ 1
!Xũ.

Glottalized nasalized velarized voiceless palatal lateral affricated click /ŋ̊
!Xũ.

Nasalized voiceless aspirated palatal lateral affricated click /ŋ̊ʖ^ʎh/ 1
!Xũ.

Voiced palatal lateral affricated click /gʖ^ʎ/ 1
!Xũ.

Velarized voiced palatal lateral affricated click /gʖ^ʎ/ 1
!Xũ.

Breathy voiced palatal lateral affricated click /g̤ʖ^ʎ/ 1 (-1)
RARE !Xũ.

Glottalized velarized voiced palatal lateral affricated click /gʖ^ʎˀ/ 1
!Xũ.

Voiceless alveolar lateral affricated click /ʖ^ɬ/ 2
Zulu, Nama.

Velarized voiceless aspirated alveolar lateral affricated click /ʖ^ɬh/ 1
Nama.

Nasalized voiceless aspirated alveolar lateral affricated click /ŋ̊ʖ^ɬ/ 1
Nama.

Glottalized nasalized voiceless alveolar lateral affricated click /ŋ̊¿^{ɬʔ}/ 1
Nama.

Nasalized voiced alveolar lateral affricated click /ŋ¿^{ɬ}/ 1
Nama.

Nasalized voiced palatal lateral affricated click /ŋ¿^{ʎ}/ 1
!Xũ.

Breathy voiced palatal lateral affricated click /g̤¿^{ʎ}/ 1
!Xũ.

4. AFFRICATES
(Pulmonic and glottalic affricates are included here. Affricated clicks are listed together with other clicks in section 3.)

Voiceless labio-dental affricate /pf/ 3
German, Beembe, Teke.

Voiceless aspirated labio-dental affricate /pf^{h}/ 1
Beembe.

Voiced labio-dental affricate /bv/ 1
Teke.

Voiceless dental affricate /t̪θ/ 2
Luo, Chipewyan.

Voiceless aspirated dental affricate /t̪θ^{h}/ 1
Chipewyan.

Voiced dental affricate /d̪ð/ 1
Luo.

Voiceless dental sibilant affricate /t̪s̪/ 10
Hungarian, Tuva, Ewe, Standard Thai, Malagasy, Tamang, Tzeltal, Squamish, Gununa-Kena, Kabardian.

Voiceless aspirated dental sibilant affricate /t̪s̪^{h}/ 4
Standard Thai, Tamang, Acoma, Nama.

Voiced dental sibilant affricate /d̪z̪/ 5
Hungarian, Ewe, Malagasy, Acoma, Kabardian.

Voiceless dental/alveolar sibilant affricate /"ts"/ 46 (-5)
German, Russian, Bulgarian, Romanian, Pashto, Kashmiri, Albanian, E. Armenian, Lappish, Yurak, Kirghiz, Hebrew, Awiya, Kullo, Lakkia, Atayal, Tagalog, Tsou, Mandarin, Hakka, Changchow, Amoy, Fuchow, Kan, Jingpho, Yao, Tlingit, Chipewyan, Chontal, Mazahua, Tonkawa, Wichita, Yuchi, Wappo, Bɽibri, Ashuslay, Jivaro, Greenlandic, Aleut, Basque, Burushaski; RARE Chukchi; LOAN Lithuanian, Cheremis, Komi, Chuvash.

Long voiceless dental/alveolar affricate /"ts:"/ 3 (-1)
Wichita, Lak; ?DERIVED Japanese.

Long labialized voiceless dental/alveolar sibilant affricate /"ts^{w}:"/ 1
Lak.

Palatalized voiceless dental/alveolar sibilant affricate /"tsʲ"/ 3 (-1)
Bulgarian, Yurak; LOAN Lithuanian.

Voiceless aspirated dental/alveolar sibilant affricate /"tsʰ"/ 19
Kashmiri, E. Armenian, Mongolian, Lakkia, Adzera, Mandarin, Hakka, Changchow, Amoy, Fuchow, Kan, Yao, Chipewyan, Mazahua, Zuni, Wiyot, Yuchi, Lak, Burushaski.

Labialized voiceless aspirated dental/alveolar sibilant affricate /"tsʷʰ"/
Lak.

Voiceless dental/alveolar sibilant affricate with breathy release /"tsʱ"/
Changchow.

Laryngealized voiceless dental/alveolar sibilant affricate /"t̰s̰"/ 1
Ashuslay.

Voiced dental/alveolar sibilant affricate /"dz"/ 18 (-1)
Lithuanian, Pashto, Kashmiri, Albanian, Mongolian, Yulu, Adzera, Amoy, Jingpho, Yao, Suena, Tlingit, Puget Sound, Seneca, Yuchi, Ocaina, Telugu; RARE Awiya.

Voiceless alveolar affricate /tɹ̌/ 1
Tamang.

Voiceless aspirated alveolar affricate /tɹ̌ʰ/ 1
Tamang.

Voiceless alveolar sibilant affricate /ts/ 39
Greek, Bashkir, Lelemi, Amo, Beembe, Ik, Hamer, Margi, Sui, Javanese, Chamorro, Rukai, Tiddim Chin, Garo, Navaho, Hupa, Zoque, Tzeltal, Totonac, K'ekchi, Mixe, Mazatec, Nootka, Quileute, Puget Sound, Hopi, Pomo, Tarascan, Cayapa, Paez, Ocaina, Chacobo, Cashinahua, Jaqaru, Campa, Moxo, Guahibo, Georgian, !Xũ.

Velarized voiceless alveolar sibilant affricate /ᵵs/ 1
!Xũ.

Voiceless aspirated alveolar sibilant affricate /tsʰ/ 10
Beembe, Sui, Navaho, Hupa, Kwakw'ala, Tarascan, Jaqaru, Amuesha, Georgian, !Xũ.

Voiceless alveolar sibilant affricate with breathy release /tsʱ/ 1
Javanese.

Voiced alveolar sibilant affricate /dz/ 10
Greek, Lelemi, Ik, Margi, Chamorro, Garo, Yareba, Kwakw'ala, Puget Sound, Ocaina.

Prenasalized voiced alveolar sibilant affricate /ⁿdz/ 1
Mazatec.

Velarized voiced alveolar sibilant affricate /ᵭz/ 1
!Xũ.

Breathy voiced alveolar sibilant affricate /d̤z̤/ 1
!Xũ.

Voiceless palato-alveolar sibilant affricate /tʃ/ 141 (-5)
Irish, Lithuanian, Russian, Bulgarian, Spanish, Romanian, Farsi, Pashto, Kurdish, Hindi-Urdu, Bengali, Punjabi, Albanian, E. Armenian, Cheremis, Komi, Hungarian, Lappish, Azerbaijani, Chuvash, Yakut, Kirghiz, Khalaj, Tuva, Evenki, Goldi, Manchu, Korean, Japanese, Moro, Bambara, Dagbani, Tarok, Amo, Swahili, Luvale, Teke, Kanuri, Maasai, Luo, Nubian, Ik, Logbara, Kunama, Tigre, Amharic, Neo-Aramaic, Somali, Awiya, Kullo, Dizi, Hausa, Angas, Margi, Mundari, Kharia, Sedang, Khmer, Maranungku, Sui, Po-ai, Lungchow, Sundanese, Sa'ban, Iai, Taishan, Burmese, Lahu, Jingpho, Andamanese, Asmat, Washkuk, Haida, Tlingit, Navaho, Chipewyan, Tolowa, Hupa, Wintu, Chontal, Totonac, K'ekchi, Mazahua, Mazatec, Mixtec, Nootka, Quileute, Squamish, Puget Sound, Papago, Luiseño, Yacqui, Tiwa, Karok, Diegueño, Shasta, Tarascan, Ojibwa, Delaware, Wiyot, Dakota, Yuchi, Alabama, Wappo, Itonama, Bribri, Cayapa, Paez, Ocaina, Muinane, Apinaye, Amahuaca, Chacobo, Tacana, Cashinahua, Ashuslay, Abipon, Quechua, Jaqaru, Island Carib, Campa, Guajiro, Moxo, Siriono, Ticuna, Siona, Jivaro, Cofan, Araucanian, Malayalam, Yukaghir, Georgian, Basque, Burushaski, Brahui, !Xũ; LOAN Goldi, Hebrew, Otomi, Guarani; OBSCURE Kefa.

Long voiceless palato-alveolar sibilant affricate /tʃː/ 5 (-1)
Punjabi, Yakut, Delaware, Lak; ?DERIVED Japanese.

Labialized voiceless palato-alveolar sibilant affricate /tʃ^{w}/ 1
Ga.

Long labialized voiceless palato-alveolar sibilant affricate /tʃ^{w}ː/ 1
Lak.

Palatalized voiceless palato-alveolar sibilant affricate /tʃ^{j}/ 1
Kashmiri.

Velarized voiceless palato-alveolar sibilant affricate /t̴ʃ/ 1
!Xũ.

Voiceless aspirated palato-alveolar sibilant affricate /tʃ^{h}/ 43 (-2)
Hindi-Urdu, Bengali, Punjabi, E. Armenian, Osmanli, Mongolian, Korean, Igbo, Gã, Swahili, Kharia, Khmer, Sui, Lungchow, Taishan, Burmese, Lahu, Haida, Navaho, Chipewyan, Tolowa, Mazahua, Yana, Tarascan, Zuni, Acoma, Wiyot, Dakota, Yuchi, Tunica, Quechua, Jaqaru, Wapishana, Amuesha, Cofan, Kota, Gilyak, Georgian, Lak, Burushaski, !Xũ; RARE Jingpho; LOAN Po-ai.

Long voiceless aspirated palato-alveolar sibilant affricate /tʃ^{h}ː/ 1
Punjabi.

Labialized voiceless aspirated palato-alveolar sibilant affricate /tʃ^{wh}/ 2
Hupa, Lak.

Palatalized voiceless aspirated palato-alveolar sibilant affricate /tʃ^{jh}/ 2 (-1)
Kashmiri; OBSCURE Amuesha.

Preaspirated voiceless palato-alveolar sibilant affricate /^{h}tʃ/ 2 (-1)
Guajiro; OBSCURE Ojibwa.

Laryngealized voiceless palato-alveolar sibilant affricate /t̰ʃ̰/ 3
Korean, Mundari, Ashuslay.

Voiced palato-alveolar sibilant affricate /dʒ/ 80 (-5)
Irish, Lithuanian, Bulgarian, Romanian, Farsi, Pashto, Kurdish, Hindi-Urdu, Bengali, Punjabi, Albanian, Komi, Osmanli, Azerbaijani, Yakut, Mongolian, Evenki, Goldi, Manchu, Japanese, Moro, Bambara, Dagbani, Igbo, Gã, Tarok, Zulu, Teke, Kanuri, Fur, Luo, Nubian, Ik, Nera, Logbara, Sara, Berta, Kunama, Arabic, Tigre, Amharic, Neo-Aramaic, Awiya, Beja, Kullo, Dizi, Hausa, Angas, Margi, Mundari, Kharia, Khasi, Bandjalang, Batak, Sa'ban, Iai, Amoy, Burmese, Lahu, Jingpho, Andamanese, Tlingit, Wintu, Papago, Achumawi, Yana, Acoma, Yuchi, Muinane, Ticuna, Cofan, Kota, Malayalam, Burushaski, Brahui; RARE Puget Sound; LOAN Hungarian, Khalaj, Hebrew; OBSCURE Kefa.

Long voiced palato-alveolar sibilant affricate /dʒː/ 2
Punjabi, Yakut.

Prenasalized voiced palato-alveolar sibilant affricate /^{n}dʒ/ 5
Luvale, Sedang, Washkuk, Mazatec, Siriono.

Labialized voiced palato-alveolar sibilant affricate /dʒ^{w}/ 1
Ga.

Palatalized voiced palato-alveolar sibilant affricate /dʒ^{j}/ 1
Kashmiri.

Velarized voiced palato-alveolar sibilant affricate /d̴ʒ/ 1
!Xũ.

Breathy voiced palato-alveolar sibilant affricate /d̤ʒ̤/ 6
Hindi-Urdu, Bengali, Igbo, Mundari, Kharia, !Xũ.

Voiceless retroflex affricate /ṭɹ̣̌/ 1
Araucanian.

Voiceless retroflex sibilant affricate /ṭṣ/ 7
Ostyak, Mandarin, Mazatec, Tacana, Jaqaru, Basque, Burushaski.

Voiceless aspirated retroflex sibilant affricate /ṭṣ^{h}/ 6
Mandarin, Acoma, Wichita, Jaqaru, Amuesha, Burushaski.

Voiced retroflex sibilant affricate /ḍẓ/ 2
Acoma, Burushaski.

Prenasalized voiced retroflex sibilant affricate /^{n}ḍẓ/ 1
Mazatec.

Voiceless retroflex affricated trill /ṭṛ̌/ 1
Malagasy.

Voiced retroflex affricated trill /ḍṛ̌/ 1
Malagasy.

Voiceless palatal affricate /cç/ 9
Sinhalese, Albanian, Komi, Hungarian, Akan, Saek, Mandarin, Kan, Ao.

Labialized voiceless palatal affricate /cç^{w}/ 1
Akan.

Voiceless aspirated palatal affricate /cçʰ/ 2
Mandarin, Kan.

Voiced palatal affricate /ɟʝ/ 5
Sinhalese, Albanian, Komi, Hungarian, Akan.

Labialized voiced palatal affricate /ɟʝʷ/ 1
Akan.

Voiceless palatal sibilant affricate /cɕ/ 2 (-1)
Gununa-Kena; LOAN Telugu.

Voiceless velar affricate /kx/ 1
Tavgy.

Voiceless aspirated velar affricate /kxʰ/ 2
Chipewyan, Nama.

Labialized voiceless aspirated velar affricate /kxʷʰ/ 1
Chipewyan.

Voiceless uvular affricate /qχ/ 3
Wolof, Nez Perce, Kabardian.

Labialized voiceless uvular affricate /qχʷ/ 1
Kabardian.

Palatalized voiceless dental lateral affricate /t̪ɬ̪ʲ/ 1
Kabardian.

Voiceless dental/alveolar lateral affricate /"tɬ"/ 5
Haida, Tlingit, Chipewyan, Nootka, Squamish.

Voiceless aspirated dental/alveolar lateral affricate /"tɬʰ"/ 1
Chipewyan.

Voiced dental/alveolar lateral affricate /"dɮ"/ 2
Haida, Tlingit.

Voiceless alveolar lateral affricate /tɬ/ 3
Navaho, Wintu, Quileute.

Voiceless aspirated alveolar lateral affricate /tɬʰ/ 1
Kwakw'ala.

Voiced alveolar lateral affricate /dɮ/ 2
Navaho, Kwakw'ala.

Voiceless velar plosive with alveolar lateral fricative release /kɬ/ 1 (-1)
OBSCURE Ashuslay.

Voiceless dental ejective affricate /t̪θ'/ 1
Chipewyan.

Voiceless dental sibilant ejective affricate /t̪s̪'/ 5
Tzeltal, Squamish, Acoma, Gununa-Kena, Kabardian.

Voiceless dental/alveolar sibilant ejective affricate /"ts'"/ 11
E. Armenian, Kullo, Dizi, Tlingit, Chipewyan, Mazahua, Zuni, Wichita, Yuchi, Wappo, Lak.

Labialized voiceless dental/alveolar sibilant ejective affricate /"tsʷ'"/ 1
Lak.

Voiceless alveolar sibilant ejective affricate /ts'/ 18
Ik, Tigre, Iraqw, Navaho, Tolowa, Hupa, Wintu, Tzeltal, K'ekchi, Otomi, Nootka, Kwakw'ala, Quileute, Puget Sound, Pomo, Jaqaru, Georgian, !Xũ.

Voiced alveolar sibilant ejective affricate /dz'/ 1
!Xũ.

Voiceless palato-alveolar sibilant ejective affricate /tʃ'/ 35 (-2)
E. Armenian, Zulu, Tigre, Amharic, Dizi, Haida, Tlingit, Navaho, Chipewyan, Tolowa, Hupa, Wintu, Chontal, K'ekchi, Mazahua, Nootka, Quileute, Squamish, Puget Sound, Yana, Shasta, Zuni, Acoma, Dakota, Yuchi, Wappo, Itonama, Quechua, Jaqaru, Gununa-Kena, Georgian, Lak, !Xũ; ?DERIVED Otomi; OBSCURE Kefa.

Labialized voiceless palato-alveolar sibilant ejective affricate /tʃʷ'/ 1
Lak.

Voiced palato-alveolar sibilant ejective affricate /dʒ'/ 1
!Xũ.

Voiceless retroflex sibilant ejective affricate /ṭṣ'/ 3
Tolowa, Acoma, Jaqaru.

Voiceless palatal ejective affricate /cç'/ 1
Gununa-Kena.

Voiceless velar ejective affricate /kx'/ 1
Tlingit.

Labialized voiceless velar ejective affricate /kxʷ'/ 1
Tlingit.

Voiceless dental/alveolar lateral ejective affricate /"tɬ'"/ 6
Ik, Haida, Tlingit, Chipewyan, Nootka, Squamish.

Voiceless alveolar lateral ejective affricate /tɬ'/ 7
Iraqw, Navaho, Hupa, Wintu, Kwakw'ala, Quileute, Puget Sound.

Voiceless laterally-released velar ejective affricate /kɬ'/ 1
Zulu.

5. FRICATIVES

Voiceless bilabial fricative /ɸ/ 21 (-5)
Ewe, Hausa, Sui, Iai, Kan, Washkuk, Kewa, Fasu, Yareba, Otomi, Yuchi, Alabama, Cayapa, Ocaina, Muinane, Araucanian; RARE Kanuri; LOAN Sinhalese, Mongolian, Tarascan, Quechua.

Labialized voiceless bilabial fricative /ɸʷ/ 1
Washkuk.

Labialized velarized voiceless bilabial fricative /ɸ^{w}/ 1
Irish.

Palatalized voiceless bilabial fricative /ɸ^{j}/ 3
Irish, Hausa, Paez.

Voiced bilabial fricative /β/ 32 (-2)
Spanish, Pashto, Cheremis, Kirghiz, Evenki, Goldi, Ewe, Neo-Aramaic, Dizi, Atayal, Kaliai, Iai, Washkuk, Gadsup, Rotokas, Mazatec, Mixtec, Diegueño, Paez, Ocaina, Muinane, Carib, Chacobo, Tacana, Amuesha, Campa, Moxo, Cofan, Greenlandic, Georgian; LOAN Mongolian, Quechua.

Palatalized voiced bilabial fricative /β^{j}/ 1
Irish.

Voiceless labio-dental fricative /f/ 135 (-20)
Greek, Breton, German, Norwegian, Russian, Bulgarian, French, Spanish, Romanian, Farsi, Pashto, Kurdish, Albanian, Hungarian, Lappish, Osmanli, Azerbaijani, Kirghiz, Tuva, Manchu, Katcha, Moro, Kadugli, Kpelle, Bisa, Bambara, Dan, Wolof, Diola, Temne, Dagbani, Senadi, Tampulma, Bariba, Ewe, Akan, Igbo, Gã, Efik, Birom, Tarok, Amo, Beembe, Swahili, Zulu, Teke, Doayo, Gbeya, Zande, Songhai, Maba, Fur, Luo, Nubian, Ik, Tama, Nera, Tabi, Logbara, Berta, Kunama, Arabic, Tigre, Amharic, Hebrew, Socotri, Neo-Aramaic, Shilha, Tuareg, Somali, Awiya, Iraqw, Beja, Kullo, Dizi, Kefa, Angas, Margi, Ngizim, Vietnamese, Kunjen, Standard Thai, Lakkia, Yay, Po-ai, Lungchow, Malagasy, Chamorro, Tsou, Adzera, Iai, Maori, Mandarin, Taishan, Hakka, Changchow, Lahu, Yao, Asmat, Sentani, Telefol, Chuave, Koiari, Taoripi, Wintu, Karok, Pomo, Ashuslay, Island Carib, Guahibo, Cofan, Ket, Kabardian, Basque, Brahui; RARE Luvale, Kanuri; LOAN Hindi-Urdu, Punjabi, E. Armenian, Cheremis, Komi, Finnish, Chuvash, Yakut, Bashkir, Khalaj, Yacqui, Tarascan, Wappo, Moxo, Guarani, Ticuna, Telugu, Burushaski.

Long voiceless labio-dental fricative /f:/ 3
Arabic, Shilha, Greenlandic.

Palatalized voiceless labio-dental fricative /f^{j}/ 2
Russian, Bulgarian.

Voiced labio-dental fricative /v/ 67 (-3)
Greek, Breton, German, Lithuanian, Russian, Bulgarian, French, Romanian, Farsi, Kurdish, Albanian, E. Armenian, Komi, Finnish, Hungarian, Osmanli, Azerbaijani, Tuva, Kpelle, Bisa, Dan, Dagbani, Senadi, Tampulma, Ewe, Igbo, Gã, Lelemi, Birom, Tarok, Amo, Beembe, Swahili, Zulu, Doayo, Gbeya, Zande, Logbara, Hebrew, Angas, Margi, Ngizim, Vietnamese, Yay, Saek, Po-ai, Lungchow, Malagasy, Rukai, Tsou, Changchow, Lahu, Tiddim Chin, Yagaria, Nambakaengo, Mixe, Luiseño, Hopi, Apinaye, Guarani, Guahibo, Kota, Kabardian, Brahui; LOAN Yakut, Bashkir, Khalaj.

Palatalized voiced labio-dental fricative /v^{j}/ 3
Lithuanian, Russian, Bulgarian.

Voiceless dental fricative /θ/ 18 (-1)
Greek, Spanish, Albanian, Bashkir, Tabi, Mursi, Berta, Lakkia, Yay, Rukai, Iai, Burmese, Karen, Chipewyan, Wintu, Amahuaca, Araucanian; RARE Arabic.

Voiced dental fricative /ð/ 21 (-5)
Greek, Spanish, Albanian, Cheremis, Yurak, Tavgy, Moro, Tabi, Rukai, Iai, Burmese, Koiari, Chipewyan, Mixtec, Tacana, Aleut; RARE Arabic, Kunjen; LOAN Mazatec, Quechua, Guarani.

Palatalized voiced dental fricative /ðʲ/ 1
Yurak.

Pharyngealized voiced dental fricative /ðˤ/ 1 (-1)
RARE Arabic.

Voiceless dental sibilant fricative /s̪/ 33
Irish, Russian, French, Spanish, Kurdish, Punjabi, Sinhalese, Albanian, Hungarian, Yakut, Tuva, Manchu, Moro, Nyangi, Arabic, Tuareg, Beja, Standard Thai, Javanese, Tamang, Nimboran, Tzeltal, Mixe, Squamish, Papago, Luiseño, Karok, Diegueño, Yana, Acoma, Gununa-Kena, Guarani, Kabardian.

Long voiceless dental sibilant fricative /s̪:/ 3
Punjabi, Yakut, Arabic.

Palatalized voiceless dental sibilant fricative /s̪ʲ/ 1
Russian.

Pharyngealized voiceless dental sibilant fricative /s̪ˤ/ 1
Arabic.

Long pharyngealized voiceless dental sibilant fricative /s̪ˤ:/ 1
Arabic.

Voiced dental sibilant fricative /z̪/ 11 (-2)
Russian, French, Kurdish, Albanian, Hungarian, Tuva, Arabic, Tuareg, Kabardian; LOAN Punjabi, Yakut.

Long voiced dental sibilant fricative /z̪:/ 1
Arabic.

Palatalized voiced dental sibilant fricative /z̪ʲ/ 1
Russian.

Pharyngealized voiced dental sibilant fricative /z̪ˤ/ 2
Arabic, Tuareg.

Long pharyngealized voiced dental sibilant fricative /z̪ˤ:/ 1
Arabic.

Voiceless dental/alveolar sibilant fricative /"s"/ 131 (-3)
Breton, Norwegian, Lithuanian, Bulgarian, Romanian, Farsi, Pashto, Hindi-Urdu, Kashmiri, E. Armenian, Ostyak, Cheremis, Lappish, Yurak, Tavgy, Chuvash, Kirghiz, Khalaj, Mongolian, Goldi, Korean, Japanese, Katcha, Wolof, Dagbani, Senadi, Ewe, Akan, Igbo, Gã, Tarok, Swahili, Luvale, Doayo, Songhai, Kanuri, Maasai, Nubian, Sebei, Nera, Logbara, Berta, Amharic, Hebrew, Socotri, Shilha, Awiya, Kullo, Dizi, Hausa, Kharia, Khasi, Sedang, Khmer, Mabuiag, Yay, Sui, Atayal, Malagasy, Malay, Batak, Tagalog, Chamorro, Tsou, Adzera, Kaliai, Iai, Mandarin, Hakka, Changchow, Amoy, Fuchow, Kan, Dafla, Burmese, Jingpho, Karen, Yao, Telefol, Pawaian, Dani, Wantoat, Suena, Kunimaipa, Taoripi, Nambakaengo, Tlingit, Chipewyan, Chontal, Mazahua, Mazatec, Mixtec,

Chatino, Tiwa, Pomo, Shasta, Tarascan, Zuni, Ojibwa, Delaware, Tonkawa, Wiyot, Seneca, Wichita, Dakota, Yuchi, Wappo, Itonama, Bribri, Mura, Carib, Amahuaca, Ashuslay, Arabela, Quechua, Island Carib, Guajiro, Sirionо, Jivaro, Cofan, Greenlandic, Kurukh, Ket, Yukaghir, Gilyak, Lak, Basque, Burushaski; RARE Apinaye; LOAN Bengali, Ticuna.

Long voiceless dental/alveolar sibilant fricative /"s:"/ 4
Japanese, Shilha, Wichita, Lak.

Labialized voiceless dental/alveolar sibilant fricative /"s^{w}"/ 1
Amharic.

Palatalized voiceless dental/alveolar sibilant fricative /"s^{j}"/ 6 (-1)
Lithuanian, Bulgarian, Yurak, Ket, Chukchi; LOAN Cheremis.

Pharyngealized voiceless dental/alveolar sibilant fricative /"s^{ʕ}"/ 1
Shilha.

Voiceless aspirated dental/alveolar sibilant fricative /"s^{h}"/ 3
Burmese, Karen, Mazahua.

Preaspirated voiceless dental/alveolar sibilant fricative /"^{h}s"/ 1 (-1)
OBSCURE Ojibwa.

Laryngealized voiceless dental/alveolar sibilant fricative /"s̰"/ 2
Korean, Hausa.

Voiced dental/alveolar sibilant fricative /"z"/ 50 (-4)
Breton, Lithuanian, Bulgarian, Romanian, Farsi, Pashto, E. Armenian, Cheremis, Kirghiz, Khalaj, Japanese, Katcha, Dagbani, Senadi, Ewe, Igbo, Gã, Tarok, Swahili, Doayo, Songhai, Kanuri, Logbara, Yulu, Amharic, Hebrew, Socotri, Shilha, Tuareg, Awiya, Kullo, Dizi, Hausa, Mabuiag, Sui, Malagasy, Changchow, Burmese, Kunimaipa, Chipewyan, Mazahua, Dakota, Bribri, Apinaye, Lak, Burushaski; RARE Karen; LOAN Hindi-Urdu, Chuvash, Evenki.

Long voiced dental/alveolar sibilant fricative /"z:"/ 1
Shilha.

Prenasalized voiced dental/alveolar sibilant fricative /"^{n}z"/ 1
Wantoat.

Palatalized voiced dental/alveolar sibilant fricative /"z^{j}"/ 1
Bulgarian.

Pharyngealized voiced dental/alveolar sibilant fricative /"z^{ʕ}"/ 1
Shilha.

Voiced alveolar fricative /ɹ̌/ 3
Azerbaijani, Sa'ban, Karen.

Voiceless alveolar sibilant fricative /s/ 112 (-3)
Greek, German, Komi, Finnish, Osmanli, Azerbaijani, Bashkir, Evenki, Kadugli, Kpelle, Bisa, Bambara, Dan, Diola, Temne, Tampulma, Bariba, Lelemi, Efik, Birom, Amo, Beembe, Zulu, Teke, Gbeya, Zande, Maba, Fur, Luo, Ik, Tama, Temein, Tabi, Sara, Kunama, Koma, Tigre, Neo-Aramaic, Somali, Iraqw, Hamer, Angas, Margi, Ngizim, Mundari, Vietnamese, Saek,

Sundanese, Sa'ban, Rukai, Ao, Tiddim Chin, Garo, Boro, Asmat, Washkuk, Iwam, Selepet, Yagaria, Kewa, Chuave, Daribi, Fasu, Yareba, Navaho, Tolowa, Hupa, Nez Perce, Klamath, Maidu, Wintu, Zoque, Tzeltal, Totonac, K'ekchi, Otomi, Nootka, Kwakw'ala, Quileute, Puget Sound, Hopi, Yacqui, Karok, Diegueño, Achumawi, Tunica, Alabama, Cayapa, Paez, Muinane, Ocaina, Chacobo, Cashinahua, S. Nambiquara, Jaqaru, Wapishana, Amuesha, Campa, Moxo, Guarani, Guahibo, Siona, Tucano, Malayalam, Georgian, Nama, Brahui, Ainu, !Xũ; RARE Telugu; LOAN Barasano, Araucanian.

Long voiceless alveolar sibilant affricate /sː/ 2
Finnish, Iraqw.

Pharyngealized voiceless alveolar sibilant fricative /sˤ/ 1
Kurdish.

Laryngealized voiceless alveolar sibilant fricative /s̰/ 2
S. Nambiquara, Siona.

Voiced alveolar sibilant fricative /z/ 36 (-1)
Greek, German, Komi, Osmanli, Azerbaijani, Kpelle, Bisa, Bambara, Dan, Tampulma, Bariba, Birom, Amo, Zulu, Gbeya, Zande, Maba, Fur, Ik, Tabi, Tigre, Neo-Aramaic, Hamer, Angas, Margi, Ngizim,Vietnamese, Ao, Tiddim Chin, Boro, Navaho, Otomi, Georgian, Brahui, !Xũ; LOAN Bashkir.

Prenasalized voiced alveolar sibilant fricative /^{n}z/ 1
Paez.

Voiceless palato-alveolar fricative /ɹ̥̌/ 1
Kabardian.

Voiced palato-alveolar fricative /ɹ̠̌/ 1
Kabardian.

Voiceless palato-alveolar sibilant fricative /ʃ/ 146 (-9)
Irish, Breton, German, Norwegian, Lithuanian, Bulgarian, French, Romanian, Farsi, Pashto, Kurdish, Albanian, E. Armenian, Cheremis, Komi, Hungarian, Lappish, Osmanli, Azerbaijani, Chuvash, Kirghiz, Bashkir, Khalaj, Tuva, Mongolian, Manchu, Japanese, Bambara, Senadi, Gã, Birom, Tarok, Amo, Swahili, Luvale, Zulu, Kanuri, Maba, Fur, Maasai, Luo, Nubian, Nera, Tabi, Mursi, Berta, Kunama, Koma, Arabic, Tigre, Amharic, Hebrew, Socotri, Neo-Aramaic, Shilha, Tuareg, Somali, Awiya, Iraqw, Beja, Kullo, Dizi, Kefa, Hamer, Hausa, Angas, Margi, Ngizim, Kanakuru, Khasi, Sedang, Sui, Po-ai, Lungchow, Cham, Iai, Taishan, Burmese, Lahu, Jingpho, Washkuk, Navaho, Chipewyan, Tolowa, Chontal, Totonac, K'ekchi, Mixe, Otomi, Mazahua, Mixtec, Chatino, Nootka, Quileute, Squamish, Puget Sound, Karok, Pomo, Achumawi, Tarascan, Zuni, Acoma, Ojibwa, Delaware, Wiyot, Dakota, Yuchi, Tunica, Wappo, Bribri, Cayapa, Paez, Ocaina, Muinane, Chacobo, Tacana, Cashinahua, Ashuslay, Arabela, Quechua, Jaqaru, Gununa-Kena, Wapishana, Amuesha, Campa, Guajiro, Siriono, Jivaro, Cofan, Greenlandic, Aleut, Georgian, Kabardian, Lak, Basque, Burushaski, !Xũ; RARE Karen, Moxo; LOAN Hindi-Urdu, Sinhalese, Ostyak, Finnish, Yakut; ?DERIVED Luiseño; OBSCURE Ojibwa.

Long voiceless palato-alveolar sibilant fricative /ʃː/ 4
Japanese, Arabic, Shilha, Lak.

Labialized voiceless palato-alveolar sibilant fricative /ʃʷ/ 2
Gã, Lak.

Long labialized palato-alveolar sibilant fricative /ʃʷː/ 1
Lak.

Palatalized voiceless palato-alveolar sibilant fricative /ʃʲ/ 3
Lithuanian, Kashmiri, Paez.

Velarized voiceless palato-alveolar sibilant fricative /ʃ̴/ 1
Russian.

Voiced palato-alveolar sibilant fricative /ʒ/ 51 (-7)
Breton, Lithuanian, Bulgarian, French, Romanian, Farsi, Pashto, Kurdish, Albanian, E. Armenian, Cheremis, Komi, Hungarian, Osmanli, Azerbaijani, Khalaj, Tuva, Senadi, Tarok, Luvale, Maba, Tigre, Amharic, Socotri, Neo-Aramaic, Shilha, Tuareg, Dizi, Angas, Margi, Ngizim, Kanakuru, Navaho, Mixe, Mazahua, Mixtec, Dakota, Ocaina, Apinaye, Aleut, Georgian, Kabardian, Lak, !Xũ; RARE Atayal; LOAN German, Hindi-Urdu, Chuvash, Yakut, Bashkir, Hebrew.

Long voiced palato-alveolar sibilant fricative /ʒː/ 1
Shilha.

Prenasalized voiced palato-alveolar sibilant fricative /ⁿʒ/ 1
Paez.

Palatalized voiced palato-alveolar sibilant fricative /ʒʲ/ 1
Lithuanian.

Velarized voiced palato-alveolar sibilant fricative /ʒ̴/ 1
Russian.

Voiceless retroflex fricative /ɹ̣̌̊/ 1
Hopi.

Voiced retroflex fricative /ɹ̣̌/ 4
E. Armenian, Araucanian, Chukchi, Burushaski.

Voiceless retroflex sibilant fricative /ṣ/ 17
Pashto, Punjabi, Cham, Mandarin, Tolowa, Mazatec, Papago, Tarascan, Acoma, Chacobo, Tacana, Cashinahua, Telugu, Kota, Malayalam, Basque, Burushaski.

Voiced retroflex sibilant fricative /ẓ/ 3
Pashto, Mandarin, Amuesha.

Laryngealized voiced retroflex sibilant fricative /ẓ̰/ 1
Wapishana.

Voiceless palatal fricative /ç/ 11 (-1)
Irish, Norwegian, Bengali, Komi, Margi, Mandarin, Kan, Haida, Kwakw'ala, Paez; OBSCURE Chuvash.

Long voiceless palatal fricative /çː/ 1 (-1)
?DERIVED Japanese.

Labialized voiceless palatal fricative /$ç^{w}$/ 1
Akan.

Voiced palatal fricative /ǰ/ 7
Komi, Khalaj, Goldi, Margi, Asmat, Greenlandic, Ket.

Voiceless palatal sibilant fricative /ɕ/ 2
Gununa-Kena, Telugu.

Voiced palatal sibilant fricative /ʑ/ 2
Muinane, Cofan.

Voiceless velar fricative /x/ 76 (-7)
Greek, Irish, Breton, German, Russian, Bulgarian, Spanish, Kurdish, Yurak, Azerbaijani, Chuvash, Kirghiz, Bashkir, Mongolian, Goldi, Manchu, Hebrew, Shilha, Iraqw, Angas, Margi, Vietnamese, Sui, Atayal, Iai, Fuchow, Dafla, Tiddim Chin, Karen, Kewa, Haida, Tlingit, Navaho, Chipewyan, Tolowa, Hupa, Nez Perce, Wintu, K'ekchi, Nootka, Quileute, Luiseño, Tiwa, Karok, Pomo, Achumawi, Yana, Shasta, Tarascan, Delaware, Tonkawa, Dakota, Bribri, Ocaina, Muinane, Amahuaca, Ashuslay, Jaqaru, Gununa-Kena, Amuesha, Guarani, Guahibo, Jivaro, Aleut, Gilyak, Lak, Nama, Brahui, !Xũ; LOAN Lithuanian, Cheremis, Komi, Khalaj, Kanuri, Somali; ?DERIVED K'ekchi.

Long voiceless velar fricative /xː/ 3
Shilha, Greenlandic, Lak.

Labialized voiceless velar fricative /x^{w}/ 18 (-1)
Iraqw, Haida, Tlingit, Chipewyan, Tolowa, Hupa, Nootka, Kwakw'ala, Quileute, Squamish, Puget Sound, Luiseño, Tiwa, Diegueño, Tonkawa, Kabardian, Lak; LOAN Guarani.

Long labialized voiceless velar fricative /x^{w}ː/ 1
Lak.

Palatalized voiceless velar fricative /x^{j}/ 1
Kabardian.

Voiced velar fricative /ɣ/ 40 (-5)
Greek, Irish, Spanish, Kurdish, Ostyak, Cheremis, Azerbaijani, Kpelle, Igbo, Fur, Shilha, Angas, Margi, Vietnamese, Maung, Kunjen, Sui, Saek, Atayal, Lahu, Karen, Navaho, Chipewyan, Tolowa, Dakota, Paez, Abipon, Amuesha, Guarani, Cofan, Greenlandic, Aleut, Chukchi, Gilyak, Brahui; RARE Tiwi; LOAN Mazatec, Quechua; ?ABSTRACT Osmanli; OBSCURE Tuva.

Long voiced velar fricative /ɣː/ 1
Shilha.

Labialized voiced velar fricative /$ɣ^{w}$/ 2 (-1)
Chipewyan; LOAN Guarani.

Palatalized voiced velar fricative /$ɣ^{j}$/ 1
Kabardian.

Laryngealized voiced velar fricative /ɣ̰/ 1
Sui.

Voiceless uvular fricative /χ/ 27 (-4)
Farsi, Pashto, E. Armenian, Wolof, Arabic, Neo-Aramaic, Tuareg, Mandarin, Haida, Tlingit, Wintu, Kwakw'ala, Quileute, Squamish, Puget Sound, Pomo, Achumawi, Aleut, Kurukh, Gilyak, Georgian, Kabardian, Lak; LOAN Hindi-Urdu, Nootka, Basque, Burushaski.

Long voiceless uvular fricative /χ:/ 3
Arabic, Greenlandic, Lak.

Labialized voiceless uvular fricative /χ^{w}/ 9 (-1)
Haida, Tlingit, Kwakw'ala, Quileute, Squamish, Puget Sound, Kabardian, Lak; LOAN Nootka.

Long labialized voiceless uvular fricative /χ^{w} / 1
Lak.

Voiced uvular fricative /ʁ/ 14 (-1)
Pashto, Arabic, Hebrew, Tuareg, Sui, Abipon, Greenlandic, Aleut, Yukaghir, Gilyak, Georgian, Kabardian, Burushaski; LOAN Hindi-Urdu.

Long voiced uvular fricative /ʁ:/ 1
Arabic.

Labialized voiced uvular fricative /ʁ^{w}/ 1
Kabardian.

Voiceless pharyngeal fricative /ħ/ 13
Kurdish, Ewe, Tama, Arabic, Tigre, Socotri, Shilha, Somali, Iraqw, Atayal, Nootka, Kabardian, Lak.

Long voiceless pharyngeal fricative /ħ:/ 2
Arabic, Shilha.

Voiced pharyngeal fricative /ʕ/ 8 (-1)
Kurdish, Ewe, Arabic, Tigre, Socotri, Shilha, Somali; LOAN Kabardian.

Long voiced pharyngeal fricative /ʕ:/ 1
Arabic.

Voiceless "h" /h/ 202 (-2)
Irish, German, Norwegian, Romanian, Farsi, Pashto, Bengali, Albanian, E. Armenian, Finnish, Hungarian, Lappish, Osmanli, Azerbaijani, Bashkir, Khalaj, Korean, Japanese, Bambara, Diola, Temne, Tampulma, Bariba, Akan, Igbo, Gã, Birom, Tarok, Amo, Beembe, Luvale, Zulu, Teke, Doayo, Gbeya, Zande, Kanuri, Fur, Luo, Nubian, Ik, Tama, Nera, Tabi, Mursi, Logbara, Sara, Berta, Kunama, Koma, Arabic, Tigre, Amharic, Hebrew, Socotri, Neo-Aramaic, Shilha, Tuareg, Somali, Iraqw, Beja, Kullo, Dizi, Kefa, Hamer, Hausa, Angas, Ngizim, Mundari, Khasi, Vietnamese, Sedang, Khmer, Standard Thai, Lakkia, Yay, Sui, Saek, Po-ai, Lungchow, Sundanese, Javanese, Malagasy, Cham, Malay, Batak, Tagalog, Sa'ban, Chamorro, Rukai, Tsou, Adzera, Roro, Kaliai, Iai, Maori, Hawaiian, Taishan, Hakka, Changchow, Amoy, Kan, Tamang, Burmese, Lahu, Jingpho, Tiddim Chin, Garo, Boro, Yao, Washkuk, Sentani, Nimboran, Iwam, Selepet, Yagaria, Pawaian, Dani, Daribi, Fasu, Koiari, Taoripi, Haida, Navaho, Chipewyan, Tolowa, Hupa, Nez Perce, Klamath, Maidu, Wintu, Chontal, Zoque, Tzeltal, Totonac, Otomi, Mazahua, Mazatec, Mixtec, Chatino, Nootka, Kwakw'ala, Quileute, Squamish, Puget Sound, Papago, Luiseño, Hopi, Yacqui, Tiwa,

Karok, Pomo, Achumawi, Yana, Shasta, Tarascan, Zuni, Acoma, Delaware, Tonkawa, Seneca, Dakota, Yuchi, Tunica, Alabama, Wappo, Itonama, Mura, Cayapa, Paez, Ocaina, Carib, Amahuaca, Chacobo, Cashinahua, Abipon, S. Nambiquara, Arabela, Quechua, Gununa-Kena, Island Carib, Campa, Guajiro, Moxo, Siriono, Guahibo, Barasano, Siona, Tucano, Cofan, Aleut, Kurukh, Malayalam, Ket, Gilyak, Lak, Nama, Burushaski, Ainu, Brahui; RARE Wapishana; LOAN Georgian.

Long voiceless "h" /h:/ 2
Arabic, Delaware.

Labialized voiceless "h" /hʷ/ 4
Igbo, Amharic, Hupa, Siona.

Laryngealized voiceless "h" /h̰/ 1 (-1)
OBSCURE S. Nambiquara.

Voiced "h" /ɦ/ 13 (-1)
Hindi-Urdu, Kashmiri, Punjabi, Sinhalese, Zulu, Kharia, Changchow, Dafla, Wichita, Telugu, Kabardian, !Xũ; RARE Karen.

Long voiceless dental lateral fricative /ɬ̪:/ 1
Greenlandic.

Palatalized voiceless dental lateral fricative /ɬ̪ʲ/ 1
Kabardian.

Palatalized voiced dental lateral fricative /ɮ̪ʲ/ 1
Kabardian.

Voiceless dental/alveolar lateral fricative /"ɬ"/ 18
Ik, Socotri, Lakkia, Po-ai, Lungchow, Taishan, Haida, Tlingit, Tolowa, Nootka, Tiwa, Zuni, Wiyot, Yuchi, Alabama, Aleut, Chukchi, Brahui.

Voiced dental/alveolar lateral fricative /"ɮ"/ 2
Ik, Socotri.

Voiceless alveolar lateral fricative /ɬ/ 13
Zulu, Nyangi, Iraqw, Margi, Ngizim, Navaho, Hupa, Nez Perce, Totonac, Kwakw'ala, Quileute, Puget Sound, Diegueño.

Voiced alveolar lateral fricative /ɮ/ 4
Zulu, Margi, Ngizim, Kanakuru.

Voiceless palato-alveolar lateral fricative /ɬ̠/ 1
Diegueño.

Voiced palato-alveolar lateral fricative /ɮ̠/ 1
Pashto.

Voiced retroflex lateral fricative /ɮ̣/ 1
Ao.

Voiceless velar-alveolar lateral fricative /x͡ɬ/ 1 (-1)
OBSCURE Ashuslay.

Voiceless bilabial ejective fricative /Φ'/ 1
Yuchi.

Voiceless labio-dental ejective fricative /f'/ 1
Kabardian.

Voiceless dental/alveolar sibilant ejective fricative /"s'"/ 7
Berta, Socotri, Tlingit, Mazahua, Wichita, Dakota, Yuchi.

Voiceless alveolar sibilant ejective fricative /s'/ 1
Koma.

Voiceless palato-alveolar sibilant ejective fricative /ʃ'/ 4 (-1)
Dakota, Yuchi, Kabardian; RARE Socotri.

Voiceless retroflex sibilant ejective fricative /ṣ'/ 1
Acoma.

Voiceless palatal sibilant ejective fricative /ɕ'/ 1
Acoma.

Voiceless velar ejective fricative /x'/ 2
Tlingit, Dakota.

Labialized voiceless velar ejective fricative /x^{w}'/ 1
Tlingit.

Voiceless uvular ejective fricative /χ'/ 1
Tlingit.

Labialized voiceless uvular ejective fricative /χ^{w}'/ 1
Tlingit.

Voiceless dental/alveolar lateral ejective fricative /"ɬ'"/ 2
Tlingit, Yuchi.

6. NASALS

Voiced bilabial nasal /m/ 299 (-3)
Greek, Breton, German, Norwegian, Lithuanian, Russian, Bulgarian, French, Spanish, Romanian, Farsi, Pashto, Kurdish, Hindi-Urdu, Bengali, Kashmiri, Punjabi, Sinhalese, Albanian, E. Armenian, Ostyak, Cheremis, Komi, Finnish, Hungarian, Lappish, Yurak, Tavgy, Osmanli, Azerbaijani, Chuvash, Yakut, Kirghiz, Bashkir, Khalaj, Tuva, Mongolian, Evenki, Goldi, Manchu, Korean, Japanese, Katcha, Moro, Kadugli, Bisa, Bambara, Dan, Wolof, Diola, Temne, Dagbani, Senadi, Tampulma, Bariba, Ewe, Akan, Igbo, Gã, Lelemi, Efik, Birom, Tarok, Amo, Beembe, Swahili, Luvale, Zulu, Teke, Doayo, Gbeya, Zande, Songhai, Kanuri, Maba, Fur, Maasai, Luo, Nubian, Nyangi, Ik, Sebei, Tama, Temein, Nera, Tabi, Mursi, Logbara, Yulu, Sara, Berta, Kunama, Koma, Arabic, Tigre, Amharic, Hebrew, Socotri, Neo-Aramaic, Shilha, Tuareg, Somali, Awiya, Iraqw, Beja, Kullo, Dizi, Kefa, Hamer, Hausa, Angas, Margi, Ngizim, Kanakuru, Mundari, Kharia, Khasi, Vietnamese, Sedang, Khmer, Maung, Tiwi, Burera, Nunggubuyu, Alawa, Maranungku, Malakmalak, Bardi, Wik-Munkan, Kunjen, Western Desert, Nyangumata, Aranda, Kariera-Ngarluma, Gugu-Yalanji, Mabuiag, Arabana-Wanganura, Diyari, Bandjalang, Standard Thai, Lakkia, Yay, Sui, Saek, Po-ai, Lungchow, Atayal, Sundanese, Javanese, Malagasy,

Cham, Malay, Batak, Tagalog, Sa'ban, Chamorro, Rukai, Tsou, Adzera, Roro, Kaliai, Iai, Maori, Hawaiian, Mandarin, Taishan, Changchow, Amoy, Fuchow, Kan, Tamang, Dafla, Burmese, Lahu, Jingpho, Ao, Tiddim Chin, Garo, Boro, Karen, Yao, Andamanese, Asmat, Washkuk, Sentani, Nimboran, Iwam, Telefol, Selepet, Gadsup, Yagaria, Kewa, Chuave, Pawaian, Dani, Wantoat, Daribi, Fasu, Suena, Dera, Kunimaipa, Yareba, Taoripi, Nasioi, Nambakaengo, Haida, Tolowa, Hupa, Nez Perce, Klamath, Maidu, Wintu, Chontal, Zoque, Tzeltal, Totonac, K'ekchi, Mixe, Otomi, Mazahua, Mazatec, Chatino, Nootka, Kwakw'ala, Squamish, Papago, Luiseño, Hopi, Yacqui, Tiwa, Karok, Pomo, Diegueño, Achumawi, Yana, Shasta, Tarascan, Zuni, Acoma, Ojibwa, Delaware, Tonkawa, Wiyot, Tunica, Alabama, Wappo, Itonama, Bribri, Cayapa, Paez, Ocaina, Muinane, Carib, Amahuaca, Chacobo, Tacana, Cashinahua, Ashuslay, Abipon, Arabela, Auca, Quechua, Jaqaru, Gununa-Kena, Wapishana, Island Carib, Amuesha, Campa, Guajiro, Moxo, Guarani, Guahibo, Ticuna, Siona, Jivaro, Cofan, Araucanian, Greenlandic, Aleut, Telugu, Kota, Kurukh, Malayalam, Ket, Yukaghir, Chukchi, Gilyak, Georgian, Kabardian, Lak, Nama, Basque, Burushaski, Ainu, Brahui, !Xũ; RARE Navaho, Seneca; ?DERIVED Dakota.

Long voiced bilabial nasal /m:/ 11
Punjabi, Finnish, Chuvash, Yakut, Wolof, Arabic, Shilha, Maranungku, Delaware, Ocaina, !Xũ.

Labialized voiced bilabial nasal $/m^{w}/$ 2
Washkuk, Nambakaengo.

Labialized velarized voiced bilabial nasal $/\text{m̴}^{w}/$ 1
Irish.

Palatalized voiced bilabial nasal $/m^{j}/$ 6
Irish, Lithuanian, Russian, Bulgarian, Yurak, Amuesha.

Breathy voiced bilabial nasal /m̤/ 2
Hindi-Urdu, !Xũ.

Laryngealized voiced bilabial nasal /m̰/ 14
Gbeya, Sedang, Sui, Haida, Tolowa, Nez Perce, Klamath, Otomi, Mazahua, Nootka, Kwakw'ala, Acoma, Wappo, !Xũ.

Voiceless bilabial nasal /m̥/ 11 (-1)
Sedang, Lakkia, Sui, Iai, Burmese, Yao, Klamath, Mazahua, Hopi, Aleut; ?DERIVED Otomi.

Voiced labiodental nasal /ɱ/ 1
Teke.

Voiced dental nasal /n̪/ 55
Irish, Norwegian, Russian, French, Spanish, Farsi, Kurdish, Hindi-Urdu, Punjabi, Finnish, Hungarian, Yakut, Khalaj, Tuva, Manchu, Gbeya, Ik, Temein, Arabic, Tigre, Tuareg, Beja, Mundari, Tiwi, Nunggubuyu, Kunjen, Western Desert, Aranda, Kariera-Ngarluma, Arabana-Wanganura, Diyari, Standard Thai, Roro, Garo, Tamang, Yao, Nimboran, Selepet, Nez Perce, Tzeltal, Squamish, Papago, Luiseño, Diegueño, Yana, Acoma, Tonkawa, Gununa-Kena, Guarani, Araucanian, Greenlandic, Malayalam, Kabardian, Nama, Brahui.

Long voiced dental nasal /n̪:/ 4
Punjabi, Finnish, Yakut, Arabic.

Palatalized voiced dental nasal /n̪ʲ/ 1
Russian.

Breathy voiced dental nasal /n̪̤/ 1
Hindi-Urdu.

Laryngealized voiced dental nasal /n̪̰/ 3
Gbeya, Nez Perce, Acoma.

Voiceless dental nasal /n̪̥/ 1
Yao.

Voiced dental/alveolar nasal /"n"/ 154 (-1)
Greek, Breton, German, Lithuanian, Bulgarian, Romanian, Pashto, Bengali, Kashmiri, Sinhalese, E. Armenian, Ostyak, Cheremis, Lappish, Yurak, Tavgy, Osmanli, Azerbaijani, Chuvash, Kirghiz, Mongolian, Evenki, Goldi, Korean, Japanese, Katcha, Wolof, Dagbani, Senadi, Ewe, Akan, Igbo, Gã, Beembe, Swahili, Luvale, Doayo, Songhai, Kanuri, Maasai, Nubian, Sebei, Nera, Mursi, Logbara, Yulu, Berta, Amharic, Hebrew, Socotri, Neo-Aramaic, Shilha, Awiya, Kullo, Dizi, Kefa, Hausa, Kharia, Khasi, Vietnamese, Sedang, Khmer, Burera, Maranungku, Wik-Munkan, Kariera-Ngarluma, Gugu-Yalanji, Mabuiag, Lakkia, Yay, Sui, Po-ai, Lungchow, Atayal, Sundanese, Javanese, Malagasy, Cham, Malay, Batak, Tagalog, Tsou, Adzera, Kaliai, Iai, Hawaiian, Taishan, Changchow, Amoy, Fuchow, Kan, Dafla, Burmese, Lahu, Jingpho, Karen, Andamanese, Sentani, Telefol, Gadsup, Pawaian, Dani, Wantoat, Suena, Dera, Kunimaipa, Nasioi, Nambakaengo, Haida, Tlingit, Chipewyan, Tolowa, Chontal, Mazahua, Chatino, Nootka, Tiwa, Karok, Pomo, Achumawi, Shasta, Tarascan, Zuni, Delaware, Wiyot, Seneca, Wichita, Yuchi, Alabama, Wappo, Itonama, Bribri, Carib, Amahuaca, Ashuslay, Abipon, Arabela, Quechua, Island Carib, Guajiro, Ticuna, Jivaro, Cofan, Aleut, Kurukh, Ket, Yukaghir, Chukchi, Gilyak, Georgian, Lak, Basque, Burushaski; ?DERIVED Dakota.

Long voiced dental/alveolar nasal /"n:"/ 6
Chuvash, Wolof, Shilha, Maranungku, Delaware, Wichita.

Labialized voiced dental/alveolar nasal /"nʷ"/ 1
Nambakaengo.

Palatalized voiced dental/alveolar nasal /"nʲ"/ 5 (-1)
Irish, Bulgarian, Yurak, Chuvash; OBSCURE Nambakaengo.

Velarized voiced dental/alveolar nasal /"ᵰ"/ 1
Irish.

Laryngealized voiced dental/alveolar nasal /"n̰"/ 8
Sedang, Sui, Haida, Tolowa, Nootka, Yuchi, Wappo, S. Nambiquara.

Voiceless dental/alveolar nasal /"n̥"/ 6
Sedang, Lakkia, Sui, Burmese, Mazahua, Aleut.

Palatalized voiceless dental/alveolar nasal /"n̥ʲ"/ 1 (-1)
?DERIVED Irish.

Velarized voiceless dental/alveolar nasal /"n̪̊"/ 1 (-1)
?DERIVED Irish.

Voiced alveolar nasal /n/ 106
Albanian, Komi, Bashkir, Moro, Kadugli, Bisa, Bambara, Dan, Diola, Temne, Tampulma, Bariba, Lelemi, Efik, Birom, Tarok, Amo, Zulu, Teke, Zande, Maba, Fur, Luo, Nyangi, Tama, Tabi, Sara, Kunama, Koma, Somali, Iraqw, Hamer, Angas, Margi, Ngizim, Kanakuru, Maung, Tiwi, Nunggubuyu, Alawa, Malakmalak, Bardi, Kunjen, Western Desert, Nyangumata, Aranda, Arabana-Wanganura, Diyari, Bandjalang, Saek, Sa'ban, Chamorro, Rukai, Maori, Mandarin, Ao, Tiddim Chin, Boro, Asmat, Washkuk, Iwam, Yagaria, Kewa, Chuave, Daribi, Fasu, Yareba, Koiari, Navaho, Hupa, Wintu, Klamath, Maidu, Zoque, Totonac, K'ekchi, Mixe, Otomi, Mazatec, Kwakw'ala, Hopi, Yacqui, Diegueño, Ojibwa, Tunica, Cayapa, Paez, Ocaina, Muinane, Chacobo, Tacana, Cashinahua, S. Nambiquara, Auca, Jaqaru, Amuesha, Campa, Moxo, Guahibo, Siona, Araucanian, Telugu, Kota, Malayalam, Ainu, !Xũ.

Long voiced alveolar nasal /n:/ 2
Somali, Ocaina.

Palatalized voiced alveolar nasal /nʲ/ 1
Nyangumata.

Laryngealized voiced alveolar nasal /n̰/ 3
Klamath, Otomi, Kwakw'ala.

Voiceless alveolar nasal /n̥/ 3 (-1)
Klamath, Hopi; ?DERIVED Otomi.

Voiced palato-alveolar nasal /n̠/ 17
Albanian, Zulu, Nunggubuyu, Alawa, Malakmalak, Bardi, Wik-Munkan, Aranda, Bandjalang, Mazatec, Papago, Diegueño, Cayapa, Wapishana, Campa, Moxo, Jivaro.

Voiced retroflex nasal /ɳ/ 20 (-1)
Norwegian, Pashto, Punjabi, Ostyak, Mundari, Maung, Nunggubuyu, Alawa, Bardi, Western Desert, Nyangumata, Aranda, Kariera-Ngarluma, Arabana-Wanganura, Diyari, Iai, Telugu, Kota, Malayalam; ?DERIVED Tiwi.

Voiceless retroflex nasal /ɳ̊/ 1
Iai.

Voiced palatal nasal /ɲ/ 107 (-3)
Irish, Breton, Lithuanian, French, Spanish, Punjabi, Ostyak, Cheremis, Komi, Hungarian, Lappish, Tavgy, Yakut, Evenki, Goldi, Katcha, Moro, Kadugli, Bisa, Bambara, Wolof, Diola, Dagbani, Tampulma, Ewe, Igbo, Gã, Lelemi, Efik, Amo, Swahili, Luvale, Teke, Zande, Songhai, Kanuri, Maba, Fur, Maasai, Luo, Nubian, Nyangi, Ik, Sebei, Tama, Temein, Tabi, Mursi, Yulu, Sara, Amharic, Tuareg, Hamer, Angas, Margi, Ngizim, Kanakuru, Kharia, Khasi, Vietnamese, Sedang, Khmer, Burera, Maranungku, Kunjen, Kariera-Ngarluma, Gugu-Yalanji, Arabana-Wanganura, Diyari, Yay, Sui, Saek, Sundanese, Javanese, Cham, Malay, Sa'ban, Chamorro, Iai, Kan, Burmese, Yao, Andamanese, Washkuk, Mazahua, Hopi, Bribri, Paez, Ocaina, Muinane, Abipon, Auca, Quechua, Jaqaru, Amuesha, Guarani, Ticuna, Cofan, Araucanian, Malayalam, Ket, Yukaghir, Gilyak, Basque; RARE Karen; LOAN Sinhalese, Tarascan.

Long voiced palatal nasal /ɲː/ 2
Yakut, Ocaina.

Laryngealized voiced palatal nasal /ɲ̰/ 3
Sedang, Sui, Mazahua.

Voiceless palatal nasal /ɲ̥/ 6
Sedang, Sui, Iai, Burmese, Yao, Mazahua.

Voiced velar nasal /ŋ/ 167 (-9)
Irish, Breton, German, Norwegian, Kurdish, Bengali, Punjabi, Ostyak, Cheremis, Lappish, Yurak, Tavgy, Yakut, Kirghiz, Bashkir, Tuva, Evenki, Goldi, Manchu, Korean, Japanese, Katcha, Moro, Kadugli, Bisa, Bambara, Wolof, Diola, Dagbani, Senadi, Tampulma, Ewe, Igbo, Gã, Lelemi, Efik, Birom, Tarok, Amo, Luvale, Teke, Doayo, Gbeya, Songhai, Kanuri, Fur, Maasai, Luo, Nyangi, Ik, Sebei, Tama, Temein, Nera, Tabi, Mursi, Yulu, Berta, Kunama, Awiya, Iraqw, Hamer, Angas, Margi, Kanakuru, Kharia, Khasi, Vietnamese, Sedang, Khmer, Maung, Tiwi, Burera, Nunggubuyu, Alawa, Maranungku, Malakmalak, Bardi, Wik-Munkan, Kunjen, Western Desert, Nyangumata, Aranda, Kariera-Ngarluma, Gugu-Yalanji, Mabuiag, Arabana-Wanganura, Diyari, Bandjalang, Standard Thai, Lakkia, Yay, Sui, Saek, Po-ai, Lungchow, Atayal, Sundanese, Javanese, Cham, Malay, Batak, Tagalog, Sa'ban, Chamorro, Rukai, Tsou, Adzera, Kaliai, Iai, Maori, Mandarin, Taishan, Changchow, Amoy, Fuchow, Kan, Tamang, Dafla, Burmese, Lahu, Jingpho, Ao, Tiddim Chin, Garo, Boro, Yao, Andamanese, Nimboran, Iwam, Telefol, Selepet, Wantoat, Dera, Kunimaipa, Nambakaengo, Hupa, Zoque, Luiseño, Hopi, Tarascan, Cayapa, Carib, Auca, Jaqaru, Guarani, Ticuna, Araucanian, Greenlandic, Aleut, Kota, Malayalam, Ket, Yukaghir, Chukchi, Gilyak, Burushaski, !Xũ; RARE Swahili, Koma, Karen; LOAN French, Hebrew, Moxo; ?DERIVED Sinhalese, Mundari, Mixtec.

Long voiced velar nasal /ŋː/ 2 (-1)
Yakut; ?DERIVED Finnish.

Labialized voiced velar nasal /ŋʷ/ 7
Awiya, Iraqw, Lakkia, Wantoat, Nambakaengo, Hopi, Guarani.

Palatalized voiced velar nasal /ŋʲ/ 2
Irish, Lakkia.

Pharyngealized voiced velar nasal /ŋˤ/ 1
!Xũ.

Laryngealized voiced velar nasal /ŋ̰/ 3
Sedang, Sui, Haida.

Voiceless velar nasal /ŋ̊/ 7
Sedang, Sui, Iai, Burmese, Yao, Hopi, Aleut.

Palatalized voiceless velar nasal /ŋ̊ʲ/ 1
Lakkia.

Voiced labial-velar nasal /m͡ŋ/ 6
Dagbani, Tampulma, Igbo, Gã, Gbeya, Iai.

Voiceless labial-velar nasal /m̥͡ŋ̊/ 1
Iai.

Voiced dental-palatal nasal /n̪͡ɲ/ 1
Maung.

7. TRILLS, TAPS AND FLAPS

Voiced dental trill /r̪/ 5
Russian, Hungarian, Tuva, Tamang, Gununa-Kena.

Palatalized voiced dental trill /r̪ʲ/ 1
Russian.

Voiced dental/alveolar trill /"r"/ 52 (-4)
Bulgarian, Farsi, Pashto, Kurdish, Hindi-Urdu, Kashmiri, Punjabi, Albanian, E. Armenian, Ostyak, Komi, Finnish, Lappish, Yurak, Tavgy, Chuvash, Yakut, Kirghiz, Mongolian, Evenki, Goldi, Manchu, Katcha, Akan, Kanuri, Nubian, Nera, Sebei, Mursi, Yulu, Berta, Khasi, Sedang, Wik-Munkan, Kariera-Ngarluma, Sundanese, Malagasy, Malay, Adzera, Chipewyan, Luiseño, Arabela, Guajiro, Kurukh, Gilyak, Georgian, Lak, Basque; RARE Gã, Mixtec; LOAN Mazatec, Quechua.

Long voiced dental/alveolar trill /"r:"/ 2
Finnish, Chuvash.

Palatalized voiced dental/alveolar trill /"rʲ"/ 2
Bulgarian, Yurak.

Velarized voiced dental/alveolar trill /"ɼ"/ 1
Yukaghir.

Laryngealized voiced dental/alveolar trill /"r̰"/ 1
Sedang.

Voiceless dental/alveolar trill /r̥/ 3
Maasai, Sedang, Gilyak.

Voiced dental/alveolar fricative trill /"ř"/ 1 (-1)
LOAN Guarani.

Voiced alveolar trill /r/ 54 (-3)
Breton, Lithuanian, Spanish, Bashkir, Moro, Kadugli, Bisa, Temne, Tampulma, Amo, Maba, Fur, Nyangi, Ik, Tama, Temein, Tabi, Kunama, Koma, Tigre, Shilha, Tuareg, Hausa, Angas, Margi, Ngizim, Mundari, Maung, Nunggubuyu, Alawa, Maranungku, Malakmalak, Bardi, Kunjen, Nyangumata, Arabana-Wanganura, Diyari, Bandjalang, Javanese, Rukai, Kaliai, Maori, Dafla, Tarascan, Tunica, Guahibo, Kota, Malayalam, Kabardian, Nama, Brahui; RARE Diegueño; LOAN Swahili, Zulu.

Long voiced alveolar trill /r:/ 3
Arabic, Shilha, Somali.

Palatalized voiced alveolar trill /rʲ/ 1
Lithuanian.

Pharyngealized voiced alveolar trill /rˤ/ 1
Shilha.

Voiced retroflex trill /ṛ/ 5 (-2)
Pashto, Kariera-Ngarluma, Arabana-Wanganura; ?DERIVED Kurukh; OBSCURE Batak.

Voiced uvular trill /ʀ/ 2
German, French.

Voiced dental tap /Đ̪/ 1
Acoma.

Laryngealized voiced dental tap /Đ̰/ 1
Acoma.

Voiced dental/alveolar tap /"Đ"/ 1
Khalaj.

Voiced alveolar tap /Đ/ 5
Spanish, Bambara, Tiwi, Rotokas, Malayalam.

Voiced labio-dental flap /ⱱ/ 2 (-1)
Gbeya; RARE Margi.

Voiced dental flap /ɾ̪/ 1
Roro.

Voiced dental/alveolar flap /"ɾ"/ 26 (-1)
Greek, Norwegian, Kurdish, Cheremis, Japanese, Wolof, Ewe, Igbo, Sebei, Logbara, Sara, Awiya, Kharia, Suena, Nasioi, Chontal, Itonama, Amahuaca, Quechua, Island Carib, Amuesha, Siriono, Ticuna, Jivaro, Basque; LOAN Pomo.

Palatalized voiced dental/alveolar flap /"ɾʲ"/ 1
Igbo.

Voiced alveolar flap /ɾ/ 53 (-2)
Irish, Romanian, Bengali, Sinhalese, Osmanli, Kpelle, Diola, Bariba, Gbeya, Maasai, Luo, Tama, Arabic, Amharic, Neo-Aramaic, Somali, Hamer, Hausa, Ngizim, Burera, Western Desert, Aranda, Standard Thai, Garo, Boro, Washkuk, Selepet, Kewa, Chuave, Daribi, Fasu, Yareba, Koiari, Tzeltal, Otomi, Yacqui, Karok, Ocaina, Carib, Chacobo, Tacana, Jaqaru, Wapishana, Campa, Moxo, Guarani, Barasano, Tucano, Telugu, Lak, Brahui; RARE Asmat; LOAN Paez.

Palatalized voiced alveolar flap /ɾʲ/ 1
Irish.

Voiced alveolar fricative flap /ɾ̌/ 1
Tacana.

Palatalized voiceless alveolar flap /ɾ̥ʲ/ 1
Irish.

Velarized voiceless alveolar flap /ɾ̴̥/ 1
Irish.

Voiced retroflex flap /ɾ̣/ 11 (-1)

Bengali, Punjabi, Kharia, Khmer, Maung, Kaliai, Pawaian, Kunimaipa, Apinaye, Kota; LOAN Hindi-Urdu.

Voiced dental/alveolar lateral flap /"ɺ"/ 3
Luvale, Logbara, Guajiro.

Voiced alveolar lateral flap /ɺ/ 3
Zande, Kewa, Paez.

Palatalized voiced alveolar lateral flap /ɺʲ/ 1
Paez.

Voiced retroflex lateral flap /ɺ̣/ 3
Moro, Papago, S. Nambiquara.

Laryngealized voiced retroflex lateral flap /ɺ̰̣/ 1
S. Nambiquara.

Voiced dental r-sound /r̪r̪/ 1
Nimboran.

Voiced dental/alveolar r-sound /"rr"/ 25 (-2)
Tarok, Doayo, Songhai, Socotri, Beja, Kullo, Dizi, Kefa, Gugu-Yalanji, Mabuiag, Yay, Atayal, Cham, Jingpho, Boro, Chatino, Achumawi, Yana, Shasta, Bribri, Abipon, Cofan, Burushaski; LOAN Tiwa, Wappo.

Laryngealized voiced dental/alveolar r-sound /"r̰r̰"/ 2 (-1)
Wichita; LOAN Wappo.

Voiced alveolar r-sound /rr/ 5
Iraqw, Iwam, Cayapa, Muinane, Ainu.

Palatalized voiced alveolar r-sound /rrʲ/ 1
Muinane.

8. APPROXIMANTS

Voiced dental lateral approximant /l̪/ 26 (-1)
Lithuanian, French, Spanish, Punjabi, Finnish, Tuva, Manchu, Gbeya, Arabic, Tuareg, Mundari, Nunggubuyu, Western Desert, Aranda, Kariera-Ngarluma, Arabana-Wanganura, Diyari, Tamang, Dafla, Tzeltal, Luiseño, Tonkawa, Gununa-Kena, Araucanian, Greenlandic; LOAN Guarani.

Long voiced dental lateral approximant /l̪:/ 3
Punjabi, Finnish, Arabic.

Palatalized voiced dental lateral approximant /l̪ʲ/ 1
Russian.

Voiceless dental lateral approximant /l̪̥/ 1
Gununa-Kena.

Voiced dental/alveolar lateral approximant /"l"/ 122 (-3)
Greek, Farsi, Kurdish, Hindi-Urdu, Bengali, Kashmiri, E. Armenian, Ostyak, Hungarian, Lappish, Yurak, Tavgy, Osmanli, Azerbaijani, Chuvash, Kirghiz, Khalaj, Mongolian, Evenki, Goldi, Korean, Katcha, Wolof,

Dagbani, Senadi, Ewe, Igbo, Gã, Tarok, Beembe, Swahili, Doayo, Songhai, Kanuri, Maasai, Nubian, Ik, Sebei, Nera, Mursi, Yulu, Berta, Hebrew, Socotri, Shilha, Awiya, Beja, Kullo, Kefa, Hamer, Kharia, Vietnamese, Sedang, Maranungku, Wik-Munkan, Kariera-Ngarluma, Gugu-Yalanji, Mabuiag, Standard Thai, Lakkia, Yay, Sui, Po-ai, Lungchow, Sundanese, Javanese, Malagasy, Cham, Malay, Batak, Tagalog, Tsou, Kaliai, Hawaiian, Mandarin, Taishan, Hakka, Changchow, Fuchow, Kan, Burmese, Lahu, Jingpho, Yao, Andamanese, Telefol, Dani, Kunimaipa, Taoripi, Nambakaengo, Haida, Chipewyan, Tolowa, Nez Perce, Chontal, Mazahua, Chatino, Squamish, Tiwa, Pomo, Yana, Zuni, Delaware, Wiyot, Dakota, Yuchi, Alabama, Wappo, Itonama, Abipon, Quechua, Island Carib, Aleut, Kurukh, Yukaghir, Gilyak, Lak, Basque, Burushaski; LOAN Tarascan, Ojibwa; ?DERIVED Mixtec.

Long voiced dental/alveolar lateral approximant /"l:"/ 4
Chuvash, Wolof, Shilha, Delaware.

Palatalized voiced dental/alveolar lateral approximant /"l^{j}"/ 5
Bulgarian, Yurak, Chuvash, Amuesha, Ket.

Velarized voiced dental/alveolar lateral approximant /"ɫ"/ 6
Bulgarian, Yakut, Khmer, Ket, Yukaghir, Georgian.

Long velarized voiced dental/alveolar lateral approximant /"ɫ:"/ 1
Yakut.

Pharyngealized voiced dental/alveolar lateral approximant /"l^{ʕ}"/ 1
Shilha.

Breathy voiced dental/alveolar lateral approximant /"l̤"/ 1
Hindi-Urdu.

Laryngealized voiced dental/alveolar lateral approximant /"l̰"/ 4
Sedang, Haida, Yuchi, Wappo.

Voiceless dental/alveolar lateral approximant /"l̥"/ 5
Mongolian, Sedang, Burmese, Yao, Chipewyan.

Voiced alveolar lateral approximant /l/ 93 (-3)
Breton, German, Norwegian, Romanian, Sinhalese, Albanian, Komi, Bashkir, Moro, Kadugli, Kpelle, Bisa, Bambara, Dan, Diola, Temne, Tampulma, Bariba, Lelemi, Amo, Zulu, Teke, Maba, Fur, Luo, Nyangi, Sebei, Tama, Temein, Tabi, Sara, Kunama, Koma, Tigre, Amharic, Neo-Aramaic, Somali, Iraqw, Hamer, Hausa, Angas, Margi, Ngizim, Kanakuru, Maung, Tiwi, Burera, Nunggubuyu, Alawa, Malakmalak, Bardi, Kunjen, Western Desert, Nyangumata, Aranda, Arabana-Wanganura, Diyari, Bandjalang, Saek, Sa'ban, Chamorro, Rukai, Ao, Tiddim Chin, Boro, Karen, Selepet, Navaho, Hupa, Nez Perce, Klamath, Maidu, Wintu, Zoque, Totonac, K'ekchi, Kwakw'ala, Quileute, Yacqui, Diegueño, Achumawi, Tunica, Cayapa, Jaqaru, Guahibo, Araucanian, Telugu, Kota, Malayalam, Brahui; RARE Ashuslay; LOAN Otomi, Moxo.

Long voiced alveolar lateral approximant /l:/ 1
Somali.

Palatalized voiced alveolar lateral approximant /l^{j}/ 3
Irish, Lithuanian, Nyangumata.

Velarized voiced alveolar lateral approximant /ɫ/ 2
Irish, Albanian.

Pharyngealized voiced alveolar lateral approximant /lˤ/ 1
Kurdish.

Laryngealized voiced alveolar lateral approximant /l̰/ 4
Tiddim Chin, Nez Perce, Klamath, Kwakw'ala.

Voiceless alveolar lateral approximant /l̥/ 1
Klamath.

Palatalized voiceless alveolar lateral approximant /l̥ʲ/ 1 (-1)
?DERIVED Irish.

Velarized voiceless alveolar lateral approximant /ɫ̥/ 1 (-1)
?DERIVED Irish.

Voiced palato-alveolar lateral approximant /l̠/ 6
Alawa, Malakmalak, Bardi, Aranda, Diegueño, Cayapa.

Voiced retroflex lateral approximant /ɭ/ 22 (-1)
Norwegian, Punjabi, Ostyak, Kanuri, Mundari, Khasi, Maung, Nunggubuyu, Alawa, Bardi, Western Desert, Nyangumata, Kariera-Ngarluma, Arabana-Wanganura, Diyari, Rukai, Iai, Tarascan, Telugu, Kota, Malayalam; ?DERIVED Tiwi.

Voiceless retroflex lateral approximant /ɭ̊/ 1
Iai.

Voiced palatal lateral approximant /ʎ/ 15 (-2)
Spanish, Ostyak, Cheremis, Komi, Tavgy, Kariera-Ngarluma, Arabana-Wanganura, Diyari, Quechua, Jaqaru, Araucanian, Malayalam, Basque; LOAN Osmanli, Guarani.

Velarized voiced palatal lateral approximant /ʎ̴/ 1
Irish.

Voiced velar lateral approximant /ʟ/ 1
Yagaria.

Voiced bilabial approximant /β/ 6
Hindi-Urdu, Lappish, Lakkia, Kunimaipa, Karok, Telugu.

Long voiced bilabial approximant /β:/ 1
Telugu.

Voiced labio-dental approximant /ʋ/ 6
Norwegian, Sinhalese, Luvale, Khmer, Malayalam, Ket.

Voiced dental/alveolar approximant /"ɹ"/ 1
Andamanese.

Voiced alveolar approximant /ɹ/ 11 (-1)
Kanakuru, Maung, Burera, Maranungku, Malakmalak, Saek, Iai, Wintu, Diegueño, Wiyot; RARE Tarascan.

oiced retroflex approximant /ɻ/ 15
Tiwi, Nunggubuyu, Alawa, Bardi, Kunjen, Western Desert, Nyangumata, Aranda, Kariera-Ngarluma, Gugu-Yalanji, Arabana-Wanganura, Diyari, Chamorro, Kan, Wiyot.

oiced palatal approximant /j/ 271 (-1)
Greek, Irish, Breton, German, Norwegian, Lithuanian, Russian, Bulgarian, French, Spanish, Romanian, Farsi, Pashto, Kurdish, Hindi-Urdu, Bengali, Kashmiri, Punjabi, Sinhalese, Albanian, E. Armenian, Ostyak, Cheremis, Komi, Finnish, Hungarian, Lappish, Yurak, Tavgy, Osmanli, Chuvash, Yakut, Kirghiz, Bashkir, Tuva, Mongolian, Evenki, Manchu, Korean, Japanese, Katcha, Moro, Kadugli, Kpelle, Bisa, Bambara, Dan, Wolof, Diola, Temne, Dagbani, Senadi, Tampulma, Bariba, Ewe, Akan, Igbo, Gã, Lelemi, Efik, Birom, Tarok, Amo, Beembe, Swahili, Luvale, Zulu, Teke, Doayo, Gbeya, Zande, Songhai, Kanuri, Maba, Fur, Maasai, Luo, Nyangi, Ik, Sebei, Tama, Temein, Nera, Tabi, Mursi, Logbara, Yulu, Sara, Berta, Kunama, Koma, Arabic, Tigre, Amharic, Hebrew, Socotri, Neo-Aramaic, Shilha, Tuareg, Somali, Awiya, Iraqw, Beja, Kullo, Dizi, Kefa, Hamer, Hausa, Angas, Margi, Ngizim, Kanakuru, Mundari, Vietnamese, Sedang, Khmer, Maung, Tiwi, Burera, Nunggubuyu, Alawa, Maranungku, Malakmalak, Bardi, Wik-Munkan, Kunjen, Western Desert, Nyangumata, Aranda, Kariera-Ngarluma, Gugu-Yalanji, Mabuiag, Arabana-Wanganura, Diyari, Bandjalang, Standard Thai, Lakkia, Yay, Sui, Saek, Po-ai, Lungchow, Sundanese, Javanese, Malagasy, Cham, Batak, Tagalog, Sa'ban, Chamorro, Rukai, Adzera, Mandarin, Taishan, Changchow, Tamang, Dafla, Burmese, Lahu, Jingpho, Ao, Boro, Karen, Yao, Andamanese, Washkuk, Sentani, Iwam, Telefol, Selepet, Gadsup, Yagaria, Kewa, Chuave, Pawaian, Dani, Daribi, Fasu, Suena, Dera, Yareba, Nambakaengo, Haida, Tlingit, Navaho, Chipewyan, Tolowa, Hupa, Nez Perce, Klamath, Maidu, Wintu, Chontal, Zoque, Totonac, K'ekchi, Mixe, Otomi, Mazahua, Mazatec, Chatino, Nootka, Kwakw'ala, Quileute, Squamish, Puget Sound, Papago, Luiseño, Hopi, Yacqui, Tiwa, Karok, Pomo, Diegueño, Achumawi, Yana, Shasta, Tarascan, Zuni, Acoma, Delaware, Tonkawa, Wiyot, Seneca, Dakota, Yuchi, Tunica, Alabama, Wappo, Itonama, Bribri, Cayapa, Paez, Yukaghir, Amahuaca, Tacana, Cashinahua, Ashuslay, Abipon, S. Nambiquara, Arabela, Quechua, Jaqaru, Gununa-Kena, Island Carib, Amuesha, Campa, Guajiro, Moxo, Siriono, Guahibo, Barasano, Siona, Tucano, Jivaro, Cofan, Araucanian, Aleut, Telugu, Kota, Kurukh, Malayalam, Yukaghir, Chukchi, Gilyak, Kabardian, Lak, Burushaski, Ainu, !Xũ; ?DERIVED Atayal.

ong voiced palatal approximant /j:/ 2
Chuvash, Arabic.

asalized voiced palatal approximant /j̃/ 2
Yakut, Kharia.

aryngealized voiced palatal approximant /j̰/ 13
Logbara, Hausa, Sui, Haida, Nez Perce, Klamath, Otomi, Mazahua, Nootka, Kwakw'ala, Acoma, Yuchi, Wappo.

oiceless palatal approximant /j̥/ 7
Malagasy, Yao, Klamath, Otomi, Mazahua, Hopi, Aleut.

owered voiced palatal approximant /ɩ̞/ 1
Khasi.

Mid palatal approximant /"e̯"/ 1
Bengali.

Lower mid back approximant /ʌ̯/ 1
Vietnamese.

Voiced velar approximant /ɣ̞/ 5
Kanakuru, Aranda, Adzera, Wiyot, Cofan.

Nasalized voiced velar approximant /ɣ̞̃/ 1
Japanese.

Voiced uvular approximant /ʁ̯/ 1
E. Armenian.

Voiced labial-palatal approximant /ɥ/ 4
Breton, French, Gã, Mandarin.

Voiced labial-velar approximant /w/ 238 (-5)
Irish, Breton, French, Spanish, Romanian, Farsi, Pashto, Kurdish, Bengali, Kashmiri, Punjabi, Ostyak, Hungarian, Yurak, Chuvash, Bashkir, Korean, Katcha, Moro, Kadugli, Bisa, Bambara, Dan, Wolof, Diola, Temne, Dagbani, Senadi, Tampulma, Bariba, Ewe, Akan, Igbo, Gã, Lelemi, Efik, Birom, Tarok, Amo, Beembe, Swahili, Luvale, Zulu, Teke, Doayo, Gbeya, Zande, Songhai, Kanuri, Maba, Fur, Maasai, Luo, Nyangi, Ik, Sebei, Tama Temein, Nera, Tabi, Mursi, Logbara, Yulu, Sara, Berta, Kunama, Koma, Arabic, Tigre, Amharic, Socotri, Shilha, Tuareg, Somali, Awiya, Iraqw, Beja, Kullo, Dizi, Kefa, Hamer, Hausa, Angas, Margi, Ngizim, Kanakuru, Mundari, Kharia, Vietnamese, Sedang, Tiwi, Burera, Nunggubuyu, Alawa, Maranungku, Malakmalak, Bardi, Wik-Munkan, Kunjen, Western Desert, Nyangumata, Aranda, Kariera-Ngarluma, Gugu-Yalanji, Mabuiag, Arabana-Wanganura, Diyari, Bandjalang, Standard Thai, Lakkia, Sui, Sundanese, Javanese, Malagasy, Cham, Batak, Tagalog, Sa'ban, Chamorro, Rukai, Iai, Maori, Hawaiian, Mandarin, Taishan, Hakka, Changchow, Tamang, Burmese, Jingpho, Ao, Garo, Karen, Yao, Andamanese, Asmat, Washkuk, Sentani, Iwam, Telefol, Selepet, Kewa, Chuave, Pawaian, Dani, Daribi, Fasu, Suena, Dera, Yareba, Nambakaengo, Haida, Tlingit, Tolowa, Hupa, Nez Perce, Klamath, Maidu, Wintu, Chontal, Zoque, Tzeltal, Totonac, K'ekchi, Otomi, Mazahua, Chatino, Nootka, Kwakw'ala, Quileute, Squamish, Puget Sound, Papago, Luiseño, Hopi, Yacqui, Tiwa, Pomo, Diegueño, Achumawi, Yana, Shasta, Tarascan, Zuni, Acoma, Delaware, Tonkawa, Wiyot, Seneca, Wichita, Dakota, Yuchi, Tunica, Alabama, Itonama, Bribri, Cayapa, Paez, Carib, Amahuaca, Chacobo, Tacana, Cashinahua, Ashuslay, Abipon, S. Nambiquara, Arabela, Auca, Quechua, Jaqaru, Gununa-Kena, Wapishana, Island Carib, Amuesha, Guajiro, Siriono Ticuna, Barasano, Siona, Tucano, Jivaro, Cofan, Araucanian, Aleut, Kurukh, Yukaghir, Chukchi, Gilyak, Kabardian, Lak, Burushaski, Ainu, !Xũ; RARE Japanese, Navaho; LOAN Lahu; ?DERIVED Atayal, Moxo.

Long voiced labial-velar approximant /w:/ 3
Chuvash, Arabic, Delaware.

Nasalized voiced labial-velar approximant /w̃/ 1
Breton.

Laryngealized voiced labial-velar approximant /w̰/   14 (-1)
Logbara, Sedang, Sui, Tiddim Chin, Haida, Nez Perce, Klamath, Otomi, Mazahua, Nootka, Kwakw'ala, Acoma, Yuchi; RARE Wichita.

Voiceless labial-velar approximant /ʍ/   11 (-1)
Sedang, Lakkia, Kaliai, Iai, Yao, Klamath, Otomi, Mazahua, Hopi, Aleut; RARE Burmese.

Lowered voiced labial-velar approximant /o̞̯/   1
Khasi.

Higher mid voiced labial-velar approximant /o̯/   1
Bengali.

9. VOWELS

High front unrounded vowel /i/   271 (-1)
Greek, Breton, Russian, Bulgarian, French, Spanish, Romanian, Farsi, Pashto, Kashmiri, Punjabi, Albanian, E. Armenian, Ostyak, Cheremis, Komi, Finnish, Hungarian, Lappish, Yurak, Tavgy, Osmanli, Chuvash, Yakut, Bashkir, Khalaj, Tuva, Mongolian, Goldi, Manchu, Korean, Japanese, Katcha, Moro, Kadugli, Kpelle, Bisa, Bambara, Dan, Wolof, Diola, Temne, Dagbani, Senadi, Tampulma, Bariba, Ewe, Akan, Igbo, Gã, Lelemi, Efik, Birom, Tarok, Amo, Beembe, Swahili, Luvale, Zulu, Teke, Doayo, Gbeya, Zande, Songhai, Kanuri, Maba, Fur, Maasai, Luo, Nubian, Nyangi, Ik, Sebei, Tama, Temein, Nera, Tabi, Mursi, Logbara, Yulu, Sara, Berta, Kunama, Koma, Amharic, Socotri, Neo-Aramaic, Shilha, Tuareg, Somali, Awiya, Beja, Kullo, Dizi, Kefa, Hamer, Ngizim, Kanakuru, Kharia, Khasi, Sedang, Maung, Tiwi, Burera, Maranungku, Malakmalak, Bardi, Wik-Munkan, Kunjen, Western Desert, Nyangumata, Aranda, Kariera-Ngarluma, Gugu-Yalanji, Mabuiag, Arabana-Wanganura, Diyari, Bandjalang, Standard Thai, Lakkia, Yay, Sui, Saek, Po-ai, Lungchow, Atayal, Sundanese, Javanese, Malagasy, Cham, Malay, Batak, Sa'ban, Chamorro, Rukai, Tsou, Adzera, Roro, Kaliai, Iai, Maori, Hawaiian, Mandarin, Taishan, Hakka, Changchow, Fuchow, Kan, Tamang, Dafla, Burmese, Lahu, Jingpho, Ao, Tiddim Chin, Garo, Boro, Karen, Yao, Andamanese, Asmat, Washkuk, Sentani, Nimboran, Iwam, Telefol, Selepet, Gadsup, Yagaria, Kewa, Chuave, Pawaian, Dani, Wantoat, Daribi, Fasu, Suena, Dera, Kunimaipa, Yareba, Koiari, Taoripi, Nasioi, Rotokas, Nambakaengo, Haida, Tlingit, Chipewyan, Tolowa, Klamath, Maidu, Wintu, Chontal, Zoque, Totonac, K'ekchi, Mixe, Otomi, Mazahua, Mazatec, Mixtec, Chatino, Nootka, Kwakw'ala, Quileute, Papago, Hopi, Yacqui, Tiwa, Karok, Yana, Shasta, Tarascan, Zuni, Acoma, Delaware, Tonkawa, Wiyot, Seneca, Wichita, Dakota, Yuchi, Tunica, Wappo, Itonama, Bribri, Mura, Cayapa, Paez, Ocaina, Muinane, Carib, Apinaye, Chacobo, Tacana, Cashinahua, Ashuslay, Abipon, S. Nambiquara, Arabela, Auca, Jaqaru, Wapishana, Island Carib, Campa, Guajiro, Moxo, Guarani, Siriono, Guahibo, Ticuna, Barasano, Siona, Tucano, Jivaro, Cofan, Araucanian, Greenlandic, Aleut, Telugu, Kota, Kurukh, Malayalam, Ket, Lak, Nama, Burushaski, Ainu, Brahui, !Xũ; ?DERIVED Margi.

Long high front unrounded vowel /iː/   41 (-1)
Irish, Breton, German, Norwegian, Lithuanian, Kurdish, Hindi-Urdu, Sinhalese, Finnish, Evenki, Korean, Wolof, Dagbani, Fur, Arabic, Tigre, Neo-Aramaic, Tuareg, Iraqw, Hausa, Angas, Khmer, Bardi, Lakkia, Atayal, Adzera, Iai, Yagaria, Navaho, Chipewyan, Tolowa, Karok, Ojibwa, Delaware, Tonkawa, Telugu, Kabardian, Lak, Brahui, !Xũ; RARE Hungarian.

Overshort high front unrounded vowel /ĭ/ 3
Yurak, Po-ai, Lungchow.

Nasalized high front unrounded vowel /ĩ/ 53 (-1)
Bulgarian, Kashmiri, Punjabi, Kpelle, Bambara, Senadi, Bariba, Ewe, Akan, Igbo, Gã, Lelemi, Beembe, Doayo, Gbeya, Zande, Sara, Kharia, Changchow, Pawaian, Daribi, Fasu, Nambakaengo, Chipewyan, Tolowa, Otomi, Mazahua, Mazatec, Mixtec, Chatino, Tiwa, Dakota, Paez, Ocaina, Apinaye, Cashinahua, S. Nambiquara, Auca, Wapishana, Island Carib, Guajiro, Guarani, Siriono, Guahibo, Ticuna, Barasano, Siona, Tucano, Jivaro, Kurukh, Nama, !Xũ; RARE Karok.

Long nasalized high front unrounded vowel /ĩ:/ 8
Irish, Hindi-Urdu, Lakkia, Navaho, Chipewyan, Tolowa, Ojibwa, Delaware.

High front unrounded vowel with velar stricture /iˠ/ 1 (-1)
OBSCURE Siriono.

Nasalised high front unrounded vowel with velar stricture /ĩˠ/ 1 (-1)
OBSCURE Siriono.

Pharyngealized high front unrounded vowel /iˤ/ 1
Neo-Aramaic.

Long pharyngealized high front unrounded vowel /iˤ:/ 2
Evenki, Neo-Aramaic.

Breathy voiced high front unrounded vowel /i̤/ 1
Tamang.

Laryngealized high front unrounded vowel /ḭ/ 2
Sedang, S. Nambiquara.

Laryngealized nasalized high front unrounded vowel /ḭ̃/ 1
S. Nambiquara.

Voiceless high front unrounded vowel /i̥/ 2
Ik, Dafla.

High front rounded vowel /y/ 21
Breton, French, Albanian, Cheremis, Finnish, Hungarian, Tavgy, Osmanli, Chuvash, Yakut, Kirghiz, Bashkir, Khalaj, Tuva, Korean, Iai, Mandarin, Changchow, Fuchow, Kan, Tzeltal.

Long high front rounded vowel /y:/ 5 (-1)
Breton, German, Norwegian, Finnish; RARE Hungarian.

Lowered high front unrounded vowel /ɩ/ 54 (-1)
Irish, German, Norwegian, Lithuanian, Kurdish, Hindi-Urdu, Bengali, Punjabi, Sinhalese, Azerbaijani, Kirghiz, Evenki, Kpelle, Diola, Tampulma, Akan, Amo, Zande, Maasai, Luo, Ik, Tama, Tabi, Logbara, Kunama, Arabic, Hebrew, Somali, Iraqw, Hausa, Angas, Mundari, Vietnamese, Khmer, Nunggubuyu, Alawa, Tagalog, Dani, Navaho, Nez Perce, Tzeltal, Puget Sound, Luiseño, Pomo, Diegueño, Ojibwa, Amahuaca, Quechua, Yukaghir, Chukchi, Gilyak, Georgian, Basque; ?DERIVED Hupa.

Long lowered high front unrounded vowel /ι:/ 1
Mongolian.

Nasalized lowered high front unrounded vowel /ι̃/ 9
Irish, Hindi-Urdu, Bengali, Punjabi, Kpelle, Akan, Burmese, Navaho, Amahuaca.

Pharyngealized lowered high front unrounded vowel /ιˤ/ 2
Evenki, Hamer.

Lowered high front rounded vowel /ʏ/ 3
German, Norwegian, Azerbaijani.

Higher mid front unrounded vowel /e/ 83 (-1)
French, Romanian, Farsi, Kashmiri, Mongolian, Goldi, Korean, Katcha, Bisa, Bambara, Dan, Wolof, Diola, Temne, Senadi, Tampulma, Bariba, Ewe, Akan, Igbo, Gã, Lelemi, Efik, Birom, Amo, Swahili, Luvale, Doayo, Gbeya, Maba, Fur, Maasai, Nyangi, Ik, Sebei, Tama, Temein, Tabi, Sara, Koma, Hamer, Kharia, Vietnamese, Sedang, Standard Thai, Lakkia, Saek, Po-ai, Javanese, Cham, Malay, Iai, Amoy, Tamang, Burmese, Lahu, Ao, Garo, Boro, Karen, Yao, Asmat, Washkuk, Sentani, Kunimaipa, Chipewyan, Otomi, Mazahua, Squamish, Tiwa, Seneca, Yuchi, Tunica, Alabama, Apinaye, Campa, Guarani, Siriono, Telugu, Chukchi, Nama, Brahui; RARE Logbara.

Long higher mid front unrounded vowel /e:/ 23 (-1)
Irish, German, Norwegian, Lithuanian, Hindi-Urdu, Sinhalese, Hungarian, Mongolian, Korean, Wolof, Dagbani, Arabic, Iraqw, Khmer, Iai, Gadsup, Karok, Diegueño, Tonkawa, Wichita, Telugu, Brahui; ?DERIVED Finnish.

Nasalized higher mid front unrounded vowel /ẽ/ 9
Kashmiri, Bambara, Ewe, Igbo, Zande, Mazahua, Tiwa, Guarani, Siriono.

Long nasalized higher mid front unrounded vowel /ẽ:/ 2
Irish, Hindi-Urdu.

Higher mid retracted front unrounded vowel /e̠/ 1
Karen.

Breathy voiced higher mid front unrounded vowel /e̤/ 1
Tamang.

Laryngealized higher mid front unrounded vowel /ḛ/ 1
Sedang.

Higher mid front rounded vowel /ø/ 15 (-1)
Breton, Cheremis, Finnish, Hungarian, Azerbaijani, Kirghiz, Bashkir, Khalaj, Tuva, Manchu, Korean, Wolof, Hopi, Gilyak; OBSCURE Guajiro.

Long higher mid front rounded vowel /ø:/ 6 (-2)
Breton, German, Norwegian, Hungarian; RARE Akan; ?DERIVED Finnish.

Overshort higher mid front rounded vowel /ø̆/ 1
Chuvash.

Nasalized higher mid front rounded vowel /ø̃/ 1 (-1)
OBSCURE Guajiro.

Mid front unrounded vowel /"e"/ 113 (-2)
Irish, Breton, Norwegian, Spanish, Bengali, Sinhalese, Albanian, Ostyak Komi, Lappish, Yurak, Tavgy, Chuvash, Tuva, Manchu, Moro, Kadugli, Tarok, Teke, Zande, Songhai, Kanuri, Luo, Nubian, Nera, Mursi, Yulu, Berta, Kunama, Amharic, Socotri, Neo-Aramaic, Tuareg, Somali, Awiya, Beja, Kullo, Dizi, Kefa, Hausa, Angas, Kanakuru, Mundari, Khasi, Malakmalak, Mabuiag, Sui, Lungchow, Malagasy, Chamorro, Tsou, Roro, Kaliai, Lahu, Jingpho, Andamanese, Nimboran, Iwam, Kewa, Chuave, Dani, Wantoat, Daribi, Fasu, Dera, Yareba, Koiari, Taoripi, Rotokas, Nambakaengo, Tlingit, Tolowa, Hupa, Klamath, Maidu, Wintu, Chontal, Tzeltal, K'ekchi, Mixe, Mixtec, Chatino, Luiseño, Yacqui, Achumawi, Yana, Shasta, Wiyot, Wappo, Itonama, Bribri, Tacana, Ashuslay, Abipon, S. Nambiquara, Arabela, Auca, Gununa-Kena, Island Carib, Guahibo, Ticuna, Barasano, Siona, Tucano, Kota, Kurukh, Malayalam, Georgian, Basque, Burushaski, !Xũ; RARE Alawa, Bandjalang.

Long mid front unrounded vowel /"e:"/ 10
Pashto, Kurdish, Tigre, Tuareg, Hausa, Ngizim, Tolowa, Hupa, Kabardian, !Xũ.

Overshort mid front unrounded vowel /"ĕ"/ 1
Ostyak.

Nasalized front mid unrounded vowel /"ẽ"/ 22 (-2)
Irish, Bengali, Punjabi, Dan, Zande, Sara, Daribi, Fasu, Zoque, Chatino Yuchi, Bribri, S. Nambiquara, Auca, Island Carib, Guahibo, Barasano, Siona, Tucano, Kurukh; RARE Songhai, Mixtec.

Pharyngealized mid front unrounded vowel /"eˤ"/ 3 (-1)
Neo-Aramaic, Hamer; ?DERIVED Lak.

Laryngealized mid front unrounded vowel /"ḛ"/ 1
S. Nambiquara.

Laryngealized nasalized front mid unrounded vowel /"ḛ̃"/ 1
S. Nambiquara.

Voiceless mid front unrounded vowel /"e̥"/ 1
Ik.

Lower mid front unrounded vowel /ɛ/ 116 (-5)
Greek, German, Russian, Bulgarian, Cheremis, Finnish, Hungarian, Osmanli, Azerbaijani, Yakut, Kirghiz, Evenki, Japanese, Katcha, Kpelle, Bambara, Dan, Wolof, Diola, Temne, Senadi, Tampulma, Bariba, Ewe, Igbo, Gã, Lelemi, Efik, Birom, Amo, Beembe, Zulu, Doayo, Gbeya, Maba, Fur, Maasai, Nyangi, Ik, Tama, Temein, Tabi, Logbara, Sara, Koma, Hebrew, Somali, Iraqw, Angas, Vietnamese, Sedang, Khmer, Maung, Burera, Wik-Munkan, Kunjen, Lakkia, Yay, Saek, Po-ai, Atayal, Sundanese, Javanese, Cham, Batak, Sa'ban, Maori, Hawaiian, Hakka, Fuchow, Kan, Dafla, Burmese, Tiddim Chin, Karen, Andamanese, Washkuk, Sentani, Selepet, Yagaria, Pawaian, Suena, Nasioi, Navaho, Zoque, Mazahua, Mazatec, Nootka, Kwakw'ala, Pomo, Tarascan, Zuni, Acoma, Delaware, Tonkawa, Wichita, Dakota, Tunica, Cayapa, Paez, Ocaina, Muinane, Carib, Apinaye, Guajiro, Moxo, Cofan, Araucanian, Yukaghir, Chukchi, Ainu; RARE French, Karok; LOAN Margi, Quechua; ?DERIVED Iai.

Long lower mid front unrounded vowel /ɛː/ 12 (-2)
Breton, German, Evenki, Wolof, Khmer, Lakkia, Telefol, Navaho, Ojibwa, Wichita; RARE French; ?DERIVED Iai.

Overshort lower mid front unrounded vowel /ɛ̆/ 1
Po-ai.

Nasalized lower mid front unrounded vowel /ɛ̃/ 20
Bulgarian, Kpelle, Bambara, Senadi, Bariba, Ewe, Igbo, Gã, Lelemi, Beembe, Doayo, Kharia, Lakkia, Pawaian, Navaho, Mazatec, Seneca, Paez, Apinaye, Guajiro.

Long nasalized lower mid front unrounded vowel /ɛ̃ː/ 4 (-1)
Lakkia, Navaho, Ojibwa; LOAN Breton.

Laryngealized lower mid front unrounded vowel /ɛ̰/ 1
Sedang.

Lower mid front rounded vowel /œ/ 7
German, Norwegian, French, Osmanli, Yakut, Iai, Fuchow.

Long lower mid front rounded vowel /œː/ 1 (-1)
RARE Akan.

Nasalized lower mid front rounded vowel /œ̃/ 1
French.

Raised low front unrounded vowel /æ/ 38 (-5)
Norwegian, Bengali, Punjabi, Ostyak, Finnish, Tavgy, Bashkir, Korean, Dan, Luo, Shilha, Tuareg, Somali, Vietnamese, Maranungku, Standard Thai, Chamorro, Iai, Taishan, Burmese, Yao, Andamanese, Wantoat, Nambakaengo, Nez Perce, Mixe, Otomi, Hopi, Seneca, Yuchi, Auca, Ket, Gilyak; RARE Hungarian, Quileute; ?DERIVED Lithuanian, Awiya, Hakka.

Long raised low front unrounded vowel /æː/ 10
Norwegian, Lithuanian, Sinhalese, Finnish, Korean, Arabic, Tuareg, Iai, Delaware, Telugu.

Nasalized raised low front unrounded vowel /æ̃/ 8
French, Bengali, Punjabi, Gbeya, Changchow, Nambakaengo, Otomi, Auca.

Long nasalized raised low front unrounded vowel /æ̃ː/ 1
Delaware.

Pharyngealized raised low front unrounded vowel /æˤ/ 1
Lak.

Low front unrounded vowel /a̟/ 14
Breton, Russian, French, Farsi, Sinhalese, Azerbaijani, Kpelle, Khmer, Sentani, Pawaian, Acoma, Cashinahua, Yukaghir, Georgian.

Long low front unrounded vowel /a̟ː/ 5
Tigre, Vietnamese, Khmer, Gadsup, Kabardian.

Nasalized low front unrounded vowel /ã̟/ 3
Dan, Pawaian, Cashinahua.

High central unrounded vowel /ɨ/ 40
Romanian, Kurdish, Kashmiri, Komi, Lappish, Tavgy, Tuva, Dan, Kanuri, Amharic, Awiya, Standard Thai, Saek, Po-ai, Sundanese, Cham, Sa'ban, Rukai, Lahu, Washkuk, Nimboran, Maidu, Mixe, Otomi, Papago, Acoma, Itonama, Muinane, Chacobo, Abipon, Gununa-Kena, Wapishana, Guarani, Ticuna, Barasano, Siona, Tucano, Cofan, Ket, Kabardian.

Long high central unrounded vowel /ɨ:/ 2
Angas, Khmer.

Overshort high central unrounded vowel /ɨ̆/ 3
Kashmiri, Sebei, Po-ai.

Nasalized high central unrounded vowel /ɨ̃/ 7
Kashmiri, Wapishana, Guarani, Ticuna, Barasano, Siona, Tucano.

Overshort nasalized high central unrounded vowel /ɨ̆̃/ 1
Kashmiri.

Retroflexed high central unrounded vowel /ɨ̢/ 1
Tarascan.

High central rounded vowel /ʉ/ 6
Norwegian, Ostyak, Mongolian, Yay, Tsou, Nambakaengo.

Long high central rounded vowel /ʉ:/ 2
Norwegian, Mongolian.

Overshort high central rounded vowel /ʉ̆/ 1
Sebei.

Lowered high central unrounded vowel /ɨ̞/ 3 (-1)
Kirghiz, Karen; LOAN Hindi-Urdu.

Lowered high central rounded vowel /ʉ̞/ 1
Somali.

Higher mid central unrounded vowel /ɘ/ 6 (-1)
Goldi, Dan, Khmer, Standard Thai, Lahu; RARE Iraqw.

Retroflexed higher mid central unrounded vowel /ɘ̢/ 1
Mandarin.

Mid central unrounded vowel /"ə"/ 67 (-1)
Breton, German, Norwegian, Romanian, Pashto, Kurdish, Kashmiri, Punjabi, Albanian, E. Armenian, Cheremis, Komi, Tavgy, Bashkir, Diola, Temne, Tarok, Fur, Tabi, Sara, Koma, Tigre, Amharic, Socotri, Tuareg, Hausa, Margi, Kanakuru, Khmer, Maranungku, Malakmalak, Yay, Sui, Saek, Po-ai, Sundanese, Javanese, Cham, Malay, Tagalog, Sa'ban, Changchow, Kan, Burmese, Boro, Asmat, Sentani, Iwam, Wantoat, Dera, Nambakaengo, Tolowa, Chontal, Mixe, Otomi, Mazahua, Kwakw'ala, Squamish, Puget Sound, Tiwa, Diegueño, Achumawi, Delaware, Gununa-Kena, Kurukh, Nama; ?DERIVED Sinhalese.

Long mid central unrounded vowel /"ə:"/ 2 (-1)
Khmer; LOAN Sinhalese.

Overshort mid central unrounded vowel /"ə̆"/ 3
Sebei, Chukchi, Georgian.

Nasalized mid central unrounded vowel /"ə̃"/ 8
Kashmiri, Punjabi, Dan, Sara, Nambakaengo, Mazahua, Tiwa, Guahibo.

Long nasalized mid central unrounded vowel /"ə̃:"/ 1
Delaware.

Mid central rounded vowel /"ɵ"/ 5
Ostyak, Mongolian, Somali, Ket, Yukaghir.

Long mid central rounded vowel /"ɵ:"/ 1
Mongolian.

Overshort mid central rounded vowel /"ɵ̆"/ 2
Ostyak, Sebei.

Lower mid central unrounded vowel /ɜ/ 10
Hindi-Urdu, Dan, Zande, Logbara, Tigre, Iraqw, Sui, Gadsup, Telugu, Kabardian.

Nasalized lower mid central unrounded vowel /ɜ̃/ 2
Hindi-Urdu, Zande.

Raised low central unrounded vowel /ɐ/ 6
German, Amo, Tuareg, Dizi, Mazahua, Carib.

Overshort raised low central unrounded vowel /ɐ̆/ 1 (-1)
RARE Sebei.

Pharyngealized raised low central unrounded vowel /ɐˤ/ 1
Hamer.

Low central unrounded vowel /a/ 274
Irish, Lithuanian, Spanish, Romanian, Bengali, Kashmiri, Punjabi, Sinhalese, Albanian, E. Armenian, Ostyak, Komi, Finnish, Lappish, Yurak, Tavgy, Osmanli, Yakut, Kirghiz, Khalaj, Evenki, Goldi, Manchu, Korean, Japanese, Moro, Kadugli, Kpelle, Bisa, Bambara, Dan, Wolof, Diola, Temne, Dagbani, Senadi, Tampulma, Bariba, Ewe, Akan, Igbo, Gã, Lelemi, Efik, Birom, Tarok, Amo, Beembe, Swahili, Luvale, Zulu, Teke, Doayo, Gbeya, Zande, Songhai, Kanuri, Maba, Fur, Maasai, Luo, Nubian, Nyangi, Ik, Sebei, Tama, Temein, Nera, Tabi, Mursi, Logbara, Yulu, Sara, Berta, Kunama, Koma, Arabic, Amharic, Hebrew, Socotri, Neo-Aramaic, Somali, Awiya, Iraqw, Beja, Kullo, Dizi, Kefa, Hausa, Angas, Margi, Ngizim, Kanakuru, Mundari, Kharia, Khasi, Sedang, Maung, Tiwi, Burera, Nunggubuyu, Alawa, Maranungku, Malakmalak, Bardi, Wik-Munkan, Kunjen, Western Desert, Nyangumata, Aranda, Kariera-Ngarluma, Gugu-Yalanji, Mabuiag, Arabana-Wanganura, Diyari, Bandjalang, Standard Thai, Lakkia, Yay, Sui, Saek, Po-ai, Lungchow, Atayal, Sundanese, Javanese, Malagasy, Cham, Malay, Batak, Sa'ban, Rukai, Tsou, Adzera, Roro, Kaliai, Hawaiian, Mandarin, Taishan, Hakka, Changchow, Amoy, Fuchow, Kan, Tamang, Burmese, Lahu, Jingpho, Ao, Tiddim Chin, Garo, Boro, Karen, Yao, Andamanese, Asmat, Washkuk, Nimboran, Iwam, Telefol, Selepet, Yagaria, Kewa, Chuave, Dani, Wantoat, Daribi, Fasu, Suena, Dera, Kunimaipa, Yareba, Koiari, Taoripi, Nasioi, Rotokas, Nambakaengo, Haida, Tlingit, Navaho, Chipewyan, Tolowa, Hupa, Nez Perce, Klamath, Maidu, Wintu, Chontal,

Zoque, Tzeltal, Totonac, K'ekchi, Mixe, Otomi, Mazahua, Mazatec, Mixtec Chatino, Nootka, Kwakw'ala, Quileute, Squamish, Puget Sound, Papago, Luiseño, Hopi, Yacqui, Karok, Pomo, Diegueño, Achumawi, Yana, Shasta, Tarascan, Zuni, Ojibwa, Delaware, Tonkawa, Wiyot, Seneca, Wichita, Dakota, Yuchi, Tunica, Alabama, Wappo, Itonama, Bribri, Mura, Paez, Ocaina, Muinane, Apinaye, Amahuaca, Chacobo, Tacana, Ashuslay, Abipon, S. Nambiquara, Arabela, Auca, Quechua, Jaqaru, Gununa-Kena, Wapishana, Island Carib, Amuesha, Campa, Guajiro, Moxo, Guarani, Siriono, Guahibo, Ticuna, Barasano, Siona, Tucano, Jivaro, Cofan, Araucanian, Greenlandic Aleut, Kota, Kurukh, Malayalam, Ket, Chukchi, Lak, Nama, Basque, Burushaski, Ainu, Brahui, !Xũ.

Long low central unrounded vowel /a:/ 35 (-1)
German, Lithuanian, Kurdish, Hindi-Urdu, Sinhalese, Finnish, Hungarian, Evenki, Korean, Wolof, Dagbani, Fur, Neo-Aramaic, Angas, Ngizim, Khasi, Bardi, Lakkia, Yay, Adzera, Yao, Telefol, Navaho, Chipewyan, Tolowa, Hupa, Karok, Diegueño, Ojibwa, Delaware, Tonkawa, Telugu, Lak, !Xũ; ?DERIVED Sa'ban.

Overshort low central unrounded vowel /ǎ/ 3
Yurak, Po-ai, Lungchow.

Nasalized low central unrounded vowel /ã/ 55 (-3)
Irish, Bengali, Kashmiri, Punjabi, Kpelle, Bambara, Dan, Senadi, Bariba Ewe, Akan, Igbo, Gã, Lelemi, Beembe, Doayo, Gbeya, Zande, Sara, Kharia, Lakkia, Daribi, Fasu, Nambakaengo, Navaho, Chipewyan, Tolowa, Otomi, Mazahua, Mazatec, Mixtec, Dakota, Bribri, Paez, Ocaina, Apinaye, Amahuaca, S. Nambiquara, Auca, Wapishana, Island Carib, Guajiro, Guarani, Siriono, Guahibo, Ticuna, Siona, Tucano, Jivaro, Kurukh, Nama, !Xũ; RARE Songhai, Logbara, Karok.

Long nasalized low central unrounded vowel /ã:/ 8
Hindi-Urdu, Lakkia, Navaho, Chipewyan, Tolowa, Ojibwa, Delaware, !Xũ.

Retroflexed low central unrounded vowel /a̢/ 1 (-1)
?DERIVED Mandarin.

Pharyngealized low central unrounded vowel /aˤ/ 2
Neo-Aramaic, !Xũ.

Long pharyngealized low central unrounded vowel /aˤ:/ 2
Neo-Aramaic, !Xũ.

Nasalized pharyngealized low central unrounded vowel /ãˤ/ 1
!Xũ.

Long nasalized pharyngealized low central unrounded vowel /ãˤ:/ 1
!Xũ.

Breathy voiced low central unrounded vowel /a̤/ 1
Tamang.

Laryngealized low central unrounded vowel /a̰/ 2
Sedang, S. Nambiquara.

Laryngealized nasalized low central unrounded vowel /ã̰/ 1
S. Nambiquara.

Voiceless low central unrounded vowel /ḁ/ 1
Ik.

Overshort low central rounded vowel /ɒ̝̆/ 1 (-1)
RARE Sebei.

High back unrounded vowel /ɯ/ 20
Ostyak, Osmanli, Chuvash, Yakut, Korean, Japanese, Lungchow, Adzera, Dafla, Ao, Nimboran, Nez Perce, Ocaina, Carib, Apinaye, Amahuaca, Cashinahua, Jaqaru, Jivaro, Araucanian.

Long high back unrounded vowel /ɯ:/ 1
Korean.

Overshort high back unrounded vowel /ɯ̆/ 1
Lungchow.

Nasalized high back unrounded vowel /ɯ̃/ 5
Apinaye, Amahuaca, Cashinahua, Abipon, Jivaro.

High back rounded vowel /u/ 254 (-1)
Greek, Breton, Norwegian, Russian, Bulgarian, French, Spanish, Romanian, Farsi, Pashto, Kashmiri, Punjabi, Albanian, E. Armenian, Ostyak, Cheremis, Komi, Finnish, Hungarian, Lappish, Yurak, Tavgy, Osmanli, Chuvash, Yakut, Bashkir, Khalaj, Tuva, Evenki, Goldi, Manchu, Korean, Katcha, Moro, Kadugli, Kpelle, Bisa, Bambara, Dan, Wolof, Temne, Dagbani, Senadi, Tampulma, Bariba, Ewe, Akan, Igbo, Gã, Lelemi, Efik, Birom, Tarok, Amo, Beembe, Swahili, Luvale, Zulu, Teke, Doayo, Gbeya, Zande, Songhai, Kanuri, Maba, Fur, Maasai, Luo, Nubian, Nyangi, Ik, Tama, Temein, Nera, Tabi, Mursi, Logbara, Yulu, Sara, Berta, Kunama, Koma, Amharic, Socotri, Neo-Aramaic, Tuareg, Awiya, Beja, Kullo, Dizi, Kefa, Hamer, Angas, Margi, Ngizim, Kanakuru, Kharia, Khasi, Sedang, Maung, Tiwi, Burera, Malakmalak, Bardi, Kunjen, Western Desert, Nyangumata, Aranda, Kariera-Ngarluma, Gugu-Yalanji, Mabuiag, Arabana-Wanganura, Diyari, Bandjalang, Standard Thai, Lakkia, Yay, Sui, Saek, Po-ai, Lungchow, Atayal, Sundanese, Javanese, Cham, Malay, Batak, Sa'ban, Chamorro, Rukai, Tsou, Roro, Kaliai, Iai, Maori, Hawaiian, Mandarin, Taishan, Hakka, Changchow, Amoy, Fuchow, Kan, Tamang, Dafla, Burmese, Lahu, Jingpho, Ao, Tiddim Chin, Garo, Boro, Karen, Yao, Andamanese, Asmat, Washkuk, Sentani, Iwam, Telefol, Selepet, Gadsup, Yagaria, Kewa, Chuave, Pawaian, Dani, Wantoat, Daribi, Fasu, Suena, Dera, Kunimaipa, Yareba, Koiari, Taoripi, Nasioi, Rotokas, Nambakaengo, Tlingit, Chipewyan, Tolowa, Maidu, Wintu, Chontal, Zoque, Totonac, K'ekchi, Mixe, Otomi, Mazahua, Mixtec, Chatino, Kwakw'ala, Quileute, Papago, Yacqui, Tiwa, Achumawi, Yana, Shasta, Tarascan, Zuni, Acoma, Delaware, Tonkawa, Wiyot, Wichita, Dakota, Yuchi, Tunica, Wappo, Itonama, Bribri, Paez, Muinane, Carib, Apinaye, Cashinahua, Ashuslay, S. Nambiquara, Arabela, Gununa-Kena, Wapishana, Island Carib, Guajiro, Moxo, Guarani, Siriono, Guahibo, Ticuna, Barasano, Siona, Tucano, Jivaro, Araucanian, Greenlandic, Aleut, Telugu, Kota, Kurukh, Malayalam, Ket, Yukaghir, Chukchi, Gilyak, Lak, Nama, Basque, Burushaski, Ainu, Brahui, !Xũ; RARE Seneca.

Long high back rounded vowel /u:/ 37 (-1)
Irish, Breton, German, Norwegian, Lithuanian, Kurdish, Hindi-Urdu, Sinhalese, Finnish, Hungarian, Evenki, Korean, Wolof, Dagbani, Fur, Arabic, Tigre, Neo-Aramaic, Tuareg, Iraqw, Hausa, Khmer, Bardi, Lakkia,

Atayal, Iai, Telefol, Chipewyan, Tolowa, Delaware, Tonkawa, Telugu, Kabardian, Lak, Brahui, !Xũ; RARE Angas.

Overshort high back rounded vowel /ŭ/ 4
Yurak, Sebei, Po-ai, Lungchow.

Nasalized high back rounded vowel /ũ/ 51 (-2)
Bulgarian, Kashmiri, Punjabi, Kpelle, Bambara, Dan, Senadi, Bariba, Ewe Akan, Igbo, Gã, Lelemi, Beembe, Doayo, Gbeya, Zande, Sara, Kharia, Lakkia, Pawaian, Daribi, Fasu, Nambakaengo, Chipewyan, Tolowa, Otomi, Mazahua, Mixtec, Chatino, Dakota, Bribri, Paez, Apinaye, Cashinahua, Wapishana, Island Carib, Guajiro, Guarani, Siriono, Guahibo, Ticuna, Barasano, Siona, Tucano, Jivaro, Kurukh, Nama, !Xũ; RARE Songhai, Tiwa.

Long nasalized high back rounded vowel /ũː/ 7
Irish, Hindi-Urdu, Lakkia, Chipewyan, Hupa, Delaware, !Xũ.

Pharyngealized high back rounded vowel /uˤ/ 1
Neo-Aramaic.

Long pharyngealized high back rounded vowel /uˤː/ 1
Neo-Aramaic.

Breathy voiced high back rounded vowel /ṳ/ 1
Tamang.

Laryngealized high back rounded vowel /ṵ/ 2
Sedang, S. Nambiquara.

Voiceless high back rounded vowel /u̥/ 2
Ik, Dafla.

Lowered high back unrounded vowel /ɯ̞/ 4
Vietnamese, Nunggubuyu, Alawa, Mandarin.

Lowered high back rounded vowel /ʊ/ 48
Irish, German, Lithuanian, Kurdish, Hindi-Urdu, Bengali, Punjabi, Sinhalese, Azerbaijani, Kirghiz, Mongolian, Kpelle, Diola, Tampulma, Akan, Igbo, Amo, Zande, Maasai, Luo, Tama, Logbara, Kunama, Arabic, Hebrew, Somali, Iraqw, Hausa, Mundari, Vietnamese, Khmer, Maranungku, Wik-Munkan, Tagalog, Dani, Kunimaipa, Haida, Tzeltal, Puget Sound, Luiseño, Karok, Pomo, Diegueño, Ojibwa, Cayapa, Quechua, Georgian, Brahui.

Long lowered high back rounded vowel /ʊː/ 1
Karok.

Nasalized lowered high back rounded vowel /ʊ̃/ 7
Irish, Hindi-Urdu, Bengali, Punjabi, Akan, Igbo, Burmese.

Pharyngealized lowered high back rounded vowel /ʊˤ/ 2
Evenki, Hamer.

Long pharyngealized lowered high back rounded vowel /ʊˤː/ 1
Evenki.

Higher mid back unrounded vowel /ɤ/ 4
Vietnamese, Hopi, Apinaye, Gilyak.

Higher mid fronted back unrounded vowel /ɤ̟/ 1
Azerbaijani.

Higher mid back rounded vowel /o/ 88 (-1)
Romanian, Farsi, Bengali, Kashmiri, Komi, Finnish, Hungarian, Azerbaijani, Kirghiz, Khalaj, Goldi, Korean, Katcha, Bisa, Bambara, Dan, Diola, Temne, Senadi, Tampulma, Bariba, Ewe, Akan, Igbo, Gã, Lelemi, Efik, Birom, Amo, Swahili, Luvale, Doayo, Gbeya, Songhai, Maba, Fur, Maasai, Nyangi, Ik, Sebei, Tama, Temein, Tabi, Sara, Koma, Hamer, Sedang, Standard Thai, Saek, Javanese, Malagasy, Cham, Malay, Iai, Amoy, Tamang, Burmese, Lahu, Ao, Garo, Boro, Karen, Yao, Selepet, Nasioi, Chipewyan, Mixe, Otomi, Mazahua, Mazatec, Nootka, Squamish, Tiwa, Tarascan, Dakota, Yuchi, Tunica, Alabama, Ocaina, Apinaye, Amuesha, Campa, Guarani, Siriono, Barasano, Telugu, Nama; RARE Logbara.

Long higher mid back rounded vowel /o:/ 25 (-2)
Irish, Breton, German, Lithuanian, Hindi-Urdu, Sinhalese, Hungarian, Korean, Wolof, Dagbani, Arabic, Iraqw, Khmer, Iai, Gadsup, Navaho, Karok, Diegueño, Ojibwa, Tonkawa, Wichita, Telugu, Brahui; RARE French; ?DERIVED Finnish.

Overshort higher mid back rounded vowel /ŏ/ 1
Po-ai.

Nasalized higher mid back rounded vowel /õ/ 17 (-1)
French, Bengali, Kashmiri, Bambara, Ewe, Igbo, Zande, Lakkia, Mazahua, Mazatec, Tiwa, Ocaina, Apinaye, Guarani, Siriono, Barasano; RARE Songhai.

Long nasalized higher mid back rounded vowel /õ:/ 4
Irish, Hindi-Urdu, Navaho, Ojibwa.

Breathy voiced higher mid back rounded vowel /o̤/ 1
Tamang.

Laryngealized higher mid back rounded vowel /o̰/ 1
Sedang.

Mid back unrounded vowel /"ɤ"/ 6
Bulgarian, Bashkir, Korean, Moro, Nimboran, Island Carib.

Long mid back unrounded vowel /"ɤ:"/ 1
Korean.

Nasalized mid back unrounded vowel /"ɤ̃"/ 2
Bulgarian, Island Carib.

Nasalized mid fronted back unrounded vowel /"ɤ̟̃"/ 1
Zoque.

Mid back rounded vowel /"o"/ 133 (-3)
Irish, Breton, Russian, Spanish, Punjabi, Sinhalese, Albanian, E. Armenian, Ostyak, Cheremis, Lappish, Yurak, Tavgy, Osmanli, Bashkir, Tuva, Mongolian, Evenki, Manchu, Moro, Kadugli, Tarok, Teke, Zande,

Kanuri, Luo, Nubian, Nera, Mursi, Yulu, Berta, Kunama, Amharic, Hebrew, Socotri, Neo-Aramaic, Tuareg, Awiya, Beja, Kullo, Dizi, Kefa, Hausa, Angas, Margi, Kanakuru, Mundari, Kharia, Khasi, Vietnamese, Malakmalak, Kunjen, Mabuiag, Sui, Lungchow, Sundanese, Batak, Chamorro, Tsou, Adzera, Roro, Kaliai, Maori, Hawaiian, Changchow, Kan, Jingpho, Andamanese, Washkuk, Iwam, Yagaria, Kewa, Chuave, Pawaian, Dani, Wantoat, Daribi, Fasu, Dera, Yareba, Koiari, Taoripi, Rotokas, Nambakaengo, Tlingit, Hupa, Klamath, Maidu, Wintu, Chontal, Zoque, Tzeltal, K'ekchi, Mixtec, Chatino, Luiseño, Yacqui, Achumawi, Yana, Wiyot, Seneca, Wappo, Itonama, Bribri, Mura, Muinane, Amahuaca, Chacobo, Tacana, Ashuslay, Abipon, S. Nambiquara, Arabela, Auca, Gununa-Kena, Guahibo, Ticuna, Siona, Tucano, Cofan, Kota, Kurukh, Malayalam, Yukaghir, Chukchi, Gilyak, Georgian, Basque, Burushaski, !Xũ; RARE Tigre; LOAN Chuvash; ?DERIVED Telugu.

Long mid back rounded vowel /"o:"/ 13
Norwegian, Pashto, Kurdish, Mongolian, Manchu, Tigre, Tuareg, Hausa, Ngizim, Adzera, Hupa, Kabardian, !Xũ.

Overshort mid back rounded vowel /"ŏ"/ 1
Ostyak.

Nasalized mid back rounded vowel /"õ"/ 24
Irish, Punjabi, Dan, Zande, Sara, Kharia, Changchow, Pawaian, Daribi, Fasu, Nambakaengo, Mixtec, Chatino, Yuchi, Bribri, Amahuaca, S. Nambiquara, Auca, Guahibo, Ticuna, Siona, Tucano, Kurukh, !Xũ.

Pharyngealized mid back rounded vowel /"oˤ"/ 3
Neo-Aramaic, Lak, !Xũ.

Long pharyngealized mid back rounded vowel /"oˤ" / 1
!Xũ.

Laryngealized mid back rounded vowel /"o̰"/ 1
S. Nambiquara.

Laryngealized nasalized mid back rounded vowel /"õ̰"/ 1
S. Nambiquara.

Voiceless mid back rounded vowel /"o̥"/ 1
Ik.

Lower mid back unrounded vowel /ʌ/ 4
Cheremis, Vietnamese, Dafla, Apinaye.

Nasalized lower mid back unrounded vowel /ʌ̃/ 1
Apinaye.

Lower mid back rounded vowel /ɔ/ 100 (-3)
Greek, German, Lithuanian, Bulgarian, French, Bengali, Yakut, Mongolian, Evenki, Japanese, Katcha, Kpelle, Bisa, Bambara, Dan, Wolof, Diola, Temne, Senadi, Tampulma, Bariba, Ewe, Akan, Igbo, Gã, Lelemi, Efik, Birom, Amo, Beembe, Zulu, Doayo, Gbeya, Maba, Fur, Maasai, Nyangi, Ik, Sebei, Tama, Temein, Tabi, Logbara, Sara, Koma, Somali, Iraqw, Vietnamese, Sedang, Khmer, Maung, Burera, Bardi, Wik-Munkan, Standard Thai, Yay, Saek, Po-ai, Atayal, Javanese, Cham, Sa'ban, Iai, Taishan, Hakka, Amoy, Fuchow, Dafla, Burmese, Lahu, Tiddim Chin, Karen, Yao,

Andamanese, Asmat, Sentani, Pawaian, Suena, Taoripi, Navaho, Nez Perce, Mixe, Otomi, Mazahua, Kwakw'ala, Papago, Pomo, Zuni, Delaware, Tonkawa, Tunica, Carib, Apinaye, Guajiro, Araucanian, Ket, Ainu; RARE Diegueño; LOAN Nootka, Quechua.

Long lower mid back rounded vowel /ɔ:/ 9 (-1)
Mongolian, Evenki, Wolof, Khmer, Lakkia, Iai, Telefol, Delaware; RARE Diegueño.

Overshort lower mid back rounded vowel /ɔ̆/ 2
Chuvash, Po-ai.

Nasalized lower mid back rounded vowel /ɔ̃/ 17
Bulgarian, Bengali, Kpelle, Bambara, Senadi, Bariba, Ewe, Igbo, Gã, Beembe, Doayo, Gbeya, Sara, Pawaian, Navaho, Seneca, Guajiro.

Long nasalized lower mid back rounded vowel /ɔ̃:/ 2
Lakkia, Delaware.

Pharyngealized lower mid back rounded vowel /ɔˤ/ 1
Hamer.

Long nasalized pharyngealized lower mid back rounded vowel /ɔ̃ˤ:/ 1
!Xũ.

Laryngealized lower mid back rounded vowel /ɔ̰/ 1
Sedang.

Centralized low back unrounded vowel /ɑ̟/ 1
Selepet.

Centralized low back rounded vowel /ɒ̟/ 2
Norwegian, Kirghiz.

Low back unrounded vowel /ɑ/ 22 (-1)
Greek, Norwegian, Bulgarian, Farsi, Azerbaijani, Chuvash, Bashkir, Khalaj, Tuva, Mongolian, Dan, Temne, Hamer, Khmer, Chamorro, Maori, Dafla, Nambakaengo, Tiwa, Cayapa, Ashuslay; LOAN Hindi-Urdu.

Long low back unrounded vowel /ɑ:/ 7
Irish, Norwegian, Pashto, Mongolian, Iraqw, Khmer, Brahui.

Nasalized low back unrounded vowel /ɑ̃/ 4 (-1)
Bulgarian, Nambakaengo, Tiwa; LOAN Hindi-Urdu.

Long nasalized low back unrounded vowel /ɑ̃:/ 2
Irish, Breton.

Low back rounded vowel /ɒ/ 5
French, Punjabi, Hungarian, Luo, Wichita.

Long low back rounded vowel /ɒ:/ 2
Breton, Wichita.

Overshort low back rounded vowel /ɒ̆/ 1
Ostyak.

Nasalized low back rounded vowel /õ/ 3
French, Punjabi, Dan.

10. DIPHTHONGS

High front unrounded to mid front unrounded diphthong /ie/ 3
E. Armenian, Evenki, Lakkia.

Nasalized high front unrounded to mid front unrounded diphthong /ĩẽ/ 1
Lakkia.

High front unrounded to low front unrounded diphthong /ia̟/ 1
Evenki.

High front unrounded to low central unrounded diphthong /ia/ 2
Saek, !Xũ.

High front unrounded to mid back rounded diphthong /io/ 3
Kurdish, Acoma, !Xũ.

Long high front unrounded to mid back rounded diphthong /io:/ 1
Evenki.

High front unrounded to high back rounded diphthong /iu/ 1
Acoma.

Lowered high front unrounded to mid front unrounded diphthong /ɩe/ 1
Gilyak.

Mid front unrounded to high front unrounded diphthong /ei/ 6
Kurdish, Khmer, Dani, Nambakaengo, Acoma, !Xũ.

Nasalized mid front unrounded to high front unrounded diphthong /ẽĩ/ 2
Burmese, !Xũ.

Mid front unrounded to low central unrounded diphthong /ea/ 1
Tsou.

Mid front unrounded to mid back rounded diphthong /eo/ 2
Tsou, Acoma.

Nasalized mid front unrounded to high back rounded diphthong /ẽũ/ 1
!Xũ.

Mid front unrounded to high central rounded diphthong /eʉ/ 1
Tsou.

Lower mid front unrounded to high front unrounded diphthong /ɛi/ 2
Dagbani, Yagaria.

Low front unrounded to mid front unrounded diphthong /a̟e/ 1
Hindi-Urdu.

Nasalized low front unrounded to lower mid front unrounded diphthong /ã̟ẽ/ 1
Hindi-Urdu.

High central unrounded to high front unrounded diphthong /iɨ/ 1
Acoma.

High central unrounded to low central unrounded diphthong /ɨa/ 1
Saek.

Mid central unrounded to high central unrounded diphthong /əɨ/ 1
Khmer.

Mid central unrounded to high front unrounded diphthong /əi/ 1
Kurdish.

Mid central unrounded to high back rounded diphthong /əu/ 1
Kurdish.

Lower mid central unrounded to high front unrounded diphthong /ɜi/ 1
Angas.

Low central unrounded to high central unrounded diphthong /aɨ/ 1
Po-ai.

Low central unrounded to high front unrounded diphthong /ai/ 5
Kurdish, Dani, Yana, Acoma, Arabela.

Low central unrounded to mid front unrounded diphthong /ae/ 2
Yagaria, !Xũ.

Pharyngealized low central unrounded to mid front unrounded diphthong /aeˤ/ 1
!Xũ.

Nasalized pharyngealized low central unrounded to mid front unrounded diphthong /ãẽˤ/ 1
!Xũ.

Low central unrounded to mid back rounded diphthong /ao/ 2
Yagaria, !Xũ.

Pharyngealized low central unrounded to mid back rounded diphthong /aoˤ/ 1
!Xũ.

Nasalized pharyngealized low central unrounded to mid back rounded diphthong /ãõˤ/ 1
!Xũ.

Low central unrounded to high back rounded diphthong /au/ 5
Kurdish, Dani, Yana, Acoma, Arabela.

Low central unrounded to high back unrounded diphthong /aɯ/ 2
Lungchow, Island Carib.

High back rounded to higher mid back rounded diphthong /uo/ 1
Lakkia.

High back rounded to low central unrounded diphthong /ua/ 1
Saek.

High back rounded to high front unrounded diphthong /ui/ 4
Kurdish, Yana, Acoma, !Xũ.

Nasalized high back rounded to high front unrounded diphthong /ũĩ/ 1
!Xũ.

Mid back rounded to high back rounded diphthong /ou/ 4
Khmer, Yagaria, Dani, Hopi.

Nasalized mid back rounded to high back rounded diphthong /õũ/ 1
Burmese.

Mid back rounded to low central unrounded diphthong /oa/ 1
!Xũ.

Nasalized mid back rounded to low central unrounded diphthong /õã/ 1
!Xũ.

Pharyngealized mid back rounded to low central unrounded diphthong /oaˤ/ 1
!Xũ.

Nasalized pharyngealized mid back rounded to low central unrounded diphthong /õãˤ/ 1
!Xũ.

Mid back rounded to mid front unrounded diphthong /oe/ 1
!Xũ.

Mid back rounded to high front unrounded diphthong /oi/ 3
Kurdish, Dani, !Xũ.

Nasalized mid back rounded to high front unrounded diphthong /õĩ/ 1
!Xũ.

Pharyngealized mid back rounded to high front unrounded diphthong /oiˤ/ 1
!Xũ.

Nasalized pharyngealized mid back rounded to high front unrounded diphthong /õĩˤ/ 1
!Xũ

Lower mid back rounded to higher mid back rounded diphthong /ɔo/ 1
Hindi-Urdu.

Nasalized lower mid back rounded to higher mid back rounded diphthong /ɔ̃õ/ 1
Hindi-Urdu.

Lower mid back rounded to high back rounded diphthong /ɔu/ 1
Dagbani.

Language	bilabial	labio-dental	dental	dental/alveolar	alveolar	palatal	velar
Greek (000)							
voiceless plosive	p			"t"			k
voiced plosive	b			"d"			g
vl. sibilant affricate					ts		
vd. sibilant affricate					dz		
vl. nonsibilant fricative		f	θ				x
vd. nonsibilant fricative		v	ð				ɣ
vl. sibilant fricative					s		
vd. sibilant fricative					z		
voiced nasal	m			"n"			
voiced flap				"ɾ"			
vd. lateral approximant				"l"			
vd. central approximant						j	

Vowels

high	i		u
lower mid		ɛ	ɔ
low			ɑ

Language	bilabial palatalized	bilabial labialized and velarized	dental	dental velarized	dental/alveolar	dental/alv. palatalized	dental/alv. velarized	alveolar	alveolar palatalized	alveolar velarized	palato-alveolar	palatal	palatal palatalized	velar	velar palatalized	variable place	labial-velar
Irish (001)																	
vl. asp. plosive	p^{jh}	p^{wh}	t̪^{h2}		"t^{h}"									k^{h}	k^{jh}		
voiced plosive	b^{j}	b^{w}	d̪		"d"									g	g^{j}		
vl. sib. affric.											tʃ						
vd. sib. affric.											dʒ						
vl. nonsib fric.	ɸ^{j}	ɸ^{w}										ç		x		h	
vd. nonsib fric.	β^{j}													ɣ			
vl. sib. fric.			s̪								ʃ						
voiced nasal	m^{j}	m^{w}	n̪			"n^{j}"	"n"					ɲ		ŋ	ŋ^{j}		
vl. nasal						"n̥^{j}"^{4}	"n̥"^{4}										
voiced flap								ɾ	ɾ^{j}								
voiceless flap									ɾ̥^{j4}	ɾ̥^{4}							
vd. lat. approx.				ɫ					l^{j}	l			ʎ^{j}				
vl. lat. approx.									l̥^{j4}	l̥^{4}							
vd. cent. approx.												j					

Vowels

	short			long	
high	ɩ		ʊ	iː	uː
higher mid				eː	oː
mid	"e"	"o"			
low	a			ɑː	

	short nasalized			long nasalized	
high	ɩ̃		ʊ̃	ĩː	ũː
higher mid				ẽː	õː
mid	"ẽ"	"õ"			
low	ã			ɑ̃ː	

Language

Norwegian (006)	bilabial	labio-dental	dental	dental/alveolar	alveolar	palato-alveolar	retroflex	palatal	velar	variable place
vl. aspirated plosive	pʰ		t̪ʰ				ʈʰ		kʰ	
voiced plosive	b		d̪				ɖ		g	
vl. nonsibilant fricative		f						ç		h
vl. sibilant fricative				"s"		ʃ				
voiced nasal	m		n̪				ɳ		ŋ	
voiced flap				"ɾ"						
vd. lateral approximant					l		ɭ			
vd. central approximant		ʋ						j		

Vowels

	long				short				
high	iː, yː	ʉː		uː	ɪ, Y	ʉ		u	
higher mid	eː, øː								
mid			"oː"		"e"	"ə"			
lower mid	æː				œ	æ	ɒ̟		
low			ɑː				ɑ		

Language

Lithuanian (007)	bilabial	bilabial palatalized	labio-dental	labio-dental palatalized	dental	dental/alveolar	dental/alv. palatalized	alveolar	alveolar palatalized	palato-alveolar	palato-alv. palatalized	palatal	velar	velar palatalized
voiceless plosive	p	pʲ				"t̪"	"t̪ʲ"						k	kʲ
voiced plosive	b	bʲ				"d̪"	"d̪ʲ"						g	gʲ
vl. sibilant affricate						"ts"	"tsʲ"			tʃ				
vd. sibilant affricate						"dz"				dʒ				
vl. nonsib. fricative													x[2]	
vd. nonsib. fricative			v	vʲ										
vl. sibilant fricative						"s"	"sʲ"			ʃ	ʃʲ			
vd. sibilant fricative						"z"				ʒ	ʒʲ[2]			
voiced nasal	m	mʲ				"n"						ɲ		
voiced trill								r	rʲ					
vd. lat. approximant					l̪				lʲ					
vd. cent. approximant												j		

Vowels

	long			short		
high	iː		uː	ɪ		ʊ
higher mid	eː		oː			
lower mid					ɔ	
low	æː aː			æ a		

Language	bilabial	labio-dental	dental/alveolar	alveolar	palato-alveolar	palatal	velar	labial-palatal	labial-velar	labial-velar nasal
Breton (002)										
vl. aspirated plosive	pʰ		"tʰ"			cʰ	kʰ			
voiced plosive	b		"d"			ɟ	g			
vl. nonsibilant fricative		f					x			
vd. nonsibilant fricative		v								
vl. sibilant fricative			"s"		ʃ					
vd. sibilant fricative			"z"		ʒ					
voiced nasal	m		"n"			ɲ	ŋ			
voiced trill				r						
vd. lateral approximant				l						
vd. central approximant						j		ɥ	w	w̃

Vowels

	short	long
high	y ɩ u	y: ɩ: u:
higher mid	ø	ø: o:
mid	"e" "ə" "o"	
lower mid		ɛ:
low	a̟	ɒ:

	long nasalized
high	
higher mid	
mid	
lower mid	ɛ̃:
low	ɑ̃:

Language	bilabial	labio-dental	dental/alveolar	alveolar	palato-alveolar	palatal	velar	uvular	variable place
German (004)									
vl. aspirated plosive	pʰ		"tʰ"				kʰ		
voiced plosive	b		"d"				g		
vl. sibilant affricate			"ts"						
vl. nonsibilant affricate		pf							
vl. nonsibilant fricative		f					x		h
vd. nonsibilant fricative		v							
vl. sibilant fricative				s	ʃ				
vd. sibilant fricative				z	ʒ[2]				
voiced nasal	m		"n"				ŋ		
voiced trill								ʀ	
vd. lateral approximant				l					
vd. central approximant						j			

Vowels

	long	short
high	i:, y: u:	ɩ, Y ʊ
higher mid	e:, ø: o:	
mid		"ə"
lower mid	ɛ:	ɛ,œ ɔ
low	a:	ɐ

Language	bilabial	bilabial palatalized	labio-dental	labio-dental palatalized	dental	dental palatalized	dental velarized	dental/alveolar	palato-alveolar	palato-alv. velarized	palatal	velar	velar palatalized
Russian (008)													
voiceless plosive	p	pʲ			t̪	t̪ʲ						k	kʲ
voiced plosive	b	bʲ			d̪	d̪ʲ						g	
vl. sib. affricate								"ts"	tʃ				
vl. nonsib. fricative			f	fʲ								x	
vd. nonsib. fricative			v	vʲ									
vl. sib. fricative					s̪	s̪ʲ				ʃ̴			
vd. sib. fricative					z̪	z̪ʲ				ʒ̴			
voiced nasal	m	mʲ			n̪	n̪ʲ							
voiced trill					r̪	r̪ʲ							
vd. lateral approximant						l̪ʲ	ɫ						
vd. central approximant											j		

Vowels

high	i			u
mid			"o"	
lower mid		ɛ		
low		a̟		

Language	bilabial	bilabial palatalized	labio-dental	labio-dental palatalized	dental/alveolar	dental/alv. palatalized	dental/alv. velarized	palato-alveolar	palatal	velar	velar palatalized
Bulgarian (009)											
vl. aspirated plosive	pʰ	pʲʰ			"tʰ"	"tʲʰ"				kʰ	kʲʰ
voiced plosive	b	bʲ			"d"	"dʲ"				g	gʲ
vl. sibilant affricate					"ts"	"tsʲ"		tʃ			
vd. sibilant affricate								dʒ			
vl. nonsibilant fricative			f	fʲ						x	
vd. nonsibilant fricative			v	vʲ							
vl. sibilant fricative					"s"	"sʲ"		ʃ			
vd. sibilant fricative					"z"	"zʲ"		ʒ			
voiced nasal	m	m			"n"	"nʲ"					
voiced trill					"r"	"rʲ"					
vd. lateral approximant						"lʲ"	"ɫ"				
vd. central approximant									j		

Vowels

	oral					nasalized				
high	i				u	ĩ				ũ
mid				"ɤ"					"ɤ̃"	
lower mid		ɛ	ɔ				ɛ̃	ɔ̃		
low			ɑ					ɑ̃		

Language

French (010)	bilabial	labio-dental	dental	palato-alveolar	palatal	velar	uvular	labial-palatal	labial-velar
voiceless plosive	p		t̪			k			
voiced plosive	b		d̪			g			
vl. nonsibilant fricative		f							
vd. nonsibilant fricative		v							
vl. sibilant fricative			s̪	ʃ					
vd. sibilant fricative			z̪	ʒ					
voiced nasal	m		n̪		ɲ	ŋ			
voiced trill							ʀ		
vd. lateral approximant			l̪						
vd. central approximant					j			ɥ	w

Vowels

	short oral		long
high	i, y	u	
higher mid	e, ø		oː
lower mid	ɛ, œ	ɔ	ɛː
low	a	ɒ	

	short nasalized	
higher mid		õ
lower mid	œ̃	
low	æ̃	ɒ̃

Language

Spanish (011)	bilabial	labio-dental	dental	alveolar	palato-alveolar	palatal	velar	labial-velar
voiceless plosive	p		t̪				k	
vl. sibilant affricate					tʃ			
vl. nonsibilant fricative		f	θ				x	
vd. nonsibilant fricative	β		ð				ɣ	
vl. sibilant fricative			s̪					
voiced nasal	m		n̪			ɲ		
voiced trill				r				
voiced tap				D				
vd. lateral approximant			l̪			ʎ		
vd. central approximant						j		w

Vowels

high	i	u
mid	"e"	"o"
low	a	

Language	bilabial	labio-dental	dental/alveolar	alveolar	palato-alveolar	palatal	velar	variable place	labial-velar
Romanian (012)									
voiceless plosive	p		"t"				k		
voiced plosive	b		"d"				g		
vl. sibilant affricate			"ts"		tʃ				
vd. sibilant affricate					dʒ				
vl. nonsibilant fricative		f						h	
vd. nonsibilant fricative		v							
vl. sibilant fricative			"s"		ʃ				
vd. sibilant fricative			"z"		ʒ				
voiced nasal	m		"n"						
voiced flap				ɾ					
vd. lateral approximant				l					
vd. central approximant						j			w

Vowels

high	i				u
higher mid		e		o	
mid			"ə"		
low			a		

Language	bilabial	labio-dental	dental	dental/alveolar	palato-alveolar	palatal	velar	uvular	glottal	variable place	labial-velar
Farsi (013)											
voiceless plosive									ʔ		
vl. aspirated plosive	p^h		$t̪^h$				k^h				
voiced plosive	b		d̪				g	ɢ			
vl. sibilant affricate					tʃ						
vd. sibilant affricate					dʒ						
vl. nonsibilant fricative		f						χ		h	
vd. nonsibilant fricative		v									
vl. sibilant fricative				"s"	ʃ						
vd. sibilant fricative				"z"	ʒ						
voiced nasal	m		n̪								
voiced trill				"r"							
vd. lateral approximant				"l"							
vd. central approximant						j					w

Vowels

high	i			u
higher mid		e	o	
low		a̟	ɑ	

Language

Pashto (014)	bilabial	labio-dental	dental/alveolar	palato-alveolar	retroflex	palatal	velar	uvular	variable place	labial-velar
voiceless plosive	p		"t"		ṭ		k			
voiced plosive	b		"d"		ḍ		g			
vl. sibilant affricate			"ts"	tʃ						
vd. sibilant affricate			"dz"	dʒ						
vl. nonsibilant fricative		f						χ	h	
vd. nonsibilant fricative	β							ʁ		
vl. sibilant fricative			"s"	ʃ	ṣ					
vd. sibilant fricative			"z"	ʒ	ẓ					
voiced nasal	m		"n"		ṇ					
voiced trill			"r"		ṛ					
voiced lateral fricative				lʒ						
vd. central approximant						j				w

Vowels

	short		long	
high	i	u		
mid	"ə"		"e:"	"o:"
low	a			

Language

Kurdish (015)	bilabial	labio-dental	dental	dental/alveolar	alveolar pharyngealized	palato-alveolar	palatal	velar	uvular	pharyngeal	glottal	labial-velar
voiceless plosive	p		t̪					k	q		ʔ	
voiced plosive	b		d̪					g				
vl. sibilant affricate						tʃ						
vd. sibilant affricate						dʒ						
vl. nonsibilant fricative		f						x		ħ		
vd. nonsibilant fricative		v						ɣ		ʕ		
vl. sibilant fricative			s̪		sˤ	ʃ						
vd. sibilant fricative			z̪			ʒ						
voiced nasal	m		n̪					ŋ				
voiced trill				"r"								
voiced flap				"ɾ"								
vd. lateral approximant				"l"	lˤ							
vd. central approximant							j					w

Vowels

	short			long		Diphthongs
high	ɩ	ɨ	ʊ	i:	u:	ei
mid		"ə"		"e:"	"o:"	əi
low				a:		ai
						oi
						ui
						eu
						əu
						au

Language

Hindi-Urdu (016)	bilabial	labio-dental	dental	dental/alveolar	palato-alveolar	retroflex	palatal	velar	uvular	glottal	variable place
voiceless plosive	p		t̪			ṭ		k	q²	ʔ²	
vl. aspirated plosive	pʰ		t̪ʰ			ṭʰ		kʰ			
voiced plosive	b		d̪			ḍ		g			
breathy vd. plosive	b̤		d̪̤			ḍ̤		g̤			
vl. sibilant affricate					tʃ						
vl. asp. sib. affricate					tʃʰ						
vd. sibilant affricate					dʒ						
breathy vd. sib. affricate					d̤ʒ						
vl. nonsib. fricative		f²							χ²		
vd. nonsib. fricative									ʁ²		ɦ
vl. sibilant fricative				"s"	ʃ²						
vd. sibilant fricative				"z"²	ʒ²						
voiced nasal	m		n̪								
breathy vd. nasal	m̤		n̪̤								
voiced trill				"r"							
voiced flap					ɽ̤²						
vd. lateral approximant				"l"							
breathy vd. lat. approximant				"l̤"							
vd. central approximant	β						j				

Vowels

	long oral			short oral			Diphthongs
high	i:		u:	ɩ	ɨ	ʊ	ɨ̯ə
higher mid	e:	o:					ɔo
lower mid					ɘ		ɨ̯̃ə
low	a:				ɑ		ɔ̃o

	long nasalized		short nasalized		
high	ĩ:	ũ:	ɩ̃		ʊ̃
higher mid	e:	o:			
lower mid				ɜ̃	

Language

Bengali (017)	bilabial	dental/alveolar	alveolar	palato-alveolar	retroflex	palatal	velar	variable place	labial-velar
voiceless plosive	p	"t"			ṭ		k		
vl. aspirated plosive	pʰ	"tʰ"			ṭʰ		kʰ		
voiced plosive	b	"d"			ḍ		g		
breathy voiced plosive	b̤	"d̤"			ḍ̤		g̤		
vl. sibilant affricate				tʃ					
vl. asp. sib. affricate				tʃʰ					
vd. sibilant affricate				dʒ					
breathy vd. sib. affricate				d̤ʒ					
vl. nonsibilant fricative						ç		h	
vl. sibilant fricative		"s"²							
voiced nasal	m	"n"					ŋ		
voiced flap			ɾ		ɽ				
vd. lateral approximant		"l"							
vd. central approximant						j			w
vd. mid central approximant						e̯			o̯

Vowels

	oral			nasalized		
high	ɩ		ʊ	ɩ̃		ʊ̃
higher mid		o				õ
mid	"e"			"ẽ"		
lower mid		ɔ			ɔ̃	
low	æ	a		æ̃	ã	

Language	bilabial	dental	dental/alveolar	alveolar	palato-alv. palatalized	retroflex	palatal	velar	variable place	labial-velar
Kashmiri (018)										
voiceless plosive	p	t̪				ṭ		k		
vl. aspirated plosive	p^h	$t̪^h$				$ṭ^h$		k^h		
voiced plosive	b	d̪				ḍ		g		
vl. sibilant affricate				ts	$tʃ^j$					
vl. asp. sib. affricate				ts^h	$tʃ^h$					
vd. sibilant affricate				dz	$dʒ^j$					
vd. nonsibilant fricative									ɦ	
vl. sibilant fricative			"s"		$ʃ^j$					
voiced nasal	m			n						
voiced trill				r						
vd. lateral approximant				l						
vd. central approximant							j			w

Vowels

	short oral			short nasalized		
high	i	ɨ	u	ĩ	ɨ̃	ũ
higher mid	e		o	ẽ		õ
mid		"ə"			"ə̃"	
low		a			ã	

	overshort oral	overshort nasalized
high	ɨ̆	ɨ̆̃

Language	bilabial	labio-dental	dental	dental/alveolar	palato-alveolar	retroflex	palatal	velar	variable place	labial-velar
Punjabi (019)										
voiceless plosive	p			"t"		ṭ		k		
long voiceless plosive	p:			"t:"		ṭ:		k:		
vl. aspirated plosive	p^h			"t^h"		$ṭ^h$		k^h		
long vl. asp. plosive	p^h:			"t^h:"		$ṭ^h$:		k^h:		
voiced plosive	b			"d"		ḍ		g		
long voiced plosive	b:			"d:"		ḍ:		g:		
vl. sibilant affricate					tʃ					
long vl. sib. affricate					tʃ:					
vl. asp. sib. affricate					$tʃ^h$					
long vl. asp. sib. aff.					$tʃ^h$:					
vd. sibilant affricate					dʒ					
long vd. sib. affricate					dʒ:					
vl. nonsibilant fricative		f[2]								
vd. nonsibilant fricative									ɦ	
vl. sibilant fricative			s̪			ṣ				
long vl. sib. fricative			s̪:							
vd. sibilant fricative			z̪[2]							
voiced nasal	m		n̪			ṇ	ɲ	ŋ		
long vd. nasal	m:		n̪:							
voiced trill				"r"						
voiced flap						ɽ				
vd. lateral approximant			l̪			ḷ				
long vd. lat. approximant			l̪:							
vd. central approximant							j			w

Vowels

	oral	nasalized
high	i ɩ ɷ u	ĩ ɩ̃ ɷ̃ ũ
mid	"e""ə""o"	"ẽ""ə̃""õ"
low	æ a ɒ	æ̃ ã ɒ̃

Language	bilabial	dental	dental/alveolar	alveolar	palato-alveolar	retroflex	palatal	velar	variable place
Sinhalese (020)									
voiceless plosive	p	t̪				ʈ		k	
voiced plosive	b	d̪				ɖ		g	
vl. nonsibilant affricate							cç		
vd. nonsibilant affricate							ɟʝ		
vl. nonsibilant fricative	ɸ[2]								
vd. nonsibilant fricative									ɦ
vl. sibilant fricative		s̪			ʃ[2]				
voiced nasal	m		"n"				ɲ[2]	ŋ[4]	
voiced flap				ɾ					
vd. lateral approximant				l					
vd. central approximant	β̞						j		

Vowels

	short				long			
high	ɩ			ɷ	iː			uː
higher mid					eː			oː
mid	"e"	"ə"[4]	"o"			"əː"[2]		
low	a̟	a			æː	aː		

Language	bilabial	labio-dental	dental	dental/alveolar	alveolar	alveolar velarized	palato-alveolar	palatal	velar	variable place
Albanian (021)										
voiceless plosive	p		t̪						k	
voiced plosive	b		d̪						g	
vl. sibilant affricate				"ts"			tʃ			
vd. sibilant affricate				"dz"			dʒ			
vl. nonsibilant affricate								cç		
vd. nonsibilant affricate								ɟʝ		
vl. nonsibilant fricative		f	θ							h
vd. nonsibilant fricative		v	ð							
vl. sibilant fricative			s̪				ʃ			
vd. sibilant fricative			z̪				ʒ			
voiced nasal	m				n		n̠			
voiced trill				"r"						
vd. lateral approximant					l	ɫ				
vd. central approximant								j		

Vowels

high	i, y		u
mid	"e"	"ə"	"o"
low		a	

Language	bilabial	labio-dental	dental/alveolar	palato-alveolar	retroflex	palatal	velar	uvular	variable place
Armenian, Eastern (022)									
voiceless plosive	p		"t"				k		
vl. aspirated plosive	p^h		"t^h"				k^h		
vl. ejective stop	p’		"t’"				k’		
vl. sibilant affricate			"ts"	tʃ					
vl. asp. sib. affricate			"ts^h"	$tʃ^h$					
vl. eject. sib. affricate			"ts’"	tʃ’					
vl. nonsibilant fricative		f[2]						χ	h
vd. nonsibilant fricative		v			ɹ̣̌				
vl. sibilant fricative			"s"	ʃ					
vd. sibilant fricative			"z"	ʒ					
voiced nasal	m		"n"						
voiced trill			"r"						
vd. lateral approximant			"l"						
vd. central approximant						j		ʁ̞	

<u>Vowels</u>

high	i		u
mid	"e"	"o"	
low		a	

<u>Diphthongs</u>

ie

Language	bilabial	dental/alveolar	palato-alveolar	retroflex	palatal	velar	labial-velar
Ostyak (050)							
voiceless plosive	p	"t"			c	k	
vl. sibilant affricate				ʈʂ			
vd. nonsibilant fricative						ɣ	
vl. sibilant fricative		"s"	ʃ[2]				
voiced nasal	m	"n"		ɳ	ɲ	ŋ	
voiced trill		"r"					
vd. lateral approximant		"l"		ɭ	ʎ		
vd. central approximant					j		w

<u>Vowels</u>

	short		overshort
high	i	u, ɯ	
mid	"e" "ə" "o"		"ĕ" "ə̆" "ŏ"
low	æ a		ɒ̆

Language	bilabial	bilabial palatalized	labio-dental	dental	dental/alveolar	dental/alv. palatalized	palato-alveolar	palatal	velar
Cheremis (051)									
voiceless plosive	p	p^{j2}			"t"	$"t^{j}"^{2}$			k
vl. sibilant affricate					$"ts"^{2}$		tʃ		
vl. nonsibilant fricative			f^{2}						
vd. nonsibilant fricative	β			ð					
vl. sibilant fricative					"s"		ʃ		x^{2}
vd. sibilant fricative					"z"		ʒ		ɣ
voiced nasal	m				"n"			ɲ	ŋ
voiced flap					"ɾ"				
vd. lateral approximant					"l"			ʎ	
vd. central approximant								j	

Vowels

high	i, y			u
higher mid		ø		
mid			"ə"	"o"
lower mid		ε	ʌ	

Language	bilabial	labio-dental	dental/alveolar	alveolar	palato-alveolar	palatal	velar
Komi (052)							
voiceless plosive	p			t		c	k
voiced plosive	b			d		ɟ	g
vl. sibilant affric.			$"ts"^{2}$		tʃ		
vd. sibilant affric.					dʒ		
vl. nonsibilant affric.						cç	
vd. nonsibilant affric.						ɟʝ	
vl. nonsibilant fric.		f^{2}				ç	x^{2}
vd. nonsibilant fric.		v				ʝ	
vl. sibilant fric.				s	ʃ		
vd. sibilant fric.				z	ʒ		
voiced nasal	m			n		ɲ	
voiced trill			"r"				
vd. lateral approx.				l		ʎ	
vd. central approx.						j	

Vowels

high	i				u
higher mid				o	
mid		"e"	"ə"		
low			a		

Language Finnish (053)	bilabial	labio-dental	dental	dental/alveolar	alveolar	palato-alveolar	palatal	velar	variable place
voiceless plosive	p		t̪					k	
long voiceless plos.	p:		t̪:					k:	
voiced plosive	b[2]		d̪[4]					g[2]	
vl. nonsibilant fric.		f[2]							h
vd. nonsibilant fric.		v							
vl. sibilant fric.					s	ʃ[2]			
long vl. sib. fric.					s:				
voiced nasal	m		n̪						
long voiced nasal	m:		n̪:					ŋ:[4]	
voiced trill				"r"					
long voiced trill				"r:"					
vd. lateral approx.			l̪						
long vd. lat. approx.			l̪:						
vd. central approx.							j		

Vowels

	short		long	
high	i, y	u	i:, y:	u:
higher mid	ø	o	e:[4], ø:	o:[4]
lower mid	ɛ			
low	æ a		æ: a:	

Language Hungarian (054)	bilabial	labio-dental	dental	dental/alveolar	palato-alveolar	palatal	velar	variable place	labial-velar
voiceless plosive	p		t̪				k		
voiced plosive	b		d̪				g		
vl. sibilant affric.			t̪s̪		tʃ				
vd. sibilant fric.			d̪z̪		dʒ[2]				
vl. nonsibilant affric.						cç			
vd. nonsibilant affric.						ɟʝ			
vl. nonsibilant fric.		f						h	
vd. nonsibilant fric.		v							
vl. sibilant fric.			s̪		ʃ				
vd. sibilant fric.			z̪		ʒ				
voiced nasal	m		n̪			ɲ			
voiced trill			r̪						
vd. lateral approx.				"l"					
vd. central approx.						j			w

Vowels

	long		short	
high	i:, y:	u:	i[1], y[1]	u
higher mid	e:, ø:	o:	ø	o
lower mid			ɛ	
low	a:		æ[1] ɒ	

Language	bilabial	labio-dental	dental/alveolar	palato-alveolar	palatal	velar	variable place
Lappish (055)							
voiceless plosive	p		"t"			k	
voiced plosive	b		"d"			g	
vl. sibilant affricate			"ts"	tʃ			
vl. nonsibilant fricative		f	"s"	ʃ			h
voiced nasal	m		"n"		ɲ	ŋ	
voiced trill			"r"				
vd. lateral approximant			"l"				
vd. central approximant	β̞				j		

Vowels

high	i	ɨ	u
mid	"e"	"o"	
low		a	

Language	bilabial	bilabial palatalized	dental	dental palatalized	dental/alveolar	dental/alv. palatalized	palatal	velar	glottal	labial-velar
Yurak (056)										
voiceless plosive	p	p^j			"t"	t^j		k	ʔ	
voiced plosive	b	b^j								
vl. sibilant affricate					"ts"	ts^j				
vl. nonsibilant fricative								x		
vd. nonsibilant fricative			ð	$ð^j$						
vl. sibilant fricative					"s"	s^j				
voiced nasal	m	m^j			"n"	n^j		ŋ		
voiced trill					"r"	r^j				
vd. lateral approximant					"l"	l^j				
vd. central approximant							j			

Vowels

	short			overshort	
high	i		u	ĭ	ŭ
mid	"e"	"o"			
low		a		ă	

Language Tavgy (057)	bilabial	dental	dental/alveolar	palatal	velar	glottal
voiceless plosive	p		"t"	c	k	ʔ
voiced plosive	b		"d"	ɟ	g	
vl. nonsibilant affricate					kx	
vd. nonsibilant fricative		ð				
vl. sibilant fricative			"s"			
voiced nasal	m		"n"	ɲ	ŋ	
voiced trill			"r"			
vd. lateral approximant			"l"	ʎ		
vd. central approximant				j		

Vowels

high	i, y	ɨ		u
mid	"e"	"ə"	"o"	
low		a		

Language Osmanli (058)	bilabial	labio-dental	dental	dental/alveolar	alveolar	palato-alveolar	palatal	velar	glottal	variable place
voiceless plosive									ʔ[2]	
vl. aspirated plos.	pʰ		t̪ʰ				cʰ[2]	kʰ		
voiced plosive	b		d̪				ɟ[2]	g		
vl. sibilant affric.						tʃ				
vd. sibilant affric.						dʒ				
vl. nonsibilant fric.		f								h
vd. nonsibilant fric.		v						ɣ[2]		
vl. sibilant fric.					s	ʃ				
vd. sibilant fric.					z	ʒ				
voiced nasal	m			"n"						
voiced flap					ɾ					
vd. lateral approx.				"l"			ʎ[2]			
vd. central approx.							j			

Vowels

high	i, y				u, ɯ
mid				"o"	
lower mid		ɛ, œ			
low			a		

Language	bilabial	labio-dental	dental	dental/alveolar	alveolar	palato-alveolar	palatal	velar	variable place
Azerbaijani (059)									
voiceless plosive	p		t̪				c	k²	
vl. aspirated plos.	pʰ		t̪ʰ				cʰ	kʰ	
vl. sibilant affric.						tʃ			
vd. sibilant affric.						dʒ			
vl. nonsibilant fric.		f						x	h
vd. nonsibilant fric.		v			ɹ̌			ɣ	
vl. sibilant fric.					s	ʃ			
vd. sibilant fric.					z	ʒ			
voiced nasal	m			"n"					
vd. lateral approx.				"l"					
vd. central approx.							j		

<u>Vowels</u>

high	ɩ, ʏ				ɷ
higher mid		ø		ɨ, o	
lower mid			ɛ		
low			ə̶	a	

Language	bilabial	labio-dental	dental/alveolar	dental/alv. palatalized	palato-alveolar	palatal	velar	labial-velar
Chuvash (060)								
voiceless plosive	p		"t"	"tʲ"			k	
voiced plosive	b²		"d"²				g²	
vl. sibilant affricate			"ts"²		tʃ			
vl. nonsibilant fricative		f²				ç⁵	x	
vl. sibilant fricative			"s"		ʃ			
vd. sibilant fricative			"z"²		ʒ²			
voiced nasal	m		"n"	"nʲ"				
long voiced nasal	m:		"n:"					
voiced trill			"r"					
long voiced trill			"r:"					
vd. lateral approximant			"l"	"lʲ"				
long vd. lat. approximant			"l:"					
vd. central approximant						j		w
long vd. cent. approximant						j:		w:

<u>Vowels</u>

high	i, y				u, ɯ
higher mid	ø				
mid		"e"		"o"²	
lower mid			ɔ		
low			ɑ		

Language Yakut (061)	bilabial	labio-dental	dental	dental/alveolar	dental/alv. velarized	palato-alveolar	palatal	palatal nasalized	velar
voiceless plosive	p[2]			"t"					k
long voiceless plosive	p:			"t:"					k:
voiced plosive	b			"d"					g
vl. sibilant affric.						tʃ			
long vl. sib. affric.						tʃ:			
vd. sibilant affric.						dʒ			
long vd. sib. affric.						dʒ:			
vl. nonsibilant fric.		f[2]							
vd. nonsibilant fric.		v[2]							
vl. sibilant fric.			s̪			ʃ[2]			
long vl. sib. fric.			s̪:						
vd. sibilant fric.			z̪[2]			ʒ[2]			
voiced nasal	m		n̪				ɲ		ŋ
long voiced nasal	m:		n̪:				ɲ:		ŋ:
voiced trill				"r"					
vd. lateral approx.					"ɫ"				
long vd. lat. approx.					"ɫ:"				
vd. central approx.							j	j̃	

Vowels

high	ɪ, y		u, ɯ
lower mid	ɛ, œ	ɔ	
low		a	

Language Kirghiz (062)	bilabial	labio-dental	dental/alveolar	palato-alveolar	palatal	velar	uvular
voiceless plosive	p		"t"				q
vl. aspirated plosive	pʰ		"tʰ"				qʰ
vl. sibilant affricate			"ts"	tʃ			
vl. nonsibilant fricative		f					
vd. nonsibilant fricative	β						
vl. sibilant fricative			"s"	ʃ		x	
vd. sibilant fricative			"z"				
voiced nasal	m		"n"			ŋ	
voiced trill			"r"				
vd. lateral approximant			"l"				
vd. central approximant					j		

Vowels

high	yɩ		ɨ	ɵ
higher mid		ø		
lower mid		ɛ		ɔ
low			a ɑ̶	

Language	bilabial	labio-dental	dental	alveolar	palato-alveolar	palatal	velar	glottal	variable place	labial-velar
Bashkir (063)										
voiceless plosive	p			t			k	ʔ²		
voiced plosive	b			d			g			
vl. sibilant affricate				ts²	tʃ²					
vl. nonsibilant fricative		f²	θ				x		h	
vd. nonsibilant fricative		v²								
vl. sibilant fricative				s	ʃ					
vd. sibilant fricative				z²	ʒ²					
voiced nasal	m			n			ŋ			
voiced trill				r						
vd. lateral approximant				l						
vd. central approximant						j				w

Vowels

high	i, y		u
higher mid	ø		
mid		"ə""o""ɤ"	
low	æ	ɑ	

Language	bilabial	labio-dental	dental	dental/alveolar	palato-alveolar	palatal	velar	variable place
Khalaj (064)								
voiceless plosive	p		t̪				k	
voiced plosive	b		d̪				g	
vl. sibilant affric.					tʃ			
vd. sibilant affric.					dʒ²			
vl. nonsibilant fric.		f²					x²	h
vd. nonsibilant fric.		v²				ʝ		
vl. sibilant fric.				"s"	ʃ			
vd. sibilant fric.				"z"	ʒ			
voiced nasal	m		n̪					
voiced tap				"D"				
vd. lateral approx.				"l"				

Vowels

high	i, y		u
higher mid	ø		o
low		a	ɑ

Language	bilabial	labio-dental	dental	palato-alveolar	palatal	velar
Tuva (065)						
voiceless plosive	p		t̪			k
voiced plosive	b		d̪			g
vl. sibilant affric.			t̪s̪	tʃ		
vl. nonsibilant fric.		f				
vd. nonsibilant fric.		v				$ɣ^5$
vl. sibilant fric.			s̪	ʃ		
vd. sibilant fric.			z̪	ʒ		
voiced nasal	m		n̪			ŋ
voiced trill			r̪			
vd. lateral approx.			l̪			
vd. central approx.					j	

Vowels

high	i, y	ɨ	u
higher mid	ø		
mid		"e" "o"	
low		ɑ	

Language	bilabial	dental/alveolar	palato-alveolar	palatal	velar
Mongolian (066)					
vl. aspirated plosive	p^{h2}	"tʰ"			k^{h2}
voiced plosive	b	"d"			g
vl. sibilant affricate		"ts"	tʃ		
vd. sibilant affricate		"dz"	dʒ		
vl. nonsibilant fricative	$ɸ^2$				x
vd. nonsibilant fricative	$β^2$				
vl. sibilant fricative		"s"	ʃ		
voiced nasal	m	"n"			
voiced trill		"r"			
vd. lateral approximant		"l"			
vl. lateral approximant		"l̥"			
vd. central approximant				j	

Vowels

	short			long	
high	i̹	ʉ	ʊ		ʉː
higher mid					
mid	e	"ɵ"	"o"	e	"ɵː" "oː"
lower mid		ɔ			ɔː
low		ɑ			ɑː

Language	bilabial	dental/alveolar	alveolar	palato-alveolar	palatal	velar
Evenki (067)						
voiceless plosive	p[2]	"t"				k
voiced plosive	b	"d"				g
vl. sibilant affric.				tʃ		
vd. sibilant affric.				dʒ		
vd. nonsibilant fric.	β					
vl. sibilant fric.			s			
vd. sibilant fric.		"z"[2]				
voiced nasal	m	"n"			ɲ	ŋ
voiced trill		"r"				
vd. lateral approx.		"l"				
vd. central approx.					j	

Vowels

	short			long			Diphthongs
high	ɩ		u	i:		u:	ie
mid		"ɵ"					ia̟
lower mid	ε		ɔ	ε:		ɔ:	io
low		a			a:		

	short pharyngealized		long pharyngealized	
high	ɩˤ	ɵˤ	i:ˤ	u:ˤ

Language	bilabial	dental/alveolar	palato-alveolar	palatal	velar
Goldi (068)					
voiceless plosive	p	"t"			k
voiced plosive	b	"d"			g
vl. sibilant affricate			tʃ		
vd. sibilant affricate			dʒ		
vl. nonsibilant fricative					x
vd. nonsibilant fricative	β			ǰ	
vl. sibilant fricative		"s"			
voiced nasal	m	"n"		ɲ	ŋ
voiced trill		"r"			
vd. lateral approximant		"l"			

Vowels

high	i		u
higher mid	e	ə	o
low		a	

Language	bilabial	labio-dental	dental	dental/alveolar	palato-alveolar	palatal	velar
Manchu (069)							
voiceless plosive	p[1]		t̪				k
voiced plosive	b		d̪				g
vl. sibilant affricate					tʃ		
vd. sibilant affricate					dʒ		
vl. nonsibilant fricative		f					x
vl. sibilant fricative			s̪		ʃ		
voiced nasal	m		n̪				ŋ
voiced trill				"r"			
vd. lateral approximant			l̪				
vd. central approximant						j	

Vowels

	short	long
high	i u	
higher mid	ø	
mid	"e" "o"	"o:"
low	a	

Language	bilabial	dental/alveolar	palato-alveolar	palatal	velar	variable place	labial-velar
Korean (070)							
voiceless plosive	p	"t"			k		
vl. aspirated plosive	pʰ	"tʰ"			kʰ		
vl. laryngealized plosive	p̰	"t̰"			k̰		
vl. sibilant affricate			tʃ				
vl. aspirated sib. affric.			tʃʰ				
vl. laryngealized sib. aff.			tʃ̰				
vl. nonsibilant fricative						h	
vl. sibilant fricative		"s"					
vl. laryngealized sib. fric.		"s̰"					
voiced nasal	m	"n"			ŋ		
vd. lateral approximant		"l"					
vd. central approximant				j			w

Vowels

	short	long
high	i, y u, ɯ	i: u:, ɯ:
higher mid	e, ø o	e: o:
mid	"ɤ"	"ɤ:"
low	æ a	æ: a:

Language Japanese (071)	bilabial	dental/alveolar	palato-alveolar	palatal	velar	velar nasalized	variable place	labial-velar
voiceless plosive	p	"t"			k			
long voiceless plosive	p	"t:"			k:			
voiced plosive	b	"d"			g[4]			
vl. sibilant affricate			tʃ					
long vl. sib. affricate		"ts:"[4]	"tʃ:[4]					
vd. sibilant affricate			dʒ					
vl. nonsibilant fricative							h	
long vl. nonsib. fricative				ç:[4]				
vl. sibilant fricative		"s"	ʃ					
long vl. sib. fricative		"s:"	ʃ					
vd. sibilant fricative		"z"						
voiced nasal	m	"n"			ŋ			
voiced flap		"ɾ"						
vd. central approximant				j		ɣ̃		w[1]

Vowels

high	i				ɯ
lower mid		ɛ		ɔ	
low			a		

Language Katcha (100)	bilabial	labio-dental	dental	dental/alveolar	alveolar	palatal	velar	labial-velar
voiceless plosive			t̪		t	c	k	
voiced plosive	b		d̪		d	ɟ	g	
vd. implosive	ɓ			"ɗ"				
vl. nonsib. fricative		f						
vl. sib. fricative				"s"				
vd. sib. fricative				"z"				
voiced nasal	m			"n"		ɲ	ŋ	
voiced trill				"r"				
vd. lateral approximant				"l"				
vd. central approximant						j		w

Vowels

high	i						u
higher mid		e				o	
lower mid			ɛ		ɔ		
low				a			

Language	bilabial	labio-dental	dental	alveolar	palato-alveolar	retroflex	palatal	velar	labial-velar
Moro (101)									
voiceless plosive	p		t̪			ṭ		k	
voiced plosive	b							g	
vl. sibilant affricate					tʃ				
vd. sibilant affricate					dʒ				
vl. nonsibilant fricative		f							
vd. nonsibilant fricative			ð						
vl. sibilant fricative			s̪						
voiced nasal	m			n			ɲ	ŋ	
voiced trill				r					
voiced lateral flap						ḷ			
vd. lateral approximant				l					
vd. central approximant							j		w

Vowels

high	i		u
mid	"e"		"o", "ɤ"
low		a	

Language	bilabial	labio-dental	dental	alveolar	palatal	velar	labial-velar
Kadugli (102)							
voiceless plosive	p		t̪	t	c	k	
voiced plosive	b		d̪	d		g	
vd. implosive	ɓ		ɗ̪		ʄ		
vl. nonsibilant fricative		f					
vl. sibilant fricative				s			
voiced nasal	m			n	ɲ	ŋ	
voiced trill				r			
vd. lateral approximant				l			
vd. central approximant					j		w

Vowels

high	i		u
mid	"e"		"o"
low		a	

Language

Kpelle (103)	bilabial	labio-dental	alveolar	palatal	velar	velar labialized	labial-velar
voiceless plosive	p		t		k	kʷ	k͡p
voiced plosive	b		d		g	gʷ	g͡b
vd. implosive	ɓ						
vl. nonsibilant fricative		f					
vd. nonsibilant fricative		v				ɣ	
vl. sibilant fricative			s				
vd. sibilant fricative			z				
voiced flap			ɾ				
vd. lateral approximant			l				
vd. central approximant				j			

Vowels

	oral				nasalized			
high	i ɩ			ʊ u	ĩ ɩ̃			ũ
lower mid		ɛ	ɔ			ɛ̃	ɔ̃	
low		a				ã		

Language

Bisa (104)	bilabial	labio-dental	alveolar	palatal	velar	labial-velar
voiceless plosive	p		t		k	
voiced plosive	b		d		g	
vl. nonsibilant fricative		f				
vd. nonsibilant fricative		v				
vl. sibilant fricative			s			
vd. sibilant fricative			z			
voiced nasal	m		n	ɲ	ŋ	
voiced trill			r			
vd. lateral approximant			l			
vd. central approximant				j		w

Vowels

high	i				u
higher mid		e		o	
lower mid				ɔ	
low			a		

Language Bambara (105)	bilabial	labio-dental	alveolar	palato-alveolar	palatal	velar	variable place	labial-velar
voiceless plosive	p		t			k		
voiced plosive	b		d			g		
vl. sibilant affricate				tʃ				
vd. sibilant affricate				dʒ				
vl. nonsibilant fricative		f					h	
vl. sibilant fricative			s	ʃ				
vd. sibilant fricative			z					
voiced nasal	m		n		ɲ	ŋ		
voiced tap			D					
vd. lateral approximant			l					
vd. central approximant					j			w

Vowels

	oral			nasalized		
high	i		u	ĩ		ũ
higher mid	e		o	ẽ		õ
lower mid	ɛ		ɔ	ɛ̃		ɔ̃
low		a			ã	

Language Dan (106)	bilabial	labio-dental	alveolar	palatal	velar	labial-velar
voiceless plosive	p		t		k	k͡p
voiced plosive	b		d		g	g͡b
vd. implosive	ɓ		ɗ			
vl. nonsibilant fricative		f				
vd. nonsibilant fricative		v				
vl. sibilant fricative			s			
vd. sibilant fricative			z			
voiced nasal	m		n			
vd. lateral approximant			l			
vd. central approximant				j		w

Vowels

	oral			nasalized		
high	i		u	ĩ		ũ
higher mid	e		o			
mid				"ẽ"	"ə̃"	"ɤ̃"
lower mid	ɛ		ɔ			
low	a̟	a	ɒ	ã̟	ã	ɒ̃

Language	bilabial	labio-dental	dental/alveolar	palatal	velar	uvular	glottal	labial-velar
Wolof (107)								
voiceless plosive	p		"t"	c	k		ʔ	
voiced plosive	b		"d"	ɟ				
long voiced plosive	b:			j:				
vl. nonsibilant affricate						qχ		
vl. nonsibilant fricative		f				χ		
vl. sibilant fricative			"s"					
voiced nasal	m		"n"	ɲ	ŋ			
long voiced nasal	m		"n:"					
voiced flap			"ɾ"					
vd. lateral approximant			"l"					
long vd. lat. approximant			"l:"					
vd. central approximant				j				w

Vowels

	long			short		
high	i:		u:	i		u
higher mid	e:		o:	e, ø		
lower mid	ɛ:	ɔ:		ɛ		ɔ
low		a:			a	

Language	bilabial	labio-dental	alveolar	palatal	velar	variable place	labial-velar
Diola (108)							
voiceless plosive	p		t	c	k		
voiced plosive	b		d	ɟ	g		
vl. nonsibilant fricative		f				h	
vl. sibilant fricative			s				
voiced nasal	m		n	ɲ	ŋ		
voiced flap			ɾ				
vd. lateral approximant			l				
vd. central approximant				j			w

Vowels

high	i, ɩ		u, ʊ
higher mid	e		o
mid		"ə"	
lower mid	ɛ		ɔ
low		a	

Language	bilabial	labio-dental	dental	alveolar	palatal	velar	glottal	variable place	labial-velar
Temne (109)									
voiceless plosive	p		t̪	t		k	ʔ[1]		
voiced plosive	b			d		g			g͡b
vl. nonsibilant fricative		f						h	
vl. sibilant fricative				s					
voiced nasal	m			n					
voiced trill				r					
vd. lateral approximant				l					
vd. central approximant					j				w

Vowels

high	i				u
higher mid		e		o	
mid			"ə"		
lower mid			ɛ	ɔ	
low			a	ɑ	

Language	bilabial	labio-dental	dental/alveolar	palato-alveolar	palatal	velar	labial-velar
Dagbani (110)							
voiceless plosive	p		"t"			k	k͡p
voiced plosive	b		"d"			g	g͡b
vl. sibilant affricate				tʃ			
vd. sibilant affricate				dʒ			
vl. nonsibilant fricative		f					
vd. nonsibilant fricative		v					
vl. sibilant fricative			"s"				
vd. sibilant fricative			"z"				
voiced nasal	m		"n"		ɲ	ŋ	ŋ͡m
vd. lateral approximant			"l"				
vd. central approximant					j		w

Vowels

	long			short			Diphthongs
high	i:		u:	i		u	ɛɩ
higher mid	e:	o:					ɔu
low	a:				a		

<u>Language</u>

Senadi (111)	bilabial	labio-dental	dental/alveolar	palato-alveolar	palatal	velar	labial-velar
voiceless plosive	p		"t"		c	k	k͡p
voiced plosive	b		"d"		ɟ	g	g͡b
vl. nonsibilant fricative		f					
vd. nonsibilant fricative		v					
vl. sibilant fricative			"s"	ʃ			
vd. sibilant fricative			"z"	ʒ			
voiced nasal	m		"n"			ŋ	
vd. lateral approximant			"l"				
vd. central approximant					j		w

<u>Vowels</u>

	oral			nasalized		
high	i		u	ĩ		ũ
higher mid	e		o			
lower mid	ɛ		ɔ	ɛ̃		ɔ̃
low		a			ã	

<u>Language</u>

Tampulma (112)	bilabial	labio-dental	alveolar	palatal	velar	variable place	labial-velar
voiceless plosive	p		t	c	k		k͡p
voiced plosive	b		d	ɟ	g		g͡b
vl. nonsibilant fricative		f				h	
vd. nonsibilant fricative		v					
vl. sibilant fricative			s				
vd. sibilant fricative			z				
voiced nasal	m		n	ɲ	ŋ		m͡ŋ
voiced trill			r				
vd. lateral approximant			l				
vd. central approximant				j			w

<u>Vowels</u>

high	i ɩ		ʊ u
higher mid	e		o
lower mid	ɛ		ɔ
low		a	

Language Bariba (113)	bilabial	labio-dental	alveolar	palatal	velar	variable place	labial-velar
voiceless plosive	p		t		k		k͡g
voiced plosive	b		d		g		g͡b
vl. nonsibilant fricative		f				h	
vl. sibilant fricative			s				
vd. sibilant fricative			z				
voiced nasal	m		n				
voiced flap			ɾ				
vd. lateral approximant			l				
vd. central approximant				j			w

Vowels

	oral			nasalized		
high	i		u	ĩ		ũ
higher mid	e		o			
lower mid	ε		ɔ	ε̃		ɔ̃
low		a			ã	

Language Ewe (114)	bilabial	labio-dental	dental	dental/alveolar	palatal	velar	pharyngeal	labial-velar
voiceless plosive								k͡p
vl. aspirated plos.	p^h		$t̪^h$			k^h		
voiced plosive	b		d̪			g		g͡b
vl. sibilant affric.			t̪s̪					
vd. sibilant affric.			d̪z̪					
vl. nonsibilant fric.	ɸ	f					h	
vd. nonsibilant fric.	β	v					ʕ	
vl. sibilant fric.				"s"				
vd. sibilant fric.				"z"				
voiced nasal	m			"n"	ɲ	ŋ		
voiced flap				"ɾ"				
vd. lateral approx.				"l"				
vd. central approx.					j			w

Vowels

	oral			nasalized		
high	i		u	ĩ		ũ
higher mid	e		o	ẽ		õ
lower mid	ε		ɔ	ε̃		ɔ̃
low		a			ã	

Language Akan (115)	bilabial	labio-dental	dental/alveolar	palatal	palatal labialized	velar	variable place	labial-velar
vl. aspirated plosive	pʰ		"tʰ"			kʰ		
voiced plosive	b		"d"			g		
vl. nonsibilant affricate				cç	cçʷ			
vd. nonsibilant affricate				ɟʝ	ɟʝʷ			
vl. nonsibilant fricative		f			çʷ		h	
vl. sibilant fricative			"s"					
voiced nasal	m		"n"					
voiced trill			"r"					
vd. central approximant				j				w

Vowels

	oral				nasalized			
high	i	ɪ	u	ʊ	ĩ	ɪ̃	ũ	ʊ̃
higher mid	e		o					
lower mid		ɔ						
low	a				ã			

	long nasalized	
high		
higher mid	ø̃:[1]	
lower mid		œ̃:[1]
low		

Language Igbo (116)	bilabial	bilabial palatalized	labio-dental	dental/alveolar	dental/alv. palatalized	alveolar	palato-alveolar	palatal	velar	velar labialized	variable place	variable place labialized	labial-velar
voiceless plosive	p	pʲ		"t"					k	kʷ			
vl. asp. plos.	pʰ	pʲʰ		"tʰ"					kʰ	kʷʰ			
voiced plosive	b	bʲ		"d"					g	gʷ			
breathy vd. plos.	b̤	b̤ʲ		"d̤"					g̤	g̤ʷ			
vl. implosive	p˂					t˂							
vd. implosive	ɓ												
vl. sib. affric.							tʃ						
vd. sib. affric.							dʒ						
breathy vd. sib. af.							d̤ʒ						
vl. nonsib. fric.			f								h	hʷ	
vd. nonsib. fric.			v						ɣ				
vl. sib. fric.				"s"									
vd. sib. fric.				"z"									
voiced nasal	m			"n"				ɲ	ŋ				ŋ͡m
voiced flap				"ɾ"	"ɾʲ"								
vd. lateral approx.				"l"									
vd. central approx.								j					w

Vowels	oral				nasalized			
high	i		ʊ	u	ĩ		ʊ̃	ũ
higher mid	e		o		ẽ		õ	
lower mid	ɛ	ɔ			ɛ̃	ɔ̃		
low	a				ã			

Language

Gã (117)

	bilabial	labio-dental	dental	dental/alveolar	alveolar	palato-alveolar	palato-alv. labialized	palatal	velar	variable place	labial-palatal	labial-velar
voiceless plosive												k͡p
vl. aspirated plos.	pʰ		t̪ʰ						kʰ			
voiced plosive	b				d				g			g͡b
vl. sibilant affric.							tʃʷ					
vl. asp. sib. affric.						tʃʰ						
vd. sibilant affric.						dʒ	dʒʷ					
vl. nonsibilant fric.		f								h		
vd. nonsibilant fric.		v										
vl. sibilant fric.				"s"		ʃ	ʃʷ					
vd. sibilant fric.				"z"								
voiced nasal	m			"n"				ɲ	ŋ			m͡ŋ
voiced trill				"r"[1]								
vd. lateral approx.				"l"								
vd. central approx.								j			ɥ	w

Vowels

	oral				nasalized			
high	i			u	ĩ			ũ
higher mid	e		o					
lower mid		ɛ	ɔ			ɛ̃	ɔ̃	
low		a				ã		

Language

Lelemi (118)

	bilabial	labio-dental	alveolar	retroflex	palatal	velar	labial-velar
voiceless plosive	p[2]		t			k	k͡p
voiced plosive	b			ḍ			g͡b
vl. sibilant affricate			ts				
vd. sibilant affricate			dz				
vd. nonsibilant affricate		v					
vl. sibilant fricative			s				
voiced nasal	m		n		ɲ	ŋ	
vd. lateral approximant			l				
vd. central approximant					j		w

Vowels

	oral				nasalized			
high	i			u	ĩ			ũ
higher mid	e		o					
lower mid		ɛ	ɔ			ɛ̃	ɔ̃	
low		a				ã		

Language

Efik (119)	bilabial	labio-dental	alveolar	palatal	velar	labial-velar
voiceless plosive			t		k	k͡p
voiced plosive	b		d			
vl. nonsibilant fricative		f				
vl. sibilant fricative			s			
voiced nasal	m		n	ɲ	ŋ	
vd. central approximant				j		w

Vowels

high	i	u
higher mid	e	o
lower mid	ɛ	ɔ
low	a	

Language

Birom (120)	bilabial	labio-dental	alveolar	palato-alveolar	palatal	velar	variable place	labial-velar
voiceless plosive	p		t		c	k		k͡p
voiced plosive	b		d		ɟ	g		g͡b
vl. nonsibilant fricative		f					h	
vd. nonsibilant fricative		v						
vl. sibilant fricative			s	ʃ				
vd. sibilant fricative			z					
voiced nasal	m		n			ŋ		
vd. central approximant					j			w

Vowels

high	i	u
higher mid	e	o
lower mid	ɛ	ɔ
low	a	

Language	bilabial	labio-dental	dental/alveolar	palato-alveolar	palatal	velar	variable place	labial-velar
Tarok (121)								
voiceless plosive	p		"t"			k		k͡p
voiced plosive	b		"d"			g		g͡b
vd. implosive	ɓ		"ɗ"					
vl. sibilant affricate				tʃ				
vd. sibilant affricate				dʒ				
vl. nonsibilant fricative		f					h	
vd. nonsibilant fricative		v						
vl. sibilant fricative			"s"	ʃ				
vd. sibilant fricative			"z"	ʒ				
voiced nasal	m		"n"			ŋ		
voiced r-sound			"rr"					
vd. lateral approximant			"l"					
vd. central approximant					j			w

Vowels

high	i		u
mid	"e""ə""o"		
low		a	

Language	bilabial	labio-dental	alveolar	palato-alveolar	palatal	velar	variable place	labial-velar
Amo (122)								
voiceless plosive	p		t			k		k͡p
voiced plosive	b		d			g		g͡b
vl. sibilant affricate			ts	tʃ				
vd. sibilant affricate				dʒ				
vl. nonsibilant fricative		f					h	
vd. nonsibilant fricative		v						
vl. sibilant fricative			s	ʃ				
vd. sibilant fricative			z					
voiced nasal	m		n		ɲ	ŋ		
voiced trill			r					
vd. lateral approximant			l					
vd. central approximant					j			w

Vowels

high	i ɩ					ʊ u
higher mid		e			o	
lower mid			ɛ	ɔ		
low			ɐ a			

Language	bilabial	labio-dental	dental/alveolar	alveolar	palatal	velar	variable place	labial-velar
Beembe (123)								
voiceless plosive	p		"t"					
vl. aspirated plosive	pʰ		"tʰ"			kʰ		
vl. sibilant affricate				ts				
vl. asp. sib. affricate				tsʰ				
vl. nonsibilant affricate		pf						
vl. asp. nonsib. affricate		pfʰ						
vl. nonsibilant fricative		f					h	
vd. nonsibilant fricative		v						
vl. sibilant fricative				s				
voiced nasal	m		"n"					
vd. lateral approximant			"l"					
vd. central approximant					j			w

Vowels

	oral			nasalized		
high	i		ɷ	ĩ		ũ
lower mid	ɛ		ɔ	ɛ̃		ɔ̃
low		a			ã	

Language	bilabial	labio-dental	dental/alveolar	alveolar	palato-alveolar	palatal	velar	labial-velar
Swahili (124)								
voiceless plosive	p		"t"				k	
vl. aspirated plos.	pʰ		"tʰ"				kʰ	
vd. implosive	ɓ		"ɗ"			ʄ	ɠ	
vl. sibilant affric.					tʃ			
vl. asp. sib. affric.					tʃʰ			
vl. nonsibilant fric.		f						
vd. nonsibilant fric.		v						
vl. sibilant fric.			"s"		ʃ			
vd. sibilant fric.			"z"					
voiced nasal	m		"n"			ɲ	ŋ[1]	
voiced trill				r[2]				
vd. lateral approx.			"l"					
vd. central approx.						j		w

Vowels

high	i		u
higher mid	e		o
low		a	

Language	bilabial	bilabial prenasalize	labio-dental	dental/alveolar	dental/alv. prenasal	palato-alveolar	palato-alv. prenasal	palatal	velar	velar prenasalized	variable place	labial-velar
Luvale (125)												
voiceless plosive	p			"t"					k			
voiced plosive		^{m}b			"^{n}d"				^{ŋ}g			
vl. sibilant affricate						tʃ						
vd. sibilant affricate							^{n}dʒ					
vl. nonsibilant fricative			f								h	
vl. sibilant fricative				"s"		ʃ						
vd. sibilant fricative						ʒ						
voiced nasal	m			"n"				ɲ	ŋ			
voiced lateral flap				"ɺ"								
vd. central approximant			ʋ					j				w

Vowels

high	i				u
higher mid		e		o	
low			a		

Language	bilabial	labio-dental	alveolar	palato-alveolar	palatal	velar	variable place	labial-velar
Zulu (126)								
voiceless plosive	p		t			k		
vl. aspirated plosive	p^h		t^h			k^h		
vl. ejective stop	p'		t'			k'		
voiceless click				ǃ				
vl. aspirated click				$ǃ^h$				
vd. implosive	ɓ							
vl. affricated click			$ǀ^s$					
vl. asp. affricated click			$ǀ^{sh}$					
vl. sib. eject. affricate				tʃ'				
vd. sibilant affricate					dʒ			
vd. lateral eject. affric.						kɬ'		
vl. nonsibilant fricative		f					h	
vd. nonsibilant fricative		v					ɦ	
vl. sibilant fricative			s	ʃ				
vd. sibilant fricative			z					
vl. lateral fricative			ɬ					
vd. lateral fricative			ɮ					
voiced nasal	m		n	n̠				
voiced trill			r^2					
vd. lateral approximant			l					
vl. lat. affric. click			$ǁ^ɬ$					
vl. asp. lat. affric. click			$ǁ^{ɬh}$					
vd. central approximant					j			w

Vowels

high	i				u
lower mid		ɛ		ɔ	
low			a		

<u>Language</u>

Teke (127)	bilabial	labio-dental	alveolar	palato-alveolar	palatal	velar	variable place	labial-velar
voiceless plosive	p		t			k		
voiced plosive	b		d			g		
vl. sibilant affricate				tʃ				
vd. sibilant affricate				dʒ				
vl. nonsibilant affricate		pf						
vd. nonsibilant affricate		bv						
vl. nonsibilant fricative		f					h	
vl. sibilant fricative			s					
voiced nasal	m	ɱ	n		ɲ	ŋ		
vd. lateral approximant			l					
vd. central approximant					j			w

<u>Vowels</u>

high	i				u
mid		"e"		"o"	
low			a		

<u>Language</u>

Doayo (128)	bilabial	labio-dental	dental/alveolar	palatal	velar	variable place	labial-velar
voiceless plosive	p		"t"		k		k͡p
voiced plosive	b		"d"		g		g͡b
vd. implosive	ɓ		"ɗ"				
vl. nonsibilant fricative		f				h	
vd. nonsibilant fricative		v					
vl. sibilant fricative			"s"				
vd. sibilant fricative			"z"				
voiced nasal	m		"n"		ŋ		
voiced r-sound			"r"				
vd. lateral approximant			"l"				
vd. central approximant				j			w

<u>Vowels</u>

	oral						nasalized				
high	i					u	ĩ				ũ
higher mid		e			o						
lower mid			ɛ	ɔ				ɛ̃		ɔ̃	
low				a					ã		

Language Gbeya (129)	bilabial	bilabial prenasalized	labio-dental	dental	dental prenasalized	alveolar	palatal	velar	velar prenasalized	glottal	variable place	labial-velar	labial-velar prenasal
voiceless plosive	p			t̪				k		?		k͡p	
voiced plosive	b	ᵐb		d̪	ⁿd̪			g	ᵑg			g͡b	m͡ŋg͡b
vd. implosive	ɓ			ɗ̪									
vl. nonsibilant fricative			f								h		
vd. nonsibilant fricative			v										
vl. sibilant fricative						s							
vd. sibilant fricative						z							
voiced nasal	m			n̪				ŋ				m͡ŋ	
laryngd. vd. nasal	m̰			n̪̰									
voiced flap			ѵ			ɾ							
vd. lateral approximant				l̪									
vd. central approximant							j					w	

Vowels

	oral	nasalized
high	i u	ĩ ũ
higher mid	e o	
lower mid	ɛ ɔ	ɔ̃
low	a	æ̃ ã

Language Zande (130)	bilabial	labio-dental	alveolar	palatal	velar	variable place	labial-velar
voiceless plosive	p		t		k		k͡p
voiced plosive	b		d		g		g͡b
vl. nonsibilant fricative		f				h	
vd. nonsibilant fricative		v					
vl. sibilant fricative			s				
vd. sibilant fricative			z				
voiced nasal	m		n	ɲ			
voiced lateral flap		ɺ					
vd. central approximant				j			w

Vowels

	oral	nasalized
high	i ɩ ɷ u	Ĩ ũ
higher mid		ẽ õ
mid	"e" "o"	"ɛ̃" "ɔ̃"
lower mid	ɛ ɔ	ɔ̃ ɛ̃
low	a	ã

Language	bilabial	labio-dental	dental/alveolar	dental/alv. palatalized	palatal	velar	labial-velar
Songhai (200)							
voiceless plosive			"t"	"tʲ"[4]		k	
voiced plosive	b		"d"	"dʲ"[4]		g	
vl. nonsibilant fricative		f					
vl. sibilant fricative			"s"				
vd. sibilant fricative			"z"				
voiced nasal	m		"n"		ɲ	ŋ	
voiced r-sound			"rr"				
vd. lateral approximant			"l"				
vd. central approximant					j		w

Vowels

	oral			nasalized		
high	i		u			ũ[1]
higher mid			o			õ[1]
mid	"e"			"ẽ"[1]		
low		a			ã[1]	

Language	bilabial	labio-dental	dental/alveolar	palato-alveolar	retroflex	palatal	velar	glottal	variable place	labial-velar
Kanuri (201)										
voiceless plosive	p		"t"				k	ʔ		
voiced plosive	b		"d"				g			
vl. sibilant affric.				tʃ						
vd. sibilant affric.				dʒ						
vl. nonsibilant fric.	ɸ[1]	f[1]							h	
vl. sibilant fric.			"s"	ʃ			x[2]			
vd. sibilant fric.			"z"							
voiced nasal	m		"n"			ɲ	ŋ			
voiced trill			"r"							
vd. lateral approx.			"l"		ɭ					
vd. central approx.						j				

Vowels

high	i		ɨ		u
mid		"e"		"o"	
low			a		

Language	bilabial	labio-dental	dental/alveolar	alveolar	palato-alveolar	retroflex	palatal	velar	glottal	labial-velar
Maba (202)										
voiceless plosive			"t"			ʈ		k	ʔ	
voiced plosive	b		"d"			ɖ	ɟ	g		
vl. nonsibilant fricative		f								
vl. sibilant fricative				s	ʃ					
vd. sibilant fricative				z	ʒ					
voiced nasal	m			n			ɲ	ŋ		
voiced trill				r						
vd. lateral approximant				l						
vd. central approximant							j			w

Vowels

high	i		u
higher mid	e		o
lower mid	ɛ		ɔ
low		a	

Language	bilabial	labio-dental	alveolar	palato-alveolar	palatal	velar	variable place	labial-velar
Fur (203)								
voiceless plosive	p		t			k		
voiced plosive	b		d			g		
vd. sibilant affric.				dʒ				
vl. nonsibilant fric.		f					h	
vd. nonsibilant fric.						ɣ		
vl. sibilant fric.			s	ʃ				
vd. sibilant fric.			z					
voiced nasal	m		n		ɲ	ŋ		
voiced trill			r					
vd. lateral approx.			l					
vd. central approx.					j			w

Vowels

	short			long		
high	i		u	i:		u:
higher mid	e		o			
mid		ə				
lower mid	ɛ		ɔ			
low		a			a:	

Language Maasai (204)	bilabial	dental/alveolar	alveolar	palato-alveolar	palatal	velar	labial-velar
voiceless plosive	p	"t"				k	
vd. implosive	ɓ	"ɗ"			ʄ	ɠ	
vl. sibilant affric.				tʃ			
vl. sibilant fric.		"s"		ʃ			
voiced nasal	m	"n"			ɲ	ŋ	
voiced trill		"r"					
voiced flap			ɾ				
vd. lateral approx.		"l"					
vd. central approx.					j		w

Vowels

high	i	ɪ	ʊ	u
higher mid	e	o		
lower mid	ɛ	ɔ		
low	a			

Language Luo (205)	bilabial	labio-dental	dental	alveolar	palato-alveolar	palatal	velar	glottal	variable place	labial-velar
voiceless plosive								ʔ		
vl. aspirated plos.	pʰ			tʰ			kʰ			
voiced plosive	b			d			g			
vl. sibilant affric.					tʃ					
vd. sibilant affric.					dʒ					
vl. nonsibilant affric.			t̪θ							
vd. nonsibilant affric.			d̪ð							
vl. nonsibilant fric.		f							h	
vl. sibilant fric.				s	ʃ					
voiced nasal	m			n		ɲ	ŋ			
voiced flap				ɾ						
vd. lateral approx.				l						
vd. central approx.						j				w

Vowels

high	i	ɪ	ʊ	u
mid	"e"	"o"		
low	æ	a	ɒ	

Language Nubian (206)	bilabial	labio-dental	dental/alveolar	palato-alveolar	palatal	velar	variable place
voiceless plosive			"t"			k	
voiced plosive	b		"d"			g	
vl. sibilant affric.				tʃ			
vd. sibilant affric.				dʒ			
vl. nonsibilant fric.		f					h
vl. sibilant fric.			"s"	ʃ			
voiced nasal	m		"n"		ɲ		
voiced trill			"r"				
vd. lateral approx.			"l"				

Vowels

high	i				u
mid		"e"		"o"	
low			a		

Language Nyangi (207)	bilabial	dental	alveolar	palatal	velar	labial-velar
voiceless plosive	p		t	c	k	
vd. implosive	ɓ		ɗ	ʄ	ɠ	
vl. sibilant fric.		s̪				
vl. lateral fric.			ɬ			
voiced nasal	m		n	ɲ	ŋ	
voiced trill			r			
vd. lateral approx.			l			
vd. central approx.				j		w

Vowels

high	i						u
higher mid		e				o	
lower mid			ɛ		ɔ		
low				a			

Language	bilabial	labio-dental	dental	dental/alveolar	alveolar	palato-alveolar	palatal	velar	uvular	variable place	labial-velar
Ik (208)											
voiceless plosive	p		t̪					k			
voiced plosive	b		d̪					g			
vl. ejective stop								k'			
vd. implosive	ɓ		ɗ̪				ʄ		ɢ̆		
vl. sibilant affricate					ts	tʃ					
vd. sibilant affricate					dz	dʒ					
vl. eject. sib. affricate					ts'						
vl. eject. lat. affricate				"tɬ"							
vl. nonsibilant fricative		f								h	
vl. sibilant fricative					s						
vd. sibilant fricative					z						
vl. lateral fricative				"ɬ"							
vd. lateral fricative				"ɮ"							
voiced nasal	m		n̪				ɲ	ŋ			
voiced trill					r						
vd. lateral approximant				"l"							
vd. central approximant							j				w

Vowels

	voiced					voiceless				
high	i ɩ				u	i̥				u̥
higher mid	e			o						
mid							"e̥"		"o̥"	
lower mid		ɛ	ɔ							
low		a						ḁ		

Language	bilabial	dental/alveolar	palatal	velar	labial-velar
Sebei (209)					
voiceless plosive	p	"t"	c	k	
vl. sibilant fricative		"s"			
voiced nasal	m	"n"	ɲ	ŋ	
voiced trill		"r"			
voiced flap		"ɾ"			
vd. lateral approximant		"l"			
vd. central approximant			j		w

Vowels

	short					overshort
high	i				u	ɨ̆, ʉ̆
higher mid		e		o		
mid						"ə̆", "ɵ̆"
lower mid			ɔ			
low			a			ɐ̆, ɒ̆

<u>Language</u>

Tama (210)	bilabial	labio-dental	dental	alveolar	palatal	velar	pharyngeal	variable place	labial-velar
voiceless plosive			t̪			k			
voiced plosive	b		d̪		ɟ	g			
vd. implosive	ɓ			ɗ					
vl. nonsibilant fric.		f					ħ	h	
vl. sibilant fric.				s					
voiced nasal	m			n	ɲ	ŋ			
voiced trill				r					
voiced flap				ɾ					
vd. lateral approx.				l					
vd. central approx.					j				w

<u>Vowels</u>

high	i	ɩ						ɷ	u
higher mid			e				o		
lower mid				ɛ		ɔ			
low					a				

<u>Language</u>

Temein (211)	bilabial	dental	alveolar	palatal	velar	labial-velar
voiceless plosive	p	t̪	t		k	
voiced plosive	b	d̪	d	ɟ	g	
vl. sibilant fricative			s			
voiced nasal	m	n̪		ɲ	ŋ	
voiced trill			r			
vd. lateral approximant			l			
vd. central approximant				j		w

<u>Vowels</u>

high	i						u
higher mid		e				o	
lower mid			ɛ		ɔ		
low				a			

Language	bilabial	labio-dental	dental/alveolar	palato-alveolar	palatal	velar	variable place	labial-velar
Nera (212)								
voiceless plosive			"t"			k		
voiced plosive	b		"d"			g		
vd. sibilant affric.				dʒ				
vl. nonsibilant fric.		f					h	
vl. sibilant fric.			"s"	ʃ				
voiced nasal	m		"n"			ŋ		
voiced trill			"r"					
vd. lateral approx.			"l"					
vd. central approx.					j			w

Vowels

high	i				u
mid		"e"		"o"	
low			a		

Language	bilabial	labio-dental	dental	alveolar	palato-alveolar	palatal	velar	glottal	variable place	labial-velar
Tabi (213)										
voiceless plosive	p		t̪			c	k	ʔ		
voiced plosive	b		d̪			ɟ	g			
vl. nonsibilant fric.		f	θ						h	
vd. nonsibilant fric.			ð							
vl. sibilant fric.				s	ʃ					
vd. sibilant fric.				z						
voiced nasal	m			n		ɲ	ŋ			
voiced trill				r						
vd. lateral approx.				l						
vd. central approx.						j				w

Vowels

high	i ɩ					u
higher mid		e				o
mid				"ə"		
lower mid			ɛ		ɔ	
low				a		

Language

Mursi (214)	bilabial	dental	dental/alveolar	palato-alveolar	palatal	velar	variable place	labial-velar
voiceless plosive	p		"t"		c	k		
voiced plosive	b		"d"		ɟ	g		
vd. implosive	ɓ		"ɗ"					
vl. nonsibilant fric.		θ					h	
vl. sibilant fric.				ʃ				
voiced nasal	m		"n"		ɲ	ŋ		
voiced trill			"r"					
vd. lateral approx.			"l"					
vd. central approx.					j			w

Vowels

high	i				u
mid		"e"		"o"	
low			a		

Language

Logbara (215)	bilabial	labio-dental	dental	dental/alveolar	palato-alveolar	palatal	velar	glottal	variable place	labial-velar
voiceless plosive	p		t̪				k	ʔ		k͡p
voiced plosive	b		d̪				g			g͡b
laryngealized vd. plosive	b̰		d̪̰							
vl. sibilant affricate					tʃ					
vd. sibilant affricate					dʒ					
vl. nonsibilant fricative		f							h	
vd. nonsibilant fricative		v								
vl. sibilant fricative				"s"						
vd. sibilant fricative				"z"						
voiced nasal	m			"n"						
voiced flap				"ɾ"						
vd. lateral flap				"ɺ"						
vd. central approximant						j				w
laryngealized vd. central approximant						j̰				w̰

Vowels

	oral					nasalized
high	i ɩ				ʊ u	
higher mid		e[1]		o[1]		
lower mid		ɛ	ɜ	ɔ		
low			a			ã[1]

Language	bilabial	bilabial prenasalized	dental	dental/alveolar	dental/alv. prenasalized	palatal	palatal prenasalized	velar	velar prenasalized	labial-velar
Yulu (216)										
voiceless plosive	p		t̪			c		k		k͡p
voiced plosive	b	ᵐb	d̪		"ⁿd"		ᶮɟ	g	ᵑg	g͡b
vd. implosive	ɓ			"ɗ"		ʄ				
vd. sibilant affric.				"dz"						
vl. sibilant fric.				"s"						
voiced nasal	m			"n"		ɲ	ŋ			
voiced trill				"r"						
vd. lateral approx.				"l"						
vd. central approx.						j				w

<u>Vowels</u>

high	i				u
mid		"e"		"o"	
low			a		

Language	bilabial	bilabial prenasalized	alveolar	alveolar prenasalized	palato-alveolar	palatal	palatal prenasalized	velar	velar prenasalized	variable place	labial-velar
Sara (217)											
voiceless plosive	p		t					k			
voiced plosive	b	ᵐb	d	ⁿd			ᶮɟ	g	ᵑg		
vd. implosive	ɓ		ɗ								
vl. sibilant affric.					dʒ						
vl. nonsibilant fric.										h	
vl. sibilant fric.			s								
voiced nasal	m		n			ɲ					
voiced flap			ɾ								
vd. lateral approx.			l								
vd. central approx.						j					w

<u>Vowels</u>

	oral							nasalized					
high	i						u	ĩ					ũ
higher mid		e				o							
mid				"ə"					"ẽ"	"ə̃"		"õ"	
lower mid			ɛ		ɔ						ɔ̃		
low				a						ã			

Language													
Berta (218)	bilabial	bilabial prenasalized	labio-dental	dental	dental/alveolar	dental/alv. prenasalized	palato-alveolar	palatal	velar	velar prenasalized	glottal	variable place	labial-velar
voiceless plosive											ʔ		
voiced plosive	b	ᵐb			"d"	"ⁿd"			g	ᵑg			
vl. ejective stop	p'								k'				
vd. implosive					"ɗ"								
vl. sibilant affric.							dʒ						
vl. nonsib. fric.			f	θ								h	
vl. sibilant fric.					"s"		ʃ						
vl. sib. eject. fric.					"s'"								
voiced nasal	m				"n"				ŋ				
voiced trill					"r"								
vd. lateral approx.					"l"								
vd. central approx.								j					w

Vowels

high	i				u
mid		"e"		"o"	
low			a		

Language									
Kunama (219)	bilabial	labio-dental	dental	alveolar	palato-alveolar	palatal	velar	variable place	labial-velar
voiceless plosive			t̪				k		
voiced plosive	b		d̪				g		
vl. sibilant affric.					tʃ				
vd. sibilant affric.					dʒ				
vl. nonsibilant fric.		f						h	
vl. sibilant fric.				s	ʃ				
voiced nasal	m			n		ɲ	ŋ		
voiced trill				r					
vd. lateral approx.				l					
vd. central approx.						j			w

Vowels

high	i	ɩ				ʊ	u
mid			"e"		"o"		
low				a			

Language	bilabial	alveolar	palato-alveolar	palatal	velar	glottal	variable place	labial-velar
Koma (220)								
voiceless plosive	p	t			k	ʔ		
voiced plosive	b	d			g			
vl. ejective stop	p'	t'			k'			
vd. implosive	ɓ	ɗ						
vl. nonsibilant fric.							h	
vl. sibilant fric.		s	ʃ					
vl. sib. eject. fric.		s'						
voiced nasal	m	n			ŋ[1]			
voiced trill		r						
vd. lateral approx.		l						
vd. central approx.				j				w

Vowels

high	i				u
higher mid	e			o	
mid			"ə"		
lower mid		ɛ		ɔ	
low			a		

Language	bilabial	labio-dental	dental	dental pharyngealized	alveolar	palato-alveolar	palatal	velar	uvular	pharyngeal	glottal	variable place	labial-velar
Arabic (250)													
voiceless plosive			t̪	t̪ˤ				k	q		ʔ		
long vl. plosive			t̪:	t̪ˤ:				k:	q:		ʔ:		
voiced plosive	b		d̪	d̪ˤ				g					
long vd. plosive	b:		d̪:	d̪ˤ:				g:					
vd. sib. affricate						dʒ							
vl. nonsib. fricative		f	θ[1]			ʃ			χ	ħ		h	
long vl. nonsib. fricative		f:				ʃ:			χ:	ħ:		h:	
vd. nonsib. fricative			ð[1]	ðˤ[1]					ʁ	ʕ			
long vd. nonsib. fricative									ʁ:	ʕ:			
vl. sib. fricative			s̪	s̪ˤ									
long vl. sib. fricative			s̪:	s̪ˤ:									
vd. sib. fricative			z̪	z̪ˤ									
long vd. sib. fricative			z̪:	z̪ˤ:									
voiced nasal	m		n̪										
long vd. nasal	m:		n̪:										
long vd. trill					r:								
voiced flap					ɾ								
vd. lat. approximant			l̪										
long vd. lat. approximant			l̪:										
vd. cent. approximant							j						w
long vd. cent. approximant							j:						w:

Vowels

	long			short		
high	i:		u:	ɩ		ʊ
higher mid		e:	o:			
low		æ:			a	

Language Tigre (251)	bilabial	labio-dental	dental	alveolar	palato-alveolar	palatal	velar	pharyngeal	glottal	variable place	labial-velar
voiceless plosive			t̪				k		ʔ		
voiced plosive	b		d̪				g				
vl. ejective stop			t̪'				k'				
vl. sibilant affric.					tʃ						
vd. sibilant affric.					dʒ						
vl. sib. eject. affric.				ts'	tʃ'						
vl. nonsibilant fric.		f						ħ		h	
vd. nonsibilant fric.								ʕ			
vl. sibilant fric.				s	ʃ						
vd. sibilant fric.				z	ʒ						
vl. sib. eject. fric.				s'							
voiced nasal	m		n̪								
voiced trill				r							
vd. lateral approx.				l							
vd. central approx.						j					w

Vowels		long			short
high	i:		u:		
mid		"e:"		"o:"	"ə"
lower mid					3
low		ɐ:			

Language Amharic (252)	bilabial	labio-dental	dental/alveolar	alveolar	palato-alveolar	palatal	velar	velar labialized	variable place	variable place labialized	labial-velar
voiceless plosive	p[2]		"t"				k	kʷ			
voiced plosive	b		"d"				g	gʷ			
vl. ejective stop	p'[2]		"t'"				k'	kʷ'			
vl. sibilant affric.					tʃ						
vd. sibilant affric.					dʒ						
vl. sib. eject. affric.					tʃ'						
vl. nonsibilant fric.		f							h	hʷ	
vl. sibilant fric.			"s"		ʃ						
vd. sibilant fric.			"z"		ʒ						
vl. sib. eject. fric.			"s'"								
voiced nasal	m		"n"			ɲ					
voiced flap				ɾ							
vd. lateral approx.				l							
vd. central approx.						j					w

Vowels					
high	i		ɨ		u
mid		"e"	ə	"o"	
low			a		

Language	bilabial	labio-dental	dental/alveolar	palato-alveolar	palatal	velar	uvular	glottal	variable place
Hebrew (253)									
voiceless plosive	p		"t"			k		ʔ	
voiced plosive	b		"d"			g			
vl. sibilant affric.			"ts"	tʃ[2]					
vd. sibilant affric.				dʒ[2]					
vl. nonsibilant fric.		f				x			h
vd. nonsibilant fric.		v					ʁ		
vl. sibilant fric.			"s"	ʃ					
vd. sibilant fric.			"z"	ʒ[2]					
voiced nasal	m		"n"			ŋ[2]			
vd. lateral approx.			"l"						
vd. central approx.					j				
Vowels									
high	ɩ				ʊ				
mid				o					
lower mid		ɛ							
low			a						

Language	bilabial	labio-dental	dental/alveolar	palato-alveolar	palatal	velar	uvular	glottal	variable place	labial-velar
Socotri (254)										
voiceless plosive			"t̪"			k		ʔ		
voiced plosive	b		"d"			g				
vl. ejective stop			"t'"			k'				
vl. nonsibilant fric.		f					χ		h	
vd. nonsibilant fric.							ʁ			
vl. sibilant fric.			"s"	ʃ						
vd. sibilant fric.			"z"	ʒ						
vl. sib. eject. fric.			"s'"	ʃ'[1]						
vl. lateral fric.			"ɬ"							
vd. lateral fric.			"lʒ"							
voiced nasal	m		"n"							
voiced r-sound			"rr"							
vd. lateral approx.			"l"							
vd. central approx.					j					w
Vowels										
high	ı				ʉ					
mid		"e"	"ə"	"o"						
low			a							

Language Neo-Aramaic (255)	bilabial	labio-dental	dental	alveolar	palato-alveolar	palatal	velar	uvular	glottal	variable place
voiceless plosive	p		t̪				k	q	ʔ	
voiced plosive	b		d̪				g			
vl. sibilant affric.					tʃ					
vd. sibilant affric.					dʒ					
vl. nonsibilant fric.		f						χ		h
vd. nonsibilant fric.	β							ʁ		
vl. sibilant fric.				s	ʃ					
vd. sibilant fric.				z	ʒ					
voiced nasal	m		n̪							
voiced flap				ɾ						
vd. lateral approx.				l						
vd. central approx.						j				

Vowels

	short		long	
high	i	u	i:	u:
mid	"e"	"o"		
low	a		a:	

	short pharyngealized		long pharyngealized	
high	iˤ	uˤ	iˤ:	uˤ:
mid	"eˤ"	"oˤ"		
low	aˤ		aˤ:	

Language Shilha (256)	bilabial	labio-dental	dental/alveolar	dental/alv. pharyng	palato-alveolar	palatal	velar	velar pharyngealize	pharyngeal	variable place	labial-velar
voiceless plosive			"t"	"tˤ"			k	kˤ			
long vl. plosive			"t:"				k:				
voiced plosive	b		"d"	"dˤ"			g				
long vl. plosive	b:		"d:"				g:				
vl. nonsibilant fric.		f					x		ħ	h	
long vl. nonsib. fric.		f:					x:		ħ:		
vd. nonsibilant fric.							ɣ		ʕ		
long vd. nonsib. fric.							ɣ:				
vl. sibilant fric.			"s"	"sˤ"	ʃ						
long vl. sib. fric.			"s:"		ʃ:						
vd. sibilant fric.			"z"	"zˤ"	ʒ						
long vd. sib. fric.			"z:"		ʒ:						
voiced nasal	m		"n"								
long voiced nasal	m:		"n:"								
voiced trill			"r"	"rˤ"							
long voiced trill			"r:"								
vd. lateral approx.			"l"	"lˤ"							
long vd. lat. approx.			"l:"								
vd. central approx.						j					w

Vowels			
	high	i	u
	low	æ	

Language	bilabial	labio-dental	dental	dental pharyngealized	palato-alveolar	palatal	velar	uvular	variable place	labial-velar
Tuareg (257)										
voiceless plosive			t̪	t̪ˤ			k	q		
voiced plosive	b		d̪	d̪ˤ		ɟ	g			
vl. nonsibilant fric.		f						χ	h	
vd. nonsibilant fric.								ʁ		
vl. sibilant fric.			s̪		ʃ					
vd. sibilant fric.			z̪	z̪ˤ	ʒ					
voiced nasal	m		n̪			ɲ				
voiced trill			r̪							
vd. lateral approx.			l̪							
vd. central approx.						j				w

Vowels

	short			long	
high	i		u	i:	u:
mid	"e"	"ə"	"o"	"e:"	"o:"
low	æ	ɐ		æ:	

Language	bilabial	labio-dental	dental	alveolar	palata-alveolar	retroflex	palatal	velar	uvular	pharyngeal	glottal	variable place	labial-velar
Somali (258)													
voiceless plosive											ʔ		
vl. aspirated plosive			t̪ʰ					kʰ					
voiced plosive	b		d̪					g	ɢ				
long voiced plosive	b:		d̪:					g:	ɢ:				
laryng. vd. plosive						ɖ̰							
long laryng. vd. plosive						ɖ̰:							
vl. sibilant affricate					tʃ								
vl. nonsibilant fricative		f						x[2]		ħ	h		
vd. nonsibilant fricative										ʕ			
vl. sibilant fricative				s	ʃ								
voiced nasal	m			n									
long voiced nasal				n:									
voiced trill				r									
voiced flap				ɾ									
vd. lateral approximant				l									
long vd. lat. approximant				l:									
vd. central approximant							j						w

Vowels

high	i ɩ		ʉ	ʊ
mid	"e"		"ɵ"	
lower mid		ɛ	ɔ	
low		æ	a	

Language	bilabial	labio-dental	dental/alveolar	palato-alveolar	retroflex	palatal	velar	velar labialized	uvular	uvular labialized	labial-velar
Awiya (259)											
voiceless plosive	p		"t"				k	k^w	q	q^w	
voiced plosive	b				ḍ		g	g^w	ɢ	$ɢ^w$	
vl. sibilant affric.			"ts"	tʃ							
vd. sibilant affric.			"dz"[1]	dʒ							
vl. nonsibilant fric.		f									
vl. sibilant fric.			"s"	ʃ							
vd. sibilant fric.			"z"								
voiced nasal	m		"n"				ŋ	$ŋ^w$			
voiced flap			"ɾ"								
vd. lateral approx.			"l"								
vd. central approx.						j					w

Vowels

high	ɪ		ɨ		u
mid		"e"		"o"	
low		æ[4]	a		

Language	bilabial	labio-dental	alveolar	palato-alveolar	palatal	velar	velar labialized	uvular	uvular labialized	pharyngeal	glottal	variable place	labial-velar
Iraqw (260)													
voiceless plosive	p		t			k	k^w	q	q^w	ʕ*	ʔ		
voiced plosive	b		d			g	g^w						
vd. implosive	ɓ[1]		ɗ[1]										
vl. sib. eject. affric.			ts'										
vl. lat. eject. affric.			tɬ'										
vl. nonsibilant fricative		f				x	x^w			ħ		h	
vl. lateral fricative			ɬ										
vl. sibilant fricative			s	ʃ									
long vl. sib. fricative			s:										
voiced nasal	m		n			ŋ	$ŋ^w$						
voiced r-sound			rr										
vd. lateral approximant			l										
vd. central approximant					j								w

Vowels

	short				long		
high	ɩ			ʊ	i:		u:
higher mid		ɵ			e:		o:
lower mid	ɛ	ɜ	ɔ				
low		a				ɑ:	

Language	bilabial	labio-dental	dental	dental/alveolar	palato-alveolar	retroflex	palatal	velar	velar labialized	glottal	variable place	labial-velar
Beja (261)												
voiceless plosive			t̪			ṭ		k	k^w	?		
voiced plosive	b		d̪			ḍ		g	g^w			
vd. sibilant affricate					dʒ							
vl. nonsibilant fric.		f									h	
vl. sibilant fricative			s̪		ʃ							
voiced nasal	m		n̪									
voiced r-sound				"rr"								
vd. lateral approximant				"l"								
vd. central approximant							j					w

Vowels

high	i		u
mid		"e"	"o"
low		a	

Language	bilabial	labio-dental	dental/alveolar	palato-alveolar	palatal	velar	glottal	variable place	labial-velar
Kullo (262)									
voiceless plosive			"t"			k	?		
voiced plosive	b		"d"			g			
vl. ejective stop			"t’"			k’			
vd. implosive			"ɗ"						
vl. sibilant affric.			"ts"	tʃ					
vl. sib. eject. affric.			"ts’"						
vd. sibilant affric.				dʒ					
vl. nonsibilant fric.		f						h	
vl.sibilant fric.			"s"	ʃ					
vd. sibilant fric.			"z"						
voiced nasal	m		"n"						
voiced r-sound			"rr"						
vd. lateral approx.			"l"						
vd. central approx.					j				w

Vowels

high	i				u
mid		"e"		"o"	
low			a		

Language Dizi (263)	bilabial	labio-dental	dental/alveolar	palato-alveolar	palatal	velar	variable place	labial-velar
voiceless plosive			"t"			k		
voiced plosive	b		"d"			g		
vl. ejective stop			"t'"			k'		
vl. sibilant affric.				tʃ				
vd. sibilant affric.				dʒ				
vl. sib. eject. affric.			"ts'"	tʃ'				
vl. nonsibilant fric.		f					h	
vd. nonsibilant fric.	β							
vl. sibilant fric.			"s"	ʃ				
vd. sibilant fric.			"z"	ʒ				
voiced nasal	m		"n"					
voiced r-sound			"rr"					
vd. lateral approx.			"l"					
vd. central approx.					j			w

Vowels

high	i				u
mid		"e"		"o"	
			e		
low			a		

Language Kefa (264)	bilabial	labio-dental	dental/alveolar	palato-alveolar	palatal	velar	glottal	variable place	labial-velar
voiceless plosive	p		"t"			k	ʔ		
voiced plosive	b		"d"			g			
vl. ejective stop	p'		"t'"			k'			
vl. sibilant affric.				tʃ[5]					
vl. sib. eject. affric.				tʃ'[5]					
vd. sibilant affric.				dʒ[5]					
vl. nonsibilant fric.		f						h	
vl. sibilant fric.				ʃ					
voiced nasal	m		"n"						
voiced r-sound			"rr"						
vd. lateral approx.			"l"						
vd. central approx.					j				w

Vowels

high	i				u
mid		"e"		"o"	
low			a		

Language	bilabial	alveolar	palato-alveolar	palatal	velar	uvular	variable place	labial-velar
Hamer (265)								
voiceless plosive	p	t		c	k			
voiced plosive	b	d		ɟ	g			
vl. ejective stop					k'			
vd. implosive	ɓ	ɗ			ɠ			
vl. sibilant affricate		ts						
vd. sibilant affricate							h	
vl. sibilant fricative		s	ʃ					
vd. sibilant fricative		z						
voiced nasal	m	n		ɲ	ŋ			
voiced flap		ɾ						
vd. lateral approximant		l						
vd. central approximant				j				w

Vowels

	plain					pharyngealized				
high	i				u	ɩˤ				ʊˤ
higher mid		e		o						
mid							"eˤ"			
lower mid									ɔˤ	
low			ɑ					ɐˤ		

Language	bilabial	bilabial palatalized	dental/alveolar	alveolar	palato-alveolar	palatal	velar	velar labialized	velar palatalized	glottal	variable place	labial-velar
Hausa (266)												
voiceless plosive			t				k	k^{w}	k^{j}	ʔ		
voiced plosive	b		d				g	g^{w}	g^{j}			
vl. ejective stop							k'	k^{w}'	k^{j}'			
vd. implosive	ɓ		"ɗ"									
vl. sibilant affricate					tʃ							
vd. sibilant affricate					dʒ							
vl. nonsibilant fricative	ɸ	$ɸ^{j}$									h	
vl. sibilant fricative			"s"		ʃ							
vd. sibilant fricative			"z"									
laryngealized vl. sib. fric.			"s̰"									
voiced nasal	m		"n"									
voiced trill				r								
voiced flap				ɾ								
vd. lateral approximant				l								
vd. central approximant						j						w
laryngealized vd. central approximant						j̰						

Vowels

	short			long	
high	ɩ		ʊ	i:	u:
mid	"e"	"ə"	"o"	"e:"	"o:"
low		a			

Language	bilabial	labio-dental	alveolar	palato-alveolar	palatal	velar	variable place	labial-velar
Angas (267)								
voiceless plosive	p		t		c	k		
voiced plosive	b		d		ɟ	g		
vd. implosive	ɓ		ɗ		ʄ			
vl. sibilant affricate				tʃ				
vd. sibilant affricate				dʒ				
vl. nonsibilant fricative		f				x	h	
vd. nonsibilant fricative		v				ɣ		
vl. sibilant fricative			s	ʃ				
vd. sibilant fricative			z	ʒ				
voiced nasal	m		n		ɲ	ŋ		
voiced trill			r					
vd. lateral approximant			l					
vd. central approximant					j			w

Vowels

	short					long			Diphthongs
high	ɩ			u	i:	ɨ:		u:[1]	εi[1]
mid	"e"		"o"						
lower mid	ε								
low		a					a:		

Language	bilabial	labio-dental	alveolar	palato-alveolar	palatal	velar	glottal	labial-velar
Margi (268)								
voiceless plosive	p		t		c	k	?	
voiced plosive	b		d		ɟ	g		
vd. implosive	ɓ		ɗ					
vl. sibilant affric.			ts	tʃ				
vd. sibilant affric.			dz	dʒ				
vl. nonsibilant fric.		f			ç	x		
vd. nonsibilant fric.		v			ʝ	ɣ		
vl. sibilant fric.			s	ʃ				
vd. sibilant fric.			z	ʒ				
vl. lateral fric.			ɬ					
vd. lateral fric.			ɮ					
voiced nasal	m		n		ɲ	ŋ		
voiced trill			r					
voiced flap		ⱱ						
vd. lateral approx.			l					
vd. central approx.					j			w

Vowels

high	ɪ			u
mid			"ə"	"o"
lower mid		ε		
low			a	

Language Ngizim (269)	bilabial	bilabial prenasalized	labio-dental	alveolar	alveolar prenasalized	palato-alveolar	palatal	palatal prenasalized	velar	velar labialized	velar prenasalized	vel. labialized & prenasalized	variable place	labial-velar
voiceless plos.	p			t			c		k	k^w				
voiced plosive	b	^mb		d	nd		ɟ	$^nɟ$	g	g^w	^ŋg	$^ŋg^w$		
laryng. vd. plos.	b̰			d̰			ɟ̰							
vl. nonsib. fric.			f										h	
vd. nonsib. fric.			v											
vl. sib. fric.				s		ʃ								
vd. sib. fric.				z		ʒ								
vl. lat. fric.				ɬ										
vd. lat. fric.				ɮ										
voiced nasal	m			n			ɲ							
voiced trill				r										
voiced flap				ɾ										
vd. lat. approx.				l										
vd. cent. approx.							j							w

Vowels

	short		long		
high	i	u			
mid			"e:"		"o:"
low		a		a:	

Language Kanakuru (270)	bilabial	alveolar	palato-alveolar	palatal	velar	labial-velar
voiceless plosive	p	t			k	
voiced plosive	b	d			g	
vd. implosive	ɓ	ɗ				
vd. nonsibilant fric.					ɣ	
vl. sibilant fric.			ʃ			
vd. sibilant fric.			ʒ			
vd. lateral fric.		ɮ				
voiced nasal	m	n		ɲ	ŋ	
vd. lateral approx.		l				
vd. central approx.		ɹ		j		w

Vowels

high	i				u
mid		"e"	"ə"	"o"	
low			a		

Language Mundari (300)	bilabial	dental	alveolar	palato-alveolar	retroflex	palatal	velar	glottal	variable place	labial-velar
voiceless plosive	p	t̪			ʈ		k	ʔ[4]		
vl. aspirated plos.	pʰ	t̪ʰ			ʈʰ		kʰ			
voiced plosive	b	d̪			ɖ		g			
breathy voiced plosive	b̤	d̪̤			ɖ̤		g̤			
vl. sibilant affric.				tʃ						
vl. aspirated sib. affric.				tʃʰ						
vd. sibilant affric.				dʒ						
breathy voiced sib. affric.				dʒ̤						
vl. nonsibilant fric.									h	
vl. sibilant fric.			s							
voiced nasal	m	n̪			ɳ		ŋ[4]			
voiced trill			r							
vd. lateral approx.		l̪			ɭ					
vd. central approx.						j				w

Vowels

high	ɩ			ʊ
mid		"e"	"o"	
low			a	

Language Kharia (301)	bilabial	dental	dental/alveolar	palato-alveolar	retroflex	palatal	velar	variable place	labial-velar
voiceless plosive	p	t̪			ʈ		k		
vl. aspirated plosive	pʰ	t̪ʰ			ʈʰ		kʰ		
voiced plosive	b	d̪			ɖ		g		
breathy voiced plosive	b̤	d̪̤			ɖ̤		g̤		
vl. sibilant affricate				tʃ					
vl. asp. sib. affricate				tʃʰ					
vd. sibilant affricate				dʒ					
breathy vd. sib. affricate				dʒ̤					
vd. nonsibilant fricative								ɦ	
vl. sibilant fricative			"s"						
voiced nasal	m		"n"			ɲ	ŋ		
voiced flap			"ɾ"		ɽ				
vd. lateral approximant			"l"						
vd. central approximant						j			w

Vowels

	oral				nasalized		
high	i			u	ĩ		ũ
higher mid	e						
mid			"o"				"õ"
lower mid					ɛ̃		
low		a				ã	

Language Khasi (302)	bilabial	dental/alveolar	palato-alveolar	retroflex	palatal	velar	glottal	variable place	labial-velar
voiceless plosive	p	"t"				k	?		
vl. aspirated plos.	p^h	"t^h"				k^h			
voiced plosive	b	"d"							
vd. sibilant affric.			dʒ						
vl. nonsibilant fric.								h	
vl. sibilant fric.		"s"	ʃ						
voiced nasal	m	"n"			ɲ	ŋ			
voiced trill		"r"							
vd. lateral approx.				ḷ					
vd. lowered cent. approx.					j̞				w̞

Vowels

	short		long
high	i	u	
mid	"e"	"o"	
low	a		a:

Language Vietnamese (303)	bilabial	labio-dental	dental/alveolar	alveolar	palatal	velar	glottal	variable place	labial-velar
voiceless plosive				t	c	k	?		
vl. aspirated plos.				t^h					
vd. implosive	ɓ			ɗ					
vl. nonsibilant fric.		f				x		h	
vd. nonsibilant fric.		v				ɣ			
vl. sibilant fric.				s					
vd. sibilant fric.				z					
voiced nasal	m		"n"		ɲ	ŋ			
vd. lateral approx.			"l"						
vd. central approx.					j				w
lower mid central approx.						ʌ̯			

Vowels

	short				long
high	ι			ɯ̟, ɷ	
higher mid	e		ɤ, o		
lower mid	ɛ	ʌ, ɔ			
low	æ				a:

Language	bilabial	bilabial prenasalized	dental/alveolar	dental/alv. prenasalized	palato-alveolar	palatal	velar	velar prenasalized	glottal	variable place	labial-velar
Sedang (304)											
voiceless plosive	p		"t"				k		ʔ		
vl. aspirated plosive	pʰ		"tʰ"				kʰ				
voiced plosive		ᵐb		"ⁿd"				ᵑg			
laryng. vd. plosive	b̰		"d̰"								
vl. sibilant affricate					tʃ						
vd. sibilant affricate					dʒ						
vl. nonsibilant fricative										h	
vl. sibilant fricative			"s"		ʃ						
voiced nasal	m		"n"			ɲ	ŋ				
laryngealized vd. nasal	m̰		"n̰"			ɲ̰	ŋ̰				
voiceless nasal	m̥		"n̥"			ɲ̥	ŋ̊				
voiced trill			"r"								
laryngealized vd. trill			"r̰"								
voiceless trill			"r̥"								
vd. lateral approximant			"l"								
laryngealized vd. lat. app.			"l̰"								
vl. lateral approximant			"l̥"								
vd. central approximant											w
laryngealized vd. cent. app.											w̰
voiceless central approximant											ʍ

Vowels

	plain				laryngealized			
high	i			u	ḭ			ṵ
higher mid		e	o			ḛ	o̰	
lower mid		ε	ɔ			ɛ̰	ɔ̰	
low		a				a̰		

Language	bilabial	labio-dental	dental/alveolar	dental/alv. velarized	palato-alveolar	retroflex	palatal	velar	glottal	variable place
Khmer (306)										
voiceless plosive	p		"t"					k	ʔ	
vl. aspirated plosive	pʰ		"tʰ"					kʰ		
vd. implosive	ɓ		"ɗ"							
vl. sibilant affricate					tʃ					
vl. asp. sib. affricate					tʃʰ					
vl. nonsibilant fricative										h
vl. sibilant fricative			"s"							
voiced nasal	m		"n"				ɲ	ŋ		
voiced flap						ɽ				
vd. lateral approximant				"ɫ"						
vd. central approximant		ʋ̯					j			

Vowels

	short			long		
high	ɩ		ɷ	iː	ɨː	uː
higher mid	ə			eː		oː
mid	"ə"			"əː"		
lower mid	ε	ɔ		εː	ɔː	
low	a̟	ɑ		a̟ː	ɑː	

<u>Language</u>

Maung (350)	bilabial	alveolar	retroflex	palatal	velar	dental-palatal
voiceless plosive	p	t	ʈ		k	t̪͡c
vd. nonsibilant fric.					ɣ	
voiced nasal	m	n	ɳ		ŋ	n̪͡ɲ
voiced trill		r				
voiced flap			ɽ			
vd. lateral approx.		l	ɭ			
vd. central approx.		ɹ		j		

<u>Vowels</u>

high	i					u
lower mid		ɛ			ɔ	
low				a		

<u>Language</u>

Tiwi (351)	bilabial	dental	alveolar	retroflex	palatal	velar	labial-velar
voiceless plosive	p	t̪	t	ʈ		k	
vd. nonsibilant fric.						ɣ[1]	
voiced nasal	m	n̪	n	ɳ		ŋ	
voiced tap			D				
vd. lateral approx.			l	ɭ			
vd. central approx.				ɻ	j		w

<u>Vowels</u>

high	i				u[1]
mid				"o"	
low			a		

Language	bilabial	dental/alveolar	alveolar	palatal	velar	labial-velar
Burera (352)						
voiceless plosive	p		t	c	k	
voiced nasal	m	"n"		ɲ	ŋ	
voiced flap			ɾ			
vd. lateral approx.			l			
vd. central approx.			ɹ	j		w
<u>Vowels</u>						
high	ɪ			u		
lower mid		ɛ	ɔ			
low		a				

Language	bilabial	dental	alvedar	palato-alveolar	retroflex	palatal	velar	labial-velar
Nunggubuyu (353)								
voiceless plosive	p	t̪	t	t̠	ʈ		k	
voiced nasal	m	n̪	n	n̠	ɳ		ŋ	
voiced trill			r					
vd. lateral approx.		l̪	l		ɭ			
vd. central					ɻ	j		w
<u>Vowels</u>								
high	ɪ		ɯ̶					
low		a						

Language	bilabial	bilabial prenasalized	alveolar	alveolar prenasalized	palato-alveolar	palato-alv. prenasalized	retroflex	retroflex prenasalized	palatal	velar	velar prenasalized	labial-velar
Alawa (354)												
voiced plosive	b	^{m}b	d	^{n}d	d̠	$^{\underline{n}}\underline{d}$	ḍ	$^{ṇ}ḍ$		g	^{ŋ}g	
voiced nasal	m		n		n̠		ṇ			ŋ		
voiced trill			r									
vd. lateral approx.			l		l̠		ḷ					
vd. central approx.			ɹ						j			w
Vowels												
high	ɩ			ɯ̶								
mid		"e"[1]										
low			a									

Language	bilabial	dental/alveolar	alveolar	palato-alveolar	palatal	velar	labial-velar
Maranungku (355)							
voiceless plosive	p	"t"				k	
long vl. plosive	p:	"t:"				k:	
vl. sibilant affric.				tʃ			
voiced nasal	m	"n"			ɲ	ŋ	
long voiced nasal	m:	"n:"					
voiced trill			r				
vd. lateral approx.		"l"					
vd. central approx.			ɹ		j		w
Vowels							
high	ɪ		ɷ				
mid		"ə"					
low		æ a					

Language	bilabial	alveolar	palato-alveolar	palatal	velar	labial-velar
Malakmalak (356)						
voiceless plosive	p	t	t̠		k	
voiced nasal	m	n	n̠		ŋ	
voiced trill		r				
vd. lateral approx.		l	l̠			
vd. central approx.		ɹ		j		w

Vowels

high	i		u
mid		"e" "ə" "o"	
low		a	

Language	bilabial	alveolar	palato-alveolar	retroflex	palatal	velar	labial-velar
Bardi (357)							
voiceless plosive	p	t	t̠	ṭ		k	
voiced nasal	m	n	n̠	ṇ		ŋ	
voiced trill		r					
vd. lateral approx.		l	l̠	ḷ			
vd. central approx.		ɹ			j		w

Vowels

	short			long		
high	i		u	iː		uː
lower mid		ɔ				
low		a			aː	

Language

Wik-Munkan (358)

	bilabial	dental/alveolar	palato-alveolar	palatal	velar	glottal	labial-velar
voiceless plosive	p	"t"	t̠		k	?	
voiced nasal	m	"n"	n̠		ŋ		
voiced trill		"r"					
vd. lateral approx.		"l"					
vd. central approx.				j			w

Vowels

	bilabial	dental/alveolar	palato-alveolar	palatal	velar	glottal	labial-velar
high	ɪ				ʊ		
lower mid		ɛ		ɔ			
low			a				

Language

Kunjen (359)

	bilabial	labio-dental	dental	alveolar	retroflex	palatal	velar	labial-velar
voiceless plosive	p		t̪	t		c	k	
vl. aspirated plos.	pʰ		t̪ʰ	tʰ		cʰ	kʰ	
vl. nonsibilant fric.		f						
vd. nonsibilant fric.			ð̆[1]				ɣ	
voiced nasal	m		n̪	n		ɲ	ŋ	
voiced trill				r				
vd. lateral approx.				l				
vd. central approx.					ɻ	j		w

Vowels

	bilabial	labio-dental	dental	alveolar	retroflex	palatal	velar	labial-velar
high	ɪ				u			
mid				"o"				
lower mid		ɛ						
low			a					

<u>Language</u>

Western Desert (360)	bilabial	dental	alveolar	retroflex	palatal	velar	labial-velar
voiceless plosive	p	t̪	t	ʈ		k	
voiced nasal	m	n̪	n	ɳ		ŋ	
voiced flap			ɾ				
vd. lateral approx.		l̪	l	ɭ			
vd. central approx.				ɻ	j		

<u>Vowels</u>

high	i		u
low		a	

<u>Language</u>

Nyangumata (361)	bilabial	alveolar	alveolar palatalized	retroflex	palatal	velar	labial-velar
voiceless plosive	p	t	t^j	ʈ		k	
voiced plosive						g	
voiced nasal	m	n	n^j	ɳ		ŋ	
voiced trill		r					
vd. lateral approximant		l	l^j	ɭ			
vd. central approximant				ɻ	j		w

<u>Vowels</u>

high	i		u
low		a	

Language	bilabial	bilabial nasally-released	dental	dental nasally-released	alveolar	alveolar nasally-released	palato-alveolar	palato-alv. nasally-released	retroflex	retroflex nasally-released	palatal	velar	velar nasally-released	labial-velar
Aranda (362)														
voiceless plosive	p		t̪		t		t̠		ṭ			k		
voiced plosive		b^{m}		d̪^{n}		d^{n}		d̠^{n}		ḍ^{n}			g^{ŋ}	
voiced nasal	m		n̪		n		n̠		ṇ				ŋ	
voiced flap					ɾ									
vd. lateral approx.			l̪		l		l̠		ḷ					
vd. central approx.									ɻ		j	ɣ̞		w
Vowels														
high	i		u											
low		a												

Language	bilabial	dental	dental/alveolar	alveolar	retroflex	palatal	velar	labial-velar
Kariera-Ngarluma (363)								
voiceless plosive	p	t̪		t	ṭ	c	k	
voiced nasal	m	n̪	"n"		ṇ	ɲ	ŋ	
voiced trill			"r"		ṛ			
vd. lateral approx.		l̪	"l"		ḷ	ʎ		
vd. central approx.					ɻ	j		w
Vowels								
high	i		u					
low		a						

Language	bilabial	dental/alveolar	retroflex	palatal	velar	labial-velar
Gugu-Yalanji (364)						
voiceless plosive	p	"t"		c	k	
voiced nasal	m	"n"		ɲ	ŋ	
voiced r-sound		"rr"				
vd. lateral approx.		"l"				
vd. central approx.			ɻ	j		w

Vowels

high	i		u
low		a	

Language	bilabial	dental/alveolar	palatal	velar	labial-velar
Mabuiag (365)					
voiceless plosive	p	"t"		k	
voiced plosive	b	"d"		g	
vl. sibilant fric.		"s"			
vd. sibilant fric.		"z"			
voiced nasal	m	"n"		ŋ	
voiced r-sound		"rr"			
vd. lateral approx.		"l"			
vd. central approx.			j		w

Vowels

high	i			u
mid		"e"	"o"	
low			a	

Language	bilabial	dental	alveolar	retroflex	palatal	velar	labial-velar
Arabana-Wanganura (366)							
voiceless plosive	p	t̪	t	ṭ	c	k	
voiced nasal	m	n̪	n	ṇ	ɲ	ŋ	
voiced trill			r	ṛ			
vd. lateral approx.		l̪	l	ḷ	ʎ		
vd. central approx.				ɹ̣	j		w

<u>Vowels</u>

high	i		u
low		a	

Language	bilabial	dental	alveolar	retroflex	palatal	velar	labial-velar
Diyari (367)							
voiceless plosive	p	t̪	t	ṭ	c	k	
voiced plosive			d	ḍ			
voiced nasal	m	n̪	n	ṇ	ɲ	ŋ	
voiced trill			r				
vd. lateral approx.		l̪	l	ḷ	ʎ		
vd. central approx.				ɹ̣	j		w

<u>Vowels</u>

high	i		u
low		a	

<u>Language</u>

Bandjalang (368)	bilabial	alveolar	palato-alveolar	palatal	velar	labial-velar
voiced plosive	b	d			g	
vd. sibilant affric.			dʒ			
voiced nasal	m	n	n̠		ŋ	
voiced trill		r				
vd. lateral approx.		l				
vd. central approx.				j		w

<u>Vowels</u>

high	ɪ			u
mid		"e"[1]		
low			a	

<u>Language</u>

Standard Thai (400)	bilabial	labio-dental	dental	dental/alveolar	alveolar	palatal	velar	glottal	variable place	labial-velar
voiceless plosive	p		t̪				k	ʔ		
vl. aspirated plos.	pʰ		t̪ʰ				kʰ			
voiced plosive	b		d̪							
vl. sibilant affric.			t̪s̪							
vl.asp. sib. affric.			t̪s̪ʰ							
vl. nonsibilant fric.		f							h	
vl. sibilant fric.			s̪							
voiced nasal	m		n̪				ŋ			
voiced flap					ɾ					
vd. lateral approx.				"l"						
vd. central approx.						j				w

<u>Vowels</u>

high	ɪ				ɨ			u
higher mid		e			ə		o	
lower mid						ɔ		
low			æ	a				

Language	bilabial	labio-dental	dental	dental/alveolar	palatal	velar	velar labialized	velar palatalized	glottal	variable place	labial-velar
Lakkia (401)											
voiceless plosive	p			"t"		k	kʷ		?		
vl. aspirated plosive	pʰ			"tʰ"		kʰ	kʷʰ	kʲʰ			
laryngealized vd. plosive	b̰										
vl. sibilant affricate				"ts"							
vl. asp. sib. affricate				"tsʰ"							
vl. nonsibilant fricative		f	θ							h	
vl. lateral fricative				"ɬ"							
voiced nasal	m			"n"		ŋ	ŋʷ	ŋʲ			
voiceless nasal	m̥			"n̥"				ŋ̊ʲ			
vd. lateral approximant				"l"							
vd. central approximant	β̰				"j"						w
vl. central approximant					"j̊"						ʍ

Vowels

	short oral			long oral			Diphthongs
high	i		u	i:		u:	ie
higher mid	e						uo
lower mid	ε			ε:	ɔ:		ĩe
low		a			a:		

	short nasalized			long nasalized		
high			ũ	ĩ:		ũ:
higher mid			õ			
lower mid	ε̃			ε̃:	ɔ̃:	
low		ã			ã:	

Language	bilabial	labio-dental	dental	dental/alveolar	palatal	velar	glottal	variable place
Yay (402)								
voiceless plosive	p			"t"	c	k	?	
vl. aspirated plos.	pʰ			"tʰ"	cʰ	kʰ		
voiced plosive	b			"d"				
vl. nonsibilant fric.		f	θ					h
vd. nonsibilant fric.		v						
vl. sibilant fric.				"s"				
voiced nasal	m			"n"	ɲ	ŋ		
voiced r-sound				"rr"				
vd. lateral approx.				"l"				
vd. central approx.					j			

Vowels

	short			long
high	i	ʉ	u	
mid		"ə"		
lower mid	ε		ɔ	
low		a		a:

Language	bilabial	dental/alveolar	alveolar	palato-alveolar	palatal	velar	uvular	glottal	variable place	labial-velar
Sui (403)										
voiceless plosive	p	"t"				k	q	?		
vl. aspirated plos.	pʰ	"tʰ"				kʰ	qʰ			
voiced plosive	b	"d"								
laryngealized vd. plos.	b̰	"d̰"								
vl. sibilant affric.			ts	tʃ						
vl. asp. sib. affric.			tsʰ	tʃʰ						
vl. nonsibilant fric.	ɸ					x			h	
vd. nonsibilant fric.						ɣ	ʁ			
laryng. vd. nonsib. fric.						ɣ̰				
vl. sibilant fric.		"s"								
vd. sibilant fric.		"z"								
voiced nasal	m	"n"			ɲ	ŋ				
voiceless nasal	m̥	"n̥"			ɲ̥	ŋ̊				
laryngealized vd. nas.	m̰	"n̰"			ɲ̰	ŋ̰				
vd. lateral approx.		"l"								
vd. central approx.					j					w
laryng. vd. cent. approx.					j̰					w̰

Vowels					
high	i				u
mid		"e"	"ə"	"o"	
lower mid			3		
low			a		

Language	bilabial	labio-dental	alveolar	palatal	velar	glottal	variable place
Saek (404)							
voiceless plosive	p		t		k	?	
vl. aspirated plosive	pʰ		tʰ		kʰ		
voiced plosive	b		d				
vl. nonsibilant affricate				cç			
vl. nonsibilant fricative							h
vd. nonsibilant fricative		v			ɣ		
vl. sibilant fricative			s				
voiced nasal	m		n	ɲ	ŋ		
vd. lateral approximant			l				
vd. central approximant			ɹ	j			

Vowels						Diphthongs
high	i		ɨ		u	ia
higher mid	e			o		ɨa
mid			"ə"			ua
lower mid		ɛ		ɔ		
low			a			

Language	bilabial	labio-dental	dental/alveolar	palato-alveolar	palatal	velar	glottal	variable place
Po-Ai (405)								
voiceless plosive	p		"t"			k	?	
vl. aspirated plosive	p^{h2}		$"t^{h}"^{2}$			k^{h2}		
vl. sibilant affricate				tʃ				
vl. asp. sib. affricate				$tʃ^{h2}$				
vl. nonsibilant fricative		f						h
vd. nonsibilant fricative		v						
vl. sibilant fricative				ʃ				
vl. lateral fricative			"ɬ"					
voiced nasal	m		"n"			ŋ		
vd. lateral approximant			"l"					
vd. central approximant						j		

Vowels

	short			long			Diphthong
high	i	ɨ	u	i:		u:	aɨ
higher mid	e					o:	
mid		ə					
lower mid	ɛ		ɔ	ɛ:		ɔ:	
low		a			a:		

Language	bilabial	labio-dental	dental/alveolar	palato-alveolar	palatal	velar	glottal	variable place
Lungchow (406)								
voiceless plosive	p		"t"			k	?	
vl. aspirated plosive	p^{h}		$"t^{h}"$			k^{h}		
laryngealized vd. plosive	b̰		"d̰"					
vl. sibilant affricate				tʃ				
vd. sibilant affricate				$tʃ^{h}$				
vl. nonsibilant fricative		f						h
vd. nonsibilant fricative		v						
vl. sibilant fricative				ʃ				
vl. lateral fricative			"ɬ"					
voiced nasal	m		"n"			ŋ		
vd. lateral approximant			"l"					
vd. central approximant					j			

Vowels

	short			overshort			Diphthong
high	i		u, ɯ	ĭ		ŭ, ɯ̆	ua
mid	"e"		"o"				
low		a			ă		

Language	bilabial	dental/alveolar	palato-alveolar	palatal	velar	uvular	pharyngeal	glottal	labial-velar
Atayal (407)									
voiceless plosive	p	"t"			k	q		?	
vl. sibilant affric.		"ts"							
vl. nonsibilant fric.					x		ħ		
vd. nonsibilant fric.	β				ɣ				
vl. sibilant fric.		"s"							
vd. sibilant fric.			ʒ[1]						
voiced nasal	m	"n"			ŋ				
voiced r-sound		"rr"							
vd. central approx.				j[4]					w[4]

Vowels

	short					long	
high	i				u	i:	u:
lower mid		ɛ		ɔ			
low			a				

Language	bilabial	dental	dental/alveolar	alveolar	palato-alveolar	palatal	velar	glottal	variable place	labial-velar
Sundanese (408)										
voiceless plosive	p	t̪					k	?		
voiced plosive	b			d			g			
vl. sibilant affric.					tʃ					
vd. sibilant affric.					dʒ					
vl. nonsibilant fric.									h	
vl. sibilant fric.				s						
voiced nasal	m		"n"			ɲ	ŋ			
voiced trill			"r"							
vd. lateral approx.			"l"							
vd. central approx.						j				w

Vowels

high	i	ɨ		u
mid		"ə"	"o"	
lower mid		ɛ		
low		a		

Language	bilabial	dental	dental/alveolar	alveolar	palatal	velar	glottal	variable place	labial-velar
Javanese (409)									
voiceless plosive	p	t̪		t		k	ʔ		
vl. plos. w/breathy release	pʱ	t̪ʱ		tʱ		kʱ			
vl. sibilant affricate				ts					
vl. sib. affr. w/breathy release				tsʱ					
vl. nonsibilant fricative								h	
vl. sibilant fricative		s̪							
voiced nasal	m		"n"		ɲ	ŋ			
voiced trill				r					
vd. lateral approximant			"l"						w
vd. central approximant					j				

Vowels

high	i						u
higher mid		e				o	
mid				"ə"			
lower mid			ɛ		ɔ		
low				a			

Language	bilabial	labio-dental	dental	dental/alveolar	retroflex	palatal	velar	variable place	labial-velar
Malagasy (410)									
voiceless plosive	p		t̪				k		
voiced plosive	b		d̪				g		
vl. sibilant affric.			t̪s̪						
vd. sibilant affric.			d̪z̪						
vl. nonsibilant fric.		f						h	
vd. nonsibilant fric.		v							
vl. sibilant fric.				"s"					
vd. sibilant fric.				"z"					
voiced nasal	m			"n"					
voiced trill				"r"					
vl. affricated trill					ṭř̥				
vd. affricated trill					ḍř				
vd. lateral approx.				"l"					
vd. central approx.						j			w

Vowels

high	i			
higher mid				o
mid		"e"		
low			a	

Language	bilabial	dental/alveolar	palato-alveolar	retroflex	palatal	velar	glottal	variable place	labial-velar
Cham (411)									
voiceless plosive	p	"t"		ʈ	c	k	?		
vl. aspirated plos.	p^h	"t^h"		$ʈ^h$	c^h	k^h			
voiced plosive	b	"d"							
vl. nonsibilant fric.								h	
vl. sibilant fric.			ʃ	ʂ					
voiced nasal	m	"n"			ɲ	ŋ			
voiced r-sound		"rr"							
vd. lateral approx.		"l"							
vd. central approx.					j				w

Vowels

high	ɪ	ɨ	u
higher mid	e		o
mid		"ə"	
lower mid	ɛ		ɔ
low		a	

Language	bilabial	dental/alveolar	palatal	velar	variable place
Malay (412)					
voiceless plosive	p	"t"	c	k	
voiced plosive	b	"d"	ɟ	g	
vl. nonsibilant fric.					h
vl. sibilant fric.		"s"			
voiced nasal	m	"n"	ɲ	ŋ	
voiced trill		"r"			
vd. lateral approx.		"l"			

Vowels

high	ɪ		u
higher mid	e		o
mid		"ə"	
low		a	

Language	bilabial	dental/alveolar	palato-alveolar	palatal	velar	uvular	variable place	labial-velar
Batak (413)								
voiceless plosive	p	"t"			k			
voiced plosive	b	"d"			g			
vd. sibilant affric.			dʒ					
vl. nonsibilant fric.							h	
vl. sibilant fric.		"s"						
voiced nasal	m	"n"			ŋ			
voiced trill						ʀ[5]		
vd. lateral approx.		"l"						
vd. central approx.				j				w
Vowels								
high	i						u	
mid						"o"		
lower mid			ε					
low				a				

Language	bilabial	dental/alveolar	palatal	velar	glottal	variable place	labial-velar
Tagalog (414)							
voiceless plosive	p	"t"			?		
voiced plosive	b	"d"		g			
vl. sibilant affric.		"ts"					
vl. nonsibilant fric.						h	
vl. sibilant fric.		"s"					
voiced nasal	m	"n"		ŋ			
vd. lateral approx.		"l"					
vd. central approx.			j				w
Vowels							
high	ι	o					
mid		"ə"					

Language	bilabial	alveolar	palato-alveolar	palatal	velar	glottal	variable place	labial-velar
Sa'ban (415)								
voiceless plosive	p	t			k	?		
voiced plosive	b	d			g			
vl. sibilant affricate			tʃ					
vd. sibilant affricate			dʒ					
vl. nonsibilant fricative							h	
vl. sibilant fricative		s						
voiced nasal	m	n		ɲ	ŋ			
voiced flap		ɾ̪						
vd. lateral approximant		l						
vd. central approximant				j				w

Vowels

	short			long
high	i	ɨ	u	
mid		"ə"		
lower mid	ɛ		ɔ	
low		a		a:

Language	bilabial	labio-dental	dental/alveolar	alveolar	retroflex	palatal	velar	glottal	variable place	labial-velar
Chamorro (416)										
voiceless plosive	p			t			k	?		
voiced plosive	b			d			g			
vl. sibilant affric.				ts						
vd. sibilant affric.				dz						
vl. nonsibilant fric.		f							h	
vl. sibilant fric.			"s"							
voiced nasal	m			n		ɲ	ŋ			
vd. lateral approx.				l						
vd. central approx.					ɻ	j				w

Vowels

high	ɪ		u
mid	"e"	"o"	
low	æ	ɑ	

Language	bilabial	labio-dental	dental	alveolar	retroflex	palatal	velar	glottal	variable place	labial-velar
Rukai (417)										
voiceless plosive	p		t̪		ṭ		k	?		
voiced plosive	b		d̪		ḍ		g			
vl. sibilant affric.				ts						
vl. nonsibilant fric.			θ						h	
vd. nonsibilant fric.		v	ð							
vl. sibilant fric.				s						
voiced nasal	m			n			ŋ			
voiced trill				r						
vd. lateral approx.				l	ḷ					
vd. central approx.						j				w

Vowels

high	i	ɨ	u
low		a	

Language	bilabial	labio-dental	dental/alveolar	velar	glottal	variable place
Tsou (418)						
voiceless plosive	p		"t"	k	?	
voiced plosive	b					
vl. sibilant affricate			"ts"			
vl. nonsibilant fricative		f				h
vd. nonsibilant fricative		v				
vl. sibilant fricative			"s"			
vd. sibilant fricative			"z"			
voiced nasal	m		"n"	ŋ		
vd. lateral approximant			"l"			

Vowels

				Diphthongs
high	i	ʉ	u	eʉ
mid	"e"	"o"		eo
low		a		ea

Language	bilabial	labio-dental	dental/alveolar	palatal	velar	glottal	variable place
Adzera (419)							
voiceless plosive						?	
vl. aspirated plosive	p^h		"t^h"		k^h		
voiced plosive	b		"d"		g		
vl. asp. sib. affricate			"ts^h"				
vd. sibilant affricate			"dʒ"				
vl. nonsibilant fricative		f					h
vl. sibilant fricative			"s"				
voiced nasal	m		"n"		ŋ		
voiced trill			"r"				
vd. central approximant				j	ɣ̑		

Vowels

	short			long		
high	i		ɯ	i:		
mid		"o"				"o:"
low		a			a:	

Language	bilabial	dental	velar	glottal	variable place
Roro (420)					
voiceless plosive	p	t̪	k	?	
voiced plosive	b				
vl. nonsibilant fric.					h
voiced nasal	m	n̪			
voiced flap		ɾ̪			

Vowels

high	i				u
mid		"e"		"o"	
low			a		

Language	bilabial	dental/alveolar	alveolar	retroflex	velar	variable place	labial-velar
Kaliai (421)							
voiceless plosive	p	"t"			k		
voiced plosive	b[1]	"d"[1]			g[1]		
vl. nonsibilant fric.						h	
vd. nonsibilant fric.	β						
vl. sibilant fric.		"s"					
voiced nasal	m	"n"			ŋ		
voiced trill			r				
voiced flap				ɽ			
vd. lateral approx.		"l"					
vl. central approx.							ʍ

Vowels

high	i		u
mid	"e"		"o"
low		a	

Language	bilabial	labio-dental	dental	dental/alveolar	alveolar	palato-alveolar	retroflex	palatal	velar	variable place	labial-velar
Iai (422)											
voiceless plosive	p			"t"			ʈ		k		
voiced plosive	b			"d"			ɖ		g		g͡b
vl. sibilant affricate						tʃ					
vd. sibilant affricate						dʒ					
vl. nonsibilant affricate	ɸ	f	θ						x	h	
vd. nonsibilant affricate	β		ð								
vl. sibilant fricative				"s"		ʃ					
voiced nasal	m			"n"			ɳ	ɲ	ŋ		ŋ͡m
voiceless nasal	m̥						ɳ̊	ɲ̊	ŋ̊		ŋ̊͡m
vd. lateral approximant							ɭ				
vl. lateral approximant							ɭ̊				
vd. central approximant					ɹ						w
vl. central approximant											ʍ

Vowels

	short		long	
high	i, y	u	iː	uː
higher mid	e	o	eː	oː
lower mid	ɛ, œ	ɔ	ɛː	ɔː
low	æ		æː	

Language	bilabial	labio-dental	dental	alveolar	velar	variable place	labial-velar
Maori (423)							
voiceless plosive	p		t̪		k		
vl. nonsibilant fric.		f				h	
voiced nasal	m			n	ŋ		
voiced trill				r			
vd. central approx.							w
Vowels							
high	i				u		
mid				"o"			
lower mid		ε					
low				ɑ			

Language	bilabial	dental/alveolar	velar	glottal	variable place	labial-velar
Hawaiian (424)						
voiceless plosive	p		k	?		
vl. nonsibilant fric.					h	
voiced nasal	m	"n"				
vd. lateral approx.		"l"				
vd. central approx.						w
Vowels						
high	i		u			
mid			"o"			
lower mid		ε				
low		a				

Language	bilabial	labio-dental	dental/alveolar	alveolar	retroflex	palatal	velar	uvular	labial-palatal	labial-velar
Mandarin (500)										
voiceless plosive	p		"t"				k			
vl. aspirated plos.	p^h		"t^h"				k^h			
vl. sibilant affric.			"ts"		ʈʂ					
vl. asp. sib. affric.			"ts^h"		$ʈʂ^h$					
vl. nonsibilant affric.						cç				
vl. asp. nonsib. affric.						$cç^h$				
vl. nonsibilant fric.		f				ç		χ		
vl. sibilant fric.			"s"		ʂ					
vd. sibilant fric.					ʐ					
voiced nasal	m			n			ŋ			
vd. lateral approx.			"l"							
vd. central approx.						j			ɥ	w

Vowels

high	i, y				u
higher mid				ɤ	
mid			"$ə^r$"[4]		
low			a, a^r[4]		

Language	bilabial	labio-dental	dental/alveolar	palato-alveolar	palatal	velar	velar labialized	variable place	labial-velar
Taishan (501)									
voiceless plosive	p		"t"			k	k^w		
vl. aspirated plosive	p^h		"t^h"			k^h	k^{wh}		
vl. sibilant affricate				tʃ					
vl. asp. sib. affricate				$tʃ^h$					
vl. nonsibilant fricative		f						h	
vl. sibilant fricative				ʃ					
vl. lateral fricative			"ɬ"						
voiced nasal	m		"n"			ŋ			
vd. lateral approximant			"l"						
vd. central approximant					j				w

Vowels

high	i		u
lower mid			ɔ
low	æ	a	

<u>Language</u>

Hakka (502)	bilabial	bilabial prenasalized	labio-dental	dental/alveolar	dental/alv. prenasalized	velar	velar prenasalized	variable place	labial-velar
voiceless plosive	p			"t"		k			
vl. aspirated plos.	pʰ			"tʰ"		kʰ			
voiced plosive		ᵐb			ⁿd		ᵑg		
vl. sibilant affric.				"ts"					
vl. asp. sib. affric.				"tsʰ"					
vl. nonsibilant fric.			f					h	
vl. sibilant fric.				"s"					
vd. lateral approx.				"l"					
vd. central approx.									w

<u>Vowels</u>

high	i			u
lower mid		ɛ	ɔ	
low		æ[4] a		

<u>Language</u>

Changchow (503)	bilabial	labio-dental	dental/alveolar	palatal	velar	glottal	variable place	labial-velar
voiceless plosive	p		"t"		k	ʔ		
vl. aspirated plos.	pʰ		"tʰ"		kʰ			
vl. plos. w. breathy rel.	pʱ		"tʱ"		kʱ			
vl. sibilant affric.			"ts"					
vl. asp. sib. affric.			"tsʰ"					
vl. sib. af./breathy rel.			"tsʱ"					
vl. nonsibilant fric.		f					h	
vd. nonsibilant fric.		v					ɦ	
vl. sibilant fric.			"s"					
vd. sibilant fric.			"z"					
voiced nasal	m		"n"		ŋ			
vd. lateral approx.			"l"					
vd. central approx.				j				w

<u>Vowels</u>

	oral			nasalized	
high	i, y		u	ĩ	
mid		"ə" "o"			"õ"
low		æ a			

<u>Language</u>

Amoy (504)	bilabial	dental/alveolar	palato-alveolar	velar	glottal	variable place
voiceless plosive	p	"t"		k	?	
vl. aspirated plos.	pʰ	"tʰ"		kʰ		
voiced plosive	b	"d"		g		
vl. sibilant affric.		"ts"				
vl. asp. sib. affric.		"tsʰ"				
vd. sibilant affric.		"dz"	dʒ			
vl. nonsibilant fric.						h
vl. sibilant fric.		"s"				
voiced nasal	m	"n"		ŋ		

<u>Vowels</u>

high	i		u
higher mid	e		o
lower mid			ɔ
low		a	

<u>Language</u>

Fuchow (505)	bilabial	dental/alveolar	velar
voiceless plosive	p	"t"	k
vl. aspirated plos.	pʰ	"tʰ"	kʰ
vl. sibilant affric.		"ts"	
vl. asp. sib. affric.		"tsʰ"	
vl. nonsibilant fric.			x
vl. sibilant fric.		"s"	
voiced nasal	m	"n"	ŋ
vd. lateral approx.		"l"	

<u>Vowels</u>

high	i, y		u
lower mid	ε, œ		ɔ
low		a	

Language Kan (506)	bilabial	dental/alveolar	retroflex	palatal	velar	variable place
voiceless plosive	p	"t"			k	
vl. aspirated plos.	pʰ	"tʰ"			kʰ	
vl. sibilant affric.		"ts"				
vl. asp. sib. affric.		"tsʰ"				
vl. nonsibilant affric.				cç		
vl. asp. nonsib. affric.				cçʰ		
vl. nonsibilant fric.	ɸ			ç		h
vl. sibilant fric.		"s"				
voiced nasal	m	"n"		ɲ	ŋ	
vd. lateral approx.		"l"				
vd. central approx.			ɻ			

Vowels

high	ı, y				u
mid			"ə"	"o"	
lower mid		ɛ			
low			a		

Language Tamang (507)	bilabial	dental	alveolar	palatal	velar	variable place	labial-velar
voiceless plosive	p	t̪			k		
vl. aspirated plos.	pʰ	t̪ʰ			kʰ		
vl. sibilant affric.		t̪s̪					
vl. asp. sib.affric.		t̪s̪ʰ					
vl. nonsibilant affric.			tǰ̥				
vd. nonsibilant affric.			dǰ				
vl. nonsibilant fric.						h	
vl. sibilant fric.		s̪					
voiced nasal	m	n̪			ŋ		
voiced trill		r̪					
vd. lateral approx.		l̪					
vd. central approx.				j			w

Vowels

	plain					breathy				
high	ı				u	ı̤				ṳ
higher mid		e		o			e̤		o̤	
low			a					a̤		

Language	bilabial	dental	dental/alveolar	alveolar	palatal	velar	variable place
Dafla (508)							
voiceless plosive	p		"t"			k	
voiced plosive	b		"d"			g	
vd. nonsibilant fric.						x	ɦ
vl. sibilant fric.			"s"				
voiced nasal	m		"n"			ŋ	
voiced trill				r			
vd. lateral approx.		l̪					
vd. central approx.					j		

Vowels	voiced			voiceless	
high	i		u, ɯ	i̥	u̥
lower mid	ɛ	ɔ, ʌ			
low		ɑ			

Language	bilabial	dental	dental/alveolar	palato-alveolar	palatal	velar	glottal	variable place	labial-velar
Burmese (509)									
voiceless plosive	p		"t"			k	ʔ		
vl. aspirated plos.	pʰ		"tʰ"			kʰ			
voiced plosive	b		"d"			g			
vl. sibilant affric.				tʃ					
vl. asp. sib. affric.				tʃʰ					
vd. sibilant affric.				dʒ					
vl. nonsibilant fric.		θ						h	
vd. nonsibilant fric.		ð							
vl. sibilant fric.			"s"	ʃ					
vl. asp. sib. fric.			"sʰ"						
vd. sibilant fric.			"z"						
voiced nasal	m		"n"		ɲ	ŋ			
voiceless nasal	m̥		"n̥"		ɲ̊	ŋ̊			
vd. lateral approx.			"l"						
vl. lateral approx.			"l̥"						
vd. central approx.					j				w
vl. central approx.									ʍ[1]

Vowels	oral				nasalized			Diphthongs
high	i			u	ĩ		ʊ̃	ẽĩ
higher mid	e			o				õũ
mid		"ə"						
lower mid		ɛ	ɔ					
low		a				æ̃		

Language Lahu (510)	bilabial	labio-dental	dental/alveolar	palato-alveolar	palatal	velar	uvular	glottal	variable place	labial-velar
voiceless plosive	p		"t"			k	q	ʔ[1]		
vl. aspirated plos.	pʰ		"tʰ"			kʰ	qʰ			
voiced plosive	b		"d"			g				
vl. sibilant affric.				tʃ						
vl. asp. sib. affric.				tʃʰ						
vd. sibilant affric.				dʒ						
vl. nonsibilant fric.		f							h	
vd. nonsibilant fric.		v				ɣ				
vl. sibilant fric.				ʃ						
voiced nasal	m		"n"			ŋ				
vd. lateral approx.			"l"							
vd. central approx.					j					w[2]

Vowels

high	i			ɨ			u
higher mid		e		ə		o	
mid			"e"				
lower mid					ɔ		
low				a			

Language Jingpho (511)	bilabial	dental/alveolar	palato-alveolar	palatal	velar	glottal	variable place	labial-velar
voiceless plosive	p	"t"			k	ʔ		
vl. aspirated plos.	pʰ	"tʰ"			kʰ			
voiced plosive	b	"d"			g			
vl. sibilant affric.		"ts"	tʃ					
vl. asp. sib. affric.			tʃʰ[1]					
vd. sibilant affric.		"dz"	dʒ					
vl. nonsibilant fric.							h	
vl. sibilant fric.		"s"	ʃ					
voiced nasal	m	"n"			ŋ			
voiced r-sound		"rr"						
vd. lateral approx.		"l"						
vd. central approx.				j				w

Vowels

high	i				u
mid		"e"		"o"	
low			a		

Language	bilabial	alveolar	retroflex	palatal	velar	glottal	labial-velar
Ao (512)							
voiceless plosive	p	t			k	?	
vl. nonsibilant affric.				cç			
vl. sibilant fric.		s					
vd. sibilant fric.		z					
vd. lateral fric.			ɭ̣				
voiced nasal	m	n			ŋ		
vd. lateral approx.		l					
vd. central approx.				j			w

Vowels

high	i				u, ɯ
higher mid		e		o	
low			a		

Language	bilabial	labio-dental	alveolar	velar	glottal	variable place	labial-velar
Tiddin Chim (513)							
voiceless plosive	p		t	k	?		
vl. aspirated plos.	pʰ		tʰ				
voiced plosive	b		d	g			
vl. sibilant affric.			ts				
vl. nonsibilant fric.				x		h	
vd. nonsibilant fric.		v					
vl. sibilant fric.			s				
vd. sibilant fric.			z				
voiced nasal	m		n	ŋ			
vd. lateral approx.			l				
laryng. vd. lat. approx.			l̰				
laryng. vd. cent. approx.							w̰

Vowels

high	i				u
lower mid		ɛ		ɔ	
low			a		

Language Garo (514)	bilabial	dental	alveolar	velar	glottal	variable place	labial-velar
voiceless plosive	p	t̪		k	ʔ		
voiced plosive	b	d̪		g			
vl. sibilant affric.			ts				
vd. sibilant affric.			dz				
vl. nonsibilant fric.						h	
vl. sibilant fric.			s				
voiced nasal	m	n̪		ŋ			
voiced flap			ɾ				
vd. central approx.							w

Vowels

high	i		u
higher mid	e		o
low		a	

Language Boro (515)	bilabial	alveolar	palatal	velar	variable place
voiceless plosive	p	t		k	
voiced plosive	b	d		g	
vl. nonsibilant fric.					h
vl. sibilant fric.		s			
vd. sibilant fric.		z			
voiced nasal	m	n		ŋ	
voiced flap		ɾ			
vd. lateral approx.		l			
vd. central approx.			j		

Vowels

high	i		u
mid	"e"	"ə"	"o"
low		a	

Language Karen (516)	bilabial	dental	dental/alveolar	alveolar	palato-alveolar	palatal	velar	glottal	variable place	labial-velar
voiceless plosive	p		"t"			c[1]	k	ʔ		
vl. aspirated plos.	pʰ		"tʰ"			cʰ[1]	kʰ			
voiced implosive	ɓ		"ɗ"							
vl. nonsibilant fric.		θ					x		ɦ[1]	
vd. nonsibilant fric.							ɣ			
vl. sibilant fric.			"s"		ʃ[1]					
vl. asp. sib. fric.			"sʰ"							
vd. sibilant fric.			"z"[1]							
voiced nasal	m		"n"			ɲ[1]	ŋ[1]			
vd. lateral approx.				l						
vd. central approx.				ɹ		j				w

Vowels

Karen vowels	1	2	3	4	5	6	7
high	i			ɨ			u
higher mid		e				o	
lower mid			ɛ, ɛ̰		ɔ		
low				a			

Language Yao (517)	bilabial	labio-dental	dental	dental/alveolar	palatal	velar	glottal	variable place	labial-velar
voiceless plosive	p		t̪		c	k	ʔ		
vl. aspirated plos.	pʰ		t̪ʰ		cʰ	kʰ			
voiced plosive	b		d̪		ɟ	g			
vl. sibilant affric.				"ts"					
vl. asp. sib. affric.				"tsʰ"					
vd. sibilant affric.				"dz"					
vl. nonsibilant fric.		f						h	
vl. sibilant fric.				"s"					
voiced nasal	m	n̪			ɲ	ŋ			
voiceless nasal	m̥	n̪̊			ɲ̊	ŋ̊			
vd. lateral approx.				"l"					
vl. lateral approx.				"l̥"					
vd. central approx.					j				w
vl. central approx.					j̊				ʍ

Vowels

Yao vowels	short							long
high	i						u	
higher mid		e				o		
lower mid					ɔ			
low			æ	a				a:

Language	bilabial	dental/alveolar	palato-alveolar	palatal	velar	labial-velar
Andamanese (600)						
voiceless plosive	p	"t"			k	
voiced plosive	b	"d"			g	
vl. sibilant affric.			tʃ			
vd. sibilant affric.			dʒ			
voiced nasal	m	"n"		ɲ	ŋ	
vd. lateral approx.		"l"				
vd. central approx.		"ɹ"		j		w

<u>Vowels</u>

high	i			u
mid	"e"			"o"
lower mid		ε	ɔ	
low		æ	a	

Language	bilabial	labio-dental	alveolar	palato-alveolar	palatal	velar	labial-velar
Asmat (601)							
voiceless plosive	p		t			k	
vl. sibilant affric.				tʃ			
vl. nonsibilant fric.		f			ǰ		
vl. sibilant fric.			s				
voiced nasal	m		n				
voiced flap			ɾ[1]				
vd. central approx.							w

<u>Vowels</u>

high	i			u
higher mid	e			
mid		"ə"		
lower mid			ɔ	
low		a		

Language	bilabial	bilabial labialized	bilabial prenasalized	bilab. labialized & prenas.	alveolar	alveolar prenasalized	palato-alveolar	palato-alv. prenasalized	palatal	velar	velar labialized	velar prenasalized	vel. labialized & prenasalized	glottal	variable place	labial-velar
Washkuk (602)																
voiceless plosive					t					k	kʷ			ʔ		
voiced plosive			ᵐb	ᵐbʷ		ⁿd						ŋg	ŋgʷ			
vl. sibilant affric.							tʃ									
vd. sibilant affric.								ⁿdʒ								
vl. nonsib. fric.	ɸ	ɸʷ													h	
vd. nonsib. fric.	β															
vl. sibilant fric.					s		ʃ									
voiced nasal	m	mʷ			n				ɲ							
voiced flap					ɾ											
vd. central approx.									j							w

Vowels

high	i			ɨ		u
higher mid		e				
mid					"o"	
lower mid			ɛ			
low				a		

Language	bilabial	labio-dental	dental/alveolar	palatal	velar	variable place	labial-velar
Sentani (603)							
voiceless plosive	p		"t"		k		
voiced plosive			"d"				
vl. nonsibilant fric.		f				h	
voiced nasal	m		"n"				
vd. central approx.				j			w

Vowels

high	i					u
higher mid		e				
mid				"ə"		
lower mid			ɛ		ɔ	
low			a̟			

Language				
Nimboran (604)	bilabial	dental	velar	variable place
voiceless plosive	p	t̪	k	
voiced plosive	b	d̪	g	
vl. nonsibilant fric.				h
vl. sibilant fric.		s̪		
voiced nasal	m	n̪	ŋ	
voiced r-sound		r̪r̪		

<u>Vowels</u>

high	i	ɨ	ɯ
mid	"e"		"ɤ"
low		a	

Language						
Iwam (605)	bilabial	alveolar	palatal	velar	variable place	labial-velar
voiceless plosive	p	t		k		
vl. nonsibilant fric.					h	
vl. sibilant fric.		s				
voiced nasal	m	n		ŋ		
voiced r-sound		rr				
vd. central approx.			j			w

<u>Vowels</u>

high	i		u
mid	"e"	"ə"	"o"
low		a	

Language	bilabial	labio-dental	dental/alveolar	palatal	velar	velar labialized	labial-velar
Telefol (606)							
voiceless plosive	p^2		"t"		k	k^w	
voiced plosive	b		$"d"^2$		g^2		
vl. nonsibilant fric.		f					
vl. sibilant fric.			"s"				
voiced nasal	m		"n"		ŋ		
vd. lateral approx.			"l"				
vd. central approx.				j			w

Vowels

	short			long		
high	i		u	iː		uː
lower mid				ɛː		ɔː
low		a			aː	

Language	bilabial	bilabial prenasalized	dental	dental prenasalized	alveolar	palatal	velar	velar prenasalized	variable place	labial-velar
Selepet (607)										
vl. aspirated plos.	p^h		$t̪^h$				k^h			
voiced plosive		^mb		$^nd̪$				^ŋg		
vl. nonsibilant fric.									h	
vl. sibilant fric.					s					
voiced nasal	m		n̪				ŋ			
voiced flap					ɾ					
vd. lateral approx.					l					
vd. central approx.						j				w

Vowels

high	i					u
higher mid					o	
lower mid		ɛ				
low			a	♀		

Language Gadsup (608)	bilabial	dental/alveolar	alveolar	palatal	velar	glottal
voiceless plosive	p		t		k	?
voiced plosive			d			
vd. nonsibilant fric.	β					
voiced nasal	m	"n"				
vd. central approx.				j		

Vowels	short			long	
high	i		u		
higher mid				e:	o:
lower mid		ε			
low				a̟:	

Language Yagaria (609)	bilabial	labio-dental	alveolar	palatal	velar	glottal	variable place
voiceless plosive	p		t		k	?	
voiced plosive	b		d		g		
vl. nonsibilant fric.							h
vd. nonsibilant fric.		v					
vl. sibilant fric.			s				
voiced nasal	m		n				
vd. lateral approx.					ǥ		
vd. central approx.				j			

Vowels						Diphthongs
high	i				u	εi
mid				"o"		ae
lower mid		ε				ao
low			a			ou

Language

Kewa (610)	bilabial	bilabial prenasalized	alveolar	alveolar prenasalized	palatal	velar	labial-velar
voiceless plosive			t		c		
voiced plosive		^{m}b		^{n}d		g	
vl. nonsibilant fric.	Φ					x	
vl. sibilant fric.			s				
voiced nasal	m		n		ɲ		
voiced flap			ɾ				
voiced lateral flap			ɺ				
vd. central approx.					j		w

Vowels

high	i			u
mid		"e"	"o"	
low			a	

Language

Chuave (611)	bilabial	labio-dental	alveolar	palatal	velar	labial-velar
voiceless plosive			t		k	
voiced plosive	b		d		g	
vl. nonsibilant fric.		f				
vl. sibilant fric.			s			
voiced nasal	m		n			
voiced flap			ɾ			
vd. central approx.				j		w

Vowels

high	i			u
mid		"e"	"o"	
low			a	

Language	bilabial	dental/alveolar	retroflex	palatal	velar	variable place	labial-velar
Pawaian (612)							
voiceless plosive	p	"t"			k		
vl. nonsibilant fric.						h	
vl. sibilant fric.		"s"					
voiced nasal	m	"n"					
voiced flap			ɽ				
vd. central approx.				j			w

Vowels

	oral				nasalized			
high	i		u		ĩ			ũ
mid		"o"					"õ"	
lower mid	ɛ	ɔ			ɛ̃	ɔ̃		
low	ɐ̟				ɐ̟̃			

Language	bilabial	dental/alveolar	palatal	velar	velar labialized	glottal	variable place	labial-velar
Dani (613)								
voiceless plosive	p	"t"		k	k^w	ʔ		
vl. nonsibilant fric.							h	
vl. sibilant fric.		"s"						
voiced nasal	m	"n"						
vd. lateral approx.		"l"						
vd. central approx.			j					w

Vowels

						Diphthongs	
high	i	ɪ		ʊ	u	ei	oi
mid		"e"	"o"			ai	ou
low		a				au	

Language	bilabial	bilabial prenasalized	dental/alveolar	dental/alv. prenasalized	velar	velar labialized	velar prenasalized	vel. labialized & prenasaliz
Wantoat (615)								
voiceless plosive	p		"t"		k	k^w		
voiced plosive		^mb		"nd"			^ŋg	$^ŋg^w$
vl. sibilant fric.			"s"					
vd. sibilant fric.				"^nz"				
voiced nasal	m		"n"		ŋ	$ŋ^w$		

Vowels

high	i				u
mid		"e"	"ə"	"o"	
low		æ	a		

Language	bilabial	alveolar	palatal	velar	variable place	labial-velar
Daribi (616)						
voiceless plosive	p	t		k		
vl. aspirated plos.	p^h	t^h		k^h		
vl. nonsibilant fric.					h	
vl. sibilant fric.		s				
voiced nasal	m	n				
voiced flap		ɾ				
vd. central approx.			j			w

Vowels

	oral					nasalized				
high	i				u	ĩ				ũ
mid		"e"		"o"			"ẽ"		"õ"	
low			a					ã		

Language

Fasu (617)	bilabial	alveolar	palatal	velar	variable place	labial-velar
voiceless plosive	p	t		k		
vl. nonsibilant fric.	ɸ				h	
vl. sibilant fric.		s				
voiced nasal	m	n				
voiced flap		ɾ				
vd. central approx.			j			w

Vowels

	oral			nasalized		
high	i		u	ĩ		ũ
mid	"e"		"o"	"ẽ"		"õ"
low		a			ã	

Language

Suena (618)	bilabial	dental/alveolar	palatal	velar	labial-velar
voiceless plosive	p	"t"		k	
voiced plosive	b	"d"		g	
vd. sibilant affric.		"dz"			
vl. sibilant fric.		"s"			
voiced nasal	m	"n"			
voiced flap		"ɾ"			
vd. central approx.			j		w

Vowels

high	i				u
lower mid		ɛ		ɔ	
low			a		

Language					
Dera (619)	bilabial	dental/alveolar	palatal	velar	labial-velar
voiceless plosive	p	"t"		k	
voiced plosive	b	"d"		g	
voiced nasal	m	"n"		ŋ	
vd. central approx.			j		w

<u>Vowels</u>

high	ɪ		u
mid		"e" "ə" "o"	
low		a	

Language						
Kunimaipa (620)	bilabial	dental	dental/alveolar	retroflex	velar	uvular
voiceless plosive	p		"t"		k	
voiced plosive	b	d̪			g	ɢ
vl. sibilant fric.			"s"			
vd. sibilant fric.			"z"			
voiced nasal	m		"n"		ŋ	
voiced flap				ɽ		
vd. lateral approx.			"l"			
vd. central approx.	β̞					

<u>Vowels</u>

high	ɪ		ʊ u
higher mid	e		
low		a	

<u>Language</u>

Yareba (621)	bilabial	alveolar	palatal	velar	labial-velar
voiceless plosive		t		k	
voiced plosive	b	d		g	
vd. sibilant affric.		dz			
vl. nonsibilant fric.	Φ				
vl. sibilant fric.		s			
voiced nasal	m	n			
voiced flap		ɾ			
vd. central approx.			j		w

<u>Vowels</u>

high	i		u
mid	"e"		"o"
low		a	

<u>Language</u>

Koiari (622)	bilabial	labio-dental	dental	alveolar	velar	variable place
voiceless plosive				t	k	
voiced plosive	b			d	g	
vl. nonsibilant fric.		f				h
vd. nonsibilant fric.			ð̪			
voiced nasal	m			n		
voiced flap				ɾ		

<u>Vowels</u>

high	i		u
mid	"e"		"o"
low		a	

Language Taoripi (623)	bilabial	labio-dental	dental/alveolar	velar	variable place
voiceless plosive	p		"t"	k	
vl. nonsibilant fric.		f			h
vl. sibilant fric.			"s"		
voiced nasal	m				
vd. lateral approx.			"l"		

Vowels

high	i					u
mid		"e"			"o"	
lower mid				ɔ		
low			a			

Language Nasioi (624)	bilabial	dental/alveolar	velar	glottal
voiceless plosive	p	"t"	k	ʔ
voiced plosive	b			
voiced nasal	m	"n"		
voiced flap		"ɾ"		

Vowels

high	i				u
higher mid				o	
lower mid		ɛ			
low			a		

Language			
Rotokas (625)	bilabial	alveolar	velar
voiceless plosive	p	t	k
voiced plosive			g
vd. nonsibilant fric.	β		
voiced tap		D	

Vowels

high	ɪ				u
mid		"e"		"o"	
low			a		

Language																		
Nambakaengo (626)	bilabial	bilabial labialized	bilabial palatalized	bilabial prenasalized	bilabial labialized & prenasalized	labio-dental	dental/alveolar	dental/alv. labialized	dental/alv. palatalized	dental/alv. prenasalized	dental/alv. labialized & prenasaliz	palatal	velar	velar labialized	velar palatalized	velar prenasalized	velar labialized & prenasalized	labial-velar
voiceless plosive	p	p^{w}	p^{j}				"t"	"t^{w}"	"t^{j}"				k	k^{w}	k^{j}			
vl. asp. plos.	p^{h}						"t^{h}"						k^{h}					
voiced plosive				^{m}b	^{m}b^{w}					"^{n}d"	"^{n}d^{w}"					^{ŋ}g	^{ŋ}g^{w}	
vd. nonsib. fric.						v												
vl. sib. fric.							"s"											
voiced nasal	m	m^{w}					"n"	"n^{w}"	"n^{j}"[5]				ŋ	ŋ^{w}				
vd. lat. approx.							"l"											
vd. cent. approx.												j						[illegible]

Vowels

	oral			nasalized			Diphthong
high	ɪ	ʉ	u	ɪ̃		ũ	e͡ɪ
mid	"e"	"ə"	"o"		"ẽ"	"õ"	
low	æ	a	ɑ	æ̃	ã	ɑ̃	

Language	bilabial	dental/alveolar	palato-alveolar	palatal	velar	velar labialized	uvular	uvular labialized	glottal	variable place	labial-velar
Haida (700)											
voiceless plosive	p	"t"		c	k	k^w	q	q^w	ʔ		
vl. aspirated plos.	p^h[1]	"t^h"		c^h	k^h	k^{wh}	q^h	q^{wh}			
vl. ejective stop		"t'"		c'	k'	k^w'	q'	q^w'			
vl. sibilant affric.			tʃ								
vl. asp. sib. affric.			$tʃ^h$								
vl. sib. eject. affric.			tʃ'								
vl. lateral affric.		"tɬ"									
vd. lateral affric.		"dɮ"									
vl. lat. eject. affric.		"tɬ'"									
vl. nonsibilant fric.				ç	x	x^w	χ	$χ^w$		h	
vl. lateral fric.		"ɬ"									
voiced nasal	m	"n"			ŋ						
laryngealized vd. nas.	m̰	"n̰"			ŋ̰						
vd. lateral approx.		"l"									
laryng. vd. lat. approx.		"l̰"									
vd. central approx.				j							w
laryng. vd. cent. approx.				j̰							w̰

Vowels

high	ɪ		ʊ
low		a	

Language	bilabial	dental/alveolar	palato-alveolar	palatal	velar	velar labialized	uvular	uvular labialized	glottal	labial-velar
Tlingit (701)										
voiceless plosive	p	"t"			k	k^w	q	q^w	ʔ	
voiced plosive	b	"d"			g	g^w	ɢ	$ɢ^w$		
vl. ejective stop	p'	"t'"			k'	k^w'	q'	q^w'		
vl. sibilant affric.		"ts"	tʃ							
vd. sibilant affric.		"dz"	dʒ							
vl. sib. eject. affric.		"ts'"	tʃ'							
vl. lateral affric.		"tɬ"								
vd. lateral affric.		"dɮ"								
vl. lat. eject. affric.		"tɬ'"								
vl. nonsibilant fric.					x	x^w	χ	$χ^w$		
vl. nonsib. eject. fric.					x'	x^w'	χ'	$χ^w$'		
vl. sibilant fric.		"s"								
vl. sib. eject. fric.		"s'"								
vl. lateral fric.		"ɬ"								
vl. lat. eject. fric.		"ɬ'"								
voiced nasal		"n"								
vd. central approx.				j						w

Vowels

high	ɪ			u
mid		"e"	"o"	
low			a	

Language

Navaho (702)	bilabial	alveolar	palato-alveolar	palatal	velar	velar labialized	glottal	variable place	labial-velar
voiceless plosive	p	t			k		ʔ[4]		
vl. aspirated plosive		tʰ			kʰ	kʷʰ[1]			
vl. ejective stop		t'			k'				
vl. sibilant affricate		ts	tʃ						
vl. asp. sib. affricate		tsʰ	tʃʰ						
vl. sib. eject. affricate		ts'	tʃ'						
vl. lateral affricate		tɬ							
vd. lateral affricate		dɮ							
vl. lat. eject. affricate		tɬ'							
vl. nonsibilant fricative					x			h	
vd. nonsibilant fricative					ɣ				
vl. sibilant fricative		s	ʃ						
vd. sibilant fricative		z	ʒ						
vl. lateral fricative		ɬ							
voiced nasal	m[1]	n							
vd. lateral approximant		l							
vd. central approximant				j					w[1]

Vowels

	short oral			long oral		
high	ɩ			i:		
higher mid						o:
lower mid	ɛ		ɔ	ɛ:		
low		a			a:	

	short nasalized			long nasalized		
high	ĩ			ĩ:		
higher mid						õ:
lower mid	ɛ̃		ɔ̃	ɛ̃:		
low		ã			ã:	

Language

Chipewyan (703)	bilabial	dental	dental/alveolar	dental/alveolar velari	palato-alveolar	palatal	velar	velar labialized	glottal	variable place
voiceless plosive	p		"t"	"ƫ"			k	kʷ	ʔ	
vl. ejective stop			"t'"				k'	kʷ'		
vl. nonsibilant affricate		t̪θ								
vl. asp. nonsib. affricate		t̪θʰ					kxʰ	kxʷʰ		
vl. nonsib. eject. affricate		t̪θ'								
vl. sibilant affricate			"ts"		tʃ					
vl. asp. sib. affricate			"tsʰ"		tʃʰ					
vl. sib. eject. affricate			"ts'"		tʃ'					
vl. lateral affricate			"tɬ"							
vl. asp. lat. affricate			"tɬʰ"							
vl. lat. eject. affricate			"tɬ'"							
vl. nonsibilant fricative		θ					x	xʷ		h
vd. nonsibilant fricative		ð					ɣ	ɣʷ		
vl. sibilant fricative			"s"		ʃ					
vd. sibilant fricative			"z"							
voiced nasal			"n"							
voiced trill			"r"							
vd. lateral approximant			"l"							
vl. lateral approximant			"l̥"							
vd. central approximant						j				

Vowels

	short			long		
high	i		u	i:		u:
higher mid	e		o			
low		a			a:	

	short nasalized			long nasalized		
high	ĩ		ũ	ĩ:		ũ:
higher mid						
low		ã			ã:	

Language	bilabial	dental/alveolar	alveolar	palato-alveolar	retroflex	palatal	velar	velar labialized	glottal	variable place	labial-velar
Tolowa (704)											
voiceless plosive	p	"t̪"					k	kʷ	ʔ		
vl. aspirated plosive		"t̪ʰ"									
vl. ejective stop		"t̪'"					k'	kʷ'			
vl. sibilant affricate				tʃ							
vl. asp. sib. affricate				tʃʰ							
vl. sib. eject. affricate			ts'	tʃ'	ʈʂ'						
vl. nonsibilant fricative							x	xʷ		h	
vd. nonsibilant fricative							ɣ				
vl. sibilant fricative			s	ʃ	ʂ						
vl. lateral fricative		"ɬ"									
voiced nasal	m	"n"									
laryngealized vd. nasal	m̰	"n̰"									
vd. lateral approximant		"l"									
vd. central approximant						j					w

Vowels

	short oral		long oral	
high	i	u	i:	u:
mid	"e""ə"		"e:"	
low	a		a:	

	short nasalized		long nasalized	
high	ĩ	ũ	ĩ:	ũ:
mid				
low	ã		ã:	

Language	bilabial	alveolar	palato-alveolar	palato-alv. labialized	palatal	velar	velar labialized	uvular	glottal	variable place	var. place labialized	labial-velar
Hupa (705)												
voiceless plosive		t			c			q	ʔ			
vl. aspirated plos.		tʰ			cʰ							
vl. ejective stop		t'			c'			q'				
vl. sibilant affric.		ts	tʃ									
vl. asp. sib. affric.		tsʰ		tʃʷʰ								
vl. sib. eject. affric.		ts'	tʃ'									
vl. lat. eject. affric.		tɬ'										
vl. nonsibilant fric.						x	xʷ			h	hʷ	
vl. sibilant fric.		s										
vl. lateral fric.		ɬ										
voiced nasal	m	n				ŋ						
vd. lateral approx.		l										
vd. central approx.					j							w

Vowels

	short		long	
high	ɪ			
mid	"e"	"o"	"e:"	"o:"
low	a		a:	

Language Nez Perce (706)	bilabial	dental	alveolar	palatal	velar	uvular	glottal	variable place	labial-velar
voiceless plosive	p	t̪	t		k		ʔ		
vl. ejective stop	p'	t̪'	t'		k'	q'			
vl. nonsibilant affric.						qχ			
vl. nonsibilant fric.					x			h	
vl. sibilant fric.			s						
vl. lateral fric.			ɬ						
voiced nasal	m	n̪							
laryngealized vd. nas.	m̰	n̪̰							
vd. lateral approx.			l						
laryng. vd. lat. approx.			l̰						
vd. central approx.				j					w
laryng. vd. cent. approx.				j̰					w̰

Vowels

high	ɩ				ɯ
lower mid				ɔ	
low		æ	a		

Note added in proofs: Margaret Langdon (p.c.) points out that the "apico-alveolar" stops reported by Aoki (1970) are affricates rather than stops. Apparently, in place of /t/ and /t'/ on this chart, a voiceless alveolar nonsibilant affricate /tɮ̥̌/ and a voiceless alveolar nonsibilant ejective affricate /tɮ̥̌'/ should be shown. Consequent minor alterations to Chapters 1, 2 and 7 and the segment index are required.

Language Klamath (707)	bilabial	alveolar	palatal	velar	uvular	glottal	variable place	labial-velar
voiceless plosive						ʔ		
vl. aspirated plos.	pʰ	tʰ	cʰ	kʰ	qʰ			
voiced plosive	b	d	ɟ	g	ɢ			
vl. ejective stop	p'	t'	c'	k'	q'			
vl. nonsibilant fric.							h	
vl. sibilant fric.		s						
voiced nasal	m	n						
laryngealized vd. nas.	m̰	n̰						
vl. nasal	m̥	n̥						
vd. lateral approx.		l						
laryng. vd. lat. approx.		l̰						
vl. lateral approx.		l̥						
vd. central approx.			j					w
laryng. vd. cent. approx.			j̰					w̰
vl. central approx.			j̊					w̥

Vowels

high	ɪ			
mid		"e"	"o"	
low			a	

Language	bilabial	alveolar	palatal	velar	variable place	labial-velar
Maidu (708)						
vl. aspirated plos.	p^h	t^h	c^h	k^h		
vl. ejective stop.	p'	t'	c'	k'		
vd. implosive	ɓ	ɗ				
vl. nonsibilant fric.					h	
vl. sibilant fric.		s				
voiced nasal	m	n				
vd. lateral approx.		l				
vd. central approx.			j			w

Vowels

high	i				u
mid		"e"		"o"	
low			a		

Language	bilabial	labio-dental	dental	alveolar	palato-alveolar	palatal	velar	uvular	glottal	variable place	labial-velar
Wintu (709)											
voiceless plosive	p			t			k	q	ʔ		
vl. aspirated plos.	p^h			t^h							
voiced plosive	b			d							
vl. ejective stop	p'			t'			k'	q'			
vl. sibilant affric.					tʃ						
vd. sibilant affric.					dʒ						
vl. sib. eject. affric.					tʃ'						
vl. lateral affric.				tɬ							
vl. lat. eject. affric.				tɬ'							
vl. nonsibilant fric.		f	θ				x	χ		h	
vl. sibilant fric.				s							
voiced nasal	m			n							
vd. lateral approx.				l							
vd. central approx.				ɹ		j					w

Vowels

high	i				u
mid		"e"		"o"	
low			a		

Language	bilabial	dental	alveolar	palato-alveolar	palatal	velar	glottal	variable place	labial-velar
Chontal (710)									
voiceless plosive	p	t̪				k	?		
voiced plosive	b	d̪							
vl. ejective stop	p'	t̪'				k'			
vl. sibilant affric.			ts	tʃ					
vl. sib. eject. affric.			ts'	tʃ'					
vl. nonsibilant fric.								h	
vl. sibilant fric.			s	ʃ					
voiced nasal	m		n						
voiced flap			ɾ						
vd. lateral approx.			l						
vd. central approx.					j				w

Vowels

high	i			u
mid	"e"	"ə"	"o"	
low		a		

Language	bilabial	alveolar	palatal	velar	glottal	variable place	labial-velar
Zoque (711)							
voiceless plosive	p	t		k	?		
voiced plosive	b[2]	d[2]		g[2]			
vl. sibilant affric.		ts					
vl. nonsibilant fric.						h	
vl. sibilant fric.		s					
voiced nasal	m	n		ŋ			
vd. lateral approx.		l					
vd. central approx.			j				w

Vowels

	oral					nasalized
high	i				u	
mid				"o"		"ɨ̃"
lower mid		ɛ				
low			a			

Language

Tzeltal (712)	bilabial	dental	alveolar	palatal	velar	glottal	variable place	labial-velar
voiceless plosive	p	t̪				?		
vl. aspirated plos.					kʰ			
voiced plosive	b	d̪[2]			g[2]			
vl. ejective stop	p'	t̪'			k'			
vl. sibilant affric.		t̪s	ts					
vl. sib. eject. affric.		t̪s'	ts'					
vl. nonsibilant fric.							h	
vl. sibilant fric.		s̪	s					
voiced nasal	m	n̪						
voiced flap			ɾ					
vd. lateral approx.		l̪						
vd. central approx.				j				w

Vowels

high	ι				ʊ
mid		"e"		"o"	
low			a		

Language

Totonac (713)	bilabial	alveolar	palato-alveolar	palatal	velar	uvular	glottal	variable place	labial-velar
voiceless plosive	p	t			k	q	?		
vl. sibilant affric.		ts	tʃ						
vl. nonsibilant fric.								h	
vl. sibilant fric.		s	ʃ						
vl. lateral fric.		ɬ							
voiced nasal	m	n							
vd. lateral approx.		l							
vd. central approx.				j					w

Vowels

high	ɪ		u
low		a	

Language	bilabial	alveolar	palato-alveolar	palatal	velar	uvular	glottal	labial-velar
K'ekchi (714)								
voiceless plosive	p	t			k	q	?	
laryngealized vd. plos.	b̰							
vl. ejective stop		t'			k'	q'		
vl. sibilant affric.		ts	tʃ					
vl. sib. eject. affric.		ts'	tʃ'					
vl. nonsibilant fric.					x			
vl. sibilant fric.		s	ʃ					
voiced nasal	m	n						
vd. lateral approx.		l						
vd. central approx.				j				w

Vowels

high	i				u
mid		"e"		"o"	
low			a		

Language	bilabial	labio-dental	dental	alveolar	palato-alveolar	palatal	velar	glottal
Mixe (715)								
voiceless plosive	p		t̪				k	?
voiced plosive			d̪				g	
vl. sibilant affricate				ts				
vd. nonsibilant fricative		v						
vl. sibilant fricative			s̪		ʃ			
vd. sibilant fricative					ʒ			
voiced nasal	m		n̪					
vd. central approximant						j.		

Vowels

high	i			ɨ			u
higher mid						o	
mid		"e"		"ə"			
lower mid					ɔ		
low			æ	a			

Language Otomi (716)	bilabial	alveolar	palato-alveolar	palatal	velar	velar labialized	glottal	variable place	labial-velar
voiceless plosive	p	t			k	k^{w4}	ʔ		
vl. aspirated plos.	pʰ	tʰ			kʰ				
voiced plosive	b	d			g	g^{w4}			
laryngealized vd. plos.	b̰	d̰							
vl. ejective stop	p'	t'			k'	kʷ',4			
vl. sibilant affric.			tʃ 2						
vl. sib. eject. affric.		ts'	tʃ' 4						
vl. nonsibilant fric.	ɸ				x 4			h	
vl. sibilant fric.		s	ʃ						
vd. sibilant fric.		z							
voiced nasal	m	n							
laryngealized vd. nas.	m̰	n̰							
voiceless nasal	m̥ 4	n̥ 4							
voiced flap		ɾ							
vd. lateral approx.		l 2							
vd. central approx.				j					w
laryng. vd. cent. approx.				j̰					w̰
vl. central approx.				j̊					ʍ

Vowels

	oral				nasalized			
high	i			u	ĩ			ũ
higher mid	e			o				
mid								
lower mid			ɔ					
		æ				æ̃	ã	

Language Mazahua (717)	bilabial	dental/alveolar	palato-alveolar	palatal	velar	velar labialized	glottal	variable place	labial-velar
voiceless plosive	p	"t"			k	kʷ	ʔ		
vl. aspirated plosive	pʰ	"tʰ"			kʰ	kʷʰ			
voiced plosive					g	gʷ			
vl. ejective stop		"t'"			k'	kʷ'			
vd. implosive	ɓ	"ɗ"							
vl. sibilant affricate		"ts"	tʃ						
vl. asp. sib. affricate		"tsʰ"	tʃʰ						
vl. sib. eject. affricate		"ts'"	tʃ'						
vl. nonsibilant fricative								h	
vl. sibilant fricative		"s"	ʃ						
vl. asp. sib. fricative		"sʰ"							
vd. sibilant fricative		"z"	ʒ						
vl. sib. eject. fricative		"s'"							
voiced nasal	m	"n"		ɲ					
laryngealized vd. nasal	m̰			ɲ̰					
voiceless nasal	m̥	"n̥"		ɲ̊					
voiced r-sound		"r"							
vd. lateral approximant		"l"							
vd. central approximant				j					w
laryng. vd. cent. approx.				j̰					w̰
vl. central approximant				j̊					ʍ

Vowels

high	i				u	ĩ		ũ
higher mid		e		o		ẽ		õ
mid			"ə"				"ə̃"	
lower mid		ɛ	ɔ					
low			a				ã	

Language

Mazatec (727)

	bilabial	dental	dental/alveolar	alveolar	alveolar prenasalized	palato-alveolar	palato-alv. prenasalized	retroflex	retroflex prenasalized	palatal	velar	velar prenasalized	glottal	variable place
voiceless plosive	p[2]		"t"								k		?	
voiced plosive	b[2]											ᵑg		
vl. sibilant affric.				ts		tʃ		ṭṣ						
vd. sibilant affric.					ⁿdz		ⁿdʒ		ⁿḍẓ					
vl. nonsibilant fric.														h
vd. nonsibilant fric.	β	ð[2]									ɣ[2]			
vl. sibilant fric.			"s"					ṣ						
voiced nasal	m			n						ɲ				
voiced trill			"r"[2]											
vd. lateral approx.			"l"											
vd. central approx.										j				

Vowels

	oral	nasalized
high	i	ĩ
higher mid	o	õ
lower mid	ε	ε̃
low	a	ã

Language

Mixtec (728)

	bilabial	dental	dental/alveolar	palato-alveolar	velar	velar labialized	glottal	variable place
voiceless plosive	p		"t"		k	kʷ	?	
vl. sibilant affric.				tʃ				
vl. nonsibilant fric.								h
vd. nonsibilant fric.	β	ð						
vl. sibilant fric.			"s"	ʃ				
vd. sibilant fric.				ʒ				
voiced nasal					ŋ[4]			
voiced trill			"r"					
vd. lateral approx.			"l"[4]					

Vowels

	oral			nasalized		
high	i		u	ĩ		ũ
mid	"e"	"o"		"ẽ"	"õ"	
low		a			ã	

Language Chatino (729)	bilabial	dental/alveolar	palato-alveolar	palatal	velar	glottal	variable place	labial-velar
voiceless plosive	p	"t"			k	ʔ		
voiced plosive	b	"d"			g			
vl. nonsibilant fric.							h	
vl. sibilant fric.		"s"	ʃ					
voiced nasal	m	"n"						
voiced r-sound		"rr"						
vd. lateral approx.		"l"						
vd. central approx.				j				w

Vowels

	oral					nasalized			
high	i				u	ĩ			ũ
mid		"e"		"o"			"ẽ"	"õ"	
low			a						

Language Nootka (730)	bilabial	dental	dental/alveolar	alveolar	palato-alveolar	palatal	velar	velar labialized	uvular	uvular labialized	pharyngeal	glottal	glottal pharyngealized	variable place	labial-velar
voiceless plosive	p	t̪					k	kʷ	q	qʷ		ʔ	ʔˤ		
vl. ejective stop	p'	t̪'					k'	kʷ'	q'²	qʷ'²					
vl. sibilant affric.				ts	tʃ										
vl. sib. eject. affric.				ts'	tʃ'										
vl. lateral affric.			tɬ												
vl. lat. eject. affric.			tɬ'												
vl. nonsibilant fric.							x	xʷ	χ²	χʷ²	ħ			h	
vl. sibilant fric.				s	ʃ										
vl. lateral fric.			ɬ												
voiced nasal	m	n̪													
laryngealized vd. nas.	m̰	n̪̰													
vd. central approx.						j									w
laryng. vd. cent. approx.						j̰									w̰

Vowels

high	i				
higher mid					o
lower mid		ε		ɔ²	
low			a		

Language	bilabial	alveolar	palatal	velar labialized	uvular	uvular labialized	glottal	variable place	labial-velar
Kwakw'ala (731)									
voiceless plosive							?		
vl. aspirated plosive	p^h	t^h	c^h	k^{wh}	q^h	q^{wh}			
voiced plosive	b	d	ɟ	g^w	ɢ	$ɢ^w$			
vl. ejective stop	p'	t'	c'	k^w'	q'	q^w'			
vl. asp. sibilant affric.		ts^h							
vd. sibilant affric.		dz							
vl. sib. ejective affric.		ts'							
vl. nonsibilant fric.			ç	x^w	χ	$χ^w$		h	
vl. asp. lateral affric.		$tɬ^h$							
vd. lateral affricate		dɮ							
vl. lat. ejective affric.		tɬ'							
vl. sibilant fric.		s							
vl. lateral fric.		ɬ							
voiced nasal	m	n							
laryngealized vd. nasal	m̰	n̰							
voiced lateral approx.		l							
laryngealized vd. lat. app.		l̰							
voiced central approx.			j						w
laryngealized vd. c. appr.			j̰						w̰

Vowels					
high	i				u
mid			"ə"		
lower mid		ɛ		ɔ	
low			a		

Language	bilabial	alveolar	palato-alveolar	palatal	velar	velar labialized	uvular	uvular labialized	glottal	variable place	labial-velar
Quileute (732)											
voiceless plosive	p	t			k	k^w	q	q^w	?		
voiced plosive	b	d			g[2]						
vl. ejective stop	p'	t'			k'	k^w'	q'	q^w'			
vl. sibilant affric.		ts	tʃ								
vl. sib. eject. affric.		ts'	tʃ'								
vl. lateral affric.		tɬ									
vl. lat. eject. affric.		tɬ'									
vl. nonsibilant fric.					x	x^w	χ	$χ^w$		h	
vl. sibilant fric.		s	ʃ								
vl. lateral fric.		ɬ									
vd. lateral approx.		l									
vd. central approx.				j							w

Vowels			
high	i		u
low		æ a	

Language Squamish (733)	bilabial	dental	dental/alveolar	palato-alveolar	palatal	velar	velar labialized	uvular	uvular labialized	glottal	variable place	labial-velar
voiceless plosive	p	t̲				k[1]	kʷ	q	qʷ	?		
vl. ejective stop	p'	t̲'				k'[1]	kʷ'	q'	qʷ'			
vl. sibilant affric.		t̲s̲		tʃ								
vl. sib. eject. aff.		t̲s̲'		tʃ'								
vl. lateral affric.			"tɬ"									
vl. lat. eject. aff.			"tɬ'"									
vl. nonsibilant fric.							xʷ	χ	χʷ		h	
vl. sibilant fric.		s̲		ʃ								
voiced nasal	m	n̲										
vd. lateral approx.			"l"									
vd. central approx.					j							w

Vowels

higher mid	e		o
mid		"ə"	
low		a	

Language Puget Sound (734)	bilabial	alveolar	palato-alveolar	palatal	velar	velar labialized	uvular	uvular labialized	glottal	variable place	labial-velar
voiceless plosive	p	t			k	kʷ	q	qʷ	?		
voiced plosive	b	d			g[1]	gʷ					
vl. ejective stop	p'	t'			k'	kʷ'	q'	qʷ'			
vl. sibilant affric.		ts	tʃ								
vd. sibilant affric.		dz	dʒ[1]								
vl. sib. eject. affric.		ts'	tʃ'								
vl. lat. eject. affric.		tɬ'									
vl. nonsibilant fric.						xʷ	χ	χʷ		h	
vl. sibilant fric.		s	ʃ								
vl. lateral fric.		ɬ									
vd. central approx.				j							w

Vowels

high	ɩ		ʊ
mid		"ə"	
low		a	

Language Papago (736)	bilabial	dental	palato-alveolar	retroflex	palatal	velar	glottal	variable place	labial-velar
voiceless plosive	p	t̪				k	?		
voiced plosive	b	d̪		ḍ		g			
vl. sibilant affric.			tʃ						
vd. sibilant affric.			dʒ						
vl. nonsibilant fric.								h	
vl. sibilant fric.		s̪		ṣ					
voiced nasal	m	n̪	n̠						
vd. lateral flap				ḷ					
vd. central approx.					j				w

Vowels

high	i	ɨ	u
lower mid		ɔ	
low		a	

Language Luiseño (737)	bilabial	labio-dental	dental	dental/alveolar	palato-alveolar	retroflex	palatal	velar	velar labialized	uvular	uvular labialized	glottal	variable place	labial-velar
voiceless plosive	p		t̪					k	kʷ	q	qʷ	?		
vl. sib. affric.					tʃ									
vl. nonsib. fric.								x	xʷ				h	
vd. nonsib. fric.		v	ð̪											
vl. sib. fric.			s̪		ʃ	ṣ								
voiced nasal	m		n̪					ŋ						
voiced trill				"r"										
vd. lat. approx.			l̪											
vd. cent. approx.							j							w

Vowels

high	ι				ʊ
mid		"e"		"o"	
low			a		

Language	bilabial	labio-dental	alveolar	retroflex	palatal	velar	velar labialized	uvular	glottal	variable place	labial-velar
Hopi (738)											
voiceless plosive	p		t			k	kʷ	q	ʔ		
vl. nonsibilant fric.										h	
vd. nonsibilant fric.		v		ɹ̣̌							
vl. sibilant fric.			s								
voiced nasal	m		n		ɲ	ŋ	ŋʷ				
voiceless nasal	m̥		n̥			ŋ̊					
vd. central approx.					j						w
vl. central approx.					j̊						ʍ

Vowels

high	i								
higher mid		ø		ɤ					
low		æ	a						

Diphthong

ou

Language	bilabial	labio-dental	alveolar	palato-alveolar	palatal	velar	glottal	variable place	labial-velar
Yaqui (739)									
voiceless plosive	p		t			k	ʔ		
voiced plosive	b		d[2]			g[2]			
vl. sibilant affric.				tʃ					
vl. nonsibilant fric.		f[2]						h	
vl. sibilant fric.			s						
voiced nasal	m		n						
voiced flap			ɾ						
vd. lateral approx.			l						
vd. central approx.					j				w

Vowels

high	i			u
mid		"e"	"o"	
low			a	

Language	bilabial	dental/alveolar	palato-alveolar	palatal	velar	velar labialized	glottal	variable place	labial-velar
Tiwa (740)									
voiceless plosive	p	"t"			k	k^w	ʔ		
vl. aspirated plos.	p^h	"t^h"							
voiced plosive	b^2	"d"^{2}			g^2				
vl. ejective stop	p'	"t'"			k'	$k^{w,1}$			
vl. sibilant affric.			tʃ						
vl. nonsibilant fric.					x	x^w		h	
vl. sibilant fric.		"s"							
vl. lateral fric.		"ɬ"							
voiced nasal	m	"n"							
voiced r-sound		"r"^{2}							
vd. lateral approx.		"l"							
vd. central approx.				j					w

<u>Vowels</u>

	oral			nasalized		
high	i		u	ĩ		$ũ^1$
higher mid	e		o	ẽ		õ
mid		"ə"			"ə̃"	
low		a			ã	

Language	bilabial	labio-dental	dental	dental/alveolar	alveolar	palato-alveolar	palatal	velar	glottal	variable place
Karok (741)										
voiceless plosive	p			"t"				k	ʔ	
vl. sibilant affric.						tʃ				
vl. nonsibilant fric.		f						x		h
vd. nonsibilant fric.	β									
vl. sibilant fric.			s̪		s	ʃ				
voiced nasal	m			"n"						
voiced flap					ɾ					
vd. central approx.							j			

<u>Vowels</u>

	short		long		short nasalized
high	i	ʊ	i:	ɔ:	$ĩ^1$
higher mid			e:	o:	
lower mid	$ɛ^1$				
low	a		a:		$ã^1$

Language Pomo, South Eastern (742)	bilabial	labio-dental	dental	dental/alveolar	alveolar	palato-alveolar	palatal	velar	uvular	glottal	variable place	labial-velar
voiceless plosive	p		t̪		t			k	q	ʔ		
voiced plosive	b				d							
vl. ejective stop	p'		t̪'		t'			k'	q'			
vl. sibilant affric.					ts							
vl. sib. eject. affric.					ts'							
vl. nonsibilant fric.		f						x	χ		h	
vl. sibilant fric.				"s"		ʃ						
voiced nasal	m			"n"								
voiced flap				"ɾ"[2]								
vd. lateral approx.				"l"								
vd. central approx.							j					w

Vowels

high	ɩ				ʊ
lower mid		ɛ		ɔ	
low			a		

Language Diegueño (743)	bilabial	dental	alveolar	palato-alveolar	palatal	velar	velar labialized	uvular	labial-velar	glottal
voiceless plosive	p	t̪	t			k	k^w	q[1]		ʔ
vl. sibilant affric.				tʃ						
vl. nonsibilant fric.						x	x^w			
vd. nonsibilant fric.	β									
vl. sibilant fric.		s̪	s							
vl. lateral fric.			ɬ	ɬ̠						
voiced nasal	m	n̪	n	n̠						
voiced trill			r[1]							
vd. lateral approx.			l	l̠						
vd. central approx.			ɹ		j				w	

Vowels

	short			long	
high	ɩ		ʊ		
higher mid				e:	o:
mid		"ə"			
lower mid		ɔ[1]		ɔ:[1]	
low		a		a:	

Language Achumawi (744)	bilabial	dental/alveolar	alveolar	palato-alveolar	palatal	velar	uvular	glottal	variable place	labial-velar
voiceless plosive	p		t			k	q	ʔ		
vd. sibilant affric.				dʒ						
vl. nonsibilant fric.						x	χ		h	
vl. sibilant fric.			s	ʃ						
voiced nasal	m	"n"								
voiced r-sound		"r"								
vd. lateral approx.			l							
vd. central approx.					j					w

<u>Vowels</u>

high	i			u
mid	"e"	"ə"	"o"	
low		a		

Language Yana (745)	bilabial	dental	dental/alveolar	palato-alveolar	palatal	velar	glottal	variable place	labial-velar
voiceless plosive							ʔ		
vl. aspirated plos.	pʰ	t̪ʰ				kʰ			
voiced plosive	b	d̪				g			
vl. ejective stop	p'	t̪'				k'			
vl. asp. sib. affric.				tʃʰ					
vd. sibilant affric.				dʒ					
vl. sib. eject. affric.				tʃ'					
vl. nonsibilant fric.						x		h	
vl. sibilant fric.		s̪							
voiced nasal	m	n̪							
voiced r-sound			"r"						
vd. lateral approx.			"l"						
vd. central approx.					j				w

<u>Vowels</u>

high	ɪ			u
mid		"e"	"o"	
low		a		

<u>Diphthongs</u>

aɪ
au
uɪ

Language	bilabial	dental/alveolar	palato-alveolar	palatal	velar	glottal	variable place	labial-velar
Shasta (746)								
voiceless plosive	p	"t"			k	ʔ		
vl. ejective stop	p'	"t'"			k'			
vl. sibilant affric.			tʃ					
vl. sib. eject. affric.			tʃ'					
vl. nonsibilant fric.					x		h	
vl. sibilant fric.		"s"						
voiced nasal	m	"n"						
voiced r-sound		"rr"						
vd. central approx.				j				w

Vowels

high	ɪ		u
mid	"e"		
low		a	

Language	bilabial	labio-dental	dental/alveolar	alveolar	palato-alveolar	retroflex	palatal	velar	velar labialized	glottal	variable place	labial-velar
Tarascan (747)												
voiceless plosive	p			t				k	kʷ	ʔ[1]		
vl. aspirated plos.	pʰ			tʰ				kʰ	kʷʰ			
voiced plosive	b[2]			d[2]				g[2]				
vl. sibilant affric.				ts	tʃ							
vl. asp. sib. affric.				tsʰ	tʃʰ							
vl. nonsibilant fric.	ɸ[2]	f[2]						x			h	
vl. sibilant fric.			"s"		ʃ		ʂ					
voiced nasal	m		"n"				ɲ[2]	ŋ				
voiced trill				r								
vd. lateral approx.			"l"[2]			ɭ						
vd. central approx.				ɹ[1]			j					w

Vowels

high	ɪ				u
higher mid				o	
lower mid		ɛ			
low			a		

Language	bilabial	dental/alveolar	palato-alveolar	palatal	velar	velar labialized	glottal	variable place	labial-velar
Zuni (748)									
voiceless plosive	p	"t"					ʔ		
vl. aspirated plosive					kʰ	kʷʰ			
vl. ejective stop					k'	kʷ'			
vl. asp. sib. affric.		"tsʰ"	tʃʰ						
vl. sib. eject. affric.		"ts'"	tʃ'						
vl. nonsibilant fric.								h	
vl. sibilant fric.		"s"	ʃ						
vl. lateral fric.		"ɬ"							
voiced nasal	m	"n"							
vd. lateral approx.		"l"							
vd. central approx.				j					w

Vowels

high	ɪ		u
lower mid	ɛ		ɔ
low		a	

Language	bilabial	dental	palato-alveolar	retroflex	palatal	velar	glottal	variable place	labial-velar
Acoma (749)									
voiceless plosive							ʔ		
vl. aspirated plos.	pʰ	t̪ʰ			cʰ				
voiced plosive	b	d̪			ɟ	g			
vl. ejective stop	p'	t̪'			c'	k'			
vl. asp. sib. affric.		t̪s̪ʰ	tʃʰ	ṭṣʰ					
vd. sibilant affric.		d̪z̪	dʒ	ḍẓ					
vl. sib. eject. affric.		t̪s̪'	tʃ'	ṭṣ'					
vl. nonsibilant fric.								h	
vl. sibilant fric.		s̪	ʃ	ṣ					
vl. sib. eject. fric.		s̪'	ʃ'	ṣ'					
voiced nasal	m	n̪							
laryngealized vd. nas.	m̰	n̪̰							
voiced tap		ɾ̪							
laryngealized vd. tap		ɾ̪̰							
vd. central approx.					j				w
laryng. vd. cent. app.					j̰				w̰

Vowels

high	ɪ	ɨ	u
lower mid	ɛ		
low	a̟		

Diphthongs

eɪ	iu
aɪ	eo
uɪ	au
ɨɪ	

Language Ojibwa (750)	bilabial	dental/alveolar	alveolar	palato-alveolar	velar	glottal
voiceless plosive	p		t		k	ʔ
vl. preaspirated plosive	ʰp[5]		ʰt[5]		ʰk[5]	
vl. sibilant affricate				tʃ		
vl. preasp. sib. affricate				ʰtʃ[5]		
vl. sibilant fricative		"s"		ʃ		
vl. preasp. sib. fricative		"ʰs"[5]		ʰʃ[5]		
voiced nasal	m		n			
vd. lateral approximant		"l"[2]				

Vowels

	long oral			short oral	
high	i:			ɩ	ɷ
higher mid		o:			
lower mid	ε:				
low		a:		a	

	long nasalized	
high	ĩ:	
higher mid		õ:
lower mid	ε̃:	
low	a:	

Language Delaware (751)	bilabial	dental/alveolar	palato-alveolar	palatal	velar	variable place	labial-velar
voiceless plosive	p	"t"			k		
long vl. plosive	p	"t:"			k:		
vl. sibilant affricate			tʃ				
long. vl. sib. affricate			tʃ:				
vl. nonsibilant fricative					x	h	
long vl. nonsib. fricative						h:	
vl. sibilant fricative		"s"	ʃ				
voiced nasal	m	"n"					
long vd. nasal	m:	"n:"					
vd. lateral approximant		"l"					
long vd. lat. approximant		"l:"					
vd. central approximant				j			w
long vd. cent. approximant							w:

Vowels

	short oral			long oral		
high	i		u	i:		u:
mid		"ə"				
lower mid	ε	ɔ			ɔ:	
low		a		æ:	a:	

	long nasalized		
high	ĩ:		ũ:
mid		"ə̃:"	
lower mid		ɔ̃:	
low	æ̃:	ã:	

Language	bilabial	dental	dental/alveolar	palatal	velar	velar labialized	glottal	variable place	labial-velar
Tonkawa (752)									
voiceless plosive	p		"t"		k	kʷ	ʔ		
vl. sibilant affric.			"ts"						
vl. nonsibilant fric.					x	xʷ		h	
vl. sibilant fric.			"s"						
voiced nasal	m	n̪							
vd. lateral approx.		l̪							
vd. central approx.				j					w

Vowels

	short			long			
high	ɩ		u	iː			uː
higher mid					eː	oː	
lower mid	ɛ	ɔ					
low		a			aː		

Language	bilabial	dental/alveolar	alveolar	palato-alveolar	retroflex	palatal	velar	velar labialized	glottal	labial-velar
Wiyot (753)										
voiceless plosive	p	"t"					k	kʷ	ʔ	
vl. aspirated plos.	pʰ	"tʰ"					kʰ	kʷʰ		
vl. sibilant affric.		"ts"		tʃ						
vl. asp. sib. affric.		"tsʰ"		tʃʰ						
vl. sibilant fric.		"s"		ʃ						
vl. lateral fric.		"ɬ"								
voiced nasal	m	"n"								
vd. lateral approx.		"l"								
vd. central approx.			ɹ		ɻ	j	ɣ̞			w

Vowels

high	i		u
mid	"e"		"o"
low		a	

Language	bilabial	dental/alveolar	palatal	velar	glottal	variable place	labial-velar
Seneca (754)							
voiceless plosive		"t"		k	?		
voiced plosive	b[1]						
vd. sibilant affricate		"dz"					
vl. nonsibilant fricative						h	
vl. sibilant fricative		"s"					
voiced nasal	m[1]	"n"					
vd. central approximant			j				w

Vowels

	oral					nasalized	
high	i				u[1]		
higher mid		e					
mid				"o"			
lower mid						ɛ̃	ɔ̃
low			æ	a			

Language	dental/alveolar	velar	velar labialized	glottal	variable place	labial-velar
Wichita (755)						
voiceless plosive	"t"	k	k^w	?		
vl. aspirated plos.	"t^h"	k^h	k^{wh}			
vl. ejective stop			k’			
vl. sibilant affric.	"ts"					
long vl. sib. affric.	"ts:"					
vl. asp. sib. affric.	"ts^h"					
vl. sib. eject. affric.	"ts’"					
vd. nonsibilant fric.					ɦ	
vl. sibilant fric.	"s"					
long vl. sib. fric.	"s:"					
vl. sib. eject. fric.	"s’"					
voiced nasal	"n"					
long voiced nasal	"n:"					
voiced r-sound	"r"					
vd. central approx.						w
laryngealized vd. cent. app.						w̰[1]

Vowels

	short				long			
high	ɪ			u				
higher mid					e:			o:
lower mid		ɛ				ɛ:		
low			ɒ				ɒ:	

Language Dakota (756)	bilabial	dental/alveolar	palato-alveolar	palatal	velar	variable place	labial-velar
voiceless plosive	p	"t"			k		
vl. aspirated plos.	pʰ	"tʰ"			kʰ		
voiced plosive	b						
vl. ejective stop	p'	"t'"			k'		
vl. sibilant affric.			tʃ				
vl. asp. sib. affric.			tʃʰ				
vl. sib. eject. affric.			tʃ'				
vl. nonsibilant fric.					x	h	
vl. nonsib. eject. fric.					x'		
vd. nonsibilant fric.					ɣ		
vl. sibilant fric.		"s"	ʃ				
vd. sibilant fric.		"z"	ʒ				
vl. sib. eject. fric.			ʃ'				
voiced nasal	m4	"n"4					
vd. lateral approx.		"l"					
vd. central approx.				j			w

Vowels	oral			nasalized		
high	ɪ		ʊ	ĩ		ũ
higher mid			o			
lower mid	ɛ					
low		a			ã	

Language Yuchi (757)	bilabial	dental/alveolar	palato-alveolar	palatal	velar	glottal	variable place	labial-velar
voiceless plosive	p	"t"			k	ʔ		
vl. aspirated plos.	pʰ	"tʰ"			kʰ			
voiced plosive	b	"d"			g			
vl. ejective stop	p'	"t'"			k'			
vl. sibilant affric.		"ts"	tʃ					
vl. asp. sib. affric.		"tsʰ"	tʃʰ					
vd. sibilant affric.		"dz"	dʒ					
vl. sib. eject. affric.		"ts'"	tʃ'					
vl. nonsibilant fric.	ɸ						h	
vl. nonsib. eject. fric.	ɸ'							
vl. sibilant fric.		"s"	ʃ					
vl. sib. eject. fric.		"s'"	ʃ'					
vl. lateral fric.		"ɬ"						
vl. lat. eject. fric.		"ɬ'"						
voiced nasal		"n"						
laryngealized vd. nas.		"n̰"						
vd. lateral approx.		"l"						
laryng. vd. lat. approx.		"l̰"						
vd. central approx.				j				w
laryng. vd. cent. approx.				j̰				w̰

Vowels	oral				nasalized	
high	ɩ			u		
higher mid		e	o			
mid					"ẽ"	"õ"
low		æ a				

Language	bilabial	alveolar	palato-alveolar	palatal	velar	glottal	variable place	labial-velar
Tunica (758)								
voiceless plosive						?		
vl. aspirated plos.	pʰ	tʰ			kʰ			
voiced plosive	b^2	d^2			g^2			
vl. asp. sib. affric.			tʃʰ					
vl. nonsibilant fric.							h	
vl. sibilant fric.		s	ʃ					
voiced nasal	m	n						
voiced trill		r						
vd. lateral approx.		l						
vd. central approx.				j				w

Vowels

high	i						u
higher mid		e				o	
lower mid			ɛ		ɔ		
low				a			

Language	bilabial	dental	dental/alveolar	alveolar	palato-alveolar	palatal	velar	variable place	labial-velar
Alabama (759)									
voiceless plosive	p	t̪					k		
voiced plosive	b								
vl. sibilant affric.					tʃ				
vl. nonsibilant fric.	Φ							h	
vl. sibilant fric.				s					
vl. lateral fric.			"ɬ"						
voiced nasal	m		"n"						
vd. lateral approx.			"l"						
vd. central approx.						j			w

Vowels

higher mid	ɵ		o
low		a	

Language	bilabial	labio-dental	dental	dental/alveolar	alveolar	palato-alveolar	palatal	velar	glottal	variable place
Wappo (760)										
voiceless plosive	p		t̪		t			k	ʔ	
voiced plosive	b[2]		d̪[2]					g[2]		
vl. ejective stop	p'		t̪'		t'			k'		
vl. sibilant affric.				"ts"		tʃ				
vl. sib. eject. affric.				"ts'"		tʃ'				
vl. nonsibilant fric.		f[2]								h
vl. sibilant fric.				"s"		ʃ				
voiced nasal	m			"n"						
laryngealized vd. nas.	m̰			"n̰"						
voiced r-sound				"r"[2]						
laryng. vd. r-sound				"r̰"[2]						
vd. lateral approx.				"l"						
laryng. vd. lat. app.				"l̰"						
vd. central. approx.							j			
laryng. vd. cent. app.							j̰			

Vowels

high	i		u
mid	"e"		"o"
low		a	

Language	bilabial	dental/alveolar	dent./alv. palatalized	palato-alveolar	palatal	velar	glottal	variable place	labial-velar
Itonama (800)									
voiceless plosive	p	"t"	"tʲ"			k	ʔ		
voiced plosive	b	"d"							
vl. ejective stop		"t'"				k'			
vl. sibilant affric.				tʃ					
vl. sib. eject. affric.				tʃ'					
vl. nonsibilant fric.								h	
vl. sibilant fric.		"s"							
voiced nasal	m	"n"							
voiced flap		"ɾ"							
vd. lateral approx.		"l"							
vd. central approx.					j				w

Vowels

high	i	ɨ	u
mid	"e"		"o"
low		a	

Language

Bribri (801)	bilabial	dental/alveolar	palato-alveolar	palatal	velar	labial-velar
voiceless plosive	p	"t"			k	
voiced plosive	b	"d"			g	
vl. sibilant affric.		"ts"	tʃ			
vl. nonsibilant fric.					x	
vl. sibilant fric.		"s"	ʃ			
vd. sibilant fric.		"z"				
voiced nasal	m	"n"		ɲ		
voiced r-sound		"r"				
vd. central approx.				j		w

Vowels

	oral				nasalized		
high	i			u	ĩ		ũ
mid		"e"	"o"		"ẽ"	"õ"	
low		a				ã	

Language

Mura (802)	bilabial	dental/alveolar	velar	glottal	variable place
voiceless plosive	p	"t"	k	ʔ	
voiced plosive	b		g		
vl. nonsibilant fric.					h
vl. sibilant fric.		"s"			

Vowels

high	i		
mid			"o"
low		a	

Language Cayapa (803)	bilabial	alveolar	palato-alveolar	palatal	velar	glottal	variable place	labial-velar
voiceless plosive	p	t	t̠		k	?		
voiced plosive	b	d	d̠		g			
vl. sibilant affric.		ts	tʃ					
vl.nonsibilant fric.	ɸ						h	
vl. sibilant fric.		s	ʃ					
voiced nasal	m	n	n̠		ŋ			
voiced r-sound		rr						
vd. lateral approx.		l	l̠					
vd. central approx.				j				w

Vowels

high	i				ɷ
lower mid		ɛ			
low				ɑ	

Language Paez (804)	bilabial	bilabial prenasalized	bilabial palatalized	alveolar	alveolar prenasalized	alveolar palatalized	alv prenasalized & palatal	palato-alveolar	palato-alv. prenasalized	palato-alv. palatalized	palatal	velar	velar prenasalized	glottal	variable place	labial-velar
voiceless plosive	p			t		t^{j}						k		?		
voiced plosive		^{m}b			^{n}d		$^{n}d^{j}$						^{ŋ}g			
vl. sibilant affric.				ts				tʃ								
vl. nonsib. fric.			$ɸ^{j}$												h	
vd. nonsib. fric.	β											ɣ				
vl. sibilant fric.				s				ʃ		$ʃ^{j}$	ç					
vd. sibilant fric.					^{n}z				$^{n}ʒ$							
voiced nasal	m			n							ɲ					
voiced flap				$ɾ^{2}$												
vd. lateral flap				ɺ		$ɺ^{j}$										
vd. central approx.											j					w

Vowels

	oral			nasalized		
high	i		u	ĩ		ũ
lower mid	ɛ			ɛ̃		
low		a			ã	

__Language__

Ocaina (805)	bilabial	alveolar	alveolar palatalized	palato-alveolar	palatal	velar	glottal	variable place
voiceless plosive	p	t	t^j			k	?	
voiced plosive	b		d^j			g		
vl. sibilant affric.		ts		tʃ				
vd. sibilant affric.		dz						
vl. nonsibilant fric.	Φ					x		h
vd. nonsibilant fric.	β							
vl. sibilant fric.		s		ʃ				
vd. sibilant fric.				ʒ				
voiced nasal	m	n			ɲ			
long voiced nasal	m:	n:			ɲ:			
voiced flap		ɾ						

__Vowels__

	oral					nasalized			
high	ı				ɯ	ĩ			ɯ̃
higher mid				o				õ	
lower mid		ɛ							
low			a				ã		

__Language__

Muinane (806)	bilabial	alveolar	alveolar palatalized	palato-alveolar	palatal	velar	glottal
voiceless plosive	p	t			c	k	?
voiced plosive	b	d			ɟ	g	
vl. sibilant affric.				tʃ			
vd. sibilant affric.				dʒ			
vl. nonsibilant fric.	Φ					x	
vd. nonsibilant fric.	β						
vl. sibilant fric.		s		ʃ			
vd. sibilant fric.					z		
voiced nasal	m	n			ɲ		
voiced r-sound		rr	rr^j				

__Vowels__

high	ı				u
mid				"o"	
lower mid		ɛ			
low			a		

Language Carib (807)	bilabial	dental/alveolar	alveolar	palatal	velar	glottal	variable place	labial-velar
voiceless plosive	p	"t"			k	ʔ[4]		
voiced plosive	b	"d"			g			
vl. nonsibilant fric.							h	
vd. nonsibilant fric.	β							
vl. sibilant fric.		"s"						
voiced nasal	m	"n"			ŋ			
voiced flap			ɾ					
vd. central approx.				j				w

Vowels			
high	ɪ		u, ɯ
lower mid	ɛ		ɔ
low		ɐ	

Language Apinaye (809)	bilabial	bilabial prenasalized	labio-dental	dental/alveolar	alveolar	alveolar prenasalized	palato-alveolar	retroflex	palatal prenasalized	velar	velar prenasalized	glottal
voiceless plosive	p				t					k		ʔ
voiced plosive		^{m}b				^{n}d			$^{ɲ}ɟ$		^{ŋ}g	
vl. sibilant affric.							tʃ					
vd. nonsibilant fric.			v									
vl. sibilant fric.				"s"[1]								
vd. sibilant fric.							ʒ					
voiced flap								ɽ				

Vowels	oral			nasalized		
high	ɪ		u, ɯ	ɪ̃		ũ, ɯ̃
higher mid	e		o, ɤ			õ
lower mid	ɛ		ɔ, ʌ	ɛ̃	ʌ̃	
low		a			ã	

Language	bilabial	dental	dental/alveolar	palato-alveolar	palatal	velar	glottal	variable place	labial-velar
Amahuaca (810)									
voiceless plosive	p		"t"			k	?		
vl. sibilant affric.				tʃ					
vl. nonsibilant fric.		θ				x		h	
vl. sibilant fric.			"s"						
voiced nasal	m		"n"						
voiced flap			"ɾ"						
vd. central approx.					j				w

Vowels

	oral			nasalized		
high	ι		ɯ	ĩ		ɯ̃
mid		"o"			"õ"	
low		a			ã	

Language	bilabial	alveolar	palato-alveolar	retroflex	velar	glottal	variable place	labial-velar
Chacobo (811)								
voiceless plosive	p	t			k	?		
vl. sibilant affric.		ts	tʃ					
vl. nonsibilant fric.							h	
vd. nonsibilant fric.	β							
vl. sibilant fric.		s	ʃ	ʂ				
voiced nasal	m	n						
voiced flap		ɾ						
vd. central approx.								w

Vowels

high	i	ɨ	
mid			"o"
low		a	

Language Tacana (812)	bilabial	dental	alveolar	palato-alveolar	retroflex	palatal	velar	glottal	labial-velar
voiceless plosive	p		t				k	?	
voiced plosive	b		d						
vl. sibilant affric.				tʃ	ṭṣ				
vd. nonsibilant fric.	β	ð̆							
vl. sibilant fric.				ʃ	ṣ				
voiced nasal	m		n						
vd. fricative flap			ř						
voiced flap			ɾ						
vd. central approx.						j			w

Vowels

high	i		
mid	"e"		"o"
low		a	

Language Cashinahua (813)	bilabial	alveolar	palato-alveolar	retroflex	palatal	velar	variable place	labial-velar
voiceless plosive	p	t				k		
voiced plosive		d						
vl. sibilant affric.		ts	tʃ					
vl. nonsibilant fric.							h	
vl. sibilant fric.		s	ʃ	ṣ				
voiced nasal	m	n						
vd. central approx.					j			w

Vowels

	oral		nasalized	
high	i	u, ɯ	ĩ	ũ, ɯ̃
low	a̟		ã̟	

Language	bilabial	labio-dental	dental/alveolar	palato-alveolar	palatal	velar	glottal	labial-velar	dental/alveolar-velar
Ashuslay (814)									
voiceless plosive	p		"t"			k	?		
laryngealized vl. plos.	p̰		"t̰"			k̰			
vl. sibilant affric.			"ts"	tʃ					
laryng. vl. sib. affric.			"t̰s̰"	t̰ʃ̰					
vl. nonsibilant affric.									kɬ[5]
vl. nonsibilant fric.		f				x			xɬ[5]
vl. sibilant fric.			"s"	ʃ					
voiced nasal	m		"n"						
vd. lateral approx.			"l"[1]						
vd. central approx.					j			w	

Vowels

high	i		u
mid	"e"	"o"	
low	a	ɑ	

Language	bilabial	dental/alveolar	palato-alveolar	palatal	velar	uvular	variable place	labial-velar
Abipon (815)								
voiceless plosive	p	"t"			k	q		
vl. sibilant affric.			tʃ					
vl. nonsibilant fric.							h	
vd. nonsibilant fric.					ɣ	ʁ		
voiced nasal	m	"n"		ɲ				
voiced r-sound		"rr"						
vd. lateral approx.		"l"						
vd. central approx.				j				w

Vowels

high	i	ɨ	
mid	"e"		"o"
low		a	

Language	bilabial	alveolar	retroflex	palatal	velar	velar labialized	glottal	variable place	labial-velar
Nambiquara, Southern (816)									
voiceless plosive	p	t			k	kʷ	ʔ		
vl. aspirated plosive	pʰ	tʰ			kʰ	kʷʰ			
vl. ejective stop	p’	t’			k’	kʷ’			
vd. implosive	ɓ	ɗ							
vl. nonsibilant fricative								h	
laryng. vd. nonsib. fricative								h̰[5]	
vl. sibilant fricative		s							
laryng. vl. sib. fricative		s̰							
voiced nasal		n							
laryng. vd. nasal		n̰							
voiced lateral flap			ɺ̣						
laryng. vd. lat. flap			ɺ̣̰						
vd. central approximant				j					w

Vowels

	plain oral			plain nasalized		
high	i		u	ĩ		
mid	"e"		"o"	"ẽ"		"õ"
low		a			ã	

	laryngealized oral			laryngealized nasal		
high	ḭ		ṵ	ḭ̃		
mid	"ḛ"		"o̰"	"ḛ̃"		"õ̰"
low		a̰			ã̰	

Language	bilabial	dental/alveolar	palato-alveolar	palatal	velar	variable place	labial-velar
Arabela (817)							
voicelss plosive	p	"t"			k		
vl. nonsibilant fric.						h	
vl. sibilant fric.		"s"	ʃ				
voiced nasal	m	"n"					
voiced trill		"r"					
vd. central approx.				j			w

Vowels

high	i		u
mid	"e"		"o"
low		a	

Diphthongs

ai
au

Language	bilabial	alveolar	palatal	velar	labial-velar
Auca (818)					
voiceless plosive	p	t		k	
voiced plosive	b	d		g	
voiced nasal	m	n	ɲ	ŋ	
vd. central approx.					w

Vowels

	oral			nasalized	
high	i			ĩ	
mid	"e"	"o"		"ẽ"	"õ"
low	æ	a		æ̃	ã

Language	bilabial	dental	dental/alveolar	palato-alveolar	palatal	velar	uvular	variable place	labial-velar
Quechua (819)									
voiceless plosive	p		"t"			k	q		
vl. aspirated plos.	pʰ		"tʰ"			kʰ	qʰ		
vl. ejective stop	p'		"t'"			k'	q'		
vl. sibilant affric.				tʃ					
vl. asp. sib. affric.				tʃʰ					
vl. sib. eject. affric.				tʃ'					
vl. nonsibilant fric.	ɸ²							h	
vd. nonsibilant fric.	β²	ð²				ɣ²			
vl. sibilant fric.			"s"	ʃ					
voiced nasal	m		"n"		ɲ				
voiced trill			"r"²						
voiced flap			"ɾ"						
vd. lateral approx.			"l"		ʎ				
vd. central approx.					j				w

Vowels

high	ι				ɷ
lower mid		ε²		ɔ²	
low			a		

Language	bilabial	alveolar	palato-alveolar	retroflex	palatal	velar	uvular	labial-velar
Jaqaru (820)								
voiceless plosive	p	t			c	k	q	
vl. aspirated plos.	pʰ	tʰ			cʰ	kʰ	qʰ	
vl. ejective stop	p'	t'			c'	k'	q'	
vl. sibilant affric.		ts	tʃ	tṣ				
vl. asp. sib. affric.		tsʰ	tʃʰ	tṣʰ				
vl. sib. eject. affric.		ts'	tʃ'	tṣ'				
vl. nonsibilant fric.						x		
vl. sibilant fric.		s	ʃ					
voiced nasal	m	n			ɲ	ŋ		
voiced flap		ɾ						
vd. lateral approx.		l			ʎ			
vd. central approx.					j			w

Vowels

high	i		ɯ
low		a	

Language	bilabial	dental	palato-alveolar	palatal	velar	uvular	glottal	variable place	labial-velar
Gununa-Kena (821)									
voiceless plosive	p	t̪			k	q	ʔ		
voiced plosive	b	d̪							
vl. ejective stop	p'	t̪'			k'				
vl. sibilant affric.		t̪s̪	tʃ	tɕ					
vl. sib. eject. affric.		t̪s̪'	tʃ'	tɕ'					
vl. nonsibilant fric.					x			h	
vl. sibilant fric.		s̪	ʃ	ɕ					
voiced nasal	m	n̪							
voiced trill		r̪							
vd. lateral approx.		l̪							
vl. lateral approx.		l̪̥							
vd. central approx.				j					w

Vowels

high	i			u
mid	"e"	"ə"	"o"	
low		a		

Language	bilabial	alveolar	palato-alveolar	retroflex	velar	glottal	variable place	labial-velar
Wapishana (822)								
voiceless plosive						ʔ		
vl. aspirated plos.	pʰ	tʰ			kʰ			
voiced plosive		d			g			
laryngealized vd. plos.	b̰	d̰						
vl. sibilant affric.			tʃ					
vl. nonsibilant fric.							h[1]	
vl. sibilant fric.		s	ʃ					
laryng. vd. sib. fric.				ẓ̰				
voiced nasal	m		n̠					
voiced flap		ɾ						
vd. central approx.								w

Vowels

	oral			nasalized		
high	i	ɨ	u	ĩ	ɨ̃	ũ
low		a			ã	

Language	bilabial	labio-dental	dental/alveolar	palato-alveolar	palatal	velar	variable place	labial-velar
Island Carib (823)								
voiceless plosive	p		"t"			k		
voiced plosive	b		"d"			g		
vl. sibilant affric.				tʃ				
vl. nonsibilant fric.		f					h	
vl. sibilant fric.			"s"					
voiced nasal	m		"n"					
voiced flap			"ɾ"					
vd. lateral approx.			"l"					
vd. central approx.					j			w

Vowels

	oral				nasalized			
high	i			u	ĩ			ũ
mid		"e"	"ɤ"			"ẽ"	"ɤ̃"	
low		a				ã		

Language												
Amuesha (824)	bilabial	bilabial palatalized	dental/alveolar	dental/alv. palatalized	alveolar	palato-alveolar	palato-alv. palatalized	retroflex	palatal	velar	glottal	labial-velar
voiceless plosive	p	p^j			t					k	ʔ	
vl. asp. sib. affric.					ts^h	tʃ^h	tʃ^{jh}[5]	ṭṣ^h				
vl. nonsibilant fric.										x		
vd. nonsibilant fric.	β									ɣ		
vl. sibilant fricative					s	ʃ						
vd. sibilant fricative								ẓ				
voiced nasal	m	m^j			n				ɲ			
voiced flap			"ɾ"									
vd. lateral approximant				"l^j"								
vd. central approximant									j			w

<u>Vowels</u>

higher mid	e		o
low		a	

Language						
Campa (825)	bilabial	alveolar	palato-alveolar	palatal	velar	variable place
voiceless plosive	p	t	t̠		k	
vl. sibilant affric.		ts	tʃ			
vl. nonsibilant fric.						h
vd. nonsibilant fric.	β					
vl. sibilant fric.		s	ʃ			
voiced nasal	m	n	n̠			
voiced flap		ɾ				
vd. central approx.				j		

<u>Vowels</u>

high	i		
higher mid	e		o
low		a	

Language Guajiro (826)	bilabial	dental/alveolar	palato-alveolar	palatal	velar	glottal	variable place	labial-velar
voiceless plosive	p	"t"			k	ʔ		
vl. preasp. plos.	ʰp	"ʰt"			ʰk			
vl. sibilant affric.			tʃ					
vl. preasp. sib. affric.			ʰtʃ					
vl. nonsibilant fric.							h	
vl. sibilant fric.		"s"	ʃ					
voiced nasal	m	"n"						
voiced trill		"r"						
vd. lateral flap		"ɺ"						
vd. central approx.				j				w

Vowels

	oral			nasalized		
high	i		u	ĩ		ũ
higher mid		ø[5]			ø̃[5]	
lower mid	ɛ		ɔ	ɛ̃		ɔ̃
low		a			ã	

Language Moxo (827)	bilabial	labio-dental	alveolar	palato-alveolar	palatal	velar	glottal	variable place	labial-velar
voiceless plosive	p		t			k	ʔ		
voiced plosive	b[2]		d[2]						
vl. sibilant affric.			ts	tʃ					
vl. nonsibilant fric.		f[2]						h	
vd. nonsibilant fric.	β								
vl. sibilant fric.			s	ʃ[1]					
voiced nasal	m		n	n̠		ŋ[2]			
voiced flap			ɾ						
vd. lateral approx.			l[2]						
vd. central approx.					j				w[4]

Vowels

high	i		u
lower mid	ɛ		
low		ȧ	

Language										
Guarani (828)	bilabial	labio-dental	dental	dental/alveolar	alveolar	palato-alveolar	palatal	velar	velar labialized	glottal
voiceless plosive	p		t̪					k	kʷ	ʔ
vl. sibilant affric.						tʃ[2]				
vl. nonsibilant fric.		f[2]						x	xʷ[2]	
vd. nonsibilant fric.		v	ð̪[2]					ɣ	ɣʷ[2]	
vl. sibilant fric.			s̪		s					
voiced nasal	m		n̪				ɲ	ŋ	ŋʷ	
voiced fricative trill				"r̝"[2]						
voiced flap					ɾ					
vd. lateral approx.			l̪[2]				ʎ[2]			

Vowels	oral			nasalized		
high	i	ɨ	u	ĩ	ɨ̃	ũ
higher mid	e	o		ẽ	õ	
low		a			ã	

Language												
Siriono (829)	bilabial	bilabial prenasalized	dental/alveolar	dental/alv. prenasalized	palato-alveolar	palato-alv. prenasalized	palatal	velar	velar palatalized	velar prenasalized	variable place	labial-velar
voiceless plosive	p		"t"					k	kʲ			
voiced plosive	b	ᵐb	"ⁿd"							ᵑg		
vl. sibilant affric.					tʃ							
vd. sibilant affric.						ⁿdʒ						
vl. nonsibilant fric.											h	
vl. sibilant fric.			"s"		ʃ							
voiced flap			"ɾ"									
vd. central approx.							j					w

Vowels	oral			nasalized		
high	ɣɣ[5]		u	ɣɣ[5]		ũ
higher mid		o			õ	
low	a			ã		

Language	bilabial	labio-dental	dental	alveolar	palatal	velar	variable place
Guahibo (830)							
voiceless plosive	p			t		k	
vl. aspirated plos.			t̪ʰ				
voiced plosive	b			d			
vl. sibilant affric.				ts			
vl. nonsibilant fric.		f				x	h
vd. nonsibilant fric.		v					
voiced nasal	m			n			
voiced trill				r			
vd. lateral approx.				l			
vd. central approx.					j		

Vowels

	oral			nasalized		
high	i		u	ĩ		ũ
mid	"e"	"ə"	"o"	"ẽ"	"ə̃"	"õ"
low		a			ã	

Language	bilabial	labio-dental	dental/alveolar	palato-alveolar	palatal	velar	velar labialized	glottal	labial-velar
Ticuna (831)									
voiceless plosive	p		"t"			k	kʷ	ʔ	
voiced plosive	b		"d"			g			
vl. sibilant affric.				tʃ					
vd. sibilant affric.				dʒ					
vl. nonsibilant fric.		f[2]							
vl. sibilant fric.			"s"[2]						
voiced nasal	m		"n"		ɲ	ŋ			
voiced flap			"ɾ"						
vd. central approx.									w

Vowels

	oral			nasalized		
high	i	ɨ	u	ĩ	ɨ̃	ũ
mid	"e"		"o"			"õ"
low		a			ã	

Language	bilabial	alveolar	palatal	velar	variable place	labial-velar
Barasano (832)						
voiceless plosive	p	t		k		
voiced plosive	b	d		g		
vl. nonsibilant fric.					h	
vl. sibilant fric.		s[2]				
voiced flap		ɾ				
vd. central approx.			j			w

Vowels

	oral			nasalized		
high	i	ɨ	u	ĩ		ũ
higher mid			o			õ
mid	"e"			"ẽ"		
low		a			ã	

Language	bilabial	dental	alveolar	palato-alveolar	retroflex	palatal	velar	velar labialized	glottal	variable place	variable place labialize	labial-velar
Siona (833)												
voiceless plosive	p	t̪					k	kʷ	ʔ			
laryng. vl. plosive	p̰				ṭ̰		k̰	kʷ̰				
vl. sibilant affric.				tʃ								
vl. nonsibilant fric.										h	hʷ	
vl. sibilant fric.			s									
laryng. vl. sib. fric.			s̰									
voiced nasal	m		n									
vd. central approx.						j						w

Vowels

	oral			nasalized		
high	i		u	ĩ		ũ
mid	"e"		"o"	"ẽ"		"õ"
low		a			ã	

Language	bilabial	alveolar	palatal	velar	glottal	variable place	labial-velar
Tucano (834)							
voiceless plosive	p	t		k	ʔ		
voiced plosive	b	d		g			
vl. nonsibilant fric.						h	
vl. sibilant fric.		s					
voiced flap		ɾ					
vd. central approx.			j				w

Vowels	oral			nasalized		
high	i		u	ĩ		ũ
mid		"e"	"o"		"ẽ"	"õ"
low		a			ã	

Language	bilabial	dental/alveolar	palato-alveolar	palatal	velar	glottal	labial-velar
Jivaro (835)							
voiceless plosive	p	"t"			k	ʔ[1]	
vl. sibilant affric.		"ts"	tʃ				
vl. nonsibilant fric.					x		
vl. sibilant fric.		"s"	ʃ				
voiced nasal	m	"n"	n̠				
voiced flap		"ɾ"					
vd. central approx.				j			w

Vowels	oral		nasalized	
high	i	u, ɯ	ĩ	ũ, ɯ̃
low	a		ã	

Language	bilabial	labio-dental	dental/alveolar	palato-alveolar	palatal	velar	glottal	variable place	labial-velar
Cofan (836)									
voiceless plosive	p		"t̪"		c[5]	k	ʔ		
vl. aspirated plos.	pʰ		"t̪ʰ"		cʰ[5]	kʰ			
voiced plosive	b		"d"		ɟ[5]	g			
vl. sibilant affric.				tʃ					
vl. asp. sib. affric.				tʃʰ					
vd. sibilant affric.				dʒ					
vl. nonsibilant fric.		f						h	
vd. nonsibilant fric.	β					ɣ			
vl. sibilant fric.			"s"	ʃ					
vd. sibilant fric.					ʑ				
voiced nasal	m		"n"		ɲ				
voiced r-sound			"rr"						
vd. central approx.					j	ɣ̯			w
Vowels									
high	i		ɨ						
mid				o					
lower mid		ɛ							
low			a						

Language	bilabial	dental	alveolar	palato-alveolar	retroflex	palatal	velar	labial-velar
Araucanian (837)								
voiceless plosive	p	t̪	t				k	
vl. sibilant affric.				tʃ				
vl. nonsibilant affric.					ṭẓ̌			
vl. nonsibilant fric.	ɸ	θ						
vd. nonsibilant fric.					ẓ̌			
vl. sibilant fric.			s[2]					
voiced nasal	m	n̪	n			ɲ	ŋ	
vd. lateral approx.		l̪	l			ʎ		
vd. central approx.						j		w
Vowels								
high	i			u, ɯ				
lower mid		ɛ	ɔ					
low		a						

Language	bilabial	labio-dental	dental	dental/alveolar	palato-alveolar	palatal	velar	uvular
Greenlandic (900)								
voiceless plosive	p		t̪				k	q
vl. sibilant affric.				"ts"				
long. vl. nonsib. fric.		f:					x:	χ:
vd. nonsibilant fric.	β					ʝ	ɣ	ʁ
vl. sibilant fric.				"s"	ʃ			
long vl. lateral fric.			ɬ̪:					
voiced nasal	m		n̪				ŋ	
vd. lateral approx.			l̪					

Vowels

high	i		u
low		a	

Language	bilabial	dental	dental/alveolar	palato-alveolar	palatal	velar	uvular	variable place	labial-velar
Aleut (901)									
voiceless plosive			"t"			k	q		
vl. sibilant affric.			"ts"						
vl. nonsibilant fric.						x	χ	h	
vd. nonsibilant fric.		ð				ɣ	ʁ		
vl. sibilant fric.				ʃ					
vd. sibilant fric.				ʒ					
vl. lateral fric.			"ɬ"						
voiced nasal	m		"n"			ŋ			
voiceless nasal	m̥		"n̥"			ŋ̊			
vd. lateral approx.			"l"						
vd. central approx.					j				w
vl. central approx.					j̊				ʍ

Vowels

high	i		u
low		a	

Language Telugu (902)	bilabial	labio-dental	dental	dental/alveolar	alveolar	retroflex	palatal	velar	variable place
voiceless plosive	p		t̪			ʈ		k	
vl. aspirated plosive	pʰ[2]					ʈʰ[2]		kʰ[2]	
voiced plosive	b		d̪			ɖ		g	
breathy vd. plosive	b̤[2]		d̪̤[2]			ɖ̤[2]		g̤[2]	
vl. sibilant affricate					ts		tʂ[2]		
vd. sibilant affricate					dz				
vl. nonsibilant fricative		f[2]							
vd. nonsibilant fricative									ɦ
vl. sibilant fricative					s	ʂ	ʂ		
voiced nasal	m				n	ɳ			
voiced flap					ɾ				
vd. lateral approximant				"l"		ɭ			
vd. central approximant	β̞						j		

Vowels

	short			long		
high	i		u	i:		u:
higher mid	e		o	e:		o:
lower mid		ε				
low					æ: a:	

Language Kota (903)	bilabial	labio-dental	dental	alveolar	palato-alveolar	retroflex	palatal	velar	labial-velar
vl. aspirated plos.	pʰ		t̪ʰ	tʰ		ʈʰ		kʰ	
voiced plosive	b		d̪	d		ɖ		g	
vl. sibilant affric.					tʃ				
vd. sibilant affric.					dʒ				
vd. nonsibilant fric.		v							
vl. sibilant fric.						ʂ			
voiced nasal	m			n		ɳ		ŋ	
voiced trill				r					
voiced flap						ɽ			
vd. lateral approx.				l		ɭ			
vd. central approx.							j		

Vowels

high	i		u
mid	"e"		"o"
low		a	

Language Kurukh (904)	bilabial	dental/alveolar	palato-alveolar	retroflex	palatal	velar	uvular	variable place	labial-velar
voiceless plosive	p	"t"		ṭ		k			
voiced plosive	b	"d"		ḍ		g			
vl. sibilant affric.			tʃ						
vd. sibilant affric.			dʒ						
vl. nonsibilant fric.							x	h	
vl. sibilant fric.		"s"							
voiced nasal	m	"n"							
voiced trill		"r"		ṛ[4]					
vd. lateral approx.		"l"							
vd. central approx.					j				w

Vowels

	oral			nasalized		
high	i		u	ĩ		ũ
mid	"e"		"o"	"ẽ"		"õ"
low		a			ã	

Language Malayalam (905)	bilabial	labio-dental	dental	alveolar	palato-alveolar	retroflex	palatal	velar	variable place
voiceless plosive	p		t̪			ṭ		k	
voiced plosive	b		d̪			ḍ		g	
vl. sibilant affric.					tʃ				
vd. sibilant affric.					dʒ				
vl. nonsibilant fric.									h
vl. sibilant fric.				s		ṣ			
voiced nasal	m		n̪	n		ṇ	ɲ	ŋ	
voiced trill				r					
voiced flap				D					
vd. lateral approx.				l		ḷ	ʎ		
vd. central approx.		ʋ					j		

Vowels

high	i		u
mid	"e"		"o"
low		a	

Language	bilabial	dental/alveolar	dental/alv. palatalized	palatal	velar	uvular	glottal	variable place
Ket (906)								
voiceless plosive		"t"	"tʲ"		k	q	?	
voiced plosive	b	"d"	"dʲ"					
vl. sibilant affric.		"s"	"sʲ"					
vl. nonsibilant fric.								h
vd. nonsibilant fric.				ǰ				
voiced nasal	m	"n"		ɲ	ŋ			
vd. lateral approx.		"l"	"lʲ"					
Vowels								
high	i		ɨ	u				
mid			"ɵ"					
lower mid			ɔ					
low		æ	a					

Language	bilabial	dental/alveolar	dental/alv. velarized	palato-alveolar	palatal	velar	uvular	labial-velar
Yukaghir (907)								
voiceless plosive	p	"t"				k	q	
voiced plosive	b	"d"				g		
vl. sibilant affric.				tʃ				
vd. sibilant affric.				dʒ				
vd. nonsibilant fric.							ʁ	
vl. sibilant fric.		"s"						
voiced nasal	m	"n"			ɲ	ŋ		
voiced trill		"r"						
vd. lateral approx.		"l"	"ɫ"					
vd. central approx.					j			w
Vowels								
high	ɩ			u̠				
mid			"ɵ" "o"					
lower mid		ɛ						
low		a̟						

Language Chukchi (908)	bilabial	dental/alveolar	retroflex	palatal	velar	uvular	glottal	labial-velar
voiceless plosive	p	"t"			k	q	?	
vl. sibilant affric.		"ts"[1]						
vd. nonsibilant fric.			ɹ̣̌		ɣ			
vl. sibilant fric.		"s"						
vl. lateral fric.		"ɬ"						
voiced nasal	m	"n"			ŋ			
vd. central approx.				j				w

Vowels

high	ι			-		u
higher mid		e				
mid				"ə"	"o"	
lower mid			ɛ			
low				a		

Language Gilyak (909)	bilabial	labio-dental	dental/alveolar	palato-alveolar	palatal	velar	uvular	variable place	labial-velar
voiceless plosive	p		"t"		c	k	q		
vl. aspirated plos.	pʰ		"tʰ"			kʰ	qʰ		
vl. asp. sib. affric.				tʃʰ					
vl. nonsibilant fric.		f				x	χ	h	
vd. nonsibilant fric.						ɣ	ʁ		
vl. sibilant fric.			"s"						
vd. sibilant fric.			"z"						
voiced nasal	m		"n"		ɲ	ŋ			
voiced trill			"r"						
voiceless trill			"ɾ̥"						
vd. lateral approx.			"l"						
vd. central approx.		v̭			j				w

Vowels						Diphthong
high	ι				u	ιe
higher mid				ɤ		
mid			"o"			
low		æ				

Language	bilabial	dental	dental/alveolar	dental/alv. velarized	alveolar	palato-alveolar	velar	uvular	variable place
Georgian (910)									
voiceless plosive	p	t̪					k		
vl. aspirated plosive	pʰ	t̪ʰ					kʰ		
vl. ejective stop	p'	t̪'					k'	q'	
vl. sibilant affricate					ts	tʃ			
vl. asp. sib. affricate					tsʰ	tʃʰ			
vl. sib. eject. affricate					ts'	tʃ'			
vl. nonsibilant fricative								χ	h[2]
vd. nonsibilant fricative	β							ʁ	
vl. sibilant fricative					s	ʃ			
vd. sibilant fricative					z	ʒ			
voiced nasal	m		"n"						
voiced trill			"r"						
vd. lateral approximant				"ɫ"					

Vowels

	short		overshort
high	ɩ	ʊ	
mid	"e"	"o"	"ɤ̆"
low	a̟		

Language	bilabial	labio-dental	dental	dental palatalized	alveolar	palato-alveolar	palatal	velar	velar labialized	velar palatalized	uvular	uvular labialized	pharyngeal	glottal	glottal labialized	labial-velar
Kabardian (911)																
voiceless plosive														ʔ	ʔʷ	
vl. asp. plosive	pʰ		t̪ʰ					kʰ	kʷʰ							
voiced plosive	b		d̪					g	gʷ							
vl. eject. stop	p'		t̪'					k'	kʷ'		q'	qʷ'				
vl. sib. affricate			ts̪													
vd. sib. affricate			dz̪													
vl. sib. eject. affr.			ts̪'													
vl. nonsib. affric.											qχ	qχʷ				
vl. nonsib. fric.		f				[illegible]			xʷ	xʲ	χ	χʷ	ħ			
vd. nonsib. fric.		v				[illegible]				ɣʲ	ʁ	ʁʷ	ʕ[2]	ɦ		
vl. " " ejt. fric.		f'														
vl. sibilant fric.			s̪			ʃ										
vd. sibilant fric.			z̪			ʒ										
vl. sib. ejt. fric.						ʃ'										
voiced nasal	m		n̪													
vl. lateral fric.				ɬʲ												
vd. lateral fric.				ɮʲ												
voiced trill					r											
vd. central approx.							j									w

Vowels

	long		short
high	i:	u:	ɨ
mid	"e:"	"o:"	
lower mid			ɜ
low	a̟		

Language	bilabial	dental/alveolar	dental/alv. labialized	palato-alveolar	palato-alv. labialized	palatal	velar	velar labialized	uvular	uvular labialized	pharyngeal	glottal	variable place	labial-velar
Lak (912)														
voiceless plosive												ʔ		
long vl. plosive	p:	"t̪:"					k:	k^{w}:	q:	q^{w}:				
vl. asp. plosive	p^{h}	"t̪^{h}"					k^{h}	k^{wh}	q^{h}	q^{wh}				
voiced plosive	b	"d"					g		ɢ	ɢ^{w}				
vl. eject. stop	p'	"t̪'"					k'	k^{w}'	q'	q^{w}'				
vl. asp. sib. af.		"ts^{h}"	"ts^{wh}"	tʃ^{h}	tʃ^{wh}									
long vl. sib. aff.		"ts:"	"ts^{w}:"	tʃ	tʃ^{w}									
vl. sib. ejec. af.		"ts'"	"ts^{w}'"	tʃ'	tʃ^{w}'									
vl. nonsib. fric.							x	x^{w}	χ	χ^{w}	ħ		h	
long "							x:	x^{w}:	χ:	χ^{w}:				
vl. sibilant fric.		"s"		ʃ	ʃ^{w}									
long "		"s:"		ʃ:	ʃ^{w}:									
vd. sibilant fric.		"z"		ʒ										
voiced nasal	m	"n"												
voiced trill		"r"												
vd. lat. approx.		"l"												
vd. cent. approx.						j								w

Vowels		short		long		short pharyngealized
	high	i	u	i:	u:	
	mid					"e^{ʕ}"[4], "o^{ʕ}"[4]
	low	a		a:		æ^{ʕ}[4]

Language	bilabial	dental	alveolar	velar	glottal	variable place
Nama (913)						
a) Non-click consonants and vowels						
voiceless plosive	p	t̪		k	ʔ	
vl. asp. sib. affricate		t̪s̪^{h}				
vl. asp. nonsib. affricate				kx^{h}		
vl. nonsiblant fricative			s	x		h
vl. sibilant fricative						
voiced nasal	m	n̪				
voiced trill			r			

Vowels	oral			nasalized	
high	i		u	ĩ	ũ
higher mid	e		o		
mid		"ə"			
low		a		ã	

Language	dental	dental nasalized	dental velarized	alveolar	alveolar nasalized	alveolar velarized	palato-alveolar	palato-alveolar nasalized	palato-alveolar velarized
Nama (913)									
b) Click consonants									
voiceless click				ƚ			ƚ̱		
voiceless aspirated click					ŋ̊ƚʰ	ǂʰ		ŋ̊ƚ̱ʰ	ǂ̱ʰ
glottalized vl. click					ŋ̊ƚˀ			ŋ̊ƚ̱ˀ	
voiced click					ŋƚ			ŋƚ̱	
voiceless affric. click	ƚ̪ˢ								
vl. asp. affric. click		ŋ̊ƚ̪ˢʰ	ǂ̪ˢʰ						
glottalized vl. affric. click		ŋ̊ƚ̪ˢˀ							
voiced affricated click		ŋƚ̪ˢ							
vl. lateral affric. click				ʖɬ					
vl. asp. lateral affr. click					ŋ̊ʖɬʰ	ʖ̶ɬʰ			
glottalized vl. lat. aff. cl.					ŋ̊ʖɬˀ				
voiced lat. affric. click					ŋʖɬ				

<u>Note</u>. Those clicks which are characterized as "velarized" in UPSID have a fricated release of the velaric closure. The term "affricated click" is reserved for clicks in which the front closure is released with accompanying local friction. Clicks which are described as both voiceless aspirated and nasalized are described in the literature as having "delayed aspiration". See Ladefoged and Traill (UCLA Working Papers in Phonetics 49: 1-27, 1980).

Language	bilabial	labio-dental	dental/alveolar	palato-alveolar	retroflex	palatal	velar	uvular
Basque (914)								
voiceless plosive	p		"t"			c	k	
voiced plosive	b		"d"			ɟ	g	
vl. sibilant affric.			"ts"	tʃ	ʈʂ			
vl. nonsibilant fric.		f						χ
vl. sibilant fric.			"s"	ʃ	ʂ			
voiced nasal	m		"n"			ɲ		
voiced trill			"r"					
voiced flap			"ɾ"					
vd. lateral approx.			"l"			ʎ		

<u>Vowels</u>

high	ι			u
mid		"e"	"o"	
low		a		

Language Burushaski (915)	bilabial	labio-dental	dental/alveolar	palato-alveolar	retroflex	palatal	velar	uvular	variable place	labial-velar
voiceless plosive	p		"t"		ṭ		k	q		
vl. aspirated plosive	p^h		"t^h"		$ṭ^h$		k^h	q^h		
voiced plosive	b		"d"		ḍ		g			
vl. sibilant affricate			"ts"	tʃ	ṭṣ					
vl. asp. sib. affricate			"ts^h"	$tʃ^h$	$ṭṣ^h$					
vd. sibilant affricate				dʒ	ḍẓ					
vl. nonsibilant fricative	f[2]							χ[2]	h	
vd. nonsibilant fricative					ỵ̌			ʁ		
vl. sibilant fricative			"s"	ʃ	ṣ					
vd. sibilant fricative			"z"							
voiced nasal	m		"n"				ŋ			
voiced r-sound			"rr"							
vd. lateral approximant			"l"							
vd. central approximant						j				w

Vowels

high	i		u
mid	"e"		"o"
low		a	

Language Ainu (916)	bilabial	alveolar	palato-alveolar	palatal	velar	variable place	labial-velar
voiceless plosive	p	t			k		
vl. sibilant affric.			tʃ				
vl. nonsibilant fric.						h	
vl. sibilant fric.		s					
voiced nasal	m	n					
voiced r-sound		rr					
vd. central approx.				j			w

Vowels

high	i		u
lower mid	ɛ		ɔ
low		a	

Language	bilabial	labio-dental	dental	alveolar	palato-alveolar	velar	glottal	variable place
Brahui (917)								
voiceless plosive	p		t̪	t		k	ʔ	
voiced plosive	b		d̪	d		g		
vl. sibilant affric.					tʃ			
vd. sibilant affric.					dʒ			
vl. nonsibilant fric.		f				x		h
vd. nonsibilant fric.		v				ɣ		
vl. sibilant fric.				s				
vd. sibilant fric.				z				
vl. lateral fric.				ɬ				
voiced nasal	m		n̪					
voiced trill				r				
voiced flap				ɾ				
vd. lateral approx.				l				

Vowels

	long			short		
high	iː		uː	i		u
higher mid	eː	oː			e	
low		ɑː			a	

Language	bilabial	alveolar	alveolar velarized	palato-alveolar	palato-alveolar velariz	palatal	velar	velar pharyngealized	variable place	labial-velar
!Xũ (918)										
a) Non-click consonants										
voiceless plosive	p	t	t̴				k			
vl. aspirated plosive	pʰ	tʰ					kʰ			
voiced plosive	b	d	d̴				g			
breathy voiced plosive							g̤			
vl. ejective stop		t'					k'			
voiced ejective stop	b'	d'					g'			
vl. sibilant affricate		ts	ts	tʃ	t̴ʃ					
vl. asp. sib. affricate		tsʰ		tsʰ						
voiced sib. affricate			dz		d̴ʒ					
vl. sib. eject. affricate		ts'		tʃ'						
breathy vd. sib. affricate		d̤z		d̤ʒ						
vd. sib. eject. affricate		dz'		dʒ'						
vl. nonsibilant fricative							x			
vd. nonsibilant fricative									ɦ	
vl. sibilant fricative		s		ʃ						
voiced sibilant fricative		z		ʒ						
voiced nasal	m	n					ŋ	ŋˤ		
long voiced nasal	mː									
breathy voiced nasal	m̤									
laryngealized vd. nasal	m̰									
voiced flap		ɾ								
vd. central approximant						j				w

Language

!Xũ (918)

b) Click consonants

	dental	dental nasalized	dental nasalized and velarized	dental velarized	alveolar	alveolar nasalized	alveolar nasalized and velarized	alveolar velarized	palatal	palatal nasalized	palatal nasalized and velarized	palatal velarized
voiceless click					ʇ			ǂ	ʗ			ʗ̵
vl. aspirated click					ʇʰ	ŋ̊ʇʰ			ʗʰ	ŋ̊ʗʰ		
glottalized vl. click						ŋ̊ʇ?	ŋ̊ʇ?			ŋ̊ʗ?	ŋ̊ʗ?	
voiced click					gʇ	ŋʇ		gǂ	gʗ	ŋʗ		gʗ̵
breathy voiced click					g̤ʇ	ŋ̤ʇ			g̤ʗ	ŋ̤ʗ		
glottalized vd. click								gǂ?				gʗ̵?
vl. affricated click	ʇ̠ˢ			ǂ̠ˢ								
vl. asp. affr. click	ʇ̠ˢʰ	ŋ̊ʇ̠ˢʰ										
glot. vl. aff. click		ŋ̊ʇ̠ˢ?	ŋ̊ʇ̠ˢ?									
vd. affric. click	gʇ̠ˢ	ŋʇ̠ˢ		gǂ̠ˢ								
breathy vd. aff. cl.	g̤ʇ̠ˢ	ŋ̤ʇ̠ˢ										
glot. vd. aff. click				gǂ̠ˢ?								
vl. lat. aff. click									ʗʎ			ʗ̵ʎ
vl. asp. lat. aff. c.									ʗʎʰ	ŋ̊ʗʎʰ		
gl. vl. lat. aff. cl.										ŋ̊ʗʎ?	ŋ̊ʗʎ?	
vd. lat. affr. click									gʗʎ	ŋʗʎ		gʗ̵ʎ
gl. vd. lat. aff. cl.												gʗ̵ʎ?
breathy vd. lateral affricated click									g̤ʗʎ	ŋ̤ʗʎ		

See note on the description of click consonants on the chart for Nama (913).

Language

!Xũ (918)

c) Vowels

	short oral		long oral	
high	i	u	i:	u:
mid	"e"	"o"	"e:"	"o:"
low	a		a:	

	short nasalized		long nasalized	
high	ĩ	ũ		ũ:
mid	"õ"			
low	ã		ã:	

	short pharyngealized oral	long pharyngealized oral
mid	"oˤ"	"oˤ:"
low	aˤ	aˤ:

	short pharyngealized nasalized	long pharyngealized nasalized
mid	"õˤ"	"õˤ:"
low	ãˤ	ãˤ:

Diphthongs

ia	oi	ẽĩ	aeˤ	ãẽˤ
ei	oe	ẽũ	aoˤ	ãõˤ
eu	oa	õĩ	oiˤ	õĩˤ
ae	ui	õã	oaˤ	õãˤ
ao		ũĩ		